The North Atlantic Triangle in a Changing World: Anglo-American-Canadian Relations, 1902–1956

The North Atlantic Powers – Britain, the United States, and Canada – constitute an important element in modern international history. They form a North Atlantic triangle which, despite an important French-speaking minority in Canada, is united by language, culture, liberal political beliefs, and a common economic philosophy. However, there exist significant foreign-policy differences within the triangle which derive from dissimilar perceptions of threat, the influence of public opinion on government, and economic, financial, and other constraints. The course of this tripartite relationship has therefore been marked by fluidity and divergence and has changed according to world circumstances. As the twentieth century began, Britain was the only global power; by the late 1950s the United States had emerged from isolation and, building on its leading international economic and financial position and its development of nuclear and conventional military strength, had replaced Britain as the only global power. Canada also underwent a transformation. In 1903 the northern dominion remained firmly within the British Empire. Sixty years later, by a convoluted process, Canada achieved sovereignty in foreign policy, changed direction in economic orientation, and emerged as a leading middle power. Ottawa had broken its colonial links with London and gravitated into the American orbit.

This book, by experts in Anglo-American-Canadian relations, examines North Atlantic triangle diplomacy from the Alaska boundary dispute to the Suez crisis of 1956, providing an up-to-date assessment of this important configuration of powers in twentieth-century international history.

B.J.C. McKERCHER is an associate professor in the Department of History, Royal Military College, Kingston, Ontario. He is author of *The Second Baldwin Government and the United States, 1924–1929* and *Transition: Britain's Loss of Global Preeminence to the United States, 1930–1945*.

LAWRENCE ARONSEN is an associate professor in the Department of History, University of Alberta. He is co-author, with Martin Kitchen, of *The Origins of the Cold War in Comparative Perspective*.

EDITED BY B.J.C. McKERCHER AND
LAWRENCE ARONSEN

The North Atlantic Triangle in a Changing World: Anglo-American-Canadian Relations, 1902–1956

UNIVERSITY OF TORONTO PRESS

Toronto Buffalo London

© University of Toronto Press Incorporated 1996
Toronto Buffalo London

Printed in Canada

ISBN 0-8020-0520-9 (cloth)
ISBN 0-8020-6957-6 (paper)

Printed on acid-free paper

Canadian Cataloguing in Publication Data

Main entry under title:

The North Atlantic triangle in a changing world :
  Anglo-American-Canadian relations, 1902–1956

Includes bibliographical references and index.
ISBN 0-8020-0520-9 (bound)
ISBN 0-8020-6957-6 (pbk.)

1. Canada – Foreign relations – United States.
2. United States – Foreign relations – Canada.
3. Canada – Foreign relations – Great Britain.
4. Great Britain – Foreign relations – Canada.
5. United States – Foreign relations – Great
Britain.   6. Great Britain – Foreign relations –
United States.   7. Canada – Foreign relations –
1867– .*   8. United States – Foreign relations –
20th century.   9. Great Britain – Foreign
relations – 20th century.   I. McKercher, Brian.
II. Aronsen, Lawrence, 1936– .

FC242.N67 1996   327.71   C95-932160-8
F1029.N67 1996

University of Toronto Press acknowledges the financial assistance to its
publishing program of the Canada Council and the Ontario Arts Council.

Contents

THE NORTH ATLANTIC TRIANGLE IN A
CHANGING WORLD

Introduction

B.J.C. McKERCHER and LAWRENCE ARONSEN

From a Canadian perspective, Great Britain, the United States, and Canada have constituted an important element of twentieth-century international history. The historian James Bartlett Brebner argued almost fifty years ago that these three powers formed a 'North Atlantic triangle' that, despite an increasingly important French-speaking minority in Canada, was distinguished by language, culture, liberal political beliefs, and an economic philosophy tied to capitalism.[1] This is not to say that the leaders and peoples of these three states shared the same world view, had common external interests, or worked harmoniously together in pursuing their separate diplomacies. There existed significant foreign policy differences among them that derived from dissimilar perceptions of threat, the influence of disparate public opinions on government, and economic, financial, and other constraints. Moreover, the nature of the relationships within the triangle changed over time. As the twentieth century began, Britain stood as the only global power; by the late 1950s, weakened by the economic consequences of fighting two world wars and with its formal empire shearing away, it had become junior to the United States. During the same period, the United States had emerged from political isolation. Building on its leading economic and financial position in the world and its development of nuclear and conventional military strength, and taking the point within the western alliance against perceived Soviet Russian aggression, it had replaced Britain as the only global power. Canada had also undertaken its own odyssey. In 1903, at the time of the Alaska boundary dispute, the northern dominion remained firmly within the British Empire. A little more than half a century later, by a twisted process that saw it achieve sovereignty in foreign policy, change its economic orientation, and emerge as a self-defined 'middle' power, Canada had broken its colonial links with London only to gravitate into the American orbit.

The idea of the 'North Atlantic triangle' emerged in the period before 1945. It was largely a Canadian idea, conceived in the aftermath of the granting of dominion sovereignty in foreign policy following the imperial conference of 1926.[2] Little doubt exists that it was genuinely held by those like Brebner, who provided its greatest popularity among the academic community. More important in terms of the northern dominion's position between the two English-speaking Great Powers, it reflected the views of political leaders like William Lyon Mackenzie King, the Canadian prime minister for most of the quarter-century after 1921. 'As Canadians,' he wrote in 1927, 'we can only seek to do all that lies in our power to fulfil our role as friendly interpreters of Britishers and Americans alike in a manner which may substitute good-will for ill-will.'[3] This observation had an added piquancy given that both Canada and the United States were former British colonies, that the national political elites in both countries were largely English speaking and anglocentric until after the Second World War, and that their political cultures in their formative periods had looked to Britain and its civilization as a model to emulate.

To a large degree, Canadians promoted the concept of the triangle to increase the international status of their country given its perpetual position as the least of the three powers, a notion tied to the development by Canadian diplomatists after 1941 of the 'functional principle.' King's Liberal government had been allied with Britain in the war against the Axis Powers since September 1939, when, following the Japanese attack on Pearl Harbor on 7 December 1941, the United States suddenly became a member of the Allied coalition. When Sir Winston Churchill, the British prime minister, and Franklin Roosevelt, the American president, then held discussions in Washington in December 1941 and January 1942 to establish both joint strategy and a Combined Chiefs of Staff to implement that strategy, King's ministry shunned involvement in the higher direction of the war. Wanting representation on some of the boards dealing with inter-Allied economic collaboration to which Canada was making a substantial contribution, however, the Canadians articulated the view that transnational cooperation should reflect the comparative strengths of the powers involved. Smaller allies, like Canada, could not insist on a voice equal to the voices of Britain and the United States; the Great Powers, however, could not expect unquestioned authority in decision making. Instead, depending on their individual contributions, each government should be involved to the level of its activity in each issue.[4] This was a realistic policy on Ottawa's part, though, as John English shows in his chapter, the practical result was a less than effective effort by King's government to influence the direction taken by the western half of the Allied coalition after January 1942. Still, by 1945 Canadians gave expression to the concept of the triangle in both a theoretical and a practical way; the triangle existed – and exists – as an important element in twentieth-century international history.

The idea of a triplice of English-speaking powers existing as a bloc in the swirl of modern international politics needs to be tempered with the realization that Great Britain, the United States, and Canada had differing national interests and thus pursued foreign policies that did not always mesh. Indeed, at particular times, such as the initial two and a half years of the First World War, the late 1920s, and during the Suez crisis of 1956, London and Washington pursued antithetical policies vis-à-vis one another, which poisoned Anglo-American relations. This deviation comes back to the point about those significant differences that derived from dissimilar perceptions of threat, the influence of disparate public opinions on government, and economic, financial, and other constraints. For instance, to shore up Britain's weakening global position after the Second World War, especially in relation to the perceived threat to western Europe posed by Soviet Russia, Churchill wrote and spoke glowingly about the natural alliance between the British Commonwealth and the United States.[5] By stressing the common heritage of the English-speaking peoples, he sought to tie American economic and military resources to the defence of liberal democracy and constitutional government. In his famous 'Iron Curtain' speech at Fulton, Missouri, in March 1946, he said: 'Neither the sure prevention of war, nor the continuous rise of world organisation will be gained without what I have called the fraternal association of the English-speaking peoples. This means a special relationship between the British Commonwealth and Empire and the United States of America.'[6]

In most respects, the Anglo-American 'special relationship' was a myth.[7] The United States had won its independence at British expense in the late eighteenth century; and subsequent American political and social development had been defined in part by a rejection of British values tied to monarchial government, an aristocratic, deferential society, and 'the white man's burden' of a civilizing empire. For their part, the British did not appreciate the open nature of the American political system, looked askance at the heterogeneous nature of the American population, and saw hypocrisy in American criticism of the British Empire while the United States established what it saw as economic control and political dominance over Latin America and scattered territories like the Hawaiian Islands and the Philippines. Although himself the product of a transatlantic marriage, Churchill had been consistently critical of American policies before the Second World War because of the economic and naval threats to Britain posed by the United States. On the other hand, after the Second World War began, he emphasized the supposed Anglo-American commonality of language, culture, and political institutions to exploit American resources to bolster sagging British strength. It is just as certain that American leaders were reluctant to use American resources to support British interests unless they coincided with those of the United States. Thus, when Dwight Eisenhower was inaugurated as American president in January 1953, he observed: 'Winston is trying to relive the days of World War II ... [when] he and our president were sitting on some rather Olympian platform with respect to the rest of the world and directing world affairs from that point of vantage ... In the present international complexities, any hope of establishing such a relationship is completely fatuous.'[8]

Therefore, while the North Atlantic triangle has existed as a distinct element in international politics in this century, its course has been marked by fluidity, the divergent experiences of its constituent parts, and national histories that are as much dissimilar as similar. And what is true of the century generally is especially so in the period covered by this book. The period from 1902 to 1956 is marked by a particularly important shift in the constellation of international power. Despite the military and diplomatic problems engendered for London by the Boer War, Britain was the only truly world power as the twentieth century began and during its first four decades.[9] By 1956, as the dust settled on the Suez debacle, Britain was seen to be – even by the British – a power of the second rank.[10] In the same period, by a combination of luck, astute diplomacy, and the strength of its economy and the size of its population, the United States had replaced Britain on this lofty plane.[11] There was nothing inevitable about this transition or about the levels to which Britain fell and the United States rose. An array of factors affected the shift within the Anglo-American relationship: the impact of the two world wars on their economies and societies, the decolonization of the British Empire, the general enfeeblement of Europe, the American rejection of political isolationism, the way in which the British and American nuclear arsenals were developed, and more.

The fact remains that in the world at large between 1902 and 1956 – and in the North Atlantic triangle particularly – Britain's power declined while that of the United States increased. This change obviously had an impact on the course of international history generally and, more narrowly, on the relationships between and among the two major English-speaking powers and their Canadian confederate. Simplistic analyses produced over the last thirty years or so abound to explain the changing dynamic within the Anglo-American-Canadian world. Reaching maturity after the Second World War, when Britain's strength had shrunk sharply and perceptibly, a range of British historians have disparaged their country's leading position in Great Power politics since the latter half of the nineteenth century. This tendency reached its zenith in the late 1980s with Paul Kennedy's explanation of the rise and fall of Great Powers since 1500.[12] At the same time, American revisionist historians propounded an unadorned cause and effect between wealth and power to explain both the growing influence of the United States and the abdication of its leaders from constructing policies that reflect the ideals of the American revolution. Their focus was the 'immoral' war in Vietnam, the roots of which they traced to before 1914.[13] Canadian historians have succumbed to a Whigish interpretation of Canada's development as a sovereign nation: the idea that progress for their country – political, economic, and social progress – came about only through breaking the shackles of the British Empire.[14] But buffeted by British decline, on the one hand, and the rise of the 'imperial' American republic, on the other, they have sought to explain how and why Canada went from being a British satellite to an American one in less than a generation; the answer supposedly resides in British failings rather than in those of Canadian leaders, notably King, the darling of the Canadian Whigs.[15]

These studies represent the dominant schools of thought and, admittedly, there were dissenting voices.[16] But the dominant schools had the greatest impact on the approach to historical study and its results; and, largely, they were an attempt to project the politics of the present – or, at least, the politics at the moment when the histories they produced were written – into the past. A particularly blatant example was the comic attempt by one American historian in the early 1970s to show that British difficulties in the Middle East during the First World War were attributable to the region's remoteness from the centre of policy making at London.[17] The argument was that effective policy could not be made by policy-makers who were so far removed from the events. But this analysis must be read as an allegory for American policies and Washington's failure in Vietnam in the late 1960s. More recent studies – those published since about 1980, primarily by younger historians – are more balanced. In the typology of historiographical development outlined by Donald Cameron Watt,[18] they are part of a natural evolution in studying the past and have reached the stage whereby they are less encumbered by the domestic debates and mythologies in their countries that earlier dominated academic life.

Using a mixture of archival sources and published secondary materials, the studies in this book examine the intertwined fates of Britain, the United States, and Canada from 1902 to 1956 in a more detached way than have previous studies. Individually and collectively, they show that the process of change was complex; that the implications of particular questions, such as economic rivalry and wartime collaboration, were far reaching; and that the survival of the political and economic ideology on which the governments and societies of the three powers were based was uncertain. Britain, the United States, and Canada have always had a 'special relationship' based on history, culture, and language. In a general sense, these bonds have not been sundered by national interests that have not always been the same; indeed, they have not been broken over the strains that have developed at particular times in the past. But as one of the leading 'post-revisionist' American diplomatic historians has recently argued, the natural state of international politics is one in which, depending on the issue at hand, powers sometimes cooperate and sometimes conflict.[19] Thus, the 'special relationship' has not existed much – if ever – in the political realm. When the United States joined with Britain during the first and second World Wars, it did so not out of any conviction that the English-speaking powers should act in concert against perceived enemies. It did so for narrow national interests. When Britain sought American assistance in both wars, the motivation of men like Churchill was to augment the British war effort and make easier the defence of the home islands and the empire. When Canadians decided to support Britain in general wars against Germany, their leaders did so to enhance Canada's position internationally. At the same time, when differences divided the three powers – Britain and the United States over the naval question in the interwar period, for instance, or Canada and Britain during the Suez crisis – the same motivation stimulated policy-makers in London, Washington, and Ottawa: defending national interests. There was no altruism in the North Atlantic triangle, although, as each contributor to this volume shows, the ties of culture and kinship were not unimportant. Understanding the North Atlantic triangle in the changing world between 1902 and 1956 lies in examining how the complex relationship of Britain, the United States, and Canada evolved during this crucial time, how that relationship matured, and how the triangle influenced global politics beyond its confines at a difficult time in international history.

NOTES

1 J.B. Brebner, *North Atlantic Triangle: The Interplay of Canada, the United States and Great Britain* (Toronto, 1945).

2 Cf. Cmd. 2768; N. Mansergh, *Survey of British Commonwealth Affairs: Problems of External Policy, 1931–1939* (London, 1952), 3–48; P.G. Wigley, *Canada and the Transition to Commonwealth: British-Canadian Relations, 1917–1926* (Cambridge, 1977).

3 King to Thomas King [a friend], 1 September 1927, King MSS [National Archives of Canada, Ottawa] MG 26 J1 Vol. 44.

4 Cf. J.L. Granatstein, 'Hume Wrong's Road to the Functional Principle,' in *Coalition Warfare: An Uneasy Accord*, ed. K.E. Neilson and R.A. Prete, (Waterloo, Ont., 1983); A.J. Miller, 'The Functional Principle in Canada's External Relations,' *International Journal*, 35(1980), 309–28.

5 Winston Churchill, *The History of the English-Speaking Peoples*, 4 vols (Toronto, 1956–8).

6 R. Rhodes James, *Winston S. Churchill: His Complete Speeches, 1897–1963* (New York, London, 1974), 72–89. Cf. H.B. Ryan, 'A New Look at Churchill's "Iron Curtain" Speech,' *Historical Journal*, 22(1979).

7 M. Beloff, 'The Special Relationship: An Anglo-American Myth,' in *A Century of Conflict, 1850–1950: Essays for A.J.P. Taylor*, ed. M. Gilbert (London 1966), 149–71; A. Buchan, 'Mothers and Daughters (or Greeks and Romans),' *Foreign Affairs*, 54(1976), 645–69; D. Reynolds, 'A "Special Relationship"?: America, Britain and International Order since World War Two,' *International Affairs*, 62(1985–6), 1–20.

8 Eisenhower diary, 6 January 1953, in *The Eisenhower Diaries*, ed. R.H. Ferrell (New York, 1981), 223.

9 See Gordon Martel, 'The Meaning of Power: Rethinking the Decline and Fall of Great Britain'; Keith Neilson, '"Greatly Exaggerated": The Myth of the Decline of Great Britain before 1914'; J.R. Ferris, '"The Greatest Power on Earth": Great Britain in the 1920s'; B.J.C. McKercher, '"Our Most Dangerous Enemy": Great Britain Pre-eminent in the 1930s'; all in *International History Review*, 13(1991).

10 David Reynolds, *Britannia Overruled: British Policy and World Power in the 20th Century* (London, 1991) is the best overview.
11 There is no American equivalent of Reynolds, *Britannia Overruled*. However, the older Stephen Ambrose, *Rise to Globalism: American Foreign Policy, 1938–1970* (Harmondsworth, 1971) is instructive. The relevant volumes of the recent 'Cambridge History of American Foreign Relations' are unhelpful, a result of their tendency to subsume foreign policy in U.S. domestic history instead of in 'international history.' Cf. Walter LaFeber, *The Search for American Opportunity, 1865–1913*, Akira Iriye, *The Globalizing of America, 1913–1945*, and Warren Cohen, *America in the Age of Soviet Power, 1945–1991*, all (Cambridge, MA, 1993). On the parochial nature of American foreign relations history, see S. Marks, 'The World According to Washington,' *Diplomatic History*, 11(1987), 265–82.
12 C. Barnett, *The Audit of War: The Illusion and Reality of Britain as a Great Nation* (London, 1986); C.J. Bartlett, *The Long Retreat: A Short History of British Defence Policy, 1945–1970* (London, 1972); P. Haggie, *Britannia at Bay: The Defence of the British Empire against Japan, 1931–1941* (Oxford, 1981). Then see P.M. Kennedy, *The Rise and Fall of Great Powers: Economic Change and Military Conflict from 1500 to 2000* (London, 1989).
13 Cf. L.C. Gardner, *Economic Aspects of New Deal Diplomacy* (Madison, WI, 1964); Gabriel and Joyce Kolko, *The Limits of Power: The World and United States Foreign Policy, 1945–1954* (New York, 1972); C.P. Parrini, *Heir to Empire: United States Economic Diplomacy, 1916–1923* (Pittsburgh, 1969). Then see William A. Williams, *The Tragedy of American Diplomacy* (New York, 1959).
14 The classic study is H. Butterfield, *The Whig Interpretation of History* (London, 1931), which discusses the notion that political progress in Britain occurred with the triumph of Parliament over the crown. For an example of this notion, placed in a Canadian nationalist context, cf. R. Bothwell, I.M. Drummond, and J. English, *Canada, 1900–1945* (Toronto, 1987); idem, *Canada since 1945: Power, Politics, and Provincialism* (Toronto, 1989).
15 Cf. Bothwell, Drummond, and English, *Canada, 1900–1945*; Desmond Morton, *Ministers and Generals: Politics and the Canadian Militia, 1868–1904* (Toronto, 1970). H.B. Neatby, *William Lyon Mackenzie King*, Vol. 2 (London, 1963). Then see J.L. Granatstein, *How Britain's Weakness Forced Canada into the Arms of the United States* (Toronto, 1989).
16 For Britain, see D. Cameron Watt, *Succeeding John Bull. America in Britain's Place 1900–75* (Cambridge, 1984), chs 1–5; for the United States, see Ernest May, *'Lessons' of the Past: The Use and Misuse of History in American Foreign Policy* (New York, 1973); for Canada, see James Eayrs, *In Defence of Canada*, Vols I, II (Toronto, 1964, 1965).

17 R.A. Adelson, 'The Formation of British Policy towards the Middle East, 1914–1918,' PhD thesis, Washington University, 1965.

18 D. Cameron Watt, 'Britain and the Historiography of the Yalta Conference and the Cold War,' *Diplomatic History*, 13(1989), 67–98. For examples of newer work, see J.R. Ferris, 'Worthy of Some Better Enemy? The British Estimate of the Imperial Japanese Army, 1919–41, and the Fall of Singapore,' *Canadian Journal of History*, 28(1993); Greg C. Kennedy, 'The 1930 London Naval Conference and Anglo-American Maritime Strength, 1927–1930,' in *Arms Limitation and Disarmament: Restraints on War, 1899–1939*, ed. B.J.C. McKercher (Westport, CT, 1992); B.J.C. McKercher, 'Wealth, Power, and the New International Order: Britain and the American Challenge in the 1920s,' *Diplomatic History*, 12(1988).

19 J.L. Gaddis, 'International Relations Theory and the End of the Cold War,' *International Security*, 17(1992–3), 5–58.

1

Canada and the Great Rapprochement, 1902–1914

ROGER SARTY

Britain's pursuit of American friendship from the late 1890s was a tacit recognition of harsh new international realities that had profound implications for Canada.[1] Britain abandoned the policy of containing American power, a policy to which Canada owed its existence, and sought military assistance from the dominion to support imperial forces elsewhere in the world. Canadian initiatives in military and external affairs were significant but often obscured by being so closely hedged and compartmentalized – sometimes intentionally. In this chapter recent research is presented on the land and maritime aspects of Canadian defence, and the frequently misunderstood relationship between them,[2] in order to suggest their place in Canada's relations with Britain and the United States. Those relations were tremendously important. They constituted the only world that mattered to Canada, the world in which it defined itself. Shifts in British or American policy could easily send shock waves through Canadian politics, sharpening disagreement as to the nation's status and destiny. Leaders, therefore, tended to cling cautiously to the status quo or, when changing circumstances compelled action, endeavoured to keep to a middle ground defined largely in domestic political terms. It was not only their success that makes it difficult in some instances to discern a Canadian position. The country, whose colonial status was most evident in defence and foreign affairs, lacked policy-making institutions and even an effective records-keeping organization. It did not help that British policy statements to Canada attempted to hide important disagreements among departments of the imperial government, while officials in Ottawa in their direct dealings with those departments, received contradictory messages.

THE CIVIL WAR, CONFEDERATION, AND PARTIAL BRITISH WITHDRAWAL

Aside from these matters, issues seemed more complex when viewed from Ottawa rather than London or Washington. Familial ties with Britain, with the heat as well as the warmth that that expression implies, and life in the shadow of the leviathan republic meant that changes at the strategic or grand strategic level touched Canada through a tangle of long-standing questions. Many of these questions and Canada's understanding of them originated in the Anglo-American relationship during and after the American Civil War. Canada's defence had always depended upon interior defence by permanent frontier garrisons from Britain's relatively small regular army and upon maritime offence against the long, exposed U.S. coastline by the Royal Navy (RN), the strongest navy in the world. The rapid mobilization of American mass armies during the Civil War had shown that even the greatly reinforced British garrisons in the interior might become no more than hostages. In addition, at this time the wars of German unification caused Britain anxiety about its military position in Europe. The imperial government therefore strongly supported confederation of the disparate North American colonies in the expectation that, united into the new dominion, they could better flourish and defend themselves. Then, in 1869–71 the frontier garrisons departed.[3]

Britain did not abandon Canada. In 1865 the province of Canada had pledged to 'devote all her resources ... to the maintenance of her connection with the mother country,' and the British government 'fully acknowledged the reciprocal obligation of defending every portion of the Empire with all the resources at its command.' Britain renewed the pledge during the withdrawal,[4] securing the naval means of fulfilment by fortifying RN bases at Halifax and Bermuda and maintaining regular army garrisons of 2,000 to 3,000 at each place. There was a smaller RN base at Esquimalt, British Columbia, which Britain later fortified and garrisoned on a more modest scale.[5] The British, moreover, did not complete the withdrawal from the frontier until, in 1871, the most dangerous questions in Anglo-American relations had been resolved by the Treaty of Washington. By that time, Washington had all but written off its armed forces as the nation concentrated on reconstruction and internal development.

The changes of the late 1860s and early 1870s assured the survival and growth of Canada but, perhaps for that very reason, did not ease Anglo-

Canadian disagreements over military and foreign policy. Defence of the inland border now fell entirely to the Canadian militia, at least until British army reinforcements could rush back to the scene in the event of a crisis. Sir John A. Macdonald, the Canadian prime minister for all but six years from 1867 until his death in 1891, did not take the new military responsibility seriously. He believed that war with the United States was 'in the highest degree improbable,' and that, in any event, the country was indefensible against a full-scale invasion from the south.[6] Always intended as reinforcements for the British regular garrisons, the Canadian militia lacked the services, organization, and training to field a substantial army. Nor was a regular army a priority, since the only foreseeable requirement would be for modest forces to quell riots or uprisings, such as the North-West Rebellion of 1885. For those purposes, the service was adequate, if barely so. The departure of the British regulars, meagre annual budgets in the order of $1 million, and pervasive political patronage ensured the decline of efficiency.

Although admitting the need for British professional soldiers as expert advisers, Ottawa was determined that their presence should not diminish its supreme authority. Canadian leaders grasped the link between control of armed forces and self-government. The appointment of the general officer commanding the militia (GOC) was reserved for a British regular of at least colonel's rank, but he and all other seconded British officers derived their powers solely from separate Canadian commissions. It was a point of constant contention. The officers, the governor-general, and British authorities tended to regard Canada as a subordinate district of the imperial army, and the reform schemes they urged built upon that concept.[7] Those schemes, moreover, looked like the thin edge of much greater commitments. From the late 1870s, when Britain faced heavier military burdens in Asia and Africa, both official and influential elements of British public opinion began to regard the stable settlement colonies as a source of reinforcements. As Macdonald warned Lord Carnarvon's commission on imperial defence in 1880, a permanent overseas obligation would seriously divide Canadians.[8] It would be far better to await the spontaneous outpouring of patriotism that would certainly be aroused by any major crisis and assure generous help. This advice would guide Canadian governments for the next sixty years.

Calls for the dominion's assistance seemed a one-way street given Britain's habit of appeasing the United States at Canada's expense. In 1866 the Americans had denounced the Reciprocity Treaty of 1854 in which they had gained access to the inshore fisheries of the Maritimes and Gulf of St Lawrence in exchange for free trade in natural goods with the North American colonies. Both Canadian federal parties dreamed of reinstating this beneficial arrangement. In the Treaty of Washington, however, Britain had conceded the fisheries without fighting for reciprocal trade. The real problem was opposition by American interests to the trade deal, but Macdonald blamed Britain's 'craven fear of the United States.'[9] When Washington was slow to ratify the fisheries articles of the treaty, and again in the late 1880s when the Americans denounced those articles and then failed to ratify new ones, armed Canadian vessels arrested American poachers. Not wanting to provoke a major crisis, Britain responded cautiously to Canada's demands for RN participation in these operations.[10]

Dominion boldness did not achieve reciprocal trade, but it did assert sovereignty over territorial waters. It also confirmed Canadian leaders in their prejudice that in their firm but neighbourly fashion they could better deal with the Americans than could the British. Further, the success of the modest Fisheries Protection Service (FPS), a civil rather than a military organization, appeared to justify Ottawa's conviction that the dominion had little need for substantial armed forces. Yet it was also true that Canadian confidence relied in no small way upon the reassuring presence of the RN and its fortified bases. One of the main reasons the dominion government resisted military reform and expansion, even assisting the British garrison at Halifax, was fear that it might provide the imperial government with an excuse for further withdrawal.[11] Certainly Americans were aware of the bases and squadrons of warships that ringed their coasts. When in the late 1880s the United States began to rebuild its moribund forces, advocates of rearmament pointed to the menace posed by Halifax, Esquimalt, Bermuda, and the Caribbean establishments.

NAVAL RACES AND ANGLO-AMERICAN FRIENDSHIP

The British confronted the revival of American military strength in the aftermath of a brief war scare in the winter of 1895–6 over U.S. intervention in a dispute over the boundary between Venezuela and British Guiana. The British government soon agreed to an American participation in the settlement, in part because of simultaneous difficulties with Germany. Nevertheless, senior British army officers made determined efforts to rescue the defence of Canada from the limbo in which it had been allowed to lapse by both the British and the Canadian governments. The growing preponderance of American strength in border regions made the Canadian interior more vulnerable than ever, and the army stressed to the RN the importance of maritime action. Believing that any hope for successful action was disappearing because of the American naval program, the Admiralty did its best to ignore the whole question.[12]

The attitude of British naval and political leaders was a first step in the strategic revolution that would slash and reorient commitments to focus on Europe. The army learned the truth only slowly, and then it resisted, rightly seeing naval domination of policy. For Britain, the international balance of power to a considerable extent had become based on counting the number of the most modern, expensive battleships possessed by each nation. During the 1880s, as the empire's competitors industrialized, the revolution in warship construction from wood to steel and from wind to steam propulsion had threatened British predominance. The navy had capitalized on the resulting concern and intense popular and official interest in naval strategy in order to win increased funds in 1889 for a loosely defined 'Two-Power Standard.' In practice this slogan came to mean that the RN should have as many battleships as the combined total of the next two largest fleets, those of France and Russia.[13]

The speed and good seakeeping qualities of the latest warship designs bolstered Admiralty confidence that the fleet could intercept any substantial enemy force on the high seas before it reached British territory. That view substantially became government policy. In the words of the Colonial Defence Committee (CDC), a body of officials from the services and the Colonial Office, in an empire-wide circular that was released to the public: 'The maintenance of sea supremacy has been assumed as the basis of the system of Imperial defence against attack from over the sea. This is the determining factor in shaping the whole defensive policy of the Empire, and is fully recognized by the Admiralty, who have accepted the responsibility of protecting all British territory abroad against organized invasion from the sea.'[14] Implicit in this strategy was the RN's need to match any likely combination of adversaries, and already the two-power standard was beginning to seem inadequate. Not only the United States, but Japan and Germany also had begun to build major navies. The reluctance of the politicians and the Admiralty to confront the problem of Anglo-American war in 1896 and after pointed towards international settlements based primarily on the naval balance;

diplomacy was the means to avoid a financially crippling requirement for a three- or four-power standard for the RN.

In Canada, the effect of the big-ship, big-fleet strategy was to make seapower seem a more remote and exclusively British affair. As the Admiralty made clear, costly, sophisticated warships and the need for centralized control over worldwide deployments left no scope for colonial initiative. London had urged the colonies to make annual cash contributions to support the imperial fleet, a move New Zealand and the Australian colonies had made with the proviso the money be spent to augment the squadron in their area; Canada had rejected the idea out of hand. Even ardent Canadian proponents of imperial cooperation found such proposals for taxation without representation repugnant. From the mid-1890s the Toronto branch of the British Navy League promoted alternative schemes for a modest Canadian-controlled force to relieve the RN in Canadian waters. These ideas, however, remained on the periphery of influence for some years.[15]

The dominion was prepared, instead, to do something about land forces. In the wake of the Venezuelan crisis, militia reform had become an issue in the general election of 1896 that brought the Liberal government of Wilfrid Laurier to power. To the extent that Laurier, a French-Canadian lawyer, thought about military questions at all, he agreed with Macdonald that geographical isolation from the world's trouble spots and friendship with the United States guaranteed Canadian security.[16] He gave the militia portfolio to Frederick W. Borden, a Nova Scotian, who like many from that province found it impossible to take seriously the Loyalist anti-American hyperbole often voiced in central Canada. Nevertheless, Borden was genuinely interested in reform. Perhaps most important, money was available, the Canadian economy having finally begun to prosper after the dreary conditions that had prevailed since the early 1870s.

British advice was available in profusion. In London, Joseph Chamberlain, the colonial secretary since 1895, had transformed the Colonial Office into a powerful ministry. As one of the leading pessimists about the state of British international power, he was determined to seek new alliances and unite the empire more closely. In 1897 Laurier startled British authorities by accepting a commission, under Major-General E.P. Leach, a senior British officer at Halifax, to investigate Canadian defence against the United States. Reinforcing this success, Chamberlain used his influence in 1898 to assign the aggressive Colonel Edward T.H. Hutton as GOC in Ottawa and, as governor-general, the Fourth Earl of

Minto. Minto, who had served in Canada as an army officer in the 1880s, was fully committed to his friend Hutton's bold design for imperial military integration.[17]

A CANADIAN NATIONAL ARMY AND WAR IN SOUTH AFRICA

Previously, British schemes to integrate the militia into the imperial army had focused on improving and assigning particular units for overseas service. Hutton seized one important element in Canada's complex allegiances by calling for the creation of a 'National Army' of 100,000 men capable of taking the field and defending the frontier against the United States according to the requirements laid down by the Leach Commission. Canada would be much less dependent upon British support in a crisis and, should Britain need help abroad, a pool of trained manpower would be available. As it turned out, the first expression of the 'National Army' was not preparations for border defence, but was the dispatch of an expeditionary force overseas. The outbreak of war in South Africa in October 1899 unleashed a flood of pro-empire sentiment in Canada, as Macdonald had predicted, and demands for active Canadian participation. There was also, as Macdonald had feared, a profound division of opinion. Laurier was in a particularly delicate position, since his power base was Quebec and French-Canadians were lukewarm or openly hostile towards imperial adventures that had no direct relation to Canadian security. Facing a divided cabinet, the prime minister tried to stand pat on established practice: Canadians could volunteer for British service.[18]

London promoted a 'national' Canadian force in the face of a cautious, 'colonial' attitude in Ottawa. Chamberlain, seeking imperial integration, had pressed the settlement colonies to offer official contingents. The War Office envisioned these contingents as small 125-man units that could be plugged into larger British units. Hutton, however, prepared plans for a Canadian formation that could take the field as a distinct entity, a proposal Minto strongly supported, as did Borden when he belatedly learned of it. Thus, the first Canadian contingent was organized as a full 1,200-man battalion, the 2nd (Special Service) Battalion, Royal Canadian Regiment (RCR). The name established its place in the Canadian militia as a unit of the RCR, the infantry component of the 'permanent force,' the small regular cadre Canada had raised in the 1870s and 1880s to instruct the part-time militia. Many of its personnel, including the commanding officer, Colonel W.D. Otter, came from the permanent force.

On this model, subsequent contingents – more than 7,000 Canadians served in South Africa in 1900–2 – were organized as special service battalion-size units.

Canadian participation did not ease tensions in the Militia Department. Although Borden welcomed many of Hutton's recommended reforms, the general spoke publicly against the evils of political meddling in military administration. This stance and other defiances of the minister's authority, together with Minto's refusal to bridle Hutton, brought Laurier and his colleagues to dismiss the difficult general in February 1900. Minto feared that Laurier's government would name as GOC an unqualified Canadian officer, who would be a puppet of the politicians. He was especially alarmed at the 'appalling self confidence'[19] with which Canadians contrasted the creditable performance of Canadian troops in South Africa with the early disasters suffered by British forces. This attitude accentuated a strain of chauvinist conviction in Canadian imperialism about the northern dominion's destiny to save the empire from Britain's old-world decadence. Although the government accepted the diplomatic Major-General Richard O'Grady Haly as Hutton's replacement, Minto suspected that the return of the heroes from South Africa would make pressure for change irresistible.[20]

With a sense of foreboding, the governor-general seized upon the appointment of Canadian officers to desirable positions at Halifax and Esquimalt in exchange for continued employment of British officers as GOC in Ottawa. The GOC appointment, he suggested to St John Brodrick, the British war secretary, could be upgraded to include the coastal garrisons. Such an arrangement would increase GOC prestige and eliminate the struggles for authority between British officers in Halifax and Ottawa which had sometimes embarrassed London's campaign for Canadian reform. Minto further endorsed the view of Colonel Gerald Kitson, a British officer serving in Canada who had made the original proposal, that the Canadians should assume full responsibility for the coastal garrisons. By compelling Ottawa to multiply the size of the meagre permanent force and organize the whole range of support services, the garrisons would provide 'a good nucleus for the whole Militia.'[21] Minto was guardedly optimistic as he informally promoted these ideas in Britain and Canada, because the Laurier administration had already shown an interest in the garrisons. When early in 1900 the War Office announced its intention of removing the regular infantry battalion from Halifax to South Africa, Laurier's ministry swiftly replaced it. The 3rd (Special Service) Battalion, RCR, remained on full-time garrison duty at

Halifax under British command until, when the war ended in 1902, it was relieved by an imperial battalion.

Laurier had actually been motivated by domestic politics. A wide consensus in the press and Parliament had emerged whereby the logical way for Canada to support the effort in South Africa would be action at home to relieve British units. Given the timing – soon after the political crisis over the dispatch of the first contingent – it seems likely that the prime minister hoped to ease the rifts and, simultaneously, to avoid further commitments in South Africa.[22] Laurier's renewed interest in the fortresses in 1902 was similarly inspired by a desire to avoid imperial entanglements. Chamberlain convened a colonial conference in London that summer to draw on the wartime spirit of solidarity to extract increased naval subsidies and the closer integration of land forces. On this occasion, he pathetically called on the overseas premiers to relieve the 'weary Titan staggering under the too vast orb of his own fate.'[23] Laurier had responded in advance in the Canadian House of Commons by promising not to embroil the dominion in the 'vortex of militarism which is now the curse and the blight of Europe.'[24] At the conference, however, the Canadian delegation acknowledged 'the duty of the Dominion, as it advances in population and wealth, to make more liberal outlay for those necessary preparations of self-defence which every country has to assume and bear.'[25] Canada was willing to take over the Halifax and Esquimalt garrisons and consider its own naval defence requirements.

The reference to naval action was a clever rejoinder to the Admiralty's call for subsidizing big ships. The Canadians wanted to improve the FPS, which had proved useful in asserting sovereignty in coastal waters. Perhaps intentionally, the proposal touched a sore point between the British armed services. Both Hutton and the Leach Commission, tied to the army, had recommended that the FPS should be better trained and equipped. Its small ships could also pass through the St Lawrence canals to provide vital support on the Great Lakes for defending the frontier against an American invasion. This role and this theatre were of no interest to the Admiralty.[26] Laurier's government ordered two new fisheries cruisers in 1903. With a good turn of speed, all-steel construction, and quick-firing guns, they were superior to other vessels in the Canadian government inventory. They could be useful as minor patrol vessels in wartime, but the RN paid no attention to the scheme. It was becoming impossible, however, to ignore the widening gulf between the British armed services over the general question of preparation for war with the United States. During the Boer War, when all the European powers had been antagonistic towards Britain, the Admiralty had been hard pressed to maintain the naval balance in home waters and the eastern Atlantic. Thus London set out to limit possible complications from competitors overseas, concluding an alliance with Japan in January 1902 and pressing as far as was possible in this direction with the determinedly isolationist United States. During the Spanish-American war of 1898, Britain had been the only European power friendly to the United States, and when Britain became embroiled in South Africa the following year, the Americans had returned the favour. Beyond popular hoopla about Anglo-Saxon brotherhood and destiny (in which Canadians fully shared), British and American interests were proving to be similar. More to the point, there was now no hope that the RN could match the United States Navy (USN) in the western hemisphere while maintaining the minimum force needed at home to secure the British Isles against the expanding European fleets.[27]

The army became aware of this situation during the latter part of 1902 when the CDC reviewed the standard of the western hemisphere garrisons. The defences at those stations had been developed on the basis of RN commitments to ensure that an attack would be limited to a coup de main. The Admiralty now announced that in a crisis no naval reinforcements could be dispatched until supremacy had been assured in European waters. The issue was soon taken up in the Committee of Imperial Defence (CID), a coordinating body recently organized to overcome the shortcomings of defence administration revealed by the Boer War, on which the prime minister sat with the service ministers, senior officers, and other officials.[28] In the case of Halifax, the army warned that the Admiralty's position was tantamount to abandoning Canada. Existing infantry and mobile artillery for landward defence of the fortress were inadequate against the large troop formations the Americans might put ashore if free to sail troop transports to Nova Scotia. The Canadians – the only source of reinforcements for the fortress if the Admiralty's views were accepted – would be powerless because all units not already assigned to Halifax would be urgently needed on the international border in Quebec and Ontario.[29]

While the army and navy wrangled, Frederick Borden informed Minto in April 1903 that he would introduce a new militia act. Among other reforms, it would end the requirement that the GOC be a British officer. Minto persuaded Borden to go to London for consultations, and to delay the legislation until he had considered British advice. In the

British cabinet, however, the balance shifted against Minto and the army. Chamberlain had resigned from the government, and the sympathetic Brodrick had been replaced by H.O. Arnold-Forster, formerly parliamentary secretary at the Admiralty and an adherent of the navalist Europe-focused strategy. So, too, was Arthur Balfour, the new prime minister. During the autumn of 1903 the CID essentially decided to leave Canadian defence to the Canadians. The committee raised no major objections to Borden's new militia bill and, without addressing army concerns about the standard of defence at Halifax and Esquimalt, decided to invite the dominion to take over the bases.[30]

Borden learned of these developments when he visited London in December 1903. In an ill-fated experiment aimed at broadening the CID to include colonial representation, Borden was made a member of that august body. The minutes of the meeting that he attended recorded the Balfour government's acceptance of the new militia bill and Borden's agreement to the transfer of the imperial bases. Minto was apoplectic when he discovered what had happened, but he was relieved to learn that the minutes of the meeting had stirred up a hornet's nest in Ottawa. The CID secretary had transformed Borden's expression of interest in the bases into a commitment. Borden formally asked that the reference be stricken from the record, but in a private note he explained that Ottawa's objection was purely procedural. The lack of prior consultation with the Canadian government about both Borden's participation in the CID and the bases question made it appear that Britain was dictating to Canada, a possibility that raised the ire of Laurier and his Quebec colleagues. Borden enjoined the British to pursue 'immediately' and directly the offer Canada had made at the 1902 Colonial Conference: 'I know a favourable answer would be given.'[31]

Minto advised the Colonial Office to ignore Borden's encouraging message. Determined that Britain must maintain the imperial garrisons in order to preserve some influence, the governor-general reported that Borden was isolated in the cabinet. This left the false impression in London that the Canadians had no interest in the bases.[32] Yet, Minto was right that the imperial connection was under severe strain in Ottawa. Britain's drive for Anglo-American settlement had swept into its train long-standing Canadian-American issues in which Canadian leaders already felt ill served by British supineness. The process had begun encouragingly enough. In 1898–9, British friendliness towards the United States during the Spanish-American war had produced an Anglo-American joint high commission charged with resolving a range of Canadian-American disputes. Acknowledging Canada's initiative in relations with the Americans, Britain allowed the dominion to name four of the six imperial commissioners, including Laurier. The leading issue was now, as a result of the Klondike gold rush, the contested Alaska panhandle boundary. When a proposal for compromise foundered because of pressures from American interests, the commission adjourned – permanently as it turned out. Laurier, with his own unexpected domestic problems, was glad of a cooling-off period. During the negotiations, in which he worked closely with the imperial government, he had been shaken by public denunciations from his politically important pro-empire supporters in Ontario that he was kowtowing to Washington.[33]

Delay did nothing to strengthen Canada's position. Laurier wanted, and the imperial government was initially willing, to use the American desire to be freed of Britain's treaty rights to participate in the construction and control of the proposed Panama canal as a lever in the Alaska question. Needing to cement American friendship in the early phase of the South African War, however, London gave way completely on the canal in 1901. In so doing, British leaders acknowledged Admiralty advice that the canal, by allowing the United States to move its fleet quickly from the Atlantic to the Pacific, had sealed American military dominance of the western hemisphere.[34] Meanwhile, the assassination of the moderate president, William McKinley, brought the 'Bully Boy,' Theodore Roosevelt, to the White House. In 1902 the British government prevailed upon Laurier to accept arbitration by an Anglo-American-Canadian tribunal of 'impartial jurists.' In the tribunal, because of Roosevelt's threats of military occupation of the panhandle and London's eagerness for a settlement, the British member sided with the Americans on every contested point.

When the tribunal results were announced in the autumn of 1903, Canadians were dumbfounded. Roosevelt's threats were chilling but not out of character for the ugly politics of the republic. The shock had been Britain's sell-out. Laurier observed in the Commons: 'The difficulty ... is that so long as Canada remains a dependency of the British Crown the present powers that we have are not sufficient for the maintenance of our right. It is important that we should ask the British Parliament for more extensive power.'[35] A further imperial embarrassment followed. By early 1904 Lieutenant-General the Earl of Dundonald, another aggressive reformer in the Hutton mould, whom the War Office had appointed to the militia command, had begun publicly to criticize the government's inept and corrupt military administration. By the time he was dismissed in June 1904, his outbursts and venomous private correspondence had confirmed British officials in their growing conviction that the system of a British GOC was unworkable and brought even Minto part way around. The parallels between Canadian difficulties and the civil-military struggle within the War Office in London did not escape British observers.[36]

In the spring of 1904 Borden had modified his draft militia bill to assert more strongly the supremacy of the minister and the civil authority. He was inspired by the creation of the Army Council in Britain, a reform modelled on the Board of the Admiralty and aimed at preventing the chaos that had resulted during the South African War from the division of authority between the commander-in-chief and the war secretary. The commander-in-chief's position was abolished, and the supervision of military preparations and administration was vested in a panel of four officers, of whom the senior, the chief of the general staff, was only the first among equals. All important questions were considered collectively in the Army Council, which included the four officers, the secretary of state, and senior civil officials. Borden's Militia Council was virtually identical except that, whereas the Army Council could make decisions in the absence of the war secretary, the Militia Council was purely advisory; this difference enshrined the Canadian principle of absolute civil supremacy.[37]

Borden made promises that increased Canadian control would not mean the promotion of unqualified Canadian officers. For the new senior appointment, the chief of the general staff, he requested the services of Colonel P.H.N. Lake, a British officer who, while serving in Canada in the 1890s, had played a key role in planning for frontier defence and become a trusted friend of the Canadian minister. As he left Canada in the fall of 1904, Minto intervened to overcome War Office scruples about selecting such a junior officer.[38] His instincts were right. Borden had always been willing to accept much of Hutton's and Dundonald's advice about improvements in planning, training, and professional military standards, and in fleshing out the militia organization with the supporting services – engineers, medical, transport, and supply – essential to mobilize and maintain an army in the field. The crises that had shortened the reformers' tenure had largely been caused by their personalities. The mutual confidence between Borden and Lake allowed them to implement many of the elements of the Hutton and Dundonald programs. Such were the government's priorities – economic development, especially the construction of two new transcontinental railways – that money never was available to expand fully the non-permanent militia or acquire the necessary equipment. Nevertheless, despite the utility of the non-permanent militia as a vehicle for political patronage, Borden accepted Lake's priority for the professional development of permanent staffs and force units, including the employment of British officers in larger numbers than before. Without this nucleus of expertise for planning, organization, and instruction, equipment and additional training camps for the non-permanent militia would have been wasted.

Meanwhile, in July 1904 financial strains on the Balfour government had brought Arnold-Forster to recommend cuts at overseas stations, including Halifax. In supporting these economies, the CID spelled out a policy, though not one the army staff had advocated:

Halifax – In the event of war with the United States, it is clear that the Western coaling station could not be defended by the garrisons at present allotted to them against organised expeditionary forces such as might be brought to bear if the British Navy were not able to be employed in full strength in the Western Atlantic. From this point of view, therefore, very small garrisons are desirable. As regards any other Powers, it is not necessary to contemplate anything more serious than a raid by one or two cruisers ... The Committee considered that effective assistance was more likely to be obtained from Canada if the entire responsibility for infantry defence were thrown upon the Dominion Government.[39]

The decision to retain British artillery and engineer troops on what promised to be a greatly reduced establishment was the slenderest acknowledgment of Minto's and the army's concerns. The army officers, with Minto's support, protested that the existing defences should be maintained. Much stronger than the island bases in the western Atlantic, Halifax had some chance of holding out against any attack the Americans might make in the critical early phase of a war.[40]

The ultimate decisions were made at the political level in close conjunction with the navy and with no reference to the army. In October 1904 Balfour's government named Admiral Sir John Fisher the first sea lord, the senior professional appointment at the Admiralty. Fisher, who cultivated and wielded enormous political influence, took up this position with the government's approval to complete RN concentration in European waters – and save funds to ease the fiscal crisis. Part of his strategy involved disposing of many smaller vessels deployed overseas and calling home some larger ships. The Pacific and the North America and West Indies squadrons that had operated on Canada's coasts were to be abolished. On 23 November, as the Admiralty prepared to shut down all naval bases in the Americas except Bermuda, the CID asked the Colonial Office to negotiate with Canada to provide the infantry battalion for Halifax and take full responsibility for the garrison at Esquimalt.[41] The Colonial Office was in a bind. In the words of the permanent under-secretary, his department had 'while maintaining that garrisons are not necessary ... at the same time [invited] Canada to furnish garrisons.' He continued, '[W]e cannot give the real reason ... the necessity for reducing Army Estimates, or the ostensible reason, the assumed impossibility of war with the United States. Unfortunately Lord Minto has told us that Canada is not prepared to undertake the defence of these two fortresses: otherwise we might offer it to them as evidence of our confidence in their military capacity and in the complete efficiency of their militia.'[42]

The truth quickly spread by way of transatlantic cable news services. Fisher was notorious for press leaks to promote his causes. Very shortly, reports about the plans to withdraw the navy from the western hemisphere appeared throughout North America. There was no attempt to disguise the reason. A *New York Times* article, reprinted in Canada, declared that a 'unique compliment' was being paid to the United States 'by practically ignoring that country in the distribution of ships ... An Admiralty official is quoted as saying: "While the relations between America and Great Britain remain as they are we do not need any warships over there. It would be a waste of money to keep any there."'[43] These reports were confirmed in a parliamentary paper of 6 December that announced the fleet reorganization. It included the bald statement: 'In the Western Hemisphere the United States are forming a navy the power and size of which will be limited only by the amount of money which the American people choose to spend on it.'[44] Soon after, news of the Admiralty's orders to close the Halifax and Esquimalt dockyards hit the Canadian press.[45]

Other British press reports that Arnold-Forster's efforts to reorganize the army were being hindered by Canada's unwillingness to take over Halifax and Esquimalt inspired an angry editorial in the Toronto *Globe* on 8 December, 'No Need for British Troops':

The garrisoning of these fortresses with well-trained Canadian regulars would be a far more popular method of contributing to imperial defence than the granting of a million a year to the War Office at Whitehall [sic, apparently a reference to recurring British proposals for cash contributions to the navy] ... Canada will be not one whit less loyal than she is today when the last British soldier leaves the forts of the Atlantic and Pacific. National self-respect demands that the Canadian people shall not be indebted to the home government in the maintenance of any soldier on the soil of Canada. Self-government must be accompanied by self-support.[46]

Because the *Globe* was the leading Liberal mouthpiece in English Canada, the independent *Ottawa Citizen* suspected the editorial had been planted.[47] No evidence for this suspicion exists, but the *Globe* editorial reflected Borden's private views. The one element that had not been emphasized was Borden's hope that responsibility for the regular garrisons would provide a means to increase and improve the politically unpopular permanent force.[48]

A consensus favouring the transfer soon emerged in the Canadian press. Conservative pro-empire newspapers had initially been suspicious;[49] but their fears evaporated with news about the sweeping nature of the British reorganization and the Balfour government's financial worries.[50] *Le Nationaliste*, associated with Henri Bourassa, the leading voice of anti-imperial nationalism in Quebec, commented that Canada had no need of imperial military charity and could easily manage the bases.[51] It was the same consensus that had interested Laurier in the fortresses since 1900. The *Globe* editorial worked magic for low spirits at the Colonial Office. Alfred Lyttelton, Chamberlain's successor, wired Lord Grey, the new governor-general, to ask if the piece reflected the government's views.[52] One potential difficulty was War Office haste to remove the British infantry battalion at Halifax. The British government brooded that if the Canadians discovered the unit was slated to go regardless of what they did, they might seize the excuse to do nothing. Again, pressure for speed and secrecy was false drama. Laurier was in touch with developments at Halifax and knew the battalion would shortly be disbanded.[53]

The anxious tone of the imperial documents has suggested that Grey had difficulty in extracting a commitment.[54] The real problem was that the ministers, just having fought a successful general election, were out of town. When Grey rounded up Laurier and Borden towards the end of December, Laurier assured him with a 'chuck of the chin,' that Canada was good for the whole cost of both garrisons, $2.5 million annually.[55] Further delay occurred until the cabinet could be assembled to make a formal offer on 20 January 1905. The one sticking point involved the method of transfer, not Canada's willingness to act. General Lake wisely advised that Canada would have to retain some British units for a couple of years, since the total strength of the permanent force was less than that of the infantry battalion alone; as well, Canadian regulars lacked the necessary technical training. Lake's proposal would have saved considerable sums, since British army pay rates were lower than Canadian ones. But it would have required subsidy payments to the British government and acceptance of continued British command.[56] The difficulty was resolved by the Canadian suggestion that personnel from the technical units be allowed to transfer to the Canadian service (234 did so), and that an additional twenty-seven specialist officers be seconded. Drawing on much of the existing permanent force, Canada formally took over Halifax in January 1906 and Esquimalt in May. In response to the War Office's financial pleas, Ottawa paid all bills as of 1 July 1905.[57]

At what standard, Grey asked midway through the transfer negotiations, should the Canadians be told to maintain the fortresses? Having been directed to trim the Halifax defences on the assumption that attacks would be only hit-and-run raids by one or two cruisers, the army in late 1904 prepared to dismantle some of the forts and cut the imperial artillery, engineer, and other technical units from a total strength of 700 to about half of that figure.[58] The army, however, had simultaneously reopened the Canadian defence question, this time hammering away at the central issue: the defence of the Canadian frontier in western Quebec and eastern and southern Ontario. Here were located the great centres of population and wealth, here conditions were least favourable to defence, and here, rather than against isolated Nova Scotia, it was assumed the Americans would make their main initial offensive. Land forces alone could not defend this area because communications were dominated by the Great Lakes; as experience in the American Revolutionary War and the War of 1812 had shown, naval control of at least Lake Ontario and, preferably, Lake Erie as well was essential. The general staff pressed the Admiralty on what it could do or recommend that Canada might do to assure command of Lake Ontario, isolated as it was by the St Lawrence canals from the big-ship fleets that were the focus of Fisher's strategy.[59]

The general staff's harping on Canada was a counter-attack against the dominance of the navy that looked like downgrading the British army to little more than a reinforcement depot for the Indian army. Canada, the only other great continental possession of the empire, was the obvious theatre – the entente with France and the idea of a major expeditionary force being in their earliest stages – where the British army had a leading strategic role to play. Better still, the Admiralty's welshing on commitments to protect British territory in both the western Atlantic and the Great Lakes demonstrated the limits of the big-ship, big-fleet policy. The Admiralty did not have to concede in the CID, where the issue was thrashed out in April and July 1905.[60] The sailors and the politicians merely reiterated that a North American war was unlikely and would be an unmitigated disaster for both Canada and Britain. They reported that the best intelligence indicated (accurately) that Germany had replaced Britain as the probable enemy against which the USN was expanding.[61] At no time did the committee address the army's questions about what should be done in the event of the unexpected. Lord Selborne, the first lord of the Admiralty and one of the principal architects of rapprochement with the United States, grasped this point and, moreover, was appalled at his officers' willingness to write off Canada. In his preface to the main Admiralty paper, he emphasized that if the United States, seized by an 'attack ... of frenzy,' should strike against Canada, Britain would naturally make a total effort; he held out the hope that such determined resistance might 'give the American people time to return to righteous sanity.'[62] More inclined to the naval view, Balfour opened the discussion by 'affirming the principle that, in the event of danger, Canada has a right to the support of the whole resources of the empire. The question is, how best to distribute our imperial forces in peace time.' To this extent, CID renewal of the 1865 pledge to Canada was something more than window-dressing.[63]

Although losing on the most important issue of central Canada, the army won its case for not cutting back the Halifax defences, undoubtedly because Canada was paying the bills. The reluctance of Japan's modern battlefleet to close with Russian forts during the recent war in the Far East was further evidence that the Americans would be unlikely to rush the substantial seafront defences at Halifax. The only other possible landing places were twenty to thirty miles from the city, across terrain so forbidding and bereft of communications that the existing garrison might well be able to hold out against 10,000 men. The general staff's paper ended by declaring that, in any event, the CID's ruling that the RN could not be expected to muster supremacy over the USN in the western Atlantic had to be kept from the Canadians: 'Ministers would resent the attitude taken up ... It must be remembered that the Canadians attach a possibly exalted importance to

Halifax ... as a fortified post in their main line of communication with the rest of the Empire.'[64]

Still, the change in British strategy was perfectly clear in Ottawa. The old imperial defence scheme for Halifax, available in the Militia Department, had spoken of the RN's dominance, limiting any American landings to 1,500–2,000 troops. Now the CDC stated: 'The United States might, for an uncertain and possibly considerable period, be in possession of sufficient local command of the sea to disembark in the vicinity of Halifax and expeditionary force of, say, 10,000 or 15,000 men.'[65] The Canadian government had agreed not only to maintain the standard recommended by London, but to revise the full fortress mobilization scheme every year or two for review by the CDC. This Canada scrupulously did. Despite budget and permanent-force manpower problems, there were as many as 1,400 Canadian regulars in the garrison, and never fewer than 1,100. That figure compared favourably with the 1,700 troops of the imperial garrison, especially considering that it had been possible to reduce some services because a home army was now in charge. The CDC consistently reaffirmed the American standard of attack, recommending in 1908, for example, improvements in the searchlight and quick-fire gun defences in order to counter new USN torpedo attack craft. Although proceeding slowly because of financial restrictions, Canada carried out these changes.[66]

The Canadian government did not really care about the strategic justification for the Halifax fortress, since the defences filled British more than Canadian needs. As the military members of the Militia Council declared in June 1905 in a published statement of defence policy, Canada was 'relieving the Imperial government of the responsibility for the safety and maintenance of the two Imperial naval bases, Halifax and Esquimalt, which stand upon Canadian soil.'[67] Government members, when speaking on defence, inevitably boasted that Canada had 'relieved the British taxpayer of the burden of any military expenditure whatsoever within her borders,' and was honouring a 'pledge to the empire' by maintaining the Halifax and Esquimalt defences at the standard set by British authorities.[68] Canadian policy, in short, did not extend beyond either the nation's self-evident need for armed forces worthy of its status or the government's search for an effective rejoinder to British appeals for military assistance overseas that had so seriously divided Canadian opinion.

Ottawa's essentially domestic focus was best shown by the transfer of the Esquimalt defences. In reviewing the western hemispheric bases, the

British had no difficulty in agreeing that this minor outpost should be abandoned. Utterly exposed to the large USN naval base in nearby Puget Sound, it was also too far removed from the Far East, where British interests in the Pacific now centred. Borden received this news in September 1905 when he was in British Columbia trying to reassure a population shaken by the RN's withdrawal at the moment that Japan, which many in the Pacific province viewed with open hostility, defeated Russia. The government kept the British judgment secret and maintained the fortifications with a skeleton garrison of about 100 troops. After the anti-Japanese riots in Vancouver in 1907, the government made cosmetic improvements at the base and ignored the pleas of Lake and other members of the militia staff to develop proper defences on the west coast. Here again, Laurier's instinct to trust in the Anglo-Japanese alliance was not far removed from that of British politicians, while the Canadian staff's suspicion of Japan echoed that of important elements in the British services.[69]

In so far as Canada had a specific military interest in taking over the fortresses, Borden hoped that the initiative would stimulate further development of the 100,000-man army.[70] During the transfer, he and Lake had pressed to increase the size of the permanent force to 5,000 troops, enough to provide coastal garrisons and strengthen depots across the country. Here at last would be an adequate professional nucleus for training and mobilizing the full strength of the part-time militia.[71] In the event, because of finances, the permanent force achieved an effective strength of no more than about 2,800 troops, and that only because Borden supported Lake in unpopular decisions to limit training of the non-permanent units.[72] Early in 1908, although the government rejected Lake's plea for more money on the grounds that slow progress with the army program might incite American aggression, it did not question the program as such.[73] As it had in the case of the fortresses, the government felt no need to plunge into strategic questions, but it was willing to pay within reasonable limits – and only those limits – for respectable forces.

To a considerable extent, the government's lack of strategic policy reflected the absence of bureaucratic machinery to integrate technical military questions with the deliberations of cabinet. That machinery, after all, was only in its early stages of development in Britain. It was true that there was no urgency for Canada to build such institutions, given the abundant evidence that Britain was coming round to the Canadian government's long-standing appreciation that war with the

United States was unthinkable. The British army, cheered by the increased Canadian effort, mistrusted the domestic imperatives behind it. Senior officers, who saw in dominion land forces an important part of the empire's military potential, feared that the Canadian habit of sloth in defence and thirst for fuller autonomy might resurface. For those reasons, and out of a continuing conviction that naval policy erred in not accounting for unexpected confrontation with the Americans, the army would never admit to the Canadians, or allow the CID and CDC to admit, that war with the United States had been discounted.[74]

NAVAL QUESTIONS ON THE GREAT LAKES AND OCEANS

The Admiralty, by contrast, was satisfied with the Laurier government's backwardness in naval defence. When the Canadian defence issue had been thrashed out in the CID during 1905, Admiralty staff officers had pointed to Canada's own 'incurable optimism,' as shown in its lack of serious military preparation, as evidence that the danger of a North American war could safely be ignored. The Admiralty also endeavoured to scotch the army's idea that Canada's laughable FPS could be developed into a Great Lakes' defence force. Balfour agreed that any worthwhile effort on the lakes would arouse American ire. The first casualty would be the Rush-Bagot Treaty of 1817, under which Britain and the United States had undertaken to maintain no more than four small armed vessels on the lakes; it would produce an arms race the empire could not win. Army officers agreed about Rush-Bagot, but pressed their naval brethren to concede that Washington could not object if the Canadians developed a force of small warships on the east coast that could in a crisis deploy to the Great Lakes. The positive comments of some ministers that this fleet could be the basis for a true Canadian navy sent a chill through the Admiralty. Fisher was opposed to dominion fleets which would certainly be inefficient and an embarrassing hindrance to centralized Admiralty control of operations.[75]

He need not have worried. In 1904 Laurier's minister of marine and fisheries, Raymond Prefontaine, had prepared draft legislation for the next stage in the transformation of the FPS: raising a 'Naval Militia,' whose members would train on the fisheries cruisers. Prefontaine, however, was given to public excesses that aroused the suspicions of French-Canadian nationalists. They drew a sharp distinction between armies for defence of home soil and seagoing endeavours that would inevitably entail direct Admiralty control and foreign commitments. Thus, Laurier was glad to use the excuse of the cost of the imperial fortresses to drop the 'Naval Militia' bill.[76] Laurier also kept a low profile on the Rush-Bagot agreement. The American government had long been under pressure to revise the agreement to allow Great Lakes states to enjoy the benefits of the USN's renaissance. There were two issues: the construction of smaller types of warships that would have to exit through the Canadian canals to join the oceanic fleets; and the entry through the canals of armed vessels to serve as training ships for naval reserve units in the Great Lakes states. Pressure from these states heightened during the Spanish-American War, and revision of the agreement became one of the leading issues in the Anglo-Canadian-American joint high commission of 1898–9. The British government supported revision to avoid American abrogation of the agreement. Laurier agreed, but he was deeply worried by strident declarations from his Ontario supporters that Canadian self-respect demanded resistance to revision. The prime minister was equally concerned about pro-revision lobbying by the Great Lakes states. The manner in which American opinion had been inflamed into a crusade against Spain led him to brood about the consequences of nationalist emotion on both sides of the lakes.[77]

After the joint high commission folded, Laurier cooperated in a subterfuge whereby Britain and the United States acted as if the draft revision had been implemented. In 1907 American press reports alerted Canadian journalists to the fact that their government had authorized the entry of two additional training vessels, which inspired dark stories about Laurier's 'concurrence' in the Americans' 'mobilizing a force of gunboats' that 'can only exist for one object.'[78] Unknown to the government, a well-informed editorial about the need to control the situation on the lakes had been inspired by a leak from the militia staff, probably Lieutenant Colonel W.G. Gwatkin, a British mobilization expert brought over to develop the plans for defence against the United States. Gwatkin evidently passed confidential documents on the 1898–9 joint high commission that showed how near revision of the treaty had come. Gwatkin and the militia staff, who had not been informed about the Anglo-Canadian-American complicity, were worried that Rush-Bagot was at risk. The leak was intended to pressure Laurier to carry out the 1898–9 revisions and forestall American abrogation of the agreement.[79] The incident reflected the isolation of the staff from policy making and the lack of seriousness with which the government regarded specific preparations for border defence.

The British army's general staff, which took the controversy in Canada at face value, used the apparent threat to Rush-Bagot to get the Admiralty to admit responsibility for Lake Ontario. One hope was that the Liberal government that had replaced Balfour's Unionists in December 1905 would take a more positive view. At a CID meeting on 14 May 1908, however, Liberal ministers suggested that Rush-Bagot was primarily a Canadian concern and expressed confidence that Ottawa would avoid dangerous risks.[80] This view was consistent with the hands-off approach the British had adopted towards Canadian-American issues since the Alaska arbitration. Rush-Bagot was only the most striking example of the manner in which Laurier, despite public threats, had not pressed Canada's usual initiative for fear of domestic and international consequences. Paradoxically, British and American officials re-energized Canada's relations with the United States. Earl Grey, much more positively disposed to Americans than the frosty Minto, was convinced that 'the chief danger ... is that of Canada becoming Parochial,' of turning her back on both the United States and the United Kingdom.[81] Grey publicly and privately encouraged the efforts of Elihu Root, Roosevelt's secretary of state. An intensely practical and learned lawyer, Root saw no reason why the whole range of Canadian-American issues could not be resolved. He was a former secretary of war and one of the American 'jurists' in the Alaska arbitration; Laurier regarded his approaches with ill-disguised suspicion.[82]

The impasse was broken by the appointment of James Bryce as British ambassador to Washington in March 1907. Bryce, an expert on the American constitution, who was convinced of Anglo-American common traditions and interests, was also known as a critic of imperial centralization. Understanding Laurier's distrust of the British embassy in Washington, he endeavoured to make himself a servant of Canada, giving every encouragement to Canadian officials who capably negotiated the details of the various boundary and fisheries questions. Bryce came to see that Laurier's prevarication was chiefly the result of Canada's having no central machinery to collect documents and record action and positions on diplomatic issues that cut across the responsibilities of several departments. Pressure from Bryce and Grey brought about the creation of Canada's Department of External Affairs in 1909 to provide such a secretariat. With these initiatives, Canada and the United States 'cleaned the slate' in 1908–11 with the conclusion of eight agreements and treaties.

Revision of Rush-Bagot was not among those formal accords. The entry of the USS *Nashville* into the Great Lakes in May 1909 set off another alarm in the press, more serious than that of 1907. This was a formidable little warship, the most modern and best armed of the training flotilla. The new American president, William Howard Taft, and his inexperienced administration violated the informal rules of subterfuge by publicizing the fact. Once again, the militia staff leaked information to a journalist, who produced forceful pieces. While Laurier considered the unusual step of refusing permission for the Americans to keep the vessel armed, he received a gentle reminder from Britain of the possibility that the Americans would denounce the treaty. That danger, Laurier confessed to Bryce, had him in 'fear and trembling all the time.' Taft was sympathetic to Laurier's domestic troubles, and Bryce was able to get an American commitment not to increase the number of armed vessels on the lakes.[83]

Perhaps the most striking thing about the furore over Rush-Bagot in 1909 was that it had no impact on the naval defence question, which became a leading issue in Canada for the first time that same year. Even the most rabidly anti-American imperialists in Ontario did not take seriously the danger of war with the United States; the point of the lurid fantasy articles about Nashville's blazing away at the defenceless Toronto waterfront was to underline Canada's humiliation caused by Laurier's underhandedness. The Toronto branch of the Navy League, the only Canadian group that seriously analyzed possibilities for naval development, had always given the lakes low priority. Their interest lay in the protection of the seacoasts and shipping against European cruisers that might break loose in remote theatres as a result of the RN's concentration close to the British Isles. After 1905 the branch promoted the organization of a Canadian coastal force by the procurement of powerful, seaworthy torpedo craft that were coming into service in the RN and other navies, including that of Australia. Fisher conceded that a dominion force of torpedo craft would not disrupt the unity of Admiralty command.[84]

The Toronto branch of the Navy League had some influence in the Conservative party. Robert Borden, the leader (not to be confused with his Liberal cousin, Sir Frederick Borden), took up the navy issue reluctantly, because his French-Canadian supporters feared that any such initiative would imply imperial commitments and cause trouble in Quebec. In January 1909 George Foster, a senior Toronto Conservative MP, put forward a parliamentary resolution that tweaked the government for not carrying through with the long-promised naval program, and for not providing 'suitable protection of [Canada's] exposed coast line

and great seaports.'[85] By the time Foster's resolution was debated on
29 March 1909, the naval issue had exploded.[86] On the 16th, Britain's
Liberal prime minister, H.H. Asquith, had announced that his government might have to lay down as many as eight 'dreadnought' battleships, instead of the planned four, in the light of evidence that Germany
had accelerated its construction of these fast, all-big-gun warships. Even
with four extra ships, he warned, Germany might have seventeen of
these vessels by 1912, compared with Britain's twenty. The two-power
standard was apparently becoming a scant one-power standard. Balfour, now leader of the opposition, countered that even the expanded
program was inadequate: by 1912 Germany might have twenty-one
dreadnoughts to Britain's twenty.

NOISE ABOUT NAVIES: QUIET LAND FORCES INTEGRATION

This 'bombshell' ignited a wave of pro-empire sentiment in the dominions. The New Zealand government immediately offered to pay for an
additional dreadnought; in Canada and Australia, the federal parties
split as to whether they should make similar special grants or develop
the dominion's own naval defences. Laurier appeared to master the situation by seizing on the Foster resolution, promising to establish torpedo
craft flotillas on the Australian model already suggested by the Admiralty. Laurier disbelieved the crisis of British power. He rightly saw a
domestic political struggle over the level of defence expenditure. Moreover, he could not conceive that the RN's supremacy could so suddenly
be broken by a newcomer like Germany, or that two such supremely
civilized nations could go to war. As he had done so often before, he
framed policy by attaching a price tag to what would be a respectable
effort. Robert Borden had suggested that Canadian naval spending
should be about half of the $6 million level of the militia budget. Laurier
obliged by establishing a ceiling of $3 million for naval defences. The
government's plan still was to build on the FPS, but to acquire torpedo craft to complete the protection afforded by the army's harbour
fortifications.

Canadian representatives to the special Imperial Defence Conference
called in August 1909 received a shock. Belatedly recognizing the
dominions' willingness to spend far more on 'national' armed forces
than on imperial subsidies, Fisher urged them to establish capital ship
'fleet units.' These forces would be substantially autonomous in peacetime but could form a formidable fleet under Admiralty command in

war. His concern was not with Germany, but with the expanding Japanese navy and the danger that the Japanese would not renew the alliance when it expired in 1911. Canada rejected the Pacific concentration and the procurement of a dreadnought, but was willing to acquire other ships recommended by the British: four substantial cruisers and six destroyers. A more formidable force than had been originally intended, it came within the $3 million spending limit.[87] The Liberals were confident that they had successfully applied the same principles as had been followed with the fortresses and militia reform: accepting imperial advice, focusing on home defence, and assuring Canadian control.[88]

Laurier's government energetically began organization of the new navy on both coasts in 1910, but soon ran into political difficulties. Robert Borden played on French-Canadian suspicions by denouncing Laurier's cruiser scheme as too ambitious. He suggested limiting the Canadian service to more modest coastal vessels. At the same time, he proclaimed that because war with Germany within five years was likely, an 'emergency' battleship subsidy would have to be given to Britain. That proposal consolidated his imperialist support, as did his further argument that the Laurier Naval Service Act's provision that Canadian warships could join operations under British control only with the permission of the government and approval by Parliament amounted to separation from the empire. The swift and world-ranging nature of naval operations, he insisted, required that a Canadian navy be more closely associated than the militia with the imperial forces.

He was wrong. At the Imperial Conference of May 1911 the British accepted the Canadian Naval Service Act and similar Australian legislation. The Admiralty and experts from other departments had concluded that common equipment, training, and doctrine would provide an adequate basis for the dominion fleets to combine with the RN in wartime.[89] As to whether the dominion governments could be counted on at the moment of crisis, Richard Haldane, the war secretary, commented: 'that we should act on the assumption that the Dominions would take part in a serious war. There was very little doubt that they would, and he was sure that their statesmen were quite alive to the fact that they would really have very little choice, none unless the enemy so willed [in the eyes of the world, all the empire's territory and shipping being British]; but for reasons of internal politics, which were quite comprehensible, they declined to bind themselves beforehand.'[90] Haldane was doing nothing more than describing the existing direction of British defence relations with the dominions. He was well qualified to do so. Since taking over the War Office in 1905, in conversations with Sir Frederick Borden and other dominion politicians, he had come to appreciate their sensitivity about 'local' control of armed forces; he also recognized how their desire for British technical and professional assistance opened the door to military integration by other means. To no small extent, the opportunities for influence became evident with the reform of the British army itself, over which Haldane presided. This change involved developing and more effectively implementing mobilization procedures, doctrine for operations, and training standards. In agreements reached at the 1907, 1909, and 1911 imperial conferences, the dominions accepted that although home defence was the primary object for each one's army, the effective defence of any particular part of the empire required quick mutual support. This broad principle in no way challenged individual dominion authority to decide what or how much it would do. But the principle allowed the adoption of British military standards so that should any dominion government so decide, its forces could give effective support.[91]

Certainly, Laurier's cabinet was as cautious as ever. To preserve the supreme authority of the Canadian government, Sir Frederick Borden kept Canada out of the British scheme for an 'Imperial General Staff.' Officers holding the principal training and planning appointments in dominion forces were to qualify at the British staff college and have the right freely and directly to communicate with their colleagues throughout the empire. Borden's rejection of the formal trappings did not matter. Most of the eligible appointments in Canada were already filled by qualified British officers on loan, and more junior Canadian officers were being groomed for these senior positions by attendance at the British staff college and exchange postings in Britain and other parts of the empire. Borden, moreover, agreed to have the Canadian forces inspected by General Sir John French, the imperial inspector general, in 1910. French emphasized the need for better preparations for mobilization, and though making the case in terms of defence against an American invasion, he did not ignore readiness to support other parts of the empire. In 1911 Borden approved a scheme to raise an overseas expeditionary force of an infantry division and cavalry brigade. It was one of his last acts as militia minister.[92]

The domestic repercussions of external relations that Laurier had always feared were central in the fall of the Liberal government in the general election of September 1911. Taft's friendly cooperation over Rush-Bagot in 1909 had been only the precursor to an achievement that had been the dream of every Canadian government: reciprocity with the United States on a wide range of natural products. Under domestic pressure because of the effects of Republican high tariffs on the cost of living, the Taft administration had met most Canadian terms and pushed the agreement through Congress in July 1911. Laurier believed he had an election winner: but a rising tide of anti-Americanism in southern Ontario cost the Liberals crucial support, and hostility towards the navy scheme told against them in Quebec.

After rising to the premiership, Robert Borden had no more luck than Laurier with the naval issue. Admiralty policy was the central difficulty. Following the renewal of the Anglo-Japanese alliance early in 1911 and a war scare with Germany during the Moroccan crisis of that summer, the new first lord of the Admiralty, Winston Churchill, determined to meet the German threat by building up a 60 per cent fleet superiority. Within his party Churchill faced strong opposition to increased spending. When Borden visited England in the summer of 1912 to consult on naval policy, Churchill asked him to revive the battleship subsidy. Convinced of the depth of the European crisis, the Canadian prime minister agreed to supply $35 million for three dreadnoughts. Borden had also come prepared to discuss all aspects of what he called his 'permanent' policy for developing a Canadian service. He was particularly interested in small, coast defence craft, given the attitude of his Quebec supporters. The most obvious need for these vessels would be to hold off American vessels, but the Admiralty explained in unvarnished terms how completely the British government had ruled out the possibility of Anglo-American war, and showed how the coast defence system needed to meet the scale of an American attack would be cripplingly expensive. A more modest coastal defence would really serve no purpose, because the cruisers of a European power would not risk closing the areas where these craft could operate. Rather, such raiders would concentrate hundreds of miles off shore against the vulnerable and massive trade that plied from the Americas to Britain seaward of Nova Scotia and southern Newfoundland. The British suggested that Borden build the Laurier cruiser squadron – which only three years before Fisher had said was not needed on the Atlantic – for trade defence. Borden was reluctant, and the Admiralty was prepared to assist him by justifying the modest coastal flotilla.[93]

'Naval Aid' was a political disaster. The bill to provide $35 million was delayed for months by a Liberal filibuster in the Commons and then killed by the Liberal majority in the Senate in May 1913. Borden dropped both that initiative and his 'permanent' policy for the coastal flotilla in order to consider his options. Meanwhile, the cadre naval service that Laurier's government had organized was allowed to wither as the Conservatives turned a blind eye to desertion and cut the budget to the bone. Liberal unwillingness to compromise owed much to Borden's attack on the Laurier navy and his pledge to replace the Naval Service Act with one that would allow automatic Admiralty control in war. Still, the fact that the fire and noise of the naval debates produced such a meagre result indicated that Canadians felt no more threatened from the sea than they had felt at the time of RN withdrawal in 1904–5.

The concrete result of Borden's concern about the European situation was an increase in militia spending from $6.9 million in fiscal 1910–11 to nearly $11 million in fiscal 1913–14. Borden, distracted by the naval issue, left militia policy almost entirely in the hands of an eccentric minister, Colonel Sam Hughes. A life-long volunteer militiaman and ardent imperialist, Hughes detested professional soldiers, whether Canadian or British, whom he felt had always treated the non-permanent force with contempt while feathering their own nests. He devoted most of the increase to the volunteers: 55,000 did paid training in 1913, compared with 43,000 in 1910, and a massive program for the construction of militia drill halls went forward across the country.[94] He did nothing for the permanent force, whose meagre numbers shrank further by attrition, and he virtually ignored the militia council. Major-General Colin Mackenzie, the British officer who had served as chief of the general staff since 1911, resigned in disgust in 1913. The British made no difficulty, because Mackenzie's narrow, rigid view of civil-military relations had raised the ghosts of the Hutton and Dundonald controversies. Hughes, moreover, selected another qualified British officer, Colonel W.G. Gwatkin, to replace him.[95]

Hughes's dictatorship and the stranding of the navy deeply depressed the staffs in Ottawa. Lieutenant Colonel George Paley, a British officer serving as director of military intelligence, lamented in August 1912 that Canada still had no policy other than the 100,000-man army and maintenance of the coastal fortresses. The 100,000-man army now bore no relation to either increased American military strength or the growth of Canadian potential in wealth and manpower since 1905. Nothing had been done to resolve the question of naval defence of the Great Lakes, nor to secure the Pacific coast or complete arrangements on the Atlantic. Nothing had been done about the close cooperation among all departments of government, everything from communciations censorship to civil transport control, that would be required to put the country on a war footing. Paley noted that these matters had to be addressed if Canada were to have any hope of holding out against the United States until imperial reinforcements arrived. It was still more urgent in view of the 'political situation in Europe' to ensure that the dominion could quickly complete its home defences, organize its resources, and dispatch assistance to the main theatre of war as the government had agreed to do at the imperial conferences.[96]

Paley recommended the formation of a Canadian version of the CID with the prime minister at its head and specialist subcommittees composed of officials from interested departments. The service chiefs strongly endorsed the proposal, and Robert Borden, when he was in England, learned that the British government had suggested a similar organization to the dominions at the 1911 Imperial Conference. Laurier had agreed, but had done nothing. Borden was interested, but was too busy to follow through, and Hughes appears to have blocked action at the departmental level. Early in 1913 Asquith's government dispatched detailed information about its 'war book' for interdepartmental cooperation on mobilization, and it urged the dominions to make their own versions so as to act quickly on the receipt of coded telegrams from London in the event of a crisis. That advice led to the creation of a deputy-minister-level war book committee in Ottawa which, fortunately, had nearly completed arrangements when the first warning telegram arrived from Britain on 29 July 1914.[97] Yet Canada still had neither a defence policy nor the machinery to make one.

At one level, the story of Canadian defence and foreign affairs in 1896–1914 is one of paradox layered upon paradox. Having struggled to achieve more complete control of the land forces, the government then cooperated in closer imperial military integration than had ever existed. The justification was an American threat that Canada had long since dismissed. Having long pressed for more authority in relations with the United States, the government then had to be induced by imperial officials to grasp the opportunity. Likewise, many of the national elements of the land and naval forces had been conceived and promoted by British soldiers and sailors. Any logic must be found in Canada's colonial status and the fact that the country was, in strategic terms, secure. Under the imperial system, Canada lacked the powers, information, and mechanisms to make comprehensive foreign and defence policy. In the absence of serious external threats, there was no imperative to acquire these means. Rather, the challenges to the new nation were economic development and political stability. Not surprisingly, external and defence affairs were usually viewed through these lenses. What Canadian governments sought were armed forces and powers over external relations that were adequate for the nation's needs, and those ends were generally what they achieved. In the event, one glaring paradox, military reform on the basis of defence against the United States, proved to be not such a paradox at all. Among the first duties of the Canadian forces on the outbreak of war in 1914 was to secure the international border against German agents and others from the neutral United States and to support the RN in maintaining patrols off U.S. ports where German ships were sheltering. As a result of the preparations made since 1905, both Canadian services proved fully adequate.[98]

NOTES

1 There are classic works, strong on both the cultural and the foreign policy dimensions of the rapprochement: C.S. Campbell, Jr, *Anglo-American Understanding, 1898–1903* (Baltimore, 1957); Bradford Perkins, *The Great Rapprochement: England and the United States, 1895–1914* (New York, 1968). Cf. A.E. Campbell, *Great Britain and the United States, 1895–1903* (London, 1960). A.L. Friedberg, *The Weary Titan: Britain and the Experience of Relative Decline, 1895–1905* (Princeton, 1988) adds valuable material on military and economic issues.

2 R.A. Preston, *Canada and 'Imperial Defense': A Study of the Origins of the British Commonwealth's Defense Organization, 1867–1919* (Toronto, 1967); idem, *The Defence of the Undefended Border: Planning for War in North America, 1867–1939* (Montreal, London, 1977); D.C. Gordon, *The Dominion Partnership in Imperial Defense, 1870–1914* (Baltimore, 1965); C.P. Stacey, *Canada and the Age of Conflict: A History of Canadian External Policies*, Vol. I: *1867–1923* (Toronto, 1977); all emphasize the land aspect of Canadian defence at the expense of maritime dimensions. The standard accounts of British military policy are understandably weak on Canadian sources: Kenneth Bourne, *Britain and the Balance of Power in North America, 1815–1908* (London, 1967); S.F. Wells, Jr, 'British Strategic Withdrawal from the Western Hemisphere, 1904–1906,' *Canadian Historical Review*, 49(1968), 335–56; John Gooch, *The Prospect of War: Studies in British Defence Policy, 1847–1942* (London, 1981), esp. 35–51.

3 On Canadian defence in the 1860s, see C.P. Stacey, *Canada and the British Army, 1846–1871: A Study in the Practice of Responsible Government*, rev. ed. (Toronto, 1963); Preston, *'Imperial Defense,'* chs 1, 2; J.M. Hitsman, *Safeguarding Canada, 1763–1871* (Toronto, 1968), chs 8–11; Bourne, *Balance of Power*, chs 7–8.

4 Stacey, *Canada and the British Army*, 187, 227, 229.

5 C.S. Mackinnon, 'The Imperial Fortresses in Canada: Halifax and Esquimalt, 1871–1906,' Ph D thesis, University of Toronto, 1965.

6 A.R. Stewart, 'Sir John A. Macdonald and the Imperial Defence Commission of 1879,' *Canadian Historical Review*, 35(1954), 122.

7 Desmond Morton, *Ministers and Generals: Politics and the Canadian Militia, 1868–1904* (Toronto, 1970).

8 Stewart, 'Macdonald and Defence Commission,' 129.

9 Quoted in Stacey, *Age of Conflict*, Vol. I, 25.

10 R.D. Tallman, 'Warships and Mackerels: The North Atlantic Fisheries in Canadian-American Relations, 1867–1877,' Ph D thesis, University of Maine, 1971; R.C. Brown, *Canada's National Policy, 1883–1900: A Study in Canadian-American Relations* (Princeton, 1964), chs 1, 3.

11 Roger Sarty, 'Silent Sentry: A Military and Political History of Canadian Coast Defence, 1867–1915,' Ph D thesis, University of Toronto, 1982, 73.

12 Bourne, *Balance of Power*, 319–29, A.J. Marder, *The Anatomy of British Sea Power: A History of British Naval Policy in the Pre-Dreadnought Era, 1880–1905* (New York, 1940), 252–7; Campbell, *Great Britain and the United States*, 32–6; Gooch, *Prospect of War*, 53–5.

13 The standard works are Marder, *Anatomy*, 44–61, 105–16; D.M. Schurman, *The Education of a Navy: The Development of British Naval Thought, 1867–1914* (Chicago, 1965), chs 1–4. Cf. Friedberg, *Weary Titan*, 144–60.

14 Colonial Defence Committee memorandum [57M], 19 May 1896, CAB [Cabinet Archives, Public Record Office, Kew] 8/1; see also Gordon, *Dominion Partnership*, 103–06.

15 Roger Sarty and Michael Hadley, *Tin-Pots and Pirate Ships: Canadian Naval Forces and German Sea Raiders, 1880–1918* (Montreal, Kingston, 1991), 9–10.

16 Preston, *'Imperial Defense'*, 115. See 'Proceedings of a Conference Between the Secretary of State for the Colonies and the Premiers of the Self-Governing Colonies ... 1897,' CO [Colonial Office Archives, Public Record Office. Kew] 885/6, Misc No. 111.

17 On the militia and reform in the late 1890s, see N. Penlington, *Canada and Imperialism, 1896–1899* (Toronto, 1965); Morton, *Ministers and Generals*, chs 6, 7.

18 Carman Miller, *Painting the Map Red: Canada and the South African War, 1899–1902* (Montreal, Kingston, 1993), chs 3, 4.

19 Quoted in Carman Miller, *The Canadian Career of the Fourth Earl of Minto: The Education of A Viceroy* (Waterloo, Ont., 1980), 121.

20 Minto to Chamberlain, 5 December 1900, Minto Papers [National Archives of Canada, Ottawa] MG 27 IIB1 vol. 21; Desmond Morton, *The Canadian General: Sir William Otter* (Toronto, 1974), 242–5; Miller, *Painting the Map*, 366.

21 Kitson to Minto, 1 August 1900, Minto Papers, vol. 21; Minto to Brodrick, 19 November 1900, Minto Papers, mfm A131.

22 Sarty, 'Silent Sentry,' 107–10; Miller, *Painting the Map*, 155.

23 Michael Howard, *The Continental Commitment: The Dilemma of British Defence Policy in the Era of the Two World Wars* (Harmondsworth, 1974), 11.

24 House of Commons, *Debates*, 12 May 1902, 4726.

25 'Memorandum by the Canadian Ministers concerning Defence,' 11 August 1902, CO Misc 144 Confidential; 'Conference Between the Secretary of State for the Colonies and the Premiers of the Self-Governing Colonies,' RG [National Archives of Canada, Ottawa] 7, G-21, file 168.

26 Roger Sarty, 'Canadian Maritime Defence, 1892–1914,' *Canadian Historical Review*, 71(1990), 470–1.

27 Rhodri Williams, *Defending the Empire: The Conservative Party and British Defence Policy, 1899–1915* (New Haven, CT, 1991), 27–31; Friedberg, *Weary Titan*, 165–84; Penlington, *Canada and Imperialism*, 106–8.

28 Bourne, *Balance of Power*, 359–60.

29 War Office, 'The Adequacy of the Existing Garrison and Defences of Halifax to resist an Attack by Land,' 11 December 1903, CAB 38/3; Gooch, *Prospect of War*, 59.

30 Morton, *Ministers and Generals*, 182–4; S.J. Harris, *Canadian Brass: The Making of a Professional Army, 1860–1939* (Toronto, 1988), 69–71; Williams, *Defending the Empire*, 41–5.

31 Borden to Minto, 1 March 1904, Minto Papers, vol. 9.

32 Minto to Lyttelton, 7 March 1904, Minto Papers, mfm A–132, vol. 4; Minto dispatch to Lyttelton, 7 March 1904, CO 42/896/9602.

33 Brown, *National Policy*, 334–5, 340–51, 396–410.

34 J.A.S. Grenville, 'Great Britain and the Isthmian Canal, 1898–1901,' *American Historical Review*, 51(1955), 48–69.

35 House of Commons, *Debates*, 23 October 1903, in Stacey, *Age of Conflict*, Vol. I, 99.

36 Morton, *Ministers and Generals*, 187–92; Miller, *Minto*, 148–55.

37 'The Militia Act, 1904' [CDC 366 R25], January 1904 [but 1905], CAB 5/1, includes a detailed analysis of the act, and a copy of the order-in-council that created the Militia Council; Borden to Lake, 1 July 1904, F.W. Borden Papers [Public Archives of Nova Scotia, Halifax], Private Letter Books 8.

38 Miller, *Minto*, 154.

39 Minutes of the 48th Meeting, CID, 8 July 1904, CAB 38/5.

40 Earl Roberts and Major General Grierson, 13 July 1904, CAB 2/1.

41 Minutes of the 58th Meeting, CID, 22 November 1904, CAB 38/6; cf. CO 42/899, nos 39966S and 40544S.

42 Ommaney, 1 December 1904, CO 42/899/40544S.

43 *Montreal Gazette*, 8 December 1904.

44 Great Britain, Parliament, Selborne, 'Distribution and Mobilization of the Fleet,' 6 December 1904 (Cd. 2335).

45 *Morning Chronicle* (Halifax), 17, 21 December 1904.

46 *Globe* (Toronto), 8 December 1904.

47 *Ottawa Citizen*, 9 December 1904.

48 Cf. Borden to Jones, [?] December 1902, F.W. Borden Papers, vol. 105.

49 *Halifax Herald*, 5 December 1904; *Mail and Empire* (Toronto), 1 December 1904.

50 Cf. *Mail and Empire* (Toronto), 1, 20 December 1904; *Montreal Gazette*, 10 December 1904.

51 *Le Nationaliste*, 11 December 1904, 1, 15 January 1905.

52 Lyttelton to Grey, 9 December 1904, RG 7 G-21, vol. 169, file 295A pt. 2.

53 Jones to Laurier, 13 January 1905, Laurier Papers [National Archives, Ottawa] MG 26G, mfm C-819.

54 Wells, 'Strategic Withdrawal,' 344–5.

55 Grey to Lyttelton, 25 December 1904, Grey Papers [National Archives, Ottawa] MG 27 IIB2, vol. 12.

56 Lake to Grey, 'Future Maintenance of Halifax as an Imperial Fortress', 12 January 1905, RG 7 G-21, vol. 169, file 295A pt. 2. Cf. 'Report of Privy Council / 20 Jan. 1905,' Canada, Parliament, *Sessional Papers, 1905* (No. 128).

57 Sarty, 'Silent Sentry,' 132–3, 137–9, 144, 181–2.

58 WO [War Office Archives, Public Record Office, Kew] 32/816/058/2848.

59 General Staff, 'The Defence of Canada,' 13 December 1904, WO 106/40/B1/9.

60 Extract from minutes of 75th Meeting, CID, 13 July 1905, WO 106/40/B1/4.

61 Ottley and Battenburg, 'Naval Notes upon the Defence of Canada,' 6 January 1905, 'Remarks by Mr A.H. Lee, MP, Civil Lord of the Admiralty,' 5 February 1905, both ADM 1/7807.

62 Selborne memorandum, in Bourne, *Balance of Power*, 383. Cf. Wells, 'Strategic Withdrawal,' 348–9.

63 Extracts minutes of 69th and 70th Meetings, CID, 5, 12 April 1905, WO 106/40/B1/4.

64 General Staff, 'The Defence of Halifax and Esquimalt,' 31 March 1905, CAB 38/8.

65 Colonial Defence Committee, 'Halifax Defence Scheme revised to January 1905. Remarks' [383R], 10 October 1905, RG 7 G-21, vol. 79, file 165 pt 2.

66 Sarty, 'Silent Sentry,' 195–7, 200–2.

67 'Memorandum from the Military Members of the Militia Council to the Minister of Militia and Defence,' 14 June 1905, Canada, Parliament, *Sessional Papers 1905* (No. 150).

68 House of Commons, *Debates*, 9 March 1909, 2265; cf. ibid., 2266–70. Then see ibids 9116–17 (10 July 1905), 5648 (2 April 1907), 5734–5 (27 March 1908), 8515–16 (5 May 1911).

69 Roger Sarty, '"There will be trouble in the North Pacific": The Defence of British Columbia in the Early Twentieth Century,' *BC Studies*, 61(1984), 6–16.

70 House of Commons, *Debates*, 5 May 1911, 8515–16.

71 'Memorandum from the Military Members of the Militia Council to the Minister of Militia and Defence,' 14 June 1905, Canada, Parliament, *Sessional Papers 1905* (No. 150).

72 Sarty, 'Silent Sentry,' 174–7.

73 Harris, *Canadian Brass*, 76.

74 Gooch, *Prospect of War*, 63–70; see also CO 537/497.

75 Ottley and Battenburg, 'Naval Notes upon the Defence of Canada,' 6 January 1905, ADM [Admiralty Archives, Public Record Office, Kew] 1/7807. Cf. Minutes of the 69th, 70th and 75th Meetings, CID, 5, 12 April, 13 July 1905, WO 106/40/B1/4.

76 R.H. Gimblett, '"Tin-Pots" or Dreadnoughts?: The Evolution of the Naval Policy of the Laurier Administration, 1896–1911,' unpublished MA thesis, 1981, 80–96; Sarty and Hadley, *Tin-Pots and Pirate Ships*, 16–18.

77 A.C. Glueck, 'The Invisible Revision of the Rush-Bagot Agreement, 1898–1914,' *Canadian Historical Review*, 60(1979), 470–2; Sarty, 'Canadian Maritime Defence,' 469–70.

78 *Ottawa Citizen*, 5 September 1907, copy on HQC 624, RG 24, mfm C-5052. It was clipped by Lt Col. Gwatkin and passed up the chain to Laurier.

79 Hamilton to Willison, 4 July 1907, MG 30 D29, vol. 18, file 140; *The News* (Toronto), 5 July 1907, 6; Gwatkin, 'A Note on the Agreement of 1817,' 27 November 1907, HQC 624, RG 24, mfm C-5052.

80 Sarty, 'Canadian Maritime Defence,' 476.

81 Grey to Lyttleton, 22 December 1904, Grey Papers, vol. 12.

82 A.C. Glueck, 'Pilgrimages to Ottawa: Canadian-American Diplomacy, 1903–13,' *Canadian Historical Association Papers* (1968), 66–83; Peter Neary, 'Grey, Bryce, and the Settlement of Canadian-American Differences, 1905–1911,' *Canadian Historical Review*, 49(1968), 358–80; Stacey, *Age of Conflict*, Vol. I, 103–21; John Hilliker, *Canada's Department of External Affairs*, Vol. I: *The Early Years, 1909–1946* (Montreal and Kingston, 1990), 27–56.

83 Sarty, 'Canadian Maritime Defence,' 481–2; Glueck, 'Rush-Bagot,' 477–81.

84 Roger Sarty, 'The Origins of the Royal Canadian Navy: The Australian Connection,' in *Reflections on the Royal Australian Navy*, ed. T.R. Frame, J.V.P. Goldrick, and P.D. Jones (Kenthurst, NSW, 1990), 91–6.

85 House of Commons, *Debates*, 29 March 1909, 3484.

86 On the naval issue, 1909–1914, see Sarty and Hadley, *Tin-Pots and Pirate Ships*, chs 1, 3.

87 Gimblett, '"Tin-Pots" and Dreadnoughts,' ch. 5.

88 For example, F.W. Borden, House of Commons, *Debates*, 10 February 1910, 3342–3.

89 Roger Sarty, 'The Naval Side of Canadian Sovereignty, 1909–1923.' *The Niobe Papers*, Vol. 4: *Oceans Policy in the 1990s: An Atlantic Perspective* (St John's, Nfld, 1992), 89–92.

90 Minutes of 100th Meeting, CID, 24 March 1911, CAB 2/2.

91 E.M. Spiers, *Haldane: an Army Reformer* (Edinburgh, 1980), ch. 6; John Gooch, *The Plans of War: The General Staff and British Military Strategy c. 1900–1916* (London, 1974), 131–53. For a critical view, R.J. Gowen, 'British Legerdemain at the 1911 Imperial Conference: The Dominions, Defense Planning, and the Renewal of the Anglo-Japanese Alliance,' *Journal of Modern History*, 52(1980), 385–413.

92 Harris, *Canadian Brass*, 77–9.

93 Admiralty memoranda, October 1912, R.L. Borden Papers [National Archives, Ottawa] MG 26H, vol. 124; Admiralty 'Supplementary Note to Memorandum on Best Method of Harbour and Coast Defence,' October 1912, Director General History [National Defence Headquarters, Ottawa] 81/744.

94 *Report of the Militia Council ... Year Ending March 31, 1911* (Ottawa, 1912), 34–5; *Report of the Militia Council ... Year Ending March 31, 1914* (Ottawa, 1915), 44–5, 56–7.

95 R.G. Haycock, *Sam Hughes: The Public Career of a Controversial Canadian, 1885–1916* (Waterloo, Ont., 1986), chs 9, 10; Harris, *Canadian Brass*, ch. 5.

96 Paley, 'Memorandum upon Defence Policy,' n.d., but forwarded by Gwatkin to Stephens, 12 August 1912, RG 24 NS 1019–1–2 pt 1, vol. 3852.

97 Sarty, 'Silent Sentry,' 225–8.

98 Sarty and Hadley, *Tin-Pots and Pirate Ships*, 79–96; J.G. Armstrong, 'Canadian Home Defence, 1914–17, and the Role of Major-General Willoughby Gwatkin,' MA thesis, Royal Military College of Canada, 1982.

2

Strategy and Supply in the North Atlantic Triangle, 1914–1918

GREG C. KENNEDY

The study of the history of cooperation between Britain and its North American allies during the First World War has taken many forms. Some scholars of the British war effort have used the occasion to sing the praises of the British Empire and its strength.[1] In the aftermath of the Second World War, the Suez Crisis of 1956, and the collapse of empire, however, much of the scholarship evaluating Britain as a Great Power during the First World War took a more jaded view of Britain's performance in 1914–18. This cynical new breed of military and diplomatic historians postulated that the First World War signalled the beginning of the end of Britain's reign as the predominant world power. They asserted that Britain had enjoyed a period of security that approached absolute power during the period from 1815 to 1890 – Pax Britannica.[2] For them, the First World War was the first manifestation of inevitable British decline from its position of preponderance, a decline that was the result of a strategic overstretching of resources. The proof of this decline was the growing reliance on and subjugation of the British war effort to the expanding United States of America.

This perception that by 1918 the United States had overtaken Great Britain as the richest and most powerful nation in the world has received support from several American historical schools of thought. Realists, revisionists, left revisionists, corporatists, and others share an underlying belief that, regardless of their evaluation of the actions of President Woodrow Wilson, the United States, for better or for worse, had become the saviour of western Europe and the 'arsenal of democracy' during the First World War.[3] The manpower, naval support, access to industrial markets, and financial assistance that the United States provided to Great Britain during the war are considered vital elements in the eventual Allied victory. The British need for assistance is once again taken, as it is by the declinist school, as the primary indicator of British weakness and subordination to the United States.

This theme of growing British weakness and supposed desperation even spills over into the history of Canada and its role as an ally in Britain's war effort. Canadian military and diplomatic historians, a group recently described as 'professional Canadians,' are interested in explaining the 'birth of the nation' and thus focus almost exclusively on the Canadian war effort.[4] These historians have also been preoccupied with providing a historical basis to justify contemporary Canadian defence and foreign policy. This need to create a past that helps to explain the present has prompted Canadian scholars to manufacture a nationalistic image of Canada's role in and relationship to Great Britain during the First World War that is not contextually accurate.

Recent scholarship has begun to reassess the validity of many of these claims. In particular, the new work challenges the idea of absolute decline, the definition of what makes a nation powerful, and what factors represent sovereignty for nation-states.[5] Central to these investigations is the role of Britain and its relationship with Canada and the United States. These findings suggest that Britain was not in a state of either massive decline or dependence, that it had never been in a position of absolute dominance, and that neither the United States nor Canada was as vital to the British strategic decision-making process as had been previously thought. Rather, a wider approach is used, one that seeks to explain Britain's Allied and imperial obligations, Britain's position as the controller of the alliance's financial, industrial, and maritime matters, and the fact that the British policy-making elite constantly kept an eye on the future and on the peace that the war would produce. The result is that a larger context is created for a comparison of the efforts of all three nations.

Working within this larger perspective, the goal in this chapter is to assess the nature of the relationship between the nations of the North Atlantic triangle with regard to three vital sections of the war effort: finance, manpower, and maritime strength. By studying the war-making capabilities of the three countries and their mobilization of the resources related to these categories, one can provide some answers to a series of questions. Was Britain the leading member of the alliance in these three areas? What were the Canadian and American contributions relative to those of Britain in these areas? Did the United States eclipse the British Empire as the major world power by 1918?

FINANCES

Studies of the Anglo-American financial relationship during the First World War have centred largely on the amount of debt that Great Britain owed the United States by the war's end.[6] Such a ratio is too simplistic a measurement to describe the power relationship between nations. It is undeniable that by the time of the American entry into the war in April 1917, Britain had floated three major War Loans, had issued a number of medium bonds, and as a result was facing a borrowing policy that was too expensive.[7] Concerns regarding rates of exchange, increasing labour rates, and increased prices for goods and services combined to make meeting the balance of payments due on short-term loans a growing concern.[8] More important to the study of the relationships within the North Atlantic triangle is discovering why Britain found itself in such dire financial straits by 1917.

While the debt crisis worried the British War Cabinet as early as 9 December 1916, men like Sir Robert Chalmers, a Treasury official, still had an overwhelming confidence in the ability of Great Britain to raise the necessary funds needed to support the war effort.[9] If negative actions, such as the U.S. Federal Reserve Board's attack on British exchange rates in late 1915, could be avoided, Chalmers was sure that actions taken to enhance Britain's solvency would be successful.[10] The net effect of the American action against the exchange rate was to make the War Cabinet even more wary of U.S. markets and therefore actively attempt to curtail American orders as much as possible.[11]

The British plan to decrease its indebtedness involved a three-step approach: the raising of loans, the sale of securities, and the reduction of domestic consumption.[12] This course of action, aimed at freeing up British finances, was necessitated by the enormous support Great Britain was providing for its Allies and the dominions. By October 1915 the daily cost of the war for Britain was £3 million per day, or £1.314 billion per year. Of that total, £1 million per day, totalling £365 million per year, was being spent on the Allies and dominions.[13] Arms and munitions for Russia, for instance, were bought in Canada, Great Britain, and the United States, while shipping, food, and other war goods were also being provided for all the Allies.[14] Both France and Italy received coal, timber, shipping services, munitions, food, and other consumables from funds provided by Britain.[15] Without that nation's credit and material assistance, the continental Allies would have been exhausted by 1917, and Britain would have been left to stand alone.

British leaders, such as David Lloyd George – first as minister of munitions after May 1915 and then as prime minister after 6 December 1916 – and Reginald McKenna – chancellor of the exchequer until December 1916 – recognized that, in terms of finances and the mobilization of industry for war, the idea of conducting the war along the lines of 'business as usual' was unacceptable.[16] In October 1915 McKenna noted that while the situation called for extraordinary efforts:

we see no reason to apprehend any general breakdown in the productive energies of the world. On the contrary, the main volume of those energies is in full activity, and the proportion lost can be largely made up by normal expansion, curtailment of luxuries, and more strenuous efforts. It is certain that the financial situation can and will, in some way or another, bring itself into conformity with the natural and actual facts of the world's production which underlie it, both during the war and at its close. Convulsive movements of the financial apparatus and temporary difficulties in regard to credit and exchange will certainly be corrected and overcome so long as the natural basis of productivity is sound.[17]

By 24 October 1916, a full year later, because of considerable liquid resources, such as gold and securities, Britain was still in a position to last three months without a public issue in America, *if necessary*; but McKenna acknowledged that this would never be the case again.[18] Britain's drift towards insolvency was being forced upon it not through any weakness of its own making but rather because of the inability of its Allies to furnish sufficient funds for their war efforts.[19] This dependence on British finance forced Britain to lend to its Allies and then seek loans that only British resources could secure in America and other parts of the British Empire.

Assuming victory and that a normal economic and financial regime would be reinstated in Europe after the war, War Cabinet members continued to see the financial situation, even in the spring of 1917, as being a manageable problem.[20] McKenna's successor as chancellor, Andrew Bonar Law, foresaw no problem in raising money in the United Kingdom. He acknowledged that indebtedness would double from £4 billion to £8 billion if the war carried on for longer than a year, and that there was some danger that Britain's Allies would not be able to meet their indebtedness to Britain after the war.[21] The involvement of the United States, however, now signalled the opportunity to achieve Britain's primary war aim: to ensure that the British Empire was not weaker than any other power in the postwar period.[22] Indeed, getting America to take over the financing of the Allies so that 'we should not be the only large creditor of our present Allies,' was an important British war aim.[23] Certainly, the belief that Britain would finish the war as a creditor nation was central to their borrowing practices until Russia was forced into a separate peace. The total amount owed Great Britain by Russia, France, Italy, Belgium, and others at the end of the war was $7.014 billion, while Great Britain owed $3.696 billion to the United States.[24] Clearly, then, British war planning and its financing of the alliance was not initially seen as disadvantageous.

Britain's wartime financing called for a winning of the postwar trade revival. From the earliest days of the war the cabinet began to encourage British manufacturers to penetrate into overseas markets that had hitherto been almost monopolized by German manufacturers. Although the plan failed, nevertheless the idea of an expanded postwar share of the markets was a central theme of the British administration.[25] Winning the peace called for a re-establishment of British trade and goods in markets that had been neglected during the war. Shipping shortages, manpower demands, financial obstacles, and wartime restrictions had opened up many international trade routes and foreign markets to American and Japanese companies and goods.[26] Also, in order to keep Russia, Italy, and France in the war, Britain was forced to expend greater amounts of national wealth and material in 1917 and 1918. More bothersome, however, was the knowledge that Britain's allies were exploiting the opportunity offered them to prosper in markets previously closed to them. The British shipping controller, Sir Joseph Maclay, reported that while Britain was providing 250,000 tons of freightage every month for the transport of American army stores, the Americans continued to leave vital shipping on routes that British shipping lines had had to abandon during the war.[27] New Zealand's prime minister, W.F. Massey, agreed with Admiralty fears that the failure of the United States to meet warship construction goals, while American merchant shipbuilding progressed, had dangerous implications for the future. A prominent Australian shipowner had informed Massey that the United States was expanding and continuing to develop lines of trade with an eye to its postwar trading position.[28] Only by reasserting itself as a dominant world trading power could Britain recover the enormous cost of the war.

Wartime financial risks were assumed not only with an understanding of the postwar challenges of rising nations such as Japan and the United States, but also with the realization of what losing the war would mean. As an extended war became more likely, the fear of losing ground to the United States grew, especially if America could not be persuaded to undertake international obligations in the postwar period.[29] The Canadian prime minister, Sir Robert Borden, a trusted adviser to the British cabinet on American issues, was confident that the British Empire would always be at commercial odds with the United States. But he argued that trade rivalry could be submerged in order to ensure as great an American assumption of international responsibility as possible; doing so would assure a peaceful and prosperous world order for all.[30] Jan Smuts, the South African minister for defence, and one of Lloyd George's most trusted military advisers, cautioned that even with American aid, the war would likely continue into 1920. Such a prolonged conflict meant that 'we shall become a second or third-class Power, and the leadership, not only financially and militarily, but in every respect, will have passed on to America and Japan. Europe will have fought itself out to a finish.'[31] The unexpected arrival of the armistice in 1918 eliminated such ideas, and once again the original concept of aggressively regaining lost trading markets and routes came to the fore. On 18 December 1918 Maclay announced that Britain was flooded with foodstuffs and that an enormous amount of tonnage had become free. Targeting the American and Japanese incursions into British trading areas, Maclay was clear that the shipping fleets were ready to be returned to their rightful owners and that these fleets could now 'be placed in distant and highly profitable trades, e.g., China and the Far East.' In two or three months, the 'normal flow of raw materials and exports would begin again.'[32] The policy of re-establishing Britain's competitive position, as quickly as possible, was aimed directly at regaining at least parity with, if not dominance over, the United States in whatever world was created by the peace settlement.[33]

An important part of the British system of financing the war was the role played by Canada. In the early stages of the war, when strategic planning had been based on the idea of a short war, the material and financial worth of Canada was considered negligible.[34] Even Canadian manufacturers and government officials showed little faith in their own capacity, and neither group appreciated the opportunities that were actually before them, since all involved accepted the short-war scenario.[35] As the war progressed and as the possibility of quick victory receded, Canadian companies and businessmen bemoaned what they perceived to be a lack of British munitions orders.[36] By mid-1915, however, Canada had come to be regarded as a very important part of the overall British war effort in the areas of munitions, foodstuffs, man-power, and raw resources.[37] The financing of these goods and services was also an issue of prime importance.

By June 1918 $1.143 billion worth of munitions orders had been placed in Canada. The disbursements amounted to $943 million, of which $372 million were provided by the imperial Treasury, $460 million by the dominion government, and $100 million by the Canadian banks.[38] Nine hundred and fifty manufacturers had received contracts over the four years, but only 400 of them were now engaged in filling contracts. As well, seven national plants had been established by the Imperial Munitions Board (IMB), an institution set up in Canada to oversee all British munitions purchases.[39] There was no doubt that Canada had offered more support than had been anticipated four years earlier. Yet despite Prime Minister Borden's belief to the contrary, expressed during imperial war conferences in 1917 and 1918, Canada had not mobilized its economy to the level of total war.[40]

While it was true that Canada had made far greater efforts in the areas of finance than had ever been expected,[41] it had not taken nearly the risks or the lending measures that marked the British effort. Driven by increased demands made on its financial system by France, Russia, and Italy, Britain had accepted more obligations because they had to be accepted. The situation was no longer one of sound finance, and R.H. Brand, who served as the liaison between the Ministry of Munitions and the IMB, pointed out the short-sightedness of Canadian bankers to the chairman of the IMB, Joseph Flavelle, in mid-1916: 'If we were all finan-cial purists like the Bank of Montreal, we should have all stopped fight-ing months ago ... They forget that to lose the War is still worse than to inflate their currency.'[42] At that time, the war was costing the British £6 million per day. They had raised well over £2 billion, and estimates showed that at that rate they would have to raise something in the neighbourhood of a further £2 billion per year.[43] By July 1916 heavy lev-els of taxation in Britain had increased revenue by 154 per cent over pre-war levels, whereas Canada's receipts had increased only 18 per cent over the same period. British taxation levels had raised about £45 per capita, and the level was expected to rise to £90 per capita in 1917. In contrast, Canada, including bank credits and a New York loan, had raised about £10 per head.[44]

Flavelle expressed his reservations about the ability of the Canadian minister of finance, Sir Thomas White, to come to grips with the enor-mity of the war and, particularly, with the gigantic role being played by

Britain. The IMB chairman felt that 'In official circles there is developed no added sense of responsibility as to the actions which should be taken whereby the country will be made acquainted with its duty.'[45] In fact, Flavelle's criticism went so far as to state:

It would be a matter of very great regret, as well as concern, to me, if this body of timid, fearful financial men are encouraged in their halting position. Canada is without one dollar of short date paper; she is reaping the benefit of prices for natural products without parallel, and is enjoying a volume of new business in munitions which is enormously adding to the wealth of the country. I venture respectfully to indicate that courage and purpose directed to conserving this great wealth and making it applicable for the nations's need can be greatly quickened and served by a resolute purpose to undertake a liability to assist the Imperial Treasury, and to make all concerned plan to serve to that end. This country does not realise it is at war; no one has given them a convincing message to that effect, and no sustained effort has been made to educate our people to a knowledge of it.[46]

These sentiments were echoed by Brand and the British Treasury. As dollar exchange rates between the United States and Great Britain worsened to British disadvantage, and Canada baulked at the request to begin to pay for its own war supplies from the profits it was reaping from the British war effort, the British Treasury began to view Canadian expenditure as being as intolerable as American expenditure in terms of loan requirements.[47] Brand pointed out that to date Canada had refused to face the financial embarrassments that the European nations had confronted and in effect, financially, was refusing to fight a 'total war.'[48]

None the less, there is no doubt that Canadian monetary support of the imperial war effort was an exceedingly important part of British war financing and that the British government realized that fact. Preferential trade and borrowing conditions, even in comparison with those of other dominions, were allotted to Canada to help to sustain the increasing wealth and power of the dominion in the hope that profits would be spent on war materiel.[49] Such measures were particularly important while the Canadian effort was required to help to stabilize the exchange rate with the Americans[50] and before American industrial strength could be brought up to full speed. Because the war ended sooner than any Allied nation had anticipated,[51] American war mobilization never did reach full production. Therefore, Canadian munitions efforts remained exceedingly important until the very end of the conflict.[52] The need for financial support from Canada was eclipsed in British eyes only after difficulties in dollar credits and transportation shortfalls arose. This shift away from Canada coincided with the U.S. entry into the war and the not unnatural British desire to see that nation's vast monetary and material wealth put into the war effort.[53]

In fact, Britain had treated Canada during the war like the small sovereign ally it was. But with larger strategic considerations weighing on their shoulders, British military and political leaders did not have the luxury of soothing Canadians who complained of high-handed colonial rule every time a financial decision did not favour Canada. Canada had done well by its relationship with Britain, a fact illustrated by Borden's obvious desire to continue to exploit the wartime imperial preference Canada had happily benefited from into the postwar period. The prime minister was quick to ask for both continued preferential contracts from the British government after the war and the removal of any restrictions on trade, realizing that such efforts would be vital in avoiding a collapse of the false war economy built up in Canada.[54] British officials like Leo Amery, the under-secretary at the Colonial Office, and Sir Auckland Geddes, the minister of national service, recognized this point. And for them the situation continued to be a two-way street: British reconstruction and rejuvenation depended on the use of materials and the strong markets provided by the growing dominions; the dominions needed access to the British economy to help to sustain their postwar growth.[55] Clearly, through its financial (and, as will be shown, manpower) contributions during the war, Canada had gained more than 'a signature, slightly indented below Britain's at American insistence, on the Treaty of Versailles and another on the Charter [sic] of the League of Nations.'[56]

On the other hand, American government officials and businessmen were not quite so generous towards Canada. They did not consider Canada a principal country, owing to the fact that any money loaned by the United States for use in Canada had to come through Great Britain. As well, as the American economy grew more regulated and restricted under mobilization conditions, U.S. businessmen and government officials wanted to know why Canada was not financing its own war industries to a greater degree. Their suspicion was that Canada was not doing its share.[57]

None the less, although access to American money was important and the Canadian contribution useful, Britain's economy, its industrial production, and its financial responses had performed in an adequate fashion during First World War: 'British resources financed the entire British war effort and much of the allied, although this created a cash-flow crisis by late 1916. The British economy surmounted extraordinary challenges during Great Britain's greatest war in a century.'[58] But although finance was an important aspect of the North Atlantic relationship, it could not be divorced from concerns over the manpower supply.

MILITARY MANPOWER

The enormous increase in financial costs that occurred during the course of the war was a direct result of the huge increases in the manpower demands on the Allies. Britain, Canada, and the United States each contributed hundreds of thousands of troops to the war effort. There were, however, important differences in the amount, the type, and the conditions of employment of these troops.[59] Great Britain entered hostilities in 1914 with an army that was much inferior in size to the armies of the continental Great Powers. The British Army was to be employed in a short war, taking a 'business as usual' approach to the conflict.[60] Although the early mobilization of Britain's industrial and manpower resources was done in a haphazard and ill-considered fashion, the secretary of state for war, Lord Kitchener, persuaded the cabinet, presided over by the Liberal prime minister, Herbert Asquith, that a large, continental-style army would be required.[61] Owing to a lack of any organizational facilities that could handle the more than 1 million volunteers that flooded into Kitchener's 'New Armies' in 1914, the newly enlarged British ground forces would not be able to play a major role until 1916.[62] After its introduction into the trenches of the Western Front in 1916, however, the 'new' British Army would continue to be pressed to assume a greater role as manpower problems plagued Britain's European allies.[63]

Canada played no small part in assisting Britain to find the men required to maintain this new army. By April 1917 over 327,312 men had been raised either for the Canadian Expeditionary Force or for Allied forces.[64] The need for troops was so strong that conscription was introduced in order to maintain high levels of recruitment in the last half of 1917 and into 1918.[65] Overall, by March 1918 Canada was seen by the British policy-makers to be doing everything possible in the area of recruiting and providing manpower for the British army, in contrast to the efforts of other dominions, such as Australia, which were not performing to expectations.[66] The Canadian Corps, by the spring of 1918, was one of the most professional organizations in the British Army.[67] Despite this military proficiency and the success of Canada's manpower efforts, conflict was developing between the dominions and Great Britain over the staggering casualty lists.

The length of the war, the failed campaign in the fall of 1917 at Passchendaele, the loss of the vital Russian armies on the Eastern Front in the same year, and the German offensive victories in March 1918 created a bleak environment for discussions concerning future British Army manpower requirements. In June 1918 Borden launched a blistering attack on British army commanders at the second meeting of the Imperial War Cabinet. He accused them of being responsible for the absence of military success, owing to 'lack of foresight and preparation, and to defects in the organization and leadership of our forces.'[68] As well, the continued need to provide men for a wide range of overseas expeditions added to demands for not only British but Canadian troops.[69]

Borden's frank commentary on what he viewed as the waste of human lives and valuable resources was echoed by Lloyd George. In his remarks to the Imperial War Cabinet on 1 August 1918 the British prime minister denounced the British and Allied military commanders for being 'somewhat reckless of human life.'[70] The military, Lloyd George said, failed to realize the stresses put on other industrial areas, such as munitions, shipbuilding, and shipping, by their assumptions that the supply of men was inexhaustible.[71] Massive losses to the British army forced British strategists to consider a number of alternative plans of action.[72] Not only did Lloyd George and the dominion premiers want to control the actions of British generals, such as Haig, and French ones, such as Foch;[73] but also, as it began to appear that the war would not end until 1920, Lloyd George and Borden realized that it was imperative to assure two objectives: the staying power of Great Britain and the acknowledgment by Woodrow Wilson of the need for the United States to take a greater role in providing troops for the war effort.[74] Of the two, the second point was the more pressing in the spring of 1918, and the more difficult to attain.

American entry into the war in April 1917 had held great promise for the Allied forces struggling in the trenches of the Western Front. The priority of Britain's requirements from the United States had originally been financial assistance to Allied governments, the release of interned enemy shipping to the Allies, and the use of the United States Navy (the USN) for convoy purposes.[75] It was assumed that the American army would provide men for the trenches in Europe, but that the small size and lack of experience of these forces would limit both the speed of their deployment and their initial size.[76] After the loss of the Russian armies in the fall of 1917 and the collapse of the Italians at Caporetto in October, however, a sense of urgency pushed French and British policy-makers to seek an acceleration of the rate of America's troop involvement.[77] Unfortunately, the urgency of the Allies was not answered with action by the United States.[78]

American mobilization was a disorganized and sporadic effort, because American planners refused to utilize the vast experience and resources available from the British and French armies.[79] They insisted on attempting to provide their own artillery, light weapons, and other materiel, and they refused to amalgamate their troops with the British Expeditionary Force, all in order to create at least the appearance of a national effort that would strengthen Wilson's postwar negotiating position.[80] A lack of decision-making authority among the American military commanders also hampered the preparation of the American Expeditionary Force (AEF). Problems with training philosophies and schedules created an impression among French and British observers that the AEF was neither well trained nor organized enough to meet the demands of modern warfare.[81] In fact, as late as October 1918, during secret British War Cabinet discussions, the assessments of the American army's capability were not flattering: 'Field Marshal Haig said that the American men individually were very good material. The Staff, however, were very inexperienced and hardly knew how to feed their troops.'[82] Such delays and inefficiencies put the Western Front and the French and British forces stationed there, and therefore the entire war effort, at unnecessary risk. The lacklustre American mobilization, suspicions of French and American designs to deprive the British army of American manpower in order to weaken the British postwar position,[83] and pressure by dominion premiers to explain the defeats of the previous autumn and the spring of 1918 all combined to cause Lloyd George to describe the AEF as the 'worst disappointment' of the war.[84] American reluctance to accept British or French material assistance was seen at the strategic planning level as a primary cause of the ineffectiveness of the American units. Although British officials had not believed the inflated claims of American government departments in December 1917 regarding the output of war materiel that would flow from the 'the great[est] manufacturing country of the world,'[85] they had not foreseen that the output would be *so* small in terms of artillery, aircraft, and troops mobilized.

Recognizing that the war had become very much a war of endurance, the British had hoped to husband manpower resources, with the expectation that American aid would meet the minimum needs of the alliance in the trenches for defensive purposes, while British manpower reserves were assured for the vital war industries upon which all Alliance armies now depended.[86] British materiel would be combined with American manpower in 1918 in preparation for operations in 1919.[87] Even such limited expectations for American mobilization, however, proved overly optimistic. The American promise had been for 450,000 men in the field by the spring of 1918. In reality, only 100,000 troops could be put into the field. These troops were not able to obtain their equipment from American sources and, therefore, were largely dependent on British or French resources. Of those 100,000 troops, only 27,000 were actually put in the line.[88] Although these less-than-spectacular results caused strains between the two major North Atlantic powers, even more stress was created by the enormous demands for transport and supply that the AEF in Europe put on limited British maritime resources.[89]

MARITIME POWER

The British Empire was held together during the First World War by the strength of the world's largest merchant fleet, the British Merchant Marine. The flow of goods and trade carried on those vessels was protected by the world's largest navy, the Royal Navy (RN).[90] The ability of Great Britain to fulfil successfully its traditional role as the linchpin of an alliance – as it had during the Napoleonic wars – depended on the continued ability of that great merchant fleet to move freely and swiftly across the oceans of the world.[91] This strategic mobility reflected the worldwide responsibilities of the British Empire and the importance of imperial defence considerations to British war aims:

The main political conclusions of this survey were that the first and greatest British interest was to clear the field absolutely of the German menace to our existence as an Oceanic Empire, dependent on its sea communications, by removing from German control all colonies or territories, insular or continental, which could serve as instruments for reviving that menace. The liberation of Belgium and France in the West and of Palestine, Syria and Mesopotamia in the East, and the elimination of the German flag from South and East Africa and the Pacific, were, consequently, the indispensable *minima* to be secured at all costs.[92]

As a significant portion of the requirements for the British war effort originated in North America, the North Atlantic triangle must be considered a critical element in the maritime aspects of the war.

The Canadian contribution to the empire's maritime war effort was relatively small. The Royal Canadian Navy was still a very tiny, coastal organization whose main components were two training cruisers, *Niobe* and *Rainbow*, and other small craft used for miscellaneous and special services.[93] Canada's naval activity had reached a peak by March 1917, when Imperial War Conference discussions revealed that the *Niobe* had been transformed into a depot ship in Halifax. In addition to normal manning requirements, a scheme of recruiting in the Royal Naval Canadian Volunteer Service for the Overseas Division had been established, and over 500 men had been sent to England for service in the fleet. The dockyards at Halifax and Esquimalt and the floating dock at Prince Rupert were important for the RN, as was the Vickers yard at Montreal. In conjunction with Newfoundland, the government organized a patrol service on the Atlantic coast, and other vessels had been equipped for minesweeping. Thirty-six trawlers and 100 drifters were being built for service in Canada, the federal government undertaking the contacts and work of construction.[94]

Merchant shipbuilding in Canada ranged from the production of wooden merchant ships to the construction of modern steel merchant vessels. Forty-four steel ships of over 207,663 tons, at a cost of approximately $38 million, were contracted for construction in Canada through the offices of the IMB. However, a late recognition of the inability of Canadian shipyards to do adequate work, along with shortages of material and labour in Canada because of competing American programs, created production delays. As a result, few ships were delivered before the end of the war.[95] Forty-six wooden ships were produced in Canadian shipyards, and a number of them were launched before the war's end.[96]

Clearly, Canada's maritime role during the war was not significant in any narrow naval sense. The nation's strength lay in its port facilities and its ability to provide vital war materials, the sinews of empire, which played a part in the overall British war effort.[97] Although such a limited maritime contribution was expected of Canada by British policymakers, far greater things were expected of the USN and the American Merchant Marine.

America's entry into the war brought with it a promise of some relief for the hard-pressed RN. Until April 1917 Britain was the unchallenged director of maritime operations for the alliance. The RN provided the bulk of the main battlefleet units required to thwart German and Austrian attempts to break the Allied blockade of their coasts. As well, RN cruisers and destroyers bore the brunt of escort and patrol duties in the North Sea, Atlantic, Channel, Far Eastern, and Mediterranean waters.[98] By 1917 those cruiser and destroyer forces were protecting a vast network of routes to theatres around the world in an attempt to counter the German submarine attacks against vulnerable Allied and neutral shipping.[99]

The British cabinet's decision to continue to take imperial issues into consideration during the war had many dangerous implications, one of which was the increased demand made on merchant and transport shipping and their accompanying escorts. British maritime resources assisting French and Italian forces in the Mediterranean in 1917 were three battleships, three cruisers, nine light cruisers, two large monitors, twelve small monitors, three minelayers, thirty-seven destroyers, sixteen torpedo-boats, eight submarines, twenty-four sloops, ten armed boarding steamers, and two seaplane carriers. Supporting this main British force were a further eight yachts, 178 trawlers, ninety-four motor launches, ten patrol-paddlers, two motor boats, 163 net-drifters and four boom defence craft. Added to this list were the warships and support vessels assigned to the East Indian, China and Far Eastern, Australian, Cape, Sierra Leone, East African, Pacific, and North American and West Indian stations: 173 warships in all.[100] This naval contribution was matched by 718 naval and military transports (of some 2,108,632 tons) continually carrying troops and stores to the expeditionary forces in France, India, East Africa, Salonica, Egypt, and Mesopotamia.[101] Three hundred and ninety transports (818,456 tons) were similarly employed in supporting British operations in France, and thirty-five transports of 162,110 tons carried British troops and stores to East Africa.[102] The forces in Salonica and Egypt required 176 ships of 657,274 tons, and Mesopotamia and India used 117 vessels of 470,792 tons.[103] The result of such a dispersion of merchant and naval forces was an increased demand for a larger number of destroyers. Such growing and continuing demands for escort vessels created a dangerous overextension of the RN by May 1917.

The implementation of an effective convoy system required a large number of destroyers and elaborate organization. The Admiralty had had difficulty in achieving either prerequisite by the spring of 1917.[104] The building and repair of destroyers had been continually interrupted by strikes and labour problems. As a result, destroyer construction was not above six per month and much operational time was lost.[105] According to the first sea lord, Admiral Sir John Jellicoe, the main difficulty in providing an adequate escort system was the fact that there were simply not enough destroyers available to do all the tasks asked of them: 'It had even been necessary temporarily to reduce the destroyers with the Grand Fleet to a figure far below the safety limit, in order to afford some protection to trade ... the present intention of the Admiralty was to introduce a system whereby groups of merchant ships would be convoyed by a cruiser across the Atlantic, if the necessary cruisers could be provided, and as they entered the submarine danger zone (whether outward or homeward bound), they would be escorted by destroyers when the required number became available.'[106] The greatest threat to British sea power, however, was the continued insistence on allocating resources to overseas commitments.[107] Jellicoe insisted that the continuance of such operations was a fundamental error in the use of British maritime resources and that 'above all, the provision of escorts for the purposes of our various overseas Expeditions, were throwing an intolerable strain on the Admiralty and were dissipating our naval forces in a manner which entirely precluded our being in sufficient strength anywhere to ensure reasonable safety for our overseas communications.'[108] The first sea lord strongly urged that British commitments in overseas areas, particularly the Balkans, be reduced immediately.

The allocation of merchant and naval resources was a careful balancing act under favourable conditions. The growing threat of German U-boat operations made this strategy even more precarious. By the spring of 1917 merchant tonnage losses, plus the refusal of British strategists to discontinue overseas operations, resulted in a forecast that Britain would be 8 million tons short in terms of imports for 1918.[109] Added importance was placed on purchasing foreign vessels or hiring neutrals to operate in safer dominion waters.[110] In addition, priority was given to the shipping lanes between Great Britain and North America. The shorter routes and growing volume of goods and materiel being purchased in North America, even with a deliberate reduction in unnecessary imports such as timber, created a situation that demanded that other traditional routes and dominion markets be sacrificed for reasons of transport efficiency.[111] By April 1917, with the full knowledge of cabinet that such action would have an adverse impact on Britain's postwar economic recovery, the tonnage diverted from those routes amounted to

From:	Far East Trade	18	steamers	about	155,000	d.w.tons
	Australasian trade	13	"	"	108,000	"
	Indian trade	18	"	"	152,000	"
	N. & S. American	10	"	"	60,000	"
	South African trade	4	"	"	23,000	"
	Full requisition	7	"	"	60,000	"
				Total	558,000	

A further thirty coastal and short-trade steamers had been withdrawn from the services of Indo-China and the China Navigation companies in the eastern Seas.[112] Those thirty ships were used to replace vessels serving the Mesopotamian Expedition, thus releasing ocean-going tonnage to the North Atlantic routes.[113] Overall, the naval situation was exercising an increasing influence on the war. Although it was unlikely that the Allies would be knocked from the war in 1918 because of shipping shortages, when the United States declared war on Germany on 6 April 1917, British naval planners expected the provision of two desired resources: more escort/destroyer vessels for convoy work and an increase in the output of merchant shipbuilding. In both areas, reality fell far short of the promise.

The immediate action of the United States was to send thirty-six destroyers, under the command of Admiral William S. Sims, to serve in escort duties with the RN.[114] Following this decision, a great debate over the future of American naval policy and construction took place in Washington. This debate revolved around the wartime demands for the USN to take a larger role in immediate anti-submarine warfare (ASW) operations, and long-term, postwar strategic considerations concerning sacrificing battleship and battle-cruiser construction for destroyer construction.[115] Although the decision to put the construction of destroyers before battle-cruisers was made by 6 July 1917,[116] the actual wartime contribution of the program was slight. Labour shortages, slow program development, funding problems, continuing design changes, steel shortages, and a generally low level of mobilization within the American shipbuilding industry kept the United States from producing the desired vessels at a useful rate.[117] Indeed, the inability of the USN to provide effective combat vessels to the level and at the rate of their early claims was a serious problems for British maritime planners.[118] In September 1918 the first lord of the Admiralty, Sir Eric Geddes, considered that 'the United States promises were apparently as untrustworthy in naval as they had been in military matters, and ... only seven new destroyers had been completed by the U.S. in the first seven months of this year, and that no further new destroyers would be available from that source till January, 1919; moreover it was always possible that the Americans would retain their output for protection of their own waters.'[119] Added to the construction problem were the issues of training and deploying the American destroyer fleet. The question of training and operational experience was of particular importance with regard to the effectiveness of American forces. Sims pointed out that 'American ships, although in all respects efficient when they came to join the British naval forces, were no real addition of strength – possibly the reverse – until they had learned to adopt the same methods and work on precisely the same system as the British ships.'[120] British suspicions about America's real naval mobilization level and its plans for prosecuting the maritime aspects of the war only to U.S. advantage were heightened not only over the destroyer issue, but also with regard to America's merchant marine.

The American Merchant Marine was unable to meet the demands of American mobilization. A relatively small, coastal service, the U.S. merchant fleet suffered from a lack of ships and the inability of American industry to increase its shipbuilding capability. Despite attempts to *buy* command over the Allied maritime effort, the realities of a lack of floating tonnage, or any new tonnage coming off the quays, prevented the United States from challenging British control of maritime operations.[121] As late as March 1918 forecasts suggested that the actual American shipbuilding effort for 1918 would be only 2 million tons, as opposed to the 6 million tons originally promised.[122] As a result, British merchant shipping was put under even greater strain.

Maclay and his vessels now were responsible not only for balancing the munitions and food requirements of the alliance,[123] but also for moving over 1 million American troops across the Atlantic. The deficiencies in American marine transport were made clear during the German offensive in the spring of 1918. At that juncture, the Allies faced a manpower crisis on the continent that forced the British to implement emergency shipping measures to move more American troops to Europe. The need to assist the American's in this way came as close to undermining the British merchant fleet's ability to support the total war effort – and to crippling Britain's overall war-making ability – as did the activities of the German U-boats.[124] Even after the immediate crisis passed, the inability of American shipbuilding to increase the tonnage output necessary to meet the growing demands of the ever-increasing American forces overseas forced British shipping to continue to carry the burden. Maclay told the War Cabinet that Britain was in constant difficulty because of this situation, and that the existing precarious position was maintained only as a result of the greatest sacrifice. Australia and New Zealand were unable to ship cereal crops or meat. Coal shipments to France and Italy were being seriously impaired. American requests for coal in France and tonnage to supply the AEF were increasing.[125] During the sitting of the Imperial War Cabinet and the meeting of the Committee of Prime Ministers in August 1918, the situation was put into context by the following statement:

the British Government are constantly pressed by their Allies, and particularly by the French, to maintain the existing number of Divisions. And, on the other hand, there is no diminution in the demands made by our Allies, great and small, for shipping, repairs to shipping, coal, steel, woollen goods, railway material, and all kinds of military stores and equipment. The increase to the American Fleets and Flotillas in European waters makes an ever-heavier demand on British Dockyards for repairs. Owing to the fact that the bulk of submarine losses occur in North European waters, the increase in the American Mercantile Marine similarly involves an increased demand for repair facilities for American ships. Only lately America has asked for an increase in the supplies of British coal ... Only recently Great Britain has had to supply and ship a strategic reserve of 150,000 tons of coal for Italy. For the United States of America, Great Britain has had to undertake a great programme of textile manufacture. All these industrial claims make both a direct and indirect demand on British man-power: direct, so far as man-power is necessary for the actual manufacture; indirect, so far as it involves the importation of additional raw materials, with an increased burden on shipping, ports, and means of inland transportation.[126]

Even more disturbing for the British was that all the while there was 'clear evidence that the Americans were building up their transport organization with a view to the situation after the war.'[127]

In the final analysis, the maritime relationship among the North Atlantic Allies is clear. Britain was by far the most important maritime nation in the entire alliance. While it is arguable that the sudden end of the war may have prevented the American maritime contribution to the war from reaching its full *potential*, an enormous amount of work still would have been required to enable the United States to match the British output.[128] Had the United States been able to achieve a comparable position of maritime power, that power, along with financial and man-power considerations, would have ensured that the control of the alliance's maritime strategy would be passed from Great Britain to the United States.[129] Such an occurrence was not the reality, however. The RN and the British Merchant Marine were the backbone of British imperial power. And that power, along with the financial and man-power factors, combined to give Britain the leading role in the entire alliance framework because of that alliance's absolute need for Britain's unmatched maritime capacity.

A common thread that ran throughout the relationships among the three North Atlantic powers was the continuing desire to shape wartime commitments for postwar considerations. British policy-makers' ongoing commitment to an imperial strategy caused them great concern over the increasing American involvement in the war. Canada, in order to curry a preferred position with the United States, argued that greater American cooperation and support during and after the war was critical to the future of the empire.[130] However, Canada had also strengthened its own position, with respect to its prewar drive towards full independent status, through its wartime actions.[131] It had maintained critical economic and industrial relations with Great Britain and the empire that were necessary to maintain the momentum of Canadian economic and industrial development, critical prerequisites for full nationhood.[132]

Britain, a world power rather than an ambitious small power, was reluctant to allow the United States uncontested influence in the postwar world.[133] The United States, under Wilson's leadership, upheld a traditional American approach to foreign policy, one suspicious of British postwar interests, anti-imperialist, and wary of the continued industrial and commercial strength of Great Britain.[134] The fact that such conflicting ambitions even existed during the war brings into question the idea and the definition of total war.

Could the American and Canadian war effort be considered one of fighting a total war? The term is usually meant to indicate an all-out effort from every level of a nation's being: social, industrial, military, and financial. The American and Canadian experiences do not seem to match this definition of total war, since their financial, naval, and social sacrifices were limited in nature. Of the three North Atlantic allies, only Great Britain fought a total war in its efforts. Yet even Britain's commitment to total war must be called into question. Surely the British reluctance to sacrifice parts of the empire to expedite the military action on the Western Front (and the continued attempts to balance shipping and trade/market interests for the postwar period against wartime demands on tonnage) indicates a less than *total* commitment to the immediate prosecution of the war.[135] Such problems, however, are indicative of the complex, competitive nature of the relations among sovereign nation states even when they are operating as allies during a world crisis.

Great Britain's position after the war was only slightly changed. No longer *the* financial centre of the industrialized world, Britain now shared that position with the United States. That new reality was not indicative of impending doom, however, as declinist, professional Canadian, or Pax Americana scholars have emphasized. Britain's industries were still strong, its navy was intact and larger than ever, its merchant marine was poised to regain the dominant role it traditionally had played in world commerce, its empire was larger than ever, and the rival empires of Germany and Russia were vanquished. The struggle for domination in international markets and world affairs was now to be joined with the United States, in an attempt to continue to preserve the empire. And it would be two decades yet before 'Perfidious Albion' gave way to a new world power.

NOTES

I would like to thank Keith Neilson and David French for their advice in writing this chapter.

1 *HMSO Statistics of the Military Effort of the British Empire* (London, 1922); C.E. Fayle, *A History of the Great War: Seaborne Trade* (London, 1927); A. Hurd, *The Merchant Navy* (London, 1929); A.J. Marder, *From Dreadnought to Scapa Flow* (London, 1961); idem, *The Anatomy of British Sea Power: A History of British Naval Policy in the Pre-Dreadnought Era, 1880–1905* (London, 1964); J. Terraine, *Douglas Haig, the Educated Soldier* (London, 1963).

2 C. Barnett, *The Collapse of British Power* (London, 1972); P.M. Kennedy, *The Rise and Fall of the Great Powers* (London, 1988); idem, *The Rise and Fall of British Naval Mastery* (New York, 1976); A.L. Friedberg, *The Weary Titan: Britain and the Experience of Relative Decline, 1895–1905* (Princeton, 1988); M.G. Fry, *Illusions of Security* (Toronto, 1972); Max Beloff, *Britain's Liberal Empire, 1897–1921* (London, 1969); K.M. Burk, *Britain, America and the Sinews of War, 1914–1918* (London, 1985).

3 R.E. Osgood, *Ideals and Self-Interest in America's Foreign Relations* (Chicago, 1953); A.S. Link, *Wilson: Campaigns for Progressivism and Peace, 1916–1917* (Princeton, 1965); W.B. Fowler, *British-American Relations, 1917–1918: The Role of Sir William Wiseman* (Princeton, 1969); D.R. Beaver, *Newton D. Baker and the American War Effort, 1917–1919* (Lincoln, NE, 1966); D.C. Allard, 'Admiral William S. Sims and United States Naval Policy in World War I,' *American Neptune*, 35(1975); R.D. Cuff, *The War Industries Board* (Baltimore, 1973); D.R. Woodward, *Trial By Friendship: Anglo-American Relations, 1917–1918* (Lexington, KY, 1993).

4 For comments about the 'professional Canadians', see B.J.C. McKercher, '"A Greater and a Higher Ideal": Esme Howard, Imperial Unity, and Canadian Autonomy in Foreign Policy, 1924–27', in *Power, Personalities and Policies:*

Essays in Honour of Donald Cameron Watt, ed. M.G. Fry (London, 1992), 108.
Some of those 'professional Canadian' works are: D. Morton, *Canada and War*
(Toronto, 1981); R.C. Brown and R. Bothwell, 'The Canadian Resolution,' in
Policy by Other Means: Essays in Honour of C.P. Stacey, ed. M. Cross and R.
Bothwell (Toronto, 1972); R.D. Cuff and J.L Granatstein, *Canadian-American
Relations in Wartime* (Toronto, 1975); B.M. Gough, 'The End of Pax Britannica
and the Origins of the Royal Canadian Navy: Shifting Strategic Demands of
an Empire at Sea,' in *The RCN in Transition, 1910–1985*, ed. W.A.B. Douglas
(Vancouver, 1988); R.C. Brown, *Robert Laird Borden: A Biography*, Vols I, II
(Toronto, 1975); D. Morton and J.L.Granatstein, *Marching to Armageddon:
Canadians and the Great War, 1914–1919* (Toronto, 1989); M. Bliss, *A Canadian
Millionaire: The Life and Business Times of Sir Joseph Flavelle, Bart., 1858–1939*
(Toronto, 1978).

5 Special editions of *International History Review*, 13:4(1991) and *Canadian Journal of History*, 28:2(1993) provide an excellent introduction to the types of arguments mentioned. These editions contain essays by John Ferris, David French,
Gordon Martel, B.J.C. McKercher, and Keith Neilson. More specific are David
French, *British Economic and Strategic Planning, 1905–1915* (London, 1982);
idem, *British Strategy and War Aims, 1914–1916* (London, 1986); P.E. Rider,
'The Imperial Munitions Board and Its Relationship to Government, Business
and Labour, 1914–1920,' Ph D thesis, University of Toronto, 1974; Keith Neilson, *Strategy and Supply* (London, 1985); David Reynolds, *Britannia Overruled:
British Policy and World Power in the 20th Century* (London, 1991), ch. 4; John
Ferris, 'The Symbol and Substance of Seapower: Great Britain, the United
States, and the One-Power Standard, 1919–1921,' in *Anglo-American Relations
in the 1920s: The Struggle for Supremacy*, ed. B.J.C. McKercher (London, 1991),
81–125; A. Offer, *The First World War: An Agrarian Interpretation* (Oxford,
1989); R.G. Haycock, *Sam Hughes: The Public Career of a Controversial Canadian,
1885–1916* (Waterloo, Ont., 1986); P.G. Wigley, *Canada and the Transition to
Commonwealth: British-Canadian Relations, 1917–1926* (Cambridge, 1977).

6 Cf. K. Burk, *Britain, America, and the Sinews of War* (London, 1985); R.W. Van
Alstyne, 'Private American Loans to the Allies, 1914–1916,' *Pacific Historical
Review*, 2(1933), 180–93; C.W. Wright, 'American Economic Preparations for
War, 1914–1917 and 1939–1941,' *Canadian Journal of Economics and Political
Science*, 8(1942), 157–75; Gerd Hardach, *The First World War, 1914–1918*
(London, 1977).

7 Hardach, *First World War*, 163–6.

8 Burk, *Sinews*, 54–77.

9 Minutes of War Cabinet, Meeting 1, 9 December 1916, CAB [Cabinet
Archives, Public Record Office, Kew] 23/1.

10 Ibid.
11 Ibid.
12 War Cabinet memorandum, 'War Policy,' [G 27] 12 October 1915, Part VIII, CAB 24/1.
13 Ibid.
14 For Russia's importance in British war planning, see Neilson, *Strategy and Supply*, 171–224, 305–19.
15 War Cabinet 48, 30 January 1917, CAB 23/1; 'Note on the position with regard to the requirements of coal for France by the President of the Board of Trade' [G 104], 6 January 1917, CAB 24/3.
16 On the 'business as usual' theme, see French, *British Economic and Strategic Planning*, 98–124, 151–69.
17 'War Policy' [G 27], Part VIII, 12 October 1915, CAB 24/1.
18 'Our Financial Position in America' [G 87], 24 October 1916, CAB 24/2.
19 Ibid.
20 Imperial War Cabinet 7, 3 April 1917, CAB 23/40.
21 Ibid.
22 Ibid.; 'Memorandum on Economic Offensive, By Sir Edward Carson' [G 156], 20 September 1917, CAB 24/4; 'Notes on Sir Edward Carson's Memorandum entitled "Economic Offensive," With Some Immediate Practical Suggestions for Action by the President of the Board of Trade' [G 158], 4 October 1917; 'Proposed Economic Offensive' [G 159], 28 September 1917; 'Economic Offensive, Memorandum by the Minister of Reconstruction' [G 160], 28 September 1917; all CAB 24/4.
23 War Cabinet 7, 3 April 1917, CAB 23/40.
24 Hardach, *First World War*, 148.
25 French, *British Economic and Strategic Planning*, 109–13.
26 Procès-Verbal of Imperial War Cabinet 31, 14 August 1918, CAB 23/43. See Smuts's comments on fighting a lengthy war which might see Britain sink in status relative to the United States and Japan.
27 Secret Notes of Meetings of the Imperial War Cabinet 29b, 12 August 1918, CAB 23/44a.
28 Imperial War Cabinet 27c, 16 August 1918, CAB 23/44a.
29 War Cabinets 30, 31, 13–14 August 1918, both CAB 23/43.
30 War Cabinet 30, 13 August, 1918, CAB 23/43.
31 War Cabinet 31, 14 August 1918, CAB 23/43.
32 War Cabinet 43, 18 December 1918, CAB 23/42.
33 Continuing the story that Britain did not decline relative to other Great Powers in the interwar period are the following: Roberta A. Dayer, 'Anglo-American Monetary Policy and Rivalry in Europe and the

Far East, 1919–1931,' in McKercher, *Anglo-American Relations*, 158–86; John Ferris, '"The Greatest Power on Earth": Great Britain in the 1920s,' *International History Review*, 13(1991), 726–50; idem, 'Symbol and Substance,' 55–80; idem, 'Worthy of Some Better Enemy?: The British Estimate of the Imperial Japanese Army, 1919–41, and the Fall of Singapore,' *Canadian Journal of History*, 28(1993), 223–56; David French, '"Perfidious Albion" Faces the Powers,' *Canadian Journal of History*, 28(1993), 177–88; Greg C. Kennedy, 'The 1930 London Naval Conference and Anglo-American Maritime Strength, 1927–1930,' in *Arms Limitation and Disarmament: Restraints on War, 1899–1939*, ed. B.J.C. McKercher (Westport, CT, 1992), 149–72; Gordon Martel, 'The Meaning of Power: Rethinking the Decline and Fall of Great Britain,' *International History Review*, 13(1991), 662–94; B.J.C. McKercher, '"Our Most Dangerous Enemy": Great Britain Pre-eminent in the 1930s,' *International History Review*, 13(1991), 751–83; idem, '"No Eternal Friends or Enemies": British Defence Policy and the Problem of the United States, 1919–1939,' *Canadian Journal of History*, 28(1993), 257–93; Keith Neilson, '"Pursued by a Bear": British Estimates of Soviet Military Strength and Anglo-Soviet Relations, 1922–1939,' *Canadian Journal of History*, 28(1993), 189–222.

34 Haycock, *Hughes*, 177–97.

35 Flavelle [chairman, Imperial Munitions Board] to Brand [Ministry of Munitions], 19 March 1917, Flavelle Papers [National Archives of Canada, Ottawa], MG 30, A16, vol. 24. Cf. David Carnegie, *The History of Munitions Supply in Canada, 1914–1918* (Toronto, 1925), app. II, 309.

36 Adding to the British government's reluctance to trust Canadian munitions companies early in the war were private initiatives at profiteering such as those undertaken by the minister of militia, Sir Sam Hughes, and his associates, Colonel J. Wesley Allison, Colonel Herbert J. Mackie, and the acting Canadian high commissioner in London, George Perley, regarding the supply of shells for the Russian army. See Keith Neilson, 'Russian Foreign Purchasing in the Great War: A Test Case,' *Slavonic and East European Review*, 60(1982), 572–90.

37 For analysis of the effect of the war on Canadian farming and agricultural production, see J.H. Thompson, *The Harvests of War. The Prairie West, 1914–1918* (Toronto, 1978), 45–72; Offer, *Agrarian Interpretation*, 144–64. For the munitions aspects, see Rider, 'Munitions Board,' 66–130; Carnegie, *Munitions Supply*, app. I, 291.

38 War Cabinet 16, 13 June 1918, CAB 23/43.

39 Ibid.

40 On Borden's attempt to gain further representation for Canada in military

affairs, see G.L. Cook, 'Sir Robert Borden, Lloyd George and British Military Policy, 1917–1918,' *Historical Journal*, 14(1971), 371–95.

41 Cuff and Granatstein, *Canadian-American Relations in Wartime*, 22–23.

42 Brand to Flavelle, 8 August 1916, Flavelle Papers MG 30, A16, vol. 24.

43 Ibid., 20 July 1916.

44 Ibid.

45 Ibid., Flavelle to Brand, 24 August 1916.

46 Ibid., Flavelle to Sir Thomas White, 15 December 1916.

47 Ibid., Brand to Flavelle, 26 January 1917.

48 Ibid.

49 See 'Financial Assistance to the Dominions by His Majesty's Government' [GT 173], March 1917, CAB 24/7; Brand to Flavelle, 2 March 1917, Flavelle Papers; Chiozza Money memorandum, 'Proposal to Secure Absolutely the National Safety by Concentrating Shipping in the Atlantic' [GT 660], 4 May 1917, CAB 24/12; Hardach, *First World War*, table 33, 274.

50 'Financial Assistance Rendered by the Dominions and India to His Majesty's Government' [GT 172], March 1917, CAB 24/7.

51 See 'Possibility of Obtaining a Favorable Military Decision in 1919 or Later,' 21 March 1918, CAB 25/73, which stressed a defensive campaign to keep the alliance together while American strength was mobilized; and War Cabinet (Most Secret) 479a, 27 September 1918, CAB 23/14, in which the Admiralty warned that the Allies should brace themselves for another, more powerful submarine campaign.

52 War Cabinet 24, 12 July 1918, CAB 23/43, where Winston Churchill, minister of munitions, lists the Canadian contribution to munitions manufacturing. From no munitions factories at the beginning of the war, by July 1918, Canada supplied 55 million shells of various kinds and calibre; 45 million artillery cartridge cases; 28 million fuses and 65 million pounds of propellants; and over 47 million pounds of high explosives. At its peak, Canadian production supplied three-tenths of the total shell steel used by the British armies in the field.

53 Ibid. Cf. Burk, *Sinews*, 137–95; Rider, 'Munitions Board,' 285–319.

54 War Cabinet 47, 30 December 1918, CAB 23/14; Geddes report, 'Unemployment and the State of Trade: An Enquiry into the Question of Rehabilitating Trade and Providing Employment, Undertaken by the Minister of Reconstruction and National Service at the Request of the Prime Minister' [G 237], 14 March 1919, CAB 24/5.

55 'Imports from Canada' [GT 237], 14 March 1919, app. XXVII, CAB 24/5.

56 D. Morton, 'The Canadian Military Experience in the First World War, 1914–1918,' in *The Great War, 1914–18*, ed. R.J.Q. Adams (London, 1990), 79–98.

57 Flavelle to Brand, 11 September 1917, Brand to Flavelle, 8 September 1917, both Flavelle Papers, MG 30, A16, Vol. 24.

58 Ferris, 'Greatest Power on Earth,' 737. Ferris is also correct to point out the lack of contextual understanding that weakens Burk, *Sinews*, plus the failure 'to understand the difference between a cash-flow crisis and bankruptcy.'

59 For a full discussion of industrial mobilization, see N.F. Dreisziger, ed., *Mobilization for Total War: The Canadian, American and British Experience, 1914–1918* (Waterloo, Ont., 1981); K. Grieves, *The Politics of Manpower, 1914–1918* (Manchester, 1988); Hardach, *First World War*, ch. 7; Thompson, *Harvests of War*; Carnegie, *Munitions Supply*, ch. 26; Rider, 'Munitions Board'; Cuff, *War Industries Board*; Beaver, *Newton D. Baker*.

60 French, *Strategy and War Aims*, 1–16.

61 In August 1914 the British Expeditionary Force (BEF) amounted to only six divisions, of which four were sent to France; ibid., chs 7, 8.

62 Reynolds, *Britannia Overruled*, 94.

63 Neilson, *Strategy and Supply*, chs 5–7; P. Simpkins, 'Lord Kitchener and the Expansion of the Army,' in *Politicians and British Defence Policy, 1945–1970*, ed. I.F.W. Beckett and J. Gooch (Manchester, 1981); John Turner, *British Politics and the Great War: Coalition and Conflict, 1915–1918* (New Haven, CT, 1992), chs 3–6.

64 War Cabinet 6, 30 March 1917, CAB 23/40.

65 Many of the accepted standards such as Haycock, Granatstein, and Morton have been mentioned in the notes above. Other works include S.J. Harris, 'Canadian Brass: The Growth of the Canadian Military Profession, 1860–1919,' Ph D thesis, Duke University, 1979; G.W.L. Nicholson, *Canadian Expeditionary Force: The Canadian Army in the First World War, 1914–1919* (Ottawa, 1962); J.A. Swettenham, *To Seize the Victory: The Canadian Corps in World War I* (Toronto, 1965).

66 War Cabinet 378, March 1918, CAB 23/5. Such a favourable attitude towards the Canadian manpower effort had not always been evident. Studies in early 1917 revealed that Canada was unlikely ever to be able to send the 5th Division into France from its position as training and recruiting unit in England. There was also a great demand for Canadian troops that were familiar with railwaymen's and lumbermen's tasks. In comparison with the other self-governing dominions, Canada had enlisted only 9.6 per cent of its male population, New Zealand 11.9 per cent, Australia 10.7 per cent, and South Africa 1.7 per cent. Of the Canadian male population, 9.6 per cent, under the heading of 'per cent of total male population represented by total recruited,' 6.5 per cent were Canadian born of British extraction, 1.4 per cent were Canadian born of French extraction, 37.5 per cent were born in the

United Kingdom, and 6.7 per cent (0.2 per cent greater than those of British extraction) were born in a foreign country. See War Cabinet 41, January 23 1917, tables I, II, CAB 23/1.

67 See War Cabinet 16, 13 June 1918, CAB 23/43 on machine-gun usage and emplacement, barbed wire, artillery coordination, and manpower promotion and usage. Cf. Tim Travers, *How the War Was Won: Command and Technology in the British Army on the Western Front, 1917–1918* (London, 1992).

68 Imperial War Cabinet 16, 13 June 1918, CAB 23/43.

69 'Future Military Policy', 15 June 1918, CAB 25/87 shows planning for the movement of five Canadian railway construction battalions to Palestine and Mesopotamia in the autumn of 1918: 'If the Army in France is not likely to be in a position to spare them steps should now be taken to get them raised in Canada.'

70 Imperial War Cabinet (Most Secret Minutes) 27b, 1 August 1918, CAB 23/44a. Lloyd George's comments were directed primarily at the French general, Foch. For a look at the broader question of whether Lloyd George was deliberately starving the army of its necessary manpower, see John Gooch, 'The Maurice Debate, 1918,' *Journal of Contemporary History*, 3:4(1968), 211–28; E.B. Parsons, 'Why the British Reduced the Flow of American Troops to Europe in August–October, 1918,' *Canadian Journal of History*, 12(1977), 173–91; P.E. Dewey, 'Military Recruiting and the British Labour Force during the First World War,' *Historical Journal*, 27(1984), 199–223; David Woodward, 'Did Lloyd George Starve the British Army of Men prior to the German Offensive of 21 March, 1918?' *Historical Journal*, 27(1984), 241–52.

71 Imperial War Cabinet 27b, 1 August 1918, CAB 23/44a.

72 Woodward, 'Did Lloyd George Starve the British Army,' 248–51; Tim Travers, 'The Evolution of British Strategy and Tactics on the Western Front in 1918: GHQ, Manpower and Technology,' *Journal of Military History*, 54(1990), 173–200.

73 'Report of the Committee of Prime Ministers. Preliminary Draft as a Basis for Considerations [for the IWC in August 1918],' pt I, 7–8, CAB 23/44a: 'it is not only the right but the duty of the Government to assure itself that operations involving the probability of heavy casualties are not embarked on unless they give a probability of producing commensurate results on the final issue of the War and without wrecking the future of the Empire'. Cf. Travers, 'Evolution of British Strategy,' 176–9.

74 Imperial War Cabinet 32b, 16 August 1918, CAB 23/44ap. Borden was unimpressed with the War Cabinet's view that such enormous sacrifice would have to continue for another two years.

75 'Manner in Which U.S.A. Can Best Render Assistance in Event of Their Entry Into the War' [GT 12], 12 February 1917, CAB 24/6.

76 For some indication of the size and ability of the United States Army prior to the war, see 'Annual Report,' 26 April 1913, in *British Documents on Foreign Affairs*, ed. K. Bourne and D.C. Watt, Part I, Series C, Vol. 15, Doc. 3, 54–9.

77 War Cabinet 323, 16 January 1918, with Robertson [chief, Imperial General Staff] telegram to Pershing [commander, American Army in France), 10 January 1918, CAB 23/5

78 For the limited usefulness of the AEF see David Trask, *The AEF and Coalition Warmaking, 1917–1918* (Kansas, 1993).

79 E. Coffman, 'American Military and Strategic Policy in World War One,' in *War Aims and Strategic Policy in the Great War, 1914–1918*, ed. B.D. Hunt and A. Preston (London, 1977), 67–84; Fowler, *British-American Relations*, 126–63; D. Smythe, *Pershing: General of the Armies* (Bloomington, IN, 1986), 70–2, 234–5.

80 Cf. note 76, above, and C.R. Shrader, '"Maconochie's Stew": Logistical Support of American Forces with the BEF, 1917–18,' in Adams, *Great War*, 101–31; War Cabinet 160, 11 June 1917, CAB 23/3; Woodward, *Trial by Friendship*, 180–205.

81 War Cabinet 328 and 331, 22 and 25 January 1918, both CAB 23/5.

82 War Cabinet 498a, 21 October 1918, CAB 23/14.

83 Woodward, *Trial by Friendship*, 168–74. See also, Imperial War Cabinet 24, 12 July 1918, CAB 23/41.

84 Imperial War Cabinet 15, 11 June 1918, CAB 23/43; Woodward, *Trial by Friendship*, 175.

85 Imperial War Cabinet 15, 11 June 1918, CAB 23/43.

86 Ibid.; Grieves, *Politics of Manpower*, 180–99.

87 'Political Aspects of the Campaign of 1919,' 24 March 1918, CAB 25/73. Prepared for the British War Cabinet, this paper specifically points out that the preferred objective from the political point of view was to keep 'the Alliance together and steadily adding to the strength, by piling up American troops, and to the efficiency, by improvements in mechanical devices, of the Allied Armies on the Western Front.'

88 Imperial War Cabinet 15, CAB 23/43.

89 D.F. Trask, *Captains and Cabinets* (Columbia, 1972), 92–4; Woodward, *Trial by Friendship*, 185–206.

90 For some of the standard works on British maritime efforts during the war, see n1, above, and R.G. Albion and J.B. Pope, *Sea Lanes in Wartime: The American Experience, 1775–1945*, 2nd ed. (New York, 1968), 177–232;

D.M. Schurman, *The Education of a Navy: The Development of British Naval Strategic Thought, 1867–1914* (London, 1965); J.T. Sumida, *In Defence of Naval Supremacy* (London, 1989); Trask, *Captains and Cabinets*; G.N. Tucker, *The Naval Service of Canada*, Vol. 1 (Ottawa, 1952).

91 Offer, *Agrarian Interpretation*, 215–318.

92 The primacy of the need to maintain the empire is clearly stated in a policy paper, 'War Aims and Military Policy' [prepared for private circulation to the Imperial War Cabinet], 15 June 1918, CAB 25/87.

93 *Brassey's Naval Annual, 1919* (London, 1919), 288.

94 'General Review of the Naval Situation' [GT 277], 24 March 1917, CAB 24/8.

95 Rider, 'Munitions Board,' 151.

96 Ibid.

97 Memorandum for the Imperial War Conference, 'The Principal Supplies of Food and Feeding-Stuffs Received from the British Empire during the War' [GT 269], 17 March 1917, CAB 24/8.

98 A.C. Bell, *A History of the Blockade of Germany: and of the Countries Associated with Her in the Great War, Austria-Hungary, Bulgaria and Turkey* (London, 1937); S.W. Roskill, *The Strategy of Sea Power* (London, 1962), 101–28. Cf. 'A General Review of the Naval Situation' [GT 277], 24 March 1917, CAB 24/8.

99 As yet no comprehensive study of the destroyer and cruiser operations during the war exists. Some idea of the Royal Navy's efforts in this area may be gleaned from Paul Halpern, *A Naval History of World War I* (Annapolis, MD, 1994); J.T. Sumida, 'Forging the Trident: British Naval Industrial Logistics, 1914–1918,' in *Feeding Mars: Logistics in Western Warfare from the Middle Ages to the Present*, ed. J.A. Lynn (Boulder, CO, 1993), 217–49; idem, 'British Naval Operational Logistics, 1914–1918,' *Journal of Military History*, 57(1993), 447–81. While Professor Sumida is to be congratulated for making important steps in the study of British maritime power in the First World War, both of these studies are limited because of both a lack of contextual understanding of how naval logistics fits into the overall British war effort and a desire to overemphasize the big-battle fleet actions as the central feature of British maritime strategy.

100 'A General Review of the Naval Situation' [GT 277], 24 March 1917, CAB 24/8.

101 'Report of Cabinet Committee on War Policy' [G 179], 10 August 1917, CAB 24/44.

102 Ibid. On the naval war in the Mediterranean, see P.G. Halpern, *The Naval War in the Mediterranean, 1914–1918* (Annapolis, MD, 1987).

103 'Report of Cabinet Committee on War Policy' [G 179], 10 August 1917, CAB 24/4.

104 Difficulties in setting up the convoy system are illustrated in the problems involved with commanding civilian captains, routing, and loading/unloading facilities. On difficulties with steamer captains, see War Cabinet 26, 3 January 1917, CAB 23/1, and War Cabinet 91, 8 March 1917, CAB 23/2; on the need to improve cross-channel ferry service and movement of supplies, War Cabinet 36, 17 January 1917, CAB 23/1; on merchant vessels in convoy and unloading procedures War Cabinet 73, 19 February 1917, and App. I, CAB 23/1; on increasing merchant ships' speed to 11.5 knots using 'Howden's Forced Draught,' War Cabinet 76, 21 February 1917, CAB 23/1.

105 Imperial War Cabinet 4 and 12, 27 March and 26 April 1917, both CAB 23/40.

106 Imperial War Cabinet 12, 26 April 1917, CAB 23/40. See also A.J. Marder, *Portrait of an Admiral: The Life and Papers of Sir Herbert Richmond* (Cambridge, MA, 1952), 203, 228–36; James Goldrick and John B. Hattendorf, eds, *Mahan is not Enough* (Newport, RI, 1993), 21–4.

107 For the best overview of naval operations in the First World War, I see Halpern, *Naval History of World War I*.

108 Imperial War Cabinet 12, 26 April 1917, CAB 23/40.

109 'Restriction of Imports' [G 178], 1 December 1917, CAB 24/4.

110 Imperial War Cabinet 4, 27 March 1917, CAB 23/40; War Cabinet 45 and 62, with appendix, 25 January and 12 February 1917, both CAB 23/1; War Cabinet 83 and 100, 1 and 21 March 1917, both CAB 23/2.

111 Imperial War Cabinet 4, 27 March 1917, CAB 23/40; 'Report From Shipping Controller' [GT 388], April 1917, CAB 24/9.

112 'Report From Shipping Controller,' ibid.

113 Ibid.

114 Trask, *Captains and Cabinets*, 61–101. On Admiral Sims, see Allard, 'Admiral William S. Sims,' 97–110. For pre-1917 USN naval preparations, see Paolo E. Coletta, 'The American Naval Leaders' Preparations for War,' in Adams, *Great War*, 161–82.

115 Trask, *Captains and Cabinets*, 75–85; W.J. Williams, 'American Destroyer Programs During World War I,' unpublished paper presented at the Naval History Symposium, Annapolis, MD, 21–23 October 1993, 3–12.

116 Williams, 'Destroyer Programs,' 12.

117 Ibid., 33. For a technical assessment of the US destroyer construction program of 1917–19, see Norman Friedman, *U.S. Destroyers* (Annapolis, MD, 1982), 39–63.

118 What naval support the USN could give the Allies depended largely on British logistical support. In order to operate in European waters, the USN required coal, oil, and repair and basing facilities from Great Britain. See

'Report of the Committee of Prime Ministers,' pt II, August 1918, CAB 23/
44a.

119 Imperial War Cabinet 479a, 27 September 1918, CAB 23/41.

120 Imperial War Cabinet 21, 27 June 1918, CAB 23/41.

121 This attempt by the United States to buy control refers to an attempt to blackmail the Allies, particularly the British, into attending an inter-Allied conference to 'discuss and decide upon the relative financial, supply and transport needs of each of the Allies.' The Americans threatened to with-hold further loans after the $85 million that was due by 15 August 1917. The British responded by pointing out that if America did not cooperate within the existing system and maintain fixed rates of exchange between itself and the Allies, the result would be German victory. See War Cabinet 193, 23 July 1917, CAB 23/3.

122 'Cabinet Committee on Man-power' [G 185], 1 March 1918, CAB 24/4. For an earlier assessment, see 'Notes on Tonnage Position and the necessity for a Greatly Extended Shipbuilding Programme' [GT 982], May 1917, CAB 24/15. For background to the American position in shipbuilding in 1917–18, see W.J. Williams, *The Wilson Administration and the Shipbuilding Crisis of 1917: Steel Ships and Wooden Steamers* (Lewiston, NY, 1992).

123 War Cabinet 330, 24 January 1918, CAB 23/5: 'The Prime Minister said that the great factor of the war this year would be either military or moral, and, as far as he could see at present, he was inclined to think it would be the lat-ter. Food was our first line of defence ... He did not mean by this that the output of munitions should be dangerously reduced. There was a minimum below which it was impossible to go.'

124 War Cabinet 385 and 404, 6 April and 3 May 1918, both CAB 23/6; War Cab-inet 452, 26 July 1918, CAB 23/7; War Cabinet 487, 16 October 1918, CAB 23/8.

125 War Cabinet 452, 26 July 1918, CAB 23/7.

126 'Report of the Committee of Prime Minister,' August 1918, pt II, CAB 23/
44a.

127 War Cabinet 452, 26 July 1918, CAB 23/7.

128 The points raised here regarding British suspicion of American motives do not even begin to deal with the Admiralty's interpretation of President Wil-son's demand for 'freedom of the seas' as a direct and quite blatant assault on British sea power. The Admiralty was determined to resist this point on the grounds that in the final analysis, British imperial security rested upon the right of blockade. S.W. Roskill, *Naval Policy between the Wars*, Vol. 1 (London, 1968), 80–1, 90–1.

129 Interestingly, Wilson gave no mention of the British effort, which had

moved 1,950,513 men safely over 3,000 miles, in his address to Congress at the end of the war. Maclay and the British cabinet held a special press conference to point out the president's omission; War Cabinet 509, 4 December 1918, CAB 23/8. For the discussion of bargaining power and negotiating positions, the sudden end of the war, and the impact that this situation had had on Lloyd George and Wilson's postwar negotiations, see Erik Goldstein, *Winning the Peace* (Oxford, 1991).

130 War Cabinet 457, 13 August 1918, CAB 23/7; Imperial War Cabinet 30, 13 August, 1918, CAB 23/43.

131 John Pinder, 'Prophet Not without Honour: Lothian and the Federal Idea,' in *The Larger Idea: Lord Lothian and the Problem of National Sovereignty*, ed. John Turner (Exeter, 1988), 137–52, esp. 139.

132 Borden recognized that 'the whole fiscal system of Canada had been designed for national and Imperial purposes, and it was largely owing to its fiscal system that Canada was now a portion of the British Empire'; Imperial War Cabinet 11, April 24, 1917, CAB 23/40. Borden's request for a preferential transportation system for goods produced within the empire had been accepted by Lloyd George because such a declaration would take trade away from Russia and the United States, but 'it was a matter which could be justified on grounds of Imperial defence, and was a recognised method of development employed by the United States, Russia and France'; ibid. For a more critical view of the relationship, see Stephen Constantine, 'Anglo-Canadian Relations, the Empire Marketing Board, and Canadian National Autonomy between the Wars,' *Journal of Imperial and Commonwealth History*, 21(1993), 357–84.

133 The divergence of opinion is illustrated in postwar discussions about where the United States, if it was willing, might take responsibility for a League mandate. Palestine was thought to be a possibility. Lloyd George, however, who originally had thought the idea had merit, later thought it unwise to place 'an absolutely new and crude Power in the middle of all our complicated interests in Egypt, Arabia and Mesopotamia.' Winston Churchill and the first sea lord, Admiral Sir Roslyn E.Wemyss, wanted America involved in East Africa instead, which would obviate the temptation for the United States to develop a Mediterranean fleet or become a greater naval power, both of which might happen if the Americans became involved in Palestine or Armenia. Such strategic considerations and thinking were beyond Borden's purview. War Cabinet 44, 20 December 1918, CAB 23/42.

134 Woodward, *Trial by Friendship*, 61–3.

135 A more appropriate model for new studies of the relationship between the powers during the First World War would be a competitive-cooperative

approach, such as that used by David Reynolds, *The Creation of the Anglo-American Alliance, 1937–41: A Study in Competitive Cooperation* (London, 1981); Christopher Thorne, *Allies of a Kind: The United States, Britain, and the War against Japan, 1941–1945* (London, 1978); and M.J. Hogan, *Informal Entente: the Private Structure of Cooperation in Anglo-American Economic Diplomacy, 1918–1928* (Columbia, MO, 1978).

3

The Decade of Transition:
The North Atlantic Triangle
during the 1920s

GREGORY A. JOHNSON and DAVID A. LENARCIC

On 11 November 1918, the day the armistice ending the 'war to end all wars' was signed, Sir Robert Borden confided to his diary: 'The world has drifted far from its old anchorage and no man can with certainty prophesy what the outcome will be. I have said that another such war would destroy our civilisation. It is a grave question whether this war may not have destroyed much that we regard as necessarily incident thereto.'[1] The Canadian prime minister was right. The Great War had destroyed much that was taken for granted, and in the ensuing decade the powers made various attempts to come to terms with the changes wrought by that tremendous conflict and to prevent another upheaval.[2] For the three members of the North Atlantic triangle the ten years after the war was a period of transition. The spirit of wartime cooperation was not carried into the complicated, acrimonious, and often confusing atmosphere marked, above all, by growing rivalry and even hostility in Anglo-American relations. This rivalry was to a remarkable degree reflected in Canada. As Canadian leaders pursued their desire for increased autonomy and insulation from international problems, they often found themselves caught between the two senior partners. In the process of avoiding entanglement in Anglo-American and European squabbles, Canada often sided with the United States, and it began to reorient its economic, political, and intellectual focus away from Britain. Canada's interwar withdrawal from Imperial and international commitments and concomitant preoccupation with North American affairs mirrored a more lasting reconfiguration of the North Atlantic triangle: the general shift in power away from Britain and towards the United States.[3]

PERSONALITIES AND POLICIES

Although foreign policy is often the product of the complex interplay between domestic politics and international developments – or, as some would have it, 'structural determinants'[4] – it is still shaped and influenced by people. It is therefore important to understand in broad terms some of the attitudes and approaches of those who shaped foreign policy within the North Atlantic triangle during the 1920s. For most of the war and the early postwar period American policy was in the hands of Woodrow Wilson, Democratic president from 1913 to 1921. Wilson's basic aim was to create what has often been referred to as a 'liberal internationalist' world order based on the concepts of freer trade, open diplomacy, and national self-determination. All of these aims were embodied in the League of Nations organization created at the end of the Great War. For various reasons, about which historians still disagree,[5] the Wilsonian vision was rejected by the U.S. Senate and this defeat paved the way for the so-called Republican Ascendancy during the 1920s.[6]

That ascendancy began with the election of Warren Harding in 1920 and continued under the administrations of Calvin Coolidge and then Herbert Hoover, who served from 1928 until his defeat by Franklin Roosevelt and the Democrats in 1932. For much of this period the president did not exercise as much control over foreign policy as other members of the cabinet, most notably Charles Evans Hughes, secretary of state under Harding and Coolidge; Andrew Mellon, who served as Treasury secretary under all three Republican presidents; and Herbert Hoover, who exerted a powerful influence at Commerce until assuming office. Traditionally, historians have viewed the Republican era as the American retreat into political isolationism.[7] The rejection of Wilson's internationalist approach taught Republican leaders to pay more attention to domestic opinion, especially as it was reflected in the Senate, and to shape policy accordingly. Hence, American leaders turned inward. While it is true that the United States did not join the League of Nations and generally withdrew politically from international affairs, the country was far from detached.[8] After all, it participated in three major disarmament conferences, co-sponsored the Kellogg-Briand Pact outlawing war, and, through the Dawes and Young plans, lent its efforts to ease economic and financial problems in Europe. These forays into international diplomacy represented two significant aims in American foreign policy: promoting peace through European and American economic well-being and preventing the United States from being drawn into another major European war.

In the light of those general aims, other American goals seem somewhat contradictory. The United States sought to expand economically and pursued naval equality, if not superiority, over Great Britain.[9] American economic expansion has given rise to suspicions that policy was being directed by the business elite.[10] The reality was not that simple.[11] The State Department, for example, often disagreed with Commerce, and various bodies in the United States stood against the 'big naval' lobby in Washington. Thus, although the predominant tendency of the United States was to turn inward politically and avoid international commitments while seeking to increase economic and military power, there was a fissiparous quality to American foreign policy that led to certain misperceptions about the direction in which the United States was moving. This misunderstanding was particularly true in Great Britain.[12]

Six governments held power in Britain during the postwar decade. David Lloyd George headed a coalition that governed from 1916 until his resignation in 1922. Britain then went through three general elections in less than two years (November 1922; December 1923; October 1924). The 1922 election produced a Conservative government led by Canadian-born Andrew Bonar Law until his death from cancer in 1923, and then by Stanley Baldwin. Ramsay MacDonald led the first-ever Labour government for nine short months following the 1923 election, after which Baldwin returned to win the 1924 election; he governed until MacDonald and his Labour party regained control in 1929. Like the situation in the United States, there was a considerable division of opinion within Britain over the direction of postwar foreign policy. Old-style nationalists, such as Law, and foreign secretaries, such as the Marquess of Curzon (1919–23) and Austen Chamberlain (1924–29), were contemptuous of the United States and viewed American intrusion into British spheres of influence with suspicion. Another group, often referred to as 'Atlanticists,' which included the lord president of the council, Lord Balfour, and, off and on, Winston Churchill[13] sought cooperation and understanding with the United States. Other groupings included various politicians, bureaucrats, or intellectuals, such as Colonial and Dominions Secretary Leo Amery, Maurice Hankey, the 'man of secrets' who served as secretary of the cabinet and the Committee of Imperial Defence, British statesman Lord Robert Cecil, and Montagu Norman, governor of the Bank of England. These people wished either to transform the British Empire or to pursue the search for what D.C. Watt has termed 'a possible America,' meaning an America that would fit in with Britain's image of the world.[14]

The divisions aside, the British sought to achieve two basic aims during the 1920s. One was to preserve the European balance of power; the other was to maintain and defend the empire. For much of the postwar decade Britain concentrated on European affairs, particularly on the need to satisfy France's demand for security against a resurgent Germany in the aftermath of the American refusal to join the League of Nations. This is not to say that Britain neglected its empire. As always, British strength lay in the continued existence of a unified empire; but in seeking to fulfil this goal the British frequently locked horns with the autonomy-minded Canadians.

If the 1920s were years of the Republican ascendancy in the United States and largely Conservative domination in Britain, in Canada they marked the beginning of the Liberal ascendancy.[15] The Conservatives, led by Robert Borden – Sir Robert after 1914 – had been in power since 1911. The 1917 federal election produced a Union government headed by Borden. After ill health forced Borden to retire in 1920, Arthur Meighen led the party until his defeat at the hands of William Lyon Mackenzie King and the Liberals in 1921. Except for a brief hiatus in 1926, King dominated Canadian politics and foreign policy throughout the 1920s – in fact, excepting the period from 1930 to 1935, he dominated Canadian policy from 1921 to 1948.[16] Emphasizing the role of the prime minister in the making of Canadian foreign policy – or 'external affairs' in the Canadian lexicon – is no mistake. From 1912 to 1946 all Canadian prime minsters served as their own secretary of state for external affairs. Of course there were others who influenced the direction of foreign policy: for example, Newton Rowell, a Liberal politician who joined Borden's Union government and whose interest in Canada's international position almost exceeded that of the prime minister. Under King there were a number of notable personalities, including Ernest Lapointe, the French-Canadian justice minister, who supported the League of Nations, and J.L. Ralston, the minister of national defence. Others who deserve mention are Walter Hose, the director of the Canadian Naval Services, whose contribution and influence has been only recently recognized;[17] J.S. Ewart, a lawyer and constitutional expert who acted as an unofficial adviser to King during the 1920s; and J.W. Dafoe, the editor of what used to be the best newspaper in Canada, the *Manitoba Free Press*. But the most remarkable protagonists were Loring Christie and O.D. Skelton of the Department of External Affairs.[18]

Christie cuts a fascinating and rather tragic figure in Canadian history. He served as legal adviser under Borden and Meighen and, though he believed that Canada would eventually have to assume control over foreign policy, he shared Borden's notion of an imperial federation in which the dominions would have a say in the formulation of empire policy.[19] This idea did not endear him to King and he was eased out in 1923. (He returned in 1935 a confirmed anti-imperial isolationist.) Christie's place as a key adviser was taken by Skelton, a former university professor, who became under-secretary of state for external affairs in 1925 and King's most trusted adviser. Skelton was anti-imperialist and neutralist – if not isolationist – from the start, and he fought hard for Canadian independence throughout his career.[20] Although Borden, Meighen, and King – and Christie and Skelton – may have differed over means, they shared a common goal: the advancement of Canadian autonomy, the promotion of good Anglo-American relations, and growing disenchantment with the League of Nations. Borden and Meighen paid a great deal of lip service to the empire, but it was initially under their policies, not King's, that Canada began to move away from Britain and towards the United States.[21] King certainly carried the fight through the 1920s and beyond. Under his leadership Canadians became used to hearing the slogans 'no commitments' and 'Parliament will decide' as the country began to withdraw from European and imperial commitments.

Within the North Atlantic triangle, then, there were three broad currents. One was the gradual Canadian and American withdrawal from international commitments. The second was American economic expansion and its effect on Canadian-American and Anglo-American relations. The third was the growing Anglo-American naval rivalry and its impact on Canada's position in the triangle. These developments did not happen overnight; rather, there was a slow evolutionary change that resulted from separate responses to the new international and domestic conditions each member of the triangle faced after the Great War.

THE PEACE AND THE LEAGUE

Perhaps even more than its triangle allies, Canadian attitudes towards the postwar era were moulded by the charnel house of the Great War which had maimed and slaughtered the flower of Canadian youth. 'It was European policy, European statesmanship, European ambition, that drenched this world in blood and from which we are still suffering and will suffer for generations,' charged the Canadian delegate, Newton Rowell, at the inaugural gathering of the League of Nations in 1920. 'Fifty thousand Canadians under the soil of France and Flanders is what Canada has paid for European statesmanship trying to settle European problems.'[22] Four years later another Canadian representative at Geneva, Senator Raoul Dandurand, spoke for an entire nation baptised by fire when he declared: 'we think in terms of peace, while Europe, an armed camp, thinks in terms of war ... We live in a fire-proof house, far from inflammable materials. A vast ocean separates us from Europe.'[23]

To many Canadians, the nascent League of Nations – the brainchild of President Woodrow Wilson – symbolized a perilous affiliation. Canada had successfully lobbied at the Paris Peace Conference of 1919 to join the world body as a separate member. Yet this campaign had been based more on the ambition to see the dominion's status and voice as an autonomous nation acknowledged than on any heartfelt belief in the principles of collective security.[24] From the point of view of most Canadians the League was simply an instrument for European nations to manipulate in resolving private quarrels that in no way touched Canada. Clifford Sifton, the proprietor of the *Manitoba Free Press* and a former cabinet minister, warned that Canada's continued membership would 'do us no good and may possibly get us into trouble.' Sifton spoke for many Canadians when he asserted that the main aim of the 'people over there' was to ensnare Canadians in 'European and Imperialistic complications.'[25]

Small wonder that successive Canadian governments strove first to delete and, when that failed, to amend substantially Article X of the League Covenant. This article, which Wilson termed 'the heart of the Covenant,' pledged member states to come to the aid of any one of them who was the victim of an act of aggression. It was not a concept that appealed to many Canadians, including Prime Minister Borden, whose opposition carried an almost hysterical tone. Inclusion of the article, he said, 'might lead to great disorder, possibly rebellion on the Pacific Coast of the United States and Canada.'[26] Instead, the League must be regarded solely as a body that furnished the means to mediate, arbitrate, and adjudicate disputes. Christie argued that Canada should work towards 'a League that is a *method* of diplomacy and is not an *institution* with fighting compacts.'[27] The message here was clear. The League should provide a forum for the discussion and debate of world affairs, but it should do little more. Indeed, argued many Canadians, Canada ought to abandon the League if it remained primarily fixated on European matters. The dominion should always approach its 'obligations and interventions in regard to all regions of the earth in a sense compatible with her geographical position.'[28]

Projects designed to enlarge and fortify the collective security aspects of the League Covenant, such as the Geneva Protocol for the Pacific Settlement of International Disputes – which called for compulsory arbitration and military or economic sanctions against aggressor states – had to be avoided at all costs. According to O.D. Skelton, Canada was a country 'fortunate in its comparative isolation and its friendly neighbour.' It had nothing in common with European nations, 'heirs to centuries of feuds and fears.'[29] The Locarno Pact of 1925 was no better. By the terms of this treaty, France, Belgium, and Germany pledged to respect each other's borders and Britain and Italy guaranteed the arrangement. The renunciation by Germany and France of any wish to alter their existing boundaries, coupled with an agreement to arbitrate disputes between them, were certainly 'steps toward peace,' Skelton conceded, 'but they are Europe's steps, Europe's job and should rest for their enforcement upon the conduct of France and Germany, not upon intervention by a country four thousand miles away.' A Canadian endorsement of Locarno would pose too grave a risk to the dominion, particularly given its racial composition, its proximity to the United States, and its millstone of war debt.[30]

All in all, the prevailing sentiment in Canada during the 1920s demanded that every effort be geared towards ensuring that Canadians would not again be made 'catspaws of European imperialism.'[31] Calamity would definitely ensue through any connection with the 'legacy of warfare hate & bloodshed which makes Europe a shambles.'[32] A Liberal MP, Chubby Power, anticipated this mood, which would grip much of the country in the 1920s, in a speech to the House of Commons in September 1919:

We as Canadians have our destiny before us not in Continental Europe but here on the free soil of America. Our policy for the next hundred years should be that laid down by George Washington in the United States for the guidance of his country-men – absolute renunciation of interference in European affairs – and that laid down by the other great father of his country in Canada, Sir Wilfrid Laurier – 'freedom from the vortex of European militarism' ... let Europe be the arbiter of its own destiny while we in Canada, turning our energies to our own affairs, undertake our own peaceful development.[33]

That a Canadian should invoke the spirit of one of the founding fathers of the United States to argue the case for his own country's non-interventionism was no coincidence; for during the postwar decade many Americans were making strikingly similar arguments about the need to evade military and political commitments abroad.

Isolationist sentiment in the United States during the 1920s had many standard-bearers but its main leadership undoubtedly came from the American Senate.[34] It was a point of view first articulated in the battle waged there in 1918–20 to prevent the country from joining the League of Nations. There were several arguments advanced against member-ship that were unique to American sensibilities,[35] but certain of their essentials closely resembled Canadian attitudes. The League of Nations was 'nothing but a mind cure' and a 'pipe dream,' suggested Senator Frank Brandegee.[36] Moreover, as far as the United States was concerned, Idaho's William Borah firmly believed, it would 'finally lead us all into all kinds of entangling obligations and conditions with European affairs.'[37] Article X would see to that. Underwriting the territorial integ-rity of every nation which comprised the League was 'a very grave, a very perilous promise to make,' warned Wilson's bitter enemy and chairman of the Senate Committee on Foreign Relations, Henry Cabot Lodge: 'because there is but one way by which such guarantees, if ever invoked, can be maintained, and that way is the way of force ... If we guarantee any country on earth ... that guarantee we must maintain at any cost when our word is once given, and we must be in constant pos-session of fleets and armies capable of enforcing these guarantees at a moment's notice.'[38] In the end, the Treaty of Versailles, along with the League of Nations, was rejected by the United States Senate in March 1920. However, that body's isolationist vanguard remained ever vigilant for any other initiative that might similarly sacrifice their country's peace, prosperity, and independence on the altar of European or Asian ambitions and rivalries. An inviting target soon appeared in the form of the Four Power Pact, one of the agreements arising out of the Washing-ton Conference on naval arms limitation of 1921–2. The United States, Britain, Japan, and France agreed to respect each other's territorial rights in the Pacific, to refer disputes between them to a conference of all four nations, and to consult one another in the event of an outside attack against them.[39]

For Senate isolationists the treaty was an armed alliance pure and sim-ple through which the United States incurred dangerous obligations. It flew in the face of traditional American foreign policy, injected the republic into foreign squabbles unconnected with its own interests, and threatened its sovereignty in diplomatic affairs. Worst of all, it would one day drag the country into a war.[40] Senate opponents attacked the pact as a 'menacing little imitation league,' another example of 'the old hellish system whose frightful story is told upon a thousand battlefields of the Old World.' If it were ratified, 'American boys [would] again shed their blood on foreign fields.'[41] The Senate eventually passed the treaty, but not before its isolationist members succeeded in neutering it by attaching a reservation to American adherence that excluded any commitment to armed force, an alliance, or the obligation to assist in defence against aggression.[42] The Senate also operated against other foreign policy initiatives such as American membership in the World Court. The Senate approved American membership in the court in 1926, but only after affixing several reservations.[43] Three years later isolationist Senators were similarly able to protect America's freedom of action and limit its international obligations by so qualifying the country's adhesion to the Kellogg-Briand Pact – which renounced war as an instrument of national policy – that it amounted to nothing more than 'an international kiss.'[44]

One belief in particular underlay and unified American isolationist attitudes during the 1920s: that the decision of the United States to enter the Great War in 1917 had been a mistake. This view sprang from postwar histories of the origins of the conflict by both European and American writers that marshalled impressive evidence to support the thesis that not only had the Germans not been completely villainous or the Allies completely altruistic, but that perhaps the Allies rather than the Central Powers were primarily culpable for the war. American revisionist historians condemned their country's intervention in the conflict on that basis in the hope that the same error would not be made again.[45] Why, then, had the United States participated at all, if one side had been no more virtuous than the other, unless it had been duped? All the moral and selfless reasons for American intervention seemed to be stripped bare. The revisionist interpretation was fuelled by the conviction that the entire peace settlement was founded on a misconception, since it formally assigned Germany special responsibility for the conflict. In fact, there was much that American isolationists considered iniquitous about the Treaty of Versailles. In many ways, when it came to both the war-guilt question and the criticism of Versailles, they took their cue from European, and particularly British, opinion.[46]

Indeed, the 'thesaurus' of American isolationists was British economist John Maynard Keynes's *The Economic Consequences of the Peace*, published at the end of 1919. In a scathing critique, Keynes denounced the Versailles settlement as excessively severe towards Germany. He argued that its draconian reparations arrangements represented the triumph of political retribution over fiscal common sense. Rather than laying a solid foundation for peace, the treaty sowed the seeds of another war.[47] It was, Keynes reproached, 'one of the most outrageous acts of a cruel victor in civilised history' and would be the 'death sentence of many millions of German men, women and children.'[48] The impact of Keynes's study of the peace conference was widespread.[49] It was also immense, no more so than in his native Britain, where it soon became the rarely challenged view of the majority. 'All the phrases of the 1920's,' Martin Gilbert has observed, 'peaceful change, treaty revision, bringing Germany back to her rightful place in Europe, obtaining equality for the former foe, appeasement,' could be traced to Keynes.[50] Even though Britain's geopolitical position was radically different from that of either Canada or the United States, this frame of mind closely approximated mainstream thinking in those two countries. One might have expected that the island nation's proximity to the continent, coupled with its recent participation in the Great War, would have erased any thoughts on the part of its inhabitants that they might be able to stand aloof from Europe. Instead Keynes's assault on the injustice and immorality of Versailles resulted in a guilty population unable to justify the peace and unwilling to enforce it.[51]

From there it was but a small step to belief in the merits of 'splendid isolation.' By the mid-1920s in Britain, the concept that 'if peace is to be obtained, it must be paid for by certain sacrifices, the assumption of certain obligations,' was, one observer noted at the time, greeted with 'genuine bewilderment.'[52] In any event, the domestic situation precluded such an activist role. 'We cannot act alone as the policeman of the world,' Bonar Law announced in 1922, 'the financial and social condition of the country makes that impossible.'[53] 'Imperial isolation' became the rallying cry of many British conservatives: the repudiation of expansionism in favour of strengthening the empire, the emphasizing of nationalism over internationalism, the resolve not to permit government policy to be beholden to any supranational institution, the desire to defend existing interests rather than to seek out new responsibilities.[54] Based on these considerations, being a member of the 'League of Notions' was tantamount, one conservative organ suggested, to 'exposing England's throat to the assassin's knife.'[55] At best, 'the average conservative thought of it as a forum in which disputes could be aired and, if all went well, settled,' one observer later commented. 'The League's function was not to do but to be.'[56] At worst, many on the right viewed the organization with contempt and suspicion, scepticism and distrust, because of the threat they believed it posed to national sovereignty.[57]

Imperial isolationism perhaps found its most vocal champion during the 1920s in the Round Table movement, which included the likes of Amery, Curzon, Cecil, and Christie. During that decade the members of this group were concerned about international peace and security, but they were soon disillusioned with the League of Nations. Britain ought not to become embroiled in Europe any more than necessary. The country 'must be made to look away towards the outer world, as she always has done in the past,' Philip Kerr, later Lord Lothian, maintained. Accordingly, he and other Round Table members took as their main goals the consolidation of imperial unity and the enhancement of Anglo-American relations.[58] Indeed, it was with an eye to not alienating the dominions or the United States that the Round Table viewed the League of Nations.[59] Thus, given Canadian and American attitudes towards that body, the group looked askance at the Geneva Protocol's plan to bolster the League's collective security powers. It perhaps made sense as a pact between continental nations, but from Britain's perspective, agreeing to support compulsory arbitration and automatic sanctions might seriously impair imperial and Anglo-American collaboration. The League should confine its activities to fostering dialogue. The Round Table's assessment of Locarno was similar. On the one hand, it welcomed this rapprochement in the relationship between France and Germany as well as the treaty's limitation of Britain's continental commitment to western Europe. On the other, the group bemoaned even that obligation, not to mention the fact that, in assuming a responsibility that her dominions did not endorse, the mother country was imperilling the diplomatic unity of the empire.[60] British governments of the 1920s refused to adhere to the Geneva Protocol, signed the Locarno Pact comforted by the fact that it actually diluted the nation's continental commitment and placed conditions on British acceptance of the Kellogg-Briand Pact similar to those enacted by the American Senate.[61]

Thus, Anglo-American-Canadian diplomatic relations in the 1920s did not evolve in a vacuum but were played out against a backdrop of various domestic factors operating within all three countries. And a particular kind of collective ideological climate born of the Great War and wary of undertakings that might lead to a repetition of that ghastly experience helped to fuse the individual lines that comprised the North Atlantic triangle. Within it, however, there were differences of opinion over how best to achieve the goals of peace and security. One way for Britain to maintain its position was to promote just what the Round Table suggested: strong imperial unity and cordial Anglo-American relations. But Canada, the senior dominion, proved uncooperative and the United States hostile.

NORTH AMERICAN WITHDRAWAL

Although many have attributed to King the drive for Canadian autonomy, which resulted in the Balfour Declaration of 1926 and the Statute of Westminster of 1931, as well as the gradual shift in focus towards the United States, it is wrong to do so.[62] The pursuit of autonomy and Canada's move towards the United States began not with King but with Robert Borden and his successor, Arthur Meighen, as they sought to come to terms with the changed circumstances of the postwar world. For most of his career Robert Borden championed the British Empire and promoted the idea of a cooperative imperial commonwealth. Borden believed that through a process of continuous consultation between London and the self-governing dominions, Britain could establish a strong and unified foreign policy for the empire.[63] This goal been achieved, in part, at the Imperial War Conference of 1917, when Borden and Jan Smuts of South Africa pushed through Resolution IX. It declared that Britain 'should recognise the right of the Dominions and India to an adequate voice in foreign policy and in foreign relations, and should provide effective arrangements for continuous consultation in all important matters of common Imperial concern.'[64]

At the time Borden hailed this resolution as a major step – but in which direction? Borden himself was not sure. In one breath he told the Canadian House of Commons in 1917 that Resolution IX did 'not sacrifice in the slightest degree the autonomy of the power of self-government' in Canada; in the next he alluded to the 'opportunity for consultation, co-operation and united action' between Canada and Britain.[65] If Borden still believed that Canadian autonomy could be squared with a unified imperial foreign policy throughout 1918, he was beginning to change his view by the end of the war. The first indication came at meetings of the Imperial War Cabinet during the summer of 1918 when he launched a scathing attack on the conduct of the war and warned British leaders that unless Canada could have a 'voice in the foreign relations of the empire as a whole, she would before long have an independent voice in her own foreign affairs outside the empire.'[66]

Although the British worked hard to secure Canadian representation at the Paris Peace Conference, they had no intention of permitting Canada a full voice in imperial affairs. Lloyd George was willing to allow full Canadian participation in a series of preliminary inter-Allied conferences, but little more.[67] As he became more and more disillusioned, Borden began to believe that perhaps the time had come for Canada to take a new direction. In words that could have emanated from the pen of King, Borden wrote in his diary one late night in early December 1918: 'I am beginning to feel that in the end and perhaps sooner than later, Canada must assume full sovereignty. She can give better service to G[reat] B[ritain] & U[nited] S[tates] & to the world in that way.'[68] Borden took the first steps in this direction at the end of December 1918 when he told the British cabinet: 'if the future policy of the British Empire meant working in co-operation with some European nation as against the United States, that policy could not reckon on the approval or the support of Canada. Canada's view was that as an Empire we should keep clear, as far as possible, of European complications and alliances. This feeling had been immensely strengthened by the experience of the war, into which we had been drawn by old-standing pledges and more recent understandings, of which the Dominions had not even been aware.'[69] The same day he also announced, against British wishes, that Canada was going to withdraw the expeditionary force that had been sent to Siberia to fight the Bolsheviks.[70]

Admittedly, Borden does not appear to have abandoned completely his hope for some form of imperial unity. But in these statements there was clearly an expression of a new national awareness of Canada's position in the postwar world, a new self-interest, and a sense of the role Canada might play, namely, as potential peacemaker – or linchpin – between Britain and the United States. The chance for just such a role was not long in coming. The United States and Britain, allies of late, were entering a decade that would be characterized by growing antagonism. As one American observed in 1919: 'relations between the two countries are beginning to assume the same character as that between England and Germany before the war.'[71] One issue over which Britain and the United States disagreed was the Anglo-Japanese alliance. First negotiated in 1902, it had been renewed in 1905 and again, for ten years, in 1911. In 1921 it was up for renewal. Americans took a dim view of the alliance. It was, in the words of former secretary of state, Elihu Root, 'regarded by the people as an alliance between Great Britain and Japan against the United States.'[72]

Against this background of mounting tension Arthur Meighen travelled to London to attend the 1921 Imperial Conference. He went with one aim: to make sure the British did not renew the alliance.[73] Arguing that the renewal of the alliance would have a disastrous effect on Canadian-American relations, Meighen threatened to dissociate Canada from any British attempt to form an alliance with Japan.[74] His reasoning is instructive. 'If we now in this state of affairs renew a confidential and exclusive relationship with Japan,' he told delegates at the Imperial Conference, 'it is wholly impossible to argue convincingly, to my mind, that it is not going to affect detrimentally our relations with the United States, no matter how steadfastly the British Government sets its face to keep those relations good.'[75] Canada thus urgently and successfully helped to pressure Britain to end the alliance. It was replaced by a series of agreements reached at the Washington Conference of 1921–2, the most important of which was the Five Power Treaty limiting a tonnage ratio for capital ships – warships over 10,000 tons carrying guns larger than eight inches. The ratio was 5:5:3:1.75:1.75 for, respectively, Britain, the United States, Japan, France, and Italy. Borden was called out of retirement to represent Canada at the conference.

That the Americans had been urging Canada to oppose the alliance cannot be doubted – Root, for example, did so in the belief that the termination of the alliance and British acceptance of the Washington treaties would make Britain more dependent on American support.[76] Nevertheless, Meighen and Borden believed that they had demonstrated two things during the Imperial and Washington conferences. One was that Canada could act as a linchpin between Britain and the United States. The other was that the Imperial Conference had demonstrated the viability of a unified imperial foreign policy based on consultation. In reality, however, they had acted in the self-interest of Canada, and in so doing they had succeeded in knocking out the foundation of British policy in the Far East, demonstrated that if forced to choose between Britain and the United States Canada would choose the United States, and instilled in the British a distaste for future adventures in cooperative commonwealth experiments. In this sense they paved the way for King.

King's role has been misunderstood, an error that is understandable, since his policies generally had an opaque quality. Thus he has been variously portrayed as the great Canadian who single-handedly battled the British for Canadian autonomy or as the demon who broke the British connection and led Canada into the arms of the United States or as the crafty statesman who reversed the policies of Borden and Meighen.[77] The 'truth' – if it can be said to exist in history – probably lies somewhere between these conflicting views. King did not so much reverse policy as follow what Borden had started to its logical conclusion. He was undoubtedly a Canadian nationalist who sought autonomy, but he did not favour breaking the imperial tie. He favoured closer relations with the United States, but not too close. As one American observer later pointed out: Canada 'wished to get all the benefits out of the protection afforded her by geography, by membership in the British Empire, and by friendship with the United States without assuming any responsibilities.'[78] That may be the definitive statement of Canadian foreign policy in the interwar years.

King was not long in demonstrating where he stood on the question of Canadian autonomy. In September 1922 the British government asked each of the dominions for assistance in confronting a Turkish threat to Britain's garrison at Chanak, on the banks of the Dardanelles in Asia Minor. Owing to sloppy practices, the uncoded cable communicating this request reached Canadian newspaper offices before the government was aware of the appeal. King first learned of its contents from a newspaper reporter. Ottawa took no action. An irate King politely but stiffly notified the British that only the Canadian Parliament could decide what course the country would follow – and he had no intention of calling Parliament into session.[79] The Chanak crisis was instructive for many Canadians. Meighen's attempt to embarrass King with his 'Ready, aye, ready' speech did not succeed. For if it was true that European statesmanship had catapulted the world headlong into the Great War, it was equally true that British statesmen were European. And if bungling British diplomats had helped to plunge the world into a devastating four-year holocaust, so had the peculiar nature of the dominion's relationship to Britain automatically made it a party to the conflict. That ruinous experience, compounded now by the irksome circumstances surrounding Chanak, served during the first decade of peace to strengthen the unsettling knowledge that Canadians were not in control of starting the engine of war. Canada's ties with the mother country were quite capable of drawing the dominion into hostilities not of its own interest or making. Canada did not yet exercise full authority over the making of war and peace. The dominion could determine the nature and extent of its participation in British wars, but it was automatically a belligerent the moment Britain was one.

This lesson, of course, was not lost on King, and he certainly inflicted a further dent in the concept of a unified policy for the empire at the Imperial Conference of 1923. There, he nipped in the bud any talk of continuous consultation, coordination of defence policies, and commitments in advance to support British foreign policy. There, too, the dominions' right to sign their own treaties with other countries was enshrined.[80] Nevertheless, the prospect of joint diplomatic action with London remained a powerful bogey for many Canadians throughout the 1920s. J.S. Ewart, for example, a close friend of King, suggested that it was doubtful whether Britain really desired sincerely to confer with Canada. 'We understand you perfectly,' he wrote in a book intended for British as well as Canadian eyes, 'France wants to be able to call blacks and browns from Africa; and you want to be able to summon whites from Canada to fight blacks, browns, or other whites as you may think your interests require.'[81]

Thus the Locarno Pact, about which London had not consulted Ottawa, which appeared between two general elections in Canada, was a disturbing development. 'We cannot admit [that we are] automatically committed to all Britain's wars,' Skelton maintained. 'Canada can best decide on her course in the light of the facts and circumstances of the time, rather than give a blank cheque now to whatever men may be in power in London in 1940; their case will be more circumspect if [they are] not sure of our support in advance.'[82] For Christie, Locarno had to be the parting of company with Britain. 'I cannot escape the conviction,' he wrote to Borden in February 1926, 'that ... in order to play our unique part in the English-speaking world we must assume a more independent and detached position than existing forms allow us.'[83] That goal was achieved in large measure at the 1926 Imperial Conference, which produced the Balfour Declaration proclaiming that the dominions and Britain were 'in no way subordinate to one another in any aspect of their domestic or external affairs, though united by a common allegiance to the Crown and freely associated as members of the British Commonwealth of Nations.' The conference also agreed that the dominions could not 'be committed to the acceptance of active obligations, except with the definite consent of their own governments.'[84]

Although there were those who grumbled that the Balfour Declaration did not provide enough freedom from Downing Street, it was nevertheless a significant shift away from Britain. On the one hand, J.S. Ewart observed in 1927 regarding the Canadian outlook: 'antipathy toward Americans has decreased, and is now tending to disappear ...

making impossible the perpetuation of a Canadian felling of antagonism to the United States'.[85] On the other, 'there is an increasing disinclination to participate actively in British wars merely because they are British.' Many believed that Canada's future lay in North America and the nurturing of relations with the United States. After all, as Christie pointed out, it was 'a simple truth of geography and history that Canadians are North American and not European.'[86] So far as Skelton was concerned, Canada's future lay 'in her own reasonableness, the decency of her neighbour, and the steady development of friendly intercourse, common standards of conduct, and common points of view.'[87] In the light of this attitude it was of no small consequence that Canadian autonomy was first demonstrated by the establishment of diplomatic missions, in Washington in 1926 followed by Paris in 1928 and Tokyo a year later. British recognition of that autonomy occurred in 1928 with the appointment of a high commissioner to Ottawa.[88] As King prepared to go to Paris to sign the Kellogg-Briand Pact in 1929, he reflected proudly on his achievements in foreign policy: 'I am convinced the period of my administration will live in this particular as an epoch in the history of Canada that was formative and memorable.'[89] Indeed it was, but another epoch in Canadian history in the making was the economic shift towards the United States.

THE ECONOMIC SHIFT

The Great War's enormous impact on the international economy inevitably affected economic relations within the North Atlantic triangle. In the pre-war era Great Britain had functioned as the commercial and economic centre of the world. The war dealt a serious blow to sterling and Britain's pre-eminent economic position. The gap thus created was to a large degree filled by the United States. During the 1920s America rose to a nearly commanding position as the international financial centre. A debtor nation by nearly $4 billion in 1914, the United States emerged from the war a net creditor to the tune of about $10 billion. By 1922 this figure had risen to some $17 billion. Other indicators of America's new position are equally telling. In 1900, for example, the United States held roughly 3 per cent of the world's long-term investments; by 1929 it held more than 30 per cent. Between 1920 and 1929 American private investors lent more than $7.5 billion to foreign borrowers.[90]

By contrast, Britain emerged from the war in a weakened and precarious state. The nation faced declining trade, unemployment that ran to nearly 18 per cent in the early 1920s, shrinking gold reserves, and, at least initially, growing public unrest in the form of strikes.[91] Above all, Britain was in debt, and in debt to the United States to the tune of about $4.7 billion. British hopes for the cancellation of war debts, however, were dashed. The Americans proved unwilling to cancel, and this reluctance gave rise to the notion that the United States wanted to exert economic dominance over Britain. 'The central ambition of ... American politicians,' the British ambassador, Auckland Geddes, informed his government in 1920, 'is to win for America the position of leading nation in the world and also leader among the English-speaking nations. To do this they intend to have the strongest navy and the largest mercantile marine. They intend also to prevent us from paying our debt by sending goods to America and they look for the opportunity to treat us as a vassal State so long as the debt remains unpaid.'[92] By the mid-1920s there was considerable bad feeling in Britain. 'The debts and similar claims on the part of the United States have already made the average Englishman think the Americans are dirty swine,' wrote a senior Foreign Office official.[93]

There is little evidence to suggest that the United States wanted to reduce Britain to a vassal state, as Hughes was well aware: 'There will be no permanent peace unless economic satisfactions are enjoyed.'[94] Rather, as Frank Costigliola has pointed out, both Britain and the United States wanted to reconstruct the international economy, but each wanted to do so on terms that would fulfil its own national interests. For the United States it meant an international economy based on the concept of the free market-place, the open door, and a return to the gold standard. For Britain it meant a London-centred financial bloc, reduced war debts, stabilized prices, and internationally regulated capital flows.[95] Possessing more economic clout, the Americans won the battle during the 1920s.[96] Indications that the United States won the day were apparent in a shift in trade and investment patterns within the North Atlantic triangle, particularly with respect to Canada.

Prior to the Great War Canada had balanced its imports from the United States through exports to Britain. The United States accounted for an average of 60 per cent of all the goods Canada imported while Britain accounted for an average of 53 per cent of all the goods Canada exported between 1900 and 1914. During those same years Canada imported only 23 per cent of its goods from Britain and exported 36 per cent of all its goods to the United States. As these figures suggest, in the pre-war era the vast bulk of Canadian trade was carried out within the

North Atlantic triangle – 83 per cent of all import and 89 per cent of all export trade was with the United States and Britain.[97] The war significantly affected these trade patterns. During the 1920s Canadian imports from the United States rose from an average of 60 per cent to 68 per cent; exports to Britain declined from an average of 53 per cent to 36 per cent. During the 1920s there was also a further decline in imports, from Britain to 16.5 per cent of total imports, while exports to the United States rose to an average of 39 per cent for the decade. In terms of overall trade, 84.5 per cent of Canadian import trade and 75 per cent of export trade were done with Britain and the United States. Clearly, the most significant development was the decline in Canadian trade, especially export trade, with Britain and the increasing trade with the United States. In fact, in 1921 Canada exported more to other countries than it did to Britain – $312.845 million worth of goods were exported to Britain, $333 995 million to 'other' countries.[98] This trend would continue throughout the decade, so that by 1929 the total trade between Canada and the United States ($1.372 billion) was larger than that of the total trade between Britain and the United States ($1.178 billion).[99]

Far more significant than the changing trade pattern was the dramatic shift in investment. In 1913 British investment represented 75 per cent of the total foreign capital invested in Canada. Following the war that figure fell to 57 per cent and then declined steadily, so that by 1930 only 36 per cent of foreign investment in Canada originated in Britain. At the same time American investment in Canada grew from a pre-war rate of 23 per cent of total investment to 36 per cent in 1919 and then to 61 per cent in 1930. The turning point was 1922, when, for the first time, American investment in Canada exceeded British investment.[100] By the mid-1920s total American investment had passed the $3 billion mark and continued at an annual rate of $2.5 million for the remainder of the decade.[101] This shift was of some concern to the British, who were worried that increasing American economic influence in Canada posed a threat to the imperial link, if not to the empire itself. 'American money power is trying to get hold of the natural resources of the empire,' warned Baldwin in 1928. 'They are working like beavers.'[102] (The reference to Canada's national emblem was probably unintended.) Britain did little to rectify the situation. Sterling remained weak through much of the 1920s, and displeasure over losses suffered in railroad bankruptcies tended to make British investors shy of Canada.[103]

None of the foregoing is to imply that Canada had jumped, or was willing to jump, into America's economic bed. There were a number of problems in Canadian-American economic relations, most of them stemming from the high-tariff policies the United States employed. Moreover, throughout the 1920s King sought increased economic ties with Britain, most notably at the 1923 Imperial Economic Conference.[104] Trying to explain the aims of his budget at the end of the decade, King wrote: 'It is essential to increase, not decrease, imports from Britain if we wish to increase our exports to Britain, and the Budget ensures this by diverting trade from the United States to Britain.'[105] Further attempts to increase Canada's trade with Britain would be made during the 1930s, but the economic shift that occurred during the 1920s would never be reversed.

ANGLO-AMERICAN NAVAL RIVALRY

At one point during the Washington Conference of 1921–2 Borden had a disturbing conversation with Admiral Sir Ernle Chatfield, then serving as assistant chief of naval staff. 'Admiral Chatfield,' he recorded in his diary, 'whom personally I like, indulged in some loose and foolish talk as to his willingness to fight [the] United States with an inferior fleet. He does not seem to realise that war between the two countries would mean the destruction of a civilisation [sic] already rocking under the impact of the late war.'[106] Chatfield's comments and Borden's concern underscored what would develop into probably the most serious problem for the North Atlantic triangle during the 1920s: the Anglo-American naval rivalry. The British official naval historian, Stephen Roskill, characterized the period from 1919 to 1929 as 'the period of Anglo-American antagonism.'[107] By the autumn of 1928 Anglo-American relations had so declined as a result of the naval issue that Robert Craigie, the head of the American Department of the Foreign Office, was writing that 'war is *not* unthinkable between the two countries.'[108]

The immediate origins of the Anglo-American rivalry can be traced to the summer of 1915, when the General Board of the United States Navy recommended that 'the Navy of the United States should ultimately be equal to the most powerful maintained by any other nation of the world.'[109] Thus was born the 'second to none' naval policy that the United States sought to initiate in the naval construction programs of 1916 and 1918. As it originally stood, the 1918 program was to produce 1,000 ships, including twelve battleships and sixteen battlecruisers.[110] Although the American naval program was reduced to 156 ships after the war, in part because of the domestic opposition of the 'Mugwump' factor and the National Council for the Limitation of Armaments, it nevertheless caused considerable concern in Britain.[111] Churchill believed that there was an element of 'bluff and bluster' behind it, but he was not 'prepared to take dictation from the US.' 'We do not wish to put ourselves in the power of the United States,' he warned the cabinet.[112] This was an important consideration indeed, because the security and well-being of the empire depended upon a powerful navy, and in their weakened financial situation the British had no desire to meet new challenges. As Sir Ernle Chatfield, the first sea lord, later observed: 'We are in the remarkable position of not wanting to quarrel with anybody because we have got most of the world already, or the best parts of it, and we only want to keep what we have got and prevent others taking it away from us.'[113]

The problem was how to accomplish the task. Despite the fact that Britain had emerged from the Great War with the world's largest navy – sixty-one battleships, which was more than the American and French navies combined, 120 cruisers, and 466 destroyers – it was becoming increasingly difficult to maintain that superiority.[114] Britain had been weakened by the war and faced the difficulty of trying to finance a large military machine to oversee empire commitments. The Royal Navy alone swallowed about £160 million, or 20 per cent of government expenditure in 1919–20, at a time when budget estimates were shrinking.[115] In an effort to retrench, Britain was forced to abandon one of its long-standing policies: the 'Two-Power Standard.' Adopted in 1889, this policy held that the Royal Navy should be as strong as the combined might of any two powers. Unable to continue such a goal, Britain adopted the 'One-Power Standard' in 1920. The United States naval program was therefore viewed as a threat, or at least as a potential threat.[116]

Although the Washington Conference settled some outstanding differences in Anglo-American relations by setting limits on capital ships, the treaties said nothing about cruisers. It was over the limitation of cruiser building that the next round began. Here the British enjoyed a decided advantage over the Americans and they wanted to keep it that way. When Coolidge put forward a proposal in 1924 to hold a second Washington conference to limit construction of smaller-class ships, the British refused. The Americans kept pressing, and in 1927 the British agreed to attend the ill-fated Coolidge conference, which met in Geneva during the summer. By this time there was close to open talk of war between Britain and the United States. The basic problem was neatly summed up by Lord Jellicoe: 'The American programme has only one object in view, viz. Equality with Great Britain on the sea. We cannot help it if they build up to our required standard, but we can avoid lowering our standard to suit them.'[117] Should the Americans gain the upper hand, in Churchill's view, they would then be 'in a position to give us orders about our policy, say, in India or Egypt, or Canada or any other great matter behind which their electioneering forces were marshalled ... I would neither trust America to command, nor England to submit.'[118] It was not until the London Naval Conference of 1930 that the United States and Britain came to an agreement, and even then relations were less than cordial.[119]

This Anglo-American naval rivalry concerned Canada deeply for a number of reasons, chief of which was that Canada always suffered when Anglo-American relations soured – and a war would be an unmitigated disaster, since Canada would likely be a battleground. This was, in fact, one of the arguments Meighen advanced at the 1921 Imperial Conference.[120] Hence, during the 1920s and the 1930s Canada repeatedly sought to promote good Anglo-American relations. As Walter Hose noted: 'We, who know the U.S., should be in a position to give advice which may prevent the British Cabinet being led into playing the U.S. Big Navy Party's game by the Admiralty.'[121] Another Canadian concern rose from a general mistrust of the United States. Canada was most certainly moving towards the United States in terms of trade and attitudes to Europe, but that trend did not extend to military matters. Walter Hose strongly warned against Canada's 'placing itself entirely in the hands of the friendly neighbour.'[122] Other military figures, such as James Sutherland Brown and A.G.L. McNaughton, did not discount the possibility of war. Brown was in fact the author of 'Defence Scheme No. 1,' a plan that actually called for a 'first strike' at the United States in the event of trouble.[123]

In the end, of course, the United States and Britain did not go to war. But the Anglo-American naval rivalry served to demonstrate the precarious nature of the triangular relationship during the 1920s. Many of the problems that arose during the postwar decade would reappear during the 1930s – though there would be a different set of circumstances and, once again, different responses. Indeed, Canada would once more join the mother country in war, again temporarily leaving the Americans behind on the sidelines. But it was the last gasp of an already altered triangular relationship. The 1920s represented the beginning of a transition that would continue through the course of the twentieth century, and that was the gradual shift in power away from Britain and towards the

United States. For Canada, more than any other country, adaptation to the new order of things was imperative, controversial, and tumultuous.

NOTES

1 Borden diary, 11 November 1918, Borden Papers, National Archives of Canada, Ottawa (hereafter NAC); Henry Borden, ed., *Robert Laird Borden: His Memoirs*, Vol. II (Toronto, 1969), 157.
2 For the wider impact of the war, see Paul Fussell, *The Great War and Modern Memory* (Oxford, 1975).
3 Although dated, one of the few studies of the triangular relationship during these years is J.B. Brebner, *North Atlantic Triangle: The Interplay of Canada, the United States and Great Britain* (New York, 1945; Toronto, 1966).
4 For example, Gabriel Kolko, *The Politics of War: The World and United States Foreign Policy* (New York, 1968).
5 Cf. Arthur Link, *Woodrow Wilson: Revolution, War and Peace* (Arlington Heights, IL, 1979); N. Gordon Levin, *Woodrow Wilson and World Politics: America's Reponse to War and Revolution* (New York, 1968); Klaus Schwabe, *Woodrow Wilson, Revolutionary Germany, and Peace-Making, 1918–1919* (Chapel Hill, NC, 1985).
6 For an overview, see Warren I. Cohen, *Empire without Tears: America's Foreign Relations, 1921–1933* (New York, 1987); Frank Costigliola, *Awkward Dominion: America's Political, Economic and Cultural Relations with Europe, 1919–1933* (Ithaca, NY, 1985).
7 Selig Adler, *The Uncertain Giant, 1921–1941: American Foreign Policy between the Wars* (New York, 1965); R.E. Osgood, *Ideals and Self-Interest in America's Foreign Relations* (Chicago, 1953).
8 William Appleman Williams, 'The Legend of Isolationism in the 1920s,' *Science and Society*, 18(1954), 1–20.
9 See especially C.P. Parrini, *Heir to Empire: The United States Economic Diplomacy, 1916–1923* (Pittsburgh, 1969).
10 For example, William Appleman Williams, *The Tragedy of American Diplomacy* (New York, 1959).
11 See Joan Hoff Wilson, *American Business and Foreign Policy, 1920–1933* (Lexington, KY, 1971).
12 See D.C. Watt, *Succeeding John Bull: America in Britain's Place, 1900–1975* (Cambridge, 1984), 40–68.
13 Churchill served in a variety of positions during and after the war, including secretary for war (and air), 1918–21, colonial secretary, 1921–22, chancellor of the Exchequer, 1924–9.

14 Watt, *Succeeding John Bull*, 49–50.
15 Cf. C.P Stacey, *Canada and the Age of Conflict: A History of Canadian External Policies*, 2 vols (Toronto, 1977, 1981); P.G. Wigley, *Canada and the Transition to Commonwealth: British-Canadian Relations, 1917–1926* (Cambridge, 1977). J.L. Granatstein and Norman Hillmer, *For Better or for Worse: Canada and the United States to the 1990s* (Toronto, 1991), ch. 3, provides a good overview of Canadian-American relations.
16 Standard works include R.C. Brown, *Robert Laird Borden: A Biography*, 2 vols (Toronto, 1975, 1980); W.R. Graham, *Arthur Meighen: A Biography* (Toronto, 1960–5); R. MacGregor Dawson, *William Lyon Mackenzie King: A Political Biography, Vol. I, 1874–1923* (Toronto, 1958); H.B. Neatby, *William Lyon Mackenzie King. Vol. II, 1924–1932: The Lonely Heights* (Toronto, 1970).
17 On Hose, see Roger Sarty, 'Entirely in the Hand of the Friendly Neighbour': The Canadian Armed Forces and the Defence of the Pacific Coast, 1909–1939,' unpublished paper, 1990.
18 For a wider study, see J.L. Granatstein, *The Ottawa Men: The Civil Service Mandarins, 1935–1957* (Toronto, 1982).
19 Christie memorandum, 10 December 1914, Borden Papers, vol. 659, ff. 67875–80. Cf. Robert Bothwell, *Loring Christie: The Failure of Bureaucratic Imperialism* (New York, 1988).
20 Norman Hillmer, 'The Anglo-Canadian Neurosis: The Case of O.D. Skelton,' in *Britain and Canada: Survey of a Changing Relationship*, ed. P. Lyon (London, 1976), 61–84.
21 See J.L. Granatstein, *How Britain's Weakness Forced Canada into the Arms of the United States* (Toronto, 1989).
22 Quoted in Margaret Prang, *N.W. Rowell: Ontario Nationalist* (Toronto, 1975), 361.
23 League of Nations, *Official Journal*, Special Supplement No. 23: *Records of the Fifth Assembly* (Geneva, 1924), 222.
24 Borden, *Memoirs*, II, 180–1.
25 Ramsay Cook, ed., *The Dafoe-Sifton Correspondence, 1919–1927* (Altona, Man., 1966), 45, 74, 203.
26 Quoted in Richard Veatch, *Canada and the League of Nations* (Toronto, 1975), 8.
27 Christie to Meighen, 23 December 1925, Meighen Papers [NAC] vol. 64; Christie to Borden, 5 January 1925, Christie Papers [NAC] vol. 10, file 31.
28 Christie memorandum, 'Responsible Government: The Last Stage,' 15 June 1926, Christie Papers, vol. 26, file 106.
29 Skelton 'Notes on the Protocol of Geneva,' Department of External Affairs Records (hereafter DEA) [NAC], vol. 813, file 629 (1).

30 Skelton memorandum on Locarno, 21 October 1925, Mackenzie King Papers [NAC] vol. 141, file 1142.

31 O.D. Skelton, 'Current Events: Canada and the Making of War and Peace,' *Queen's Quarterly*, 28(July 1920), 105.

32 Cook, *Dafoe-Sifton Correspondence*, 122.

33 Canada, House of Commons, *Debates*, 11 September 1919, 230.

34 See T.N. Guinsburg, *The Pursuit of Isolationism in the United States Senate from Versailles to Pearl Harbor* (New York, 1982).

35 See Ralph Stone, *The Irreconcilables: The Fight against the League of Nations* (Lexington, KY., 1970), 82–3.

36 Ibid., 144.

37 Robert J. Maddox, *William E. Borah and American Foreign Policy* (Baton Rouge, LA, 1969), 62.

38 Quoted in W.C. Widenor, *Henry Cabot Lodge and the Search for an American Foreign Policy* (Berkeley, CA, 1980), 316.

39 Alexander De Conde, *A History of American Foreign Policy*, Vol. II: *Global Power (1900 to the present)*, 3rd ed. (New York, 1978), 86–7.

40 J.C. Vinson, *The Parchment Peace: The United States and the Washington Conference, 1921–1922* (Athens, GA, 1955), 203.

41 Ibid., 207, 208, 210.

42 Selig Adler, *The Isolationist Impulse: Its Twentieth-Century Reaction* (New York, 1957), 152.

43 Ibid., 207–10.

44 Ibid., 236–7; Guinsburg, *Pursuit of Isolationism*, 128.

45 Warren I. Cohen, *The American Revisionists: The Lessons of Intervention in World War I* (Chicago, 1967), 1–2, 233.

46 Ibid., 27–30.

47 Adler, *Isolationist Impulse*, 69–70.

48 A. Lentin, *Lloyd George, Woodrow Wilson and the Guilt of Germany: An Essay in the Pre-History of Appeasement* (Baton Rouge, LA, 1985), 137.

49 Paul Johnson, *A History of the Modern World* (London, 1983), 29–30.

50 Martin Gilbert, *The Roots of Appeasement* (London, 1966), 66.

51 Lentin, *Pre-History of Appeasement*, 140–1.

52 Quoted in K.E. Miller, *Socialism and Foreign Policy: Theory and Practice in Britain to 1931* (The Hague, 1967), 137–8.

53 Quoted in Keith Robbins, *Appeasement* (Oxford, 1988), 30.

54 G.C. Webber, *The Ideology of the British Right, 1918–1939* (London, 1986), 115–16. Cf. Watt, *Succeeding John Bull*, 51.

55 A.P. Thornton, *The Imperial Idea and Its Enemies: A Study in British Power* (London, 1959), 285.

56 R.B. McCallum, *Public Opinion and the Last Peace* (London, 1944), 146.

57 See ibid., 137–8; Robbins, *Appeasement*, 13; Thornton, *Imperial Idea*, 286–9.

58 J.E. Kendle, *The Round Table Movement and Imperial Union* (Toronto, 1975), 276–7.

59 J.R.M. Butler, *Lord Lothian* (London, 1960), 110.

60 Ibid., 112.

61 Miller, *Socialism and Foreign Policy*, 148, 184, 186; Thornton, *Imperial Idea*, 290; W.R. Rock, *British Appeasement in the 1930s* (London, 1977), 35.

62 The strongest critic of Mackenzie King is Donald Creighton, *Canada's First Century* (Toronto, 1970); idem, 'Decline and Fall of the Empire of the St Lawrence,' *Canadian Historical Association Papers* (1969).

63 Kendle, *Round Table*, 115–16.

64 Stacey, *Age of Conflict*, I, 213.

65 Ibid., 217.

66 'Report of the Committee of Prime Ministers on War Policy,' Borden Papers, file OC 628; Stacey, *Age of Conflict*, I, 225.

67 Lloyd George to Borden, 27 October 1918, *Documents on Canadian External Relations* (hereafter *DCER*), vol. I, 218.

68 Borden diary, 1 December 1918.

69 Imperial War Cabinet Minutes [IWC 47], 30 December 1918, CAB [Cabinet Archives, Public Record Office, Kew] 23/43

70 See Gaddis Smith, 'Canada and the Siberian Intervention, 1918–1919,' *American Historical Review*, 64(1959), 866–77; James Eayrs, *In Defence of Canada*, Vol. I: *From the Great War to the Great Depression* (Toronto, 1964), 27–40.

71 Quoted in Granatstein and Hillmer, *For Better or for Worse*, 76.

72 Quoted in G.P. Glazebrook, *A History of Canadian External Relations*, Vol. I (Toronto, 1966), 59.

73 On Meighen's role, see M.G. Fry, 'The North Atlantic Triangle and the Abrogation of the Anglo-Japanese Alliance,' *Journal of Modern History*, 39(1976), 46–64; Ira Klein, 'Whitehall, Washington, and the Anglo-Japanese Alliance, 1919–1921,' *Pacific Historical Review*, 41(1972), 460–83; Ian Nish, *Alliance in Decline: A Study in Anglo-Japanese Relations, 1908–1923* (London, 1972), chs 18–22.

74 Governor-General to Colonial Secretary, 1 April 1921, CO [Colonial Office Archives, Public Record Office, Kew] 42/1042

75 Minutes of the Ninth Meeting, Imperial Conference, 29 June 1921, *DCER*, III.

76 Watt, *Succeeding John Bull*, 44; M.G. Fry, *Illusions of Security: North Atlantic Diplomacy, 1918–1922* (Toronto, 1972), 91–120.

77 See A.R.M. Lower, *Colony to Nation* (Toronto, 1957); Donald Creighton, *Canada's First Century* (Toronto, 1970); Stacey, *Age of Conflict*, II.

78 'Record of meeting of Dominion Representatives,' 2 November 1937 FO [Foreign Office Archives, Public Record Office, Kew] 371/21016/06666; Moffat diary, 10 November 1937, J.P. Moffat Papers [Harvard University]. The statement was made by Norman Davis.

79 Stacey, *Age of Conflict*, II, 22–4.

80 Wigley, *Transition to Commonwealth*, 173–205.

81 J.S. Ewart, *The Independence Papers*, Vol. I (n.p., n.d.), 32–3. It is interesting to note Mackenzie King's comment on Ewart and his book: 'Ewart is very able & better informed than any one in Canada on foreign affairs,' he wrote in his diary, 'but too extreme. Is for separation. I am not, I believe in the Br[itish] Empire as a 'Co-operative Commonwealth.' Mackenzie King diary, 8 April 1922.

82 Skelton memorandum on Locarno, 21 October 1925, DEA vol. 753, file 230; Skelton memorandum, 1 January 1926, Mackenzie King Papers, vol. 92.

83 Quoted in Wigley, *Transition to Commonwealth*, 246.

84 Stacey, *Age of Conflict*, II, 86.

85 J.S. Ewart, 'Canada, the Empire, and the United States,' *Foreign Affairs*, 6(1927), 126–7.

86 Christie to Kerr, 14 December 1925, Christie Papers, vol. 11, file 35.

87 Skelton memorandum on 'The Locarno Treaties,' 1 January 1926, Mackenzie King Papers, vol. 139.

88 See Norman Hillmer, 'A British High Commissioner for Canada, 1927–28,' *Journal of Imperial and Commonwealth History*, 3(1973), 339–56.

89 Quoted in John Thompson and Allen Seager, *Canada, 1922–1939: Decades of Discord* (Toronto, 1985), 57.

90 Gabriel Kolko, *Main Currents in Modern American History* (New York, 1984), 195ff; W.R. Keylor, *The Twentieth-Century World* (Oxford, 1984), 95–111. See also C.P. Kindleberger, *The World in Depression, 1929–1939* (Los Angeles, 1973), 31–82, for what is probably the best overview.

91 See A.J.P. Taylor, *English History, 1914–1945* (Oxford, 1965), esp. xxi–xxvii, 120–6, 163; Frank Costigliola, 'Anglo-American Financial Rivalry in the 1920s,' *Journal of Economic History*, 37(1977), 911.

92 Quoted in Roberta Dayer, 'The British War Debts to the United States and the Anglo-Japanese Alliance, 1920–1923,' *Pacific Historical Review*, 45(1976), 577.

93 Hurst [FO legal adviser] minute, 28 October 1925, FO 371/10646/5376/ 1490.

94 Quoted in M. Leffler, 'Political Isolationism, Economic Expansionism, or Diplomatic Realism: American Policy toward Western Europe 1921–1933,' *Perspectives in American History*, 8(1974), 416.

95 Costigliola, 'Anglo-American Financial Rivalry,' 913–15.
96 It should be noted that the United States was unable to supplant British influence in China. See Roberta Dayer, *Finance and Empire: Sir Charles Addis, 1861–1945* (New York, 1988), xviii; Christopher Thorne, *Allies of a Kind: The United States, Britain, and the War against Japan, 1941–1945* (Oxford, 1978), 17; cf. Herbert Feis, *The Diplomacy of the Dollar: The First Era, 1919–1932* (Baltimore, 1969). B.J.C. McKercher, 'Wealth, Power, and the New International Order: Britain and the American Challenge in the 1920s,' *Diplomatic History*, 12(1988), 411–41, argues the revisionist case that Britain successfully resisted the American challenge.
97 These figures are from Stacey, *Age of Conflict*, II, 356–9. We have calculated the averages.
98 The figures are from ibid., 432–5. We have made the calculations.
99 Brebner, *North Atlantic Triangle*, 300.
100 Kenneth Norrie and Douglas Owram, *A History of the Canadian Economy* (Toronto, 1991), 450.
101 Ibid.; Stephen Scheinberg, 'Invitation to Empire: Tariffs and American Economic Expansion in Canada,' in *Enterprise and National Development: Essays in Canadian Business and Economic History*, ed. Glenn Porter and Robert D. Cuff (Toronto, 1973), 94.
102 Quoted in Watt, *Succeeding John Bull*, 60.
103 See Brebner, *North Atlantic Triangle*, 296.
104 See Wigley, *Transition to Commonwealth*, 199–205.
105 Document 13 (Mackenzie King to Morton, 14 June 1930), in I.M. Drummond, *British Economic Policy and the Empire, 1919–1939* (London, 1972), 180–2.
106 Quoted in Stacey, *Age of Conflict*, I, 352.
107 Stephen Roskill, *Naval Policy between the Wars*, Vol. I: *The Period of Anglo-American Antagonism, 1919–1929* (London, 1968).
108 Craigie memorandum, 'Outstanding Problems affecting Anglo-American Relations,' 12 November 1928 (emphasis in original), FO 371/12812/7895/39.
109 Roskill, *Naval Policy*, I, 20–1.
110 Ibid., 90–1.
111 Watt, *Succeeding John Bull*, 42.
112 Churchill memorandum, 20 July 1927, quoted in ibid., 58–9.
113 Chatfield to Fisher, 4 June 1934, quoted in Christopher Thorne, *The Limits of Foreign Policy: The West, the League and the Far Eastern Crisis of 1931–1933* (New York, 1973), 397–8.
114 Roskill, *Naval Policy*, I, 70.

115 McKercher, 'Wealth, Power, and the New International Order,' 424.

116 Roskill, *Naval Policy*, I, 70.

117 Ibid., 516.

118 Quoted in Watt, *Succeeding John Bull*, 59.

119 Raymond G. O'Connor, *Perilous Equilibrium: The United States and the London Naval Conference of 1930* (Lawrence, KS, 1962). Cf. Greg C. Kennedy, 'The 1930 London Naval Conference and Anglo-American Maritime Strength, 1927–1930', in *Arms Limitation and Disarmament: Restraints on War, 1899–1939*, ed. B.J.C. McKercher (Westport, CT, 1992), 149–71.

120 *DCER*, III, 178.

121 Quoted in B.J.C. McKercher, 'Between Two Giants: Canada, the Coolidge Conference, and Anglo-American Relations in 1927,' in *Anglo-American Relations in the 1920s: The Struggle for Supremacy*, ed. idem (Edmonton, London, 1990), 91.

122 Hose memorandum, 30 July 1926, Mackenzie King Papers, vol. 124, file 913.

123 See Stephen Harris, *Canadian Brass: The Making of a Professional Army, 1860–1939* (Toronto, 1988), 169–78.

4

World Power and Isolationism: The North Atlantic Triangle and the Crises of the 1930s

B.J.C. McKERCHER

Throughout the 1930s Britain's relationship with the two English-speaking North American powers remained largely uneasy. Between the Wall Street stock market collapse in October 1929 and the outbreak of European war in September 1939, the international order created at Paris in 1919–20 broke down via a series of European and Far Eastern crises. In the 1930s the powers' foreign policies diverged: Britain pursued a diplomacy designed to promote peace and security by active involvement in international politics – and, not coincidentally, to protect its position as the world's leading power; the United States and Canada seemed to recede further into isolationism. Although the Wall Street collapse precipitated the Great Depression of the 1930s, several foreign policy problems that distinguished the 1920s (reparations, war debts, arms limitation, and the quest for security) had yet to be resolved by 1930. These issues dominated international politics until 1933–5 when, with Japanese expansion in China, Adolph Hitler's rise to power in Germany, and Italian estrangement from Britain and France caused by the Abyssinian crisis, a new constellation of international power presented new foreign policy problems.

The latter half of the decade saw Britain attempting to come grips with these new difficulties, first by reliance on the balance of power and then through bilateral agreements at the base of which lay the late 1930s variant of appeasement.[1] American and Canadian isolationism affected British foreign policy as the international horizon darkened – London could not rely on either Washington or Ottawa as it grappled with threats portended by militaristic Japan, Nazi Germany, and fascist Italy. None the less, by the late 1930s American and Canadian leaders, chiefly Franklin Roosevelt and William Lyon Mackenzie King, gradually appreciated that the totalitarian powers had to be opposed. The question was how. The answer lay in the different perceptions that London, Washington, and Ottawa had of the changing international situation that marked the 1930s, and in why Britain and Canada declared war on Germany in September 1939 while the United States continued on the path of isolation.

The Anglo-American relationship determined the nature of the North Atlantic triangle in the 1930s. The evolution of that relationship has been adumbrated elsewhere.[2] The decade actually began auspiciously when, in the first half of 1929, new governments took office in the United States and Britain within months of each other. On 4 March Herbert Hoover, a Republican, was inaugurated as president; three months later in Britain, on 7 June, the Labour party leader, James Ramsay MacDonald, formed a minority government. Both Hoover and MacDonald wanted to end the naval rivalry that had poisoned relations since the abortive Coolidge conference in 1927. They succeeded through the medium of the London Naval Conference of January–April 1930; and, on this basis, a period of Anglo-American cooperation ensued during which London and Washington worked together in both League-of-Nations-sponsored arms limitation discussions and multilateral efforts concerned with war debts and reparations. Though the Anglo-American accord had wobbled because of differing responses to the Manchurian crisis in 1931–2, under Roosevelt, a Democrat, cooperation ended by mid-1933. Roosevelt pursued strong nationalist policies concerning international economic and financial questions – dictated by political considerations necessary for him to win Congressional backing for his program of domestic reform, the 'New Deal.' Although Roosevelt might have been an internationalist,[3] his policies created British perceptions of increasing American isolation from political issues touching European and Far Eastern security. After late 1933 the British were forced to ignore the United States in their foreign and defence policy calculations as they confronted threats in Europe, the Mediterranean, and the Far East. Only with the difficulties that arose after the Munich agreement of 30 September 1938 did they begin looking on the United States as an adjunct to British defence policy, and more particularly, as a source of economic and financial support for the anti-Axis coalition that had formed between Britain and France.

The two Canadian prime ministers of the decade, King, a Liberal, and Richard Bennett, a Conservative, doubled as their own ministers of external affairs; under their tutelage, Canadian foreign policy followed in the wake of that of the two major English-speaking powers. Despite their domestic political differences, both men had a common diplomatic goal: protecting the dominion sovereignty in foreign policy conceded by Britain in 1926. Beyond this issue of amour propre, their principal diplomatic aim centred on finding international means to assist domestic economic recovery from the Depression. Thus, they tacked behind Britain and the United States to achieve the maximum advantages for Canada.[4] Bennett expressed this attitude best in the run up to the July 1930 Canadian election, when he promised 'to blast a way into the markets that ... had been closed.'[5] As happened during the 1920s, when security questions were raised, both eschewed external commitments. As King observed as late as October 1936: 'I have long felt, however, that in these inter-imperial or international matters involving commitments in time of war, no country can too frankly express in advance what its position at the moment of crisis is pretty certain to be.'[6] Still, European events in 1938–9 confronted Canadian leaders with a hard reality. The result was the King government's decision to follow Britain into war against Germany.

The period of Anglo-American cooperation actually began following Hoover's election in November 1928.[7] A Quaker and a fiscal conservative, Hoover was disinclined to spend public money on the United States Navy (USN). He made overtures to the British Conservative government, led by Sir Stanley Baldwin, to settle the vexed matter of cruiser limitation, the focus of Anglo-American discord. Hoover was willing to give Britain an advantage in light cruisers – roughly 6,000 tons with six-inch guns – which the Royal Navy (RN) required for imperial defence; and he selected Coolidge's anglophile vice-president, Charles Dawes, as the new American ambassador to London. For its part, Baldwin's government seemed willing to accord the USN a slight edge in heavy cruisers, 'treaty' vessels with *maxima* of 10,000 tons and eight-inch guns; and Baldwin won cabinet approval to travel to Washington after the May 1929 British general election to hold talks with Hoover and his secretary of state, Henry Stimson. But when Labour won the election, MacDonald built on the diplomatic ground prepared before 7 June by conducting high-level negotiations with Hoover and Stimson. Culminating in MacDonald's visit to the United States in October, these negotiations established the principles of a naval settlement.[8] Although their actions were disingenuous given that an Anglo-American compromise had been achieved by mid-October, over the next two and one-half months MacDonald and Hoover worked to avoid the appearance of an inflexible

Anglo-American bargaining position. This approach lessened the danger of the other powers feeling confronted by a fait accompli. The British and Americans held preliminary discussions with those powers – France, Italy, and Japan; in the emerging spirit of cooperation, London and Washington kept each other abreast of what transpired in these talks.[9]

During the London Naval Conference, MacDonald and Stimson, who led the American delegation, pursued two connected goals: giving form to the principles of the compromise worked out over the preceding summer; and getting the other powers to agree to a renewed Washington treaty perpetuating the formal primacy of the RN and USN. The first goal proved easy. Since MacDonald and Hoover had already agreed on a political resolution of their naval differences – one that overrode the technical objections of naval advisers that were seen to have prevented a settlement since 1927 – the politicians dominated discussions. As MacDonald noted after his first meeting with Stimson: 'We discussed the attitude of both Japan & France & resolved that neither was to place us in an impossible position with our people if complete cooperation between us could prevent it. "If the worst comes," [Stimson] said, "we can make an agreement ourselves two."'[10]

While five-power limitation of auxiliary vessels proved fruitless, a result of Franco-Italian failure to compromise, the three major naval powers extended the Washington naval treaty to 1936. They reduced battleship numbers, agreed to limit destroyers and submarines, and, most important, reached an understanding over an improved Imperial Japanese Navy (IJN) cruiser ratio (66 per cent in numbers but only 60 per cent in total displacement).[11] Of course, no party received everything it sought. For instance, MacDonald could not induce the Americans and Japanese to abolish submarines. But in terms of the renewed treaty, the British made significant gains.[12] Holding that the USN should have only eighteen heavy cruisers to the RN's fifteen – decisive in limiting the IJN to just twelve vessels – MacDonald's firmness forced the American delegation to reduce this number from a pre-conference preference for twenty-one. In addition, the RN received 50,000 extra tons of light cruisers to compensate for the American advantage in the heavier class of this warship. The London naval treaty was ratified by October; Anglo-American naval rivalry evaporated in the growing warmth of improving relations and, from the viewpoints of London and Washington, Japanese ambitions were contained. While some difficulties remained, chiefly those tied to Franco-Italian rivalry, they could be addressed in preparatory discussions being held at Geneva for the League-of-Nations-sponsored World Disarmament Conference.

Along with the other dominions, Canada was represented at London. James Ralston, King's minister of national defence, who led the Canadian delegates, sat on the British Empire delegation; in line with the Balfour Declaration of 1926 and following a precedent established at the Coolidge conference, however, he and other dominion representatives were independent of London.[13] This separation conformed to King's desire both to avoid an 'imperial foreign policy' and to decouple Canada, especially the tiny Royal Canadian Navy (RCN), from British policies of imperial defence. King's efforts to distance Canada from Britain did not have much impact in Washington. When deciding on conference machinery, Stimson told MacDonald 'that not only would such a large representation of Dominions cause difficulty in the actual work of the Delegation but would no doubt have political repercussions in the United States where the idea of six votes of the British empire to one of the United States had always had bad political repercussions.'[14]

Ralston and allies of Canada, such as the South Africans, resisted pressures for a single dominion delegate to represent all of them at informal meetings – each could attend plenary and specialist committee meetings.[15] A Ralston-inspired formula for dominion attendance then emerged, though imperial delegates had little impact on the discussions that preoccupied MacDonald, Stimson, and Wakatsuki Reijirō, the chief Japanese delegate. The dominions signed the treaty, even though their naval forces were included in its appendices under the rubric of 'British Empire.' Given RCN weakness (two destroyers and a few smaller auxiliary vessels), Canada did not affect the naval balance worked out by the British, Americans, and Japanese. Still, MacDonald was concerned about rifts within the empire. As the conference ended, he asked Ralston to impress on King 'the great necessity of now considering the unity of the Commonwealth in conjunction with the independence of its parts.'[16] Ralston agreed, but within three months Bennett rose to the premiership.

Over the next two and one-half years, until Roosevelt's inauguration as president in March 1933, London and Washington looked for common ground concerning the unresolved issues of the 1920s. Even the fall of MacDonald's Labour government in August 1931 did not imperil Anglo-American cooperative efforts. The new ministry, the 'National Government,' a coalition of Baldwin's Conservatives, a smattering of pro-MacDonald Labourites, and a few Liberals, with MacDonald remaining as prime minister, saw every advantage in close Anglo-American ties.[17] However, while those unresolved issues became increasingly intertwined (reparations, war debts, arms limitation, and security), they were approached separately; this policy originated with Hoover, who thought it domestically impolitic to stray far from the traditions of political isolation. Prior to the Wall Street crash, the American Congress considered increased customs duties to protect the American economy – the Smoot-Hawley bill. Hoover disliked high tariffs, but he could not block this legislation from becoming law in June 1930. Subsequently, high duties on American agricultural raw materials and other goods made it difficult for foreign powers to acquire United States dollars. They played havoc with the powers' ability to honour their war debts to the United States and, in Germany's case, repay private loans contracted after 1924. While the British – and the French, Germans, and Italians – linked international economic and political security, Hoover refused to admit a connection.

Just as the London Naval Conference began, the problem of reparations finally seemed to be resolved. Private American investors had lent money to Britain and its allies during the war. Britain's 1923 debt agreement with the United States depended on German transfers and debt payments from its former allies. The former allies, in turn, relied on German reparations to make their disbursements to the British and repay their own war loans to the Americans. Additionally, after 1924 American banking houses had loaned money to Germany to aid its economic and industrial revival. An international committee of private bankers and others under the chairmanship of an American businessman, Owen Young, had been meeting in 1928 and 1929; it looked to commercialize German reparations and permit the former Allied powers to use these sums to meet their war debt payments.[18] The most important parts of the 'Young Plan' were reducing Germany's annual payment by 20 per cent; awarding Belgium, Italy, and France indemnities to cover war damages; and ensuring that German transfers to these three powers, plus Britain, covered their annual 'outpayments,' that is, their war debt payments to the United States. Young and the senior British delegate, Sir Josiah Stamp, shared similar views about solving the problem, and the plan reached the interested governments in June 1929. By January 1930, after two conferences at The Hague, it came into force. Although the sums preoccupying Britain and the United States totalled billions of dollars, Canadian investors were owed US$21 million, payable by 1988, for their share of German reparations bonds.[19] King ensured Canadian rights, but on some nettled points, such as persuading the powers to allow a consortium of Canadian banks to hold the country's bonds, rather than a single bank, he failed. He saw little benefit to Canada should its financial diplomacy 'block settlement by insistence on this point.'[20]

By the spring of 1931 strain on the German economy created by the Depression and reparations led the German chancellor, Heinrich Brüning, to argue that the political fabric of his country was imperilled. High unemployment, reduced trade, and the electoral success of the National Socialist (Nazi) and Communist parties suggested that radical government might be in the offing. Something had to be done. Under pressure from his diplomatic and economic advisers, Hoover took the courageous step on 20 June 1931 of proposing a one-year moratorium on all intergovernmental debt payments.[21] He found an ally in MacDonald, who helped to smooth its acceptance in Europe. Moreover, MacDonald's government won dominion support, especially from Bennett's ministry, for deferring payments.[22] As MacDonald told Stimson after meeting Brüning and his foreign minister in early June: 'The German Ministers thought that they could, therefore, hold on, but that if they could not, Germany with all its obligations would have to go into the melting pot. If this happens, I agree with them that the revolution and crisis can hardly be confined within German frontiers.'[23] Although Hoover refused to tie war debts and reparations formally together, his initiative implicitly united them; this point was not lost on the British Treasury.[24] Still, the moratorium was designed to buy time, to allow for what London and Washington anticipated would be an economic recovery in North America and Europe. Not only would renewed prosperity underwrite the Young Plan, but they hoped that radicalism in Germany would wither. Since reparations and war debts payments came due in June and December each year, payments would begin again at the end of 1932.

Concurrent with this economic diplomacy was another respecting arms limitation and security. At the League Assembly in the autumn of 1925 pressures from powers interested in improving international security by limiting weapons and reducing domestic arms spending produced the calling of a world disarmament conference.[25] Flowing from the signing of the Locarno treaty and Germany's admission to the League, these developments seemed to offer enough political security in Europe to begin arms reductions. Accordingly, the League established a commission to prepare a draft treaty as a basis for discussion when the main conference convened, and because of its important goal, non-

League powers, such as the United States and Bolshevik Russia, sent delegations. While the Preparatory Commission began deliberating in March 1926, the challenge of balancing arms limitation with security quickly produced stalemate. In essence, the maritime powers – Britain, the United States, and Japan – had different strategic requirements from the terrene ones – chiefly, France and its European allies, which had profited territorially at German expense in 1919. For its part, denied an air force and permitted only a small navy and a non-conscript army limited to 100,000 men, Germany sought to loosen the strictures of Versailles.

By early 1928 the Preparatory Commission was deadlocked: two competing draft treaties, one British and the other French, could not be reconciled; the effort to get a separate naval settlement foisted on the commission by means of the Coolidge conference had ended in shambles; and successive governments in Paris could not be dissuaded from seeking additional security guarantees beyond the League Covenant and Locarno.[26] Over the next three years, these impediments were slowly removed. The first breakthrough was the London naval treaty. With the British and Americans overcoming one of the major barriers to postwar international arms limitation, the French realized that a watershed had occurred. This realization stimulated a fruitful meeting of the Preparatory Commission in November-December 1930, from which a single draft treaty emerged. It blended the competing British and French proposals for air and land weapons, while incorporating the naval limitation provisions encased in the London naval treaty with the proviso that the eventual conference might amend them.

French accommodation resulted from concerted efforts by London and Washington. Through Arthur Henderson, the foreign secretary, MacDonald's government indicated that Britain could not go beyond extant security arrangements like the Covenant and Locarno to meet French concerns.[27] For its part, Hoover's administration promoted a 'derogations article' within the draft treaty: should any signatory perceive that 'a change of circumstance constitutes ... a menace to its national security,' it could 'modify temporarily' any part of the treaty to meet its particular needs.[28] Sensing that they could wring no more from the two English-speaking powers, the French caved in. By May 1931 the League Council set a date for the World Disarmament Conference to begin – 2 February 1932 – and chose Henderson as its president. Ottawa greeted these developments with little murmur. Because of Canada's membership in the League, Bennett's ministry had pro forma sent delegates to the Preparatory Commission. Although both his and King's (previous) government disparaged the covenant's sanctions provisions,[29] Bennett appreciated that arms reductions might augment international peace and security. He admitted as much to G.H. Ferguson, Canada's high commissioner at London: the 'general proposal to establish mutual confidence by abstaining[,] pending Disarmament Conference next year[,] from increase in present level of international armaments ... would be effective evidence of genuine desire of nations of the world for peace.' But in the same breath, he outlined domestic benefits in Canada 'of additional expenditure for unemployment relief on drill halls or similar works for relief purposes.'[30] As it was in Canada's interests to promote disarmament, however, his government prepared to bargain with the country's minuscule armed forces.[31]

At this juncture, arms limitation, security, and the strands of economic diplomacy converged and imposed themselves on the North Atlantic triangle. The process had begun when, within days of the disarmament conference opening, the French demanded security guarantees before embarking on arms reductions – an act of a new government in Paris dominated by the hawkish war minister, André Tardieu.[32] Almost immediately, discussion bogged down in debates that mirrored those of the Preparatory Commission before November 1930. When the conference's first session ended in early June, nothing had been accomplished.[33] The situation was not helped when Brüning's ministry fell in May and was replaced by a more conservative government led by Franz von Papen. Yet even before Brüning surrendered office, the Germans demanded 'equality of treatment' in arms limitation, which they rightly pointed out was explicit in the Treaty of Versailles.[34] British policy involved finding common ground between Paris and Berlin, for instance, not opposing 'regional guarantees between States on the Continent of Europe to meet their special anxieties.'[35] In April MacDonald and Stimson travelled to Geneva to bring the two sides together.[36] All efforts were to no avail: Tardieu was in no mood for concessions, and the Germans would not yield over equality of treatment.

When Tardieu also fell from power in May, it was surmised that progress might be possible when the conference reassembled in the autumn. On 20 June, after being renominated as the Republican candidate for the presidency, Hoover unexpectedly announced a 'plan' to guide the next session of the conference. He proposed massive qualitative and quantitative cuts to all armed forces: cutting armies by one-third; reducing aircraft carriers, cruisers, and destroyers by one-quarter;

and prohibiting bombers, tanks, and chemical and bacteriological weapons.[37] Such cuts made sense to the United States, geographically isolated from Europe and the Far East. But for other powers, surrounded by potential adversaries and having different strategic concerns, they were pregnant with danger. What was true for other powers was doubly so for Britain, adjacent to continental Europe and with a worldwide empire to defend. Sir John Simon, the new British foreign secretary, politely rebuffed Hoover's plan in early July.[38] Although Hoover's proposals made sense for Canada, Bennett refused to send instructions to the Canadian delegate, Maurice Dupré – he seems to have thought that being noncommittal would offend neither London nor Washington.[39] It did not matter. At the end of August Papen's government announced that it would boycott the conference until Germany received equality of treatment.

Hoover's 'plan' must be seen in the light of the approaching end of the debt moratorium. Hoover needed positive achievements to flourish before American voters in the November elections. The Depression had worsened; and the possibility loomed that the debtor powers could not resume payments in December. Hoover had noted when he devised the moratorium: 'I felt that one of the fundamental difficulties of all Europe was the increasing armament, which now reached the stage where the total expenditure of civilized nations was nearly $5,000,000,000 per annum; that this sum amounted to many times the whole debt weight of the world.'[40] A breakthrough at Geneva would allow for retrenchment at home and, if other powers followed suit, permit easier resumption of debt payments. But at this moment, the National Government was moving to end war debts and reparations. In British economic diplomacy, the empire would have a prominent part.

After the National Government took office in late 1931, Neville Chamberlain, the chancellor of the exchequer, and his Treasury advisers concluded that international economic and financial recovery could happen only after war debts and reparations were cancelled.[41] To his mind, Britain's rejuvenation would accelerate if, in tandem with cancellation, the government abandoned free trade to increase domestic consumption of British agricultural and industrial production. Almost immediately, the government embarked on policies of economic nationalism to protect industry and agriculture; by February 1932, with the passing of the Import Duties bill, the process of abandoning free trade had begun.[42] Chamberlain also reckoned that imperial preference tied to currency stabilization within the empire would be mutually beneficial to Britain and the dominions by creating an even larger protected market. Thus, while Simon wrestled with the World Disarmament Conference, Chamberlain pursued an economic diplomacy in the first half of 1932 to give form to his ideas. It produced two conferences during the summer of 1932. At Lausanne, in Switzerland, from 16 June to 9 July he joined with Mac-Donald to negotiate an agreement whereby the reparations-receiving powers recognized Germany's incapacity to pay once the moratorium ended. As a quid pro quo, the Germans would make a one-time disbursement of 3 billion marks – one and one-half a Young Plan annuity – and promise good behaviour.[43] The arrangement remained provisional pending Washington's agreement to suspend all intergovernmental debts owed to the United States, a concession Stimson had intimated was possible during his April visit to Geneva.[44]

On the heels of Lausanne, the Imperial Economic Conference sat at Ottawa from 20 July to 20 August; Baldwin, lord president in Mac-Donald's government, and Chamberlain led the British delegation. Although the Canadians had been marginal in the diplomacy surrounding arms limitation, security, war debts, and reparations, they played a leading role at this meeting. Soon after Bennett took office, in October 1930, the Imperial Conference at London had accepted the idea of holding a meeting dedicated to economic issues.[45] The Depression was a year old that autumn, and dominion leaders saw opportunities for imperial help to improve their economies. Bennett was prominent in advancing such ideas, even though, supported by the Australians, he talked about preferential tariffs within the empire rather than imperial free trade (in the Canadian case, for instance, there would be protection for wheat farmers).[46]

Much has been written of the resulting Ottawa conference.[47] Currency stabilization proved impossible, but the Ottawa agreement expanded markets within the empire for over 200 commodities as diverse as wheat, timber, dried fruit, automobiles, and textiles; but as tariffs were standardized rather than eliminated, the expansion of intra-imperial trade failed to materialize. By 1932, the empire imported relatively less from Britain than it had twenty years earlier; British imports from the empire in the same period remained stable. This pattern did not change to Britain's advantage after Ottawa. As a leading Canadian economic historian has remarked: 'In fact the Agreement did not prevent foreign countries from increasing their sales both to the United Kingdom, and to the empire. These rose rapidly in 1933–37.'[48] In terms of Anglo-Canadian trade, the Canadians benefited more.[49] The importance of the

Ottawa conference as it related to the North Atlantic triangle stems more from its political impact. In very tough negotiations, Bennett and his advisers assumed a guise of unbending truculence. 'Bennett has behaved to me like a pig,' Chamberlain confided to his wife, 'and I have put up with it lest I should jeopardise the Conference.'[50] Here was the rub. The British did not like the way the talks had progressed, especially over currency, but it was politically expedient to swallow bitter-tasting Canadian policies to give the appearance of success. Thus, they signed on the dotted line and departed Canada with unfavourable images of the northern dominion. Earlier, King had been the subject of private criticism among British leaders because of his sovereigntist bent and unabashed self-promotion.[51] Now Bennett, although a self-styled anglo-phile, seemed no better. The Canadians were pursuing self-interest above all else and were overly sensitive about their sovereign rights in foreign policy; they wanted all the benefits of a British connection with-out the responsibilities. Baldwin and Chamberlain, the leading members of the National Government, left Ottawa convinced that Canada would be less than reliable in confronting other equally pressing international problems that affected both Britain and the empire.[52]

These matters were crucial because, at this point, Anglo-American cooperation began weakening. A Far Eastern crisis, which erupted in September 1931 when the Japanese army began operations to conquer the Chinese province of Manchuria, created strain between London and Washington.[53] By early 1932 the Japanese had transformed Manchuria into a puppet state called Manchukuo and began lobbying other powers to give it formal recognition. The National Government worried about the security of the eastern reaches of the British Empire. After China appealed to the League to settle the crisis and restore Chinese sover-eignty over Manchuria, Simon backed a proposal to send a League com-mission of inquiry to the region to assess the situation and make recommendations for action. This decision to create a commission had the double merit of delaying an immediate League response and, per-haps, of effecting a basis for a peaceful settlement – peaceful meaning that it would not involve British forces at a time when their effectiveness in the Far East was questionable.[54] In Washington, Hoover and Stimson aligned the United States with the League inquiry, even appointing an American member to the investigating commission. But appalled at what they perceived to be an immoral act of power politics, they refused to acknowledge Japan's conquest. On 7 January 1931 Stimson stated publicly that the United States would not recognize any territorial changes resulting from military conquest; he called on other powers for support.[55] The British found the 'doctrine of non-recognition' unpalatable. Unless backed by force of arms – which Hoover abjured, given isolationist sentiment in his country and the unpreparedness of American armed forces – it amounted to a gesture that would only inflame Japanese opinion and imperil British and other western interests in the region. Refusing to endorse the American action, even after a brief outbreak of violence at Shanghai, Simon put his efforts behind the League. By March 1932 the issue receded in importance as the League awaited the report of its commission of inquiry. And although Stimson appreciated Simon's position, the British understood the limits of American will in meeting threats to the international status quo.[56]

A turning point had occurred in international politics during the autumn and winter of 1932–3. The World Disarmament Conference reconvened in September but, because of the German boycott, failed to make headway. MacDonald and Simon therefore brought extreme pressure to bear on Paris to concede 'equality of treatment.'[57] On 10 November Simon proposed replacing Section V of the Versailles Treaty – its disarmament provisions – with a convention binding on all signatories to the eventual disarmament treaty; this convention would give the Germans qualitative rather than quantitative equality.[58] In return, Berlin had to eschew territorial revisions to the Paris peace treaties. German elections held on 6 November gave this stricture especial significance. The Nazis had emerged as the largest party in the Reichstag and, during the campaign, had argued for reabsorbing the 'Polish Corridor' into Germany. Although Hitler was kept out of the new government, the French saw danger in continued rigidity. On 11 December, in line with Simon's proposal, they backed a British-sponsored declaration that promised Germany equality of treatment when the disarmament conference reconvened in late January.[59] But just days after it reconvened, Hitler was appointed chancellor.

At the same time, Roosevelt's electoral victory on 8 November made worthless Stimson's insinuation in April that it would be possible to suspend all intergovernmental debts; this possibility, which had had to await Hoover's re-election, lay at the base of the Lausanne agreement. None the less, two days after Hoover's defeat and less than two months before the end of the moratorium, the British government informed Stimson that the time had come to revise war debt payments; they suggested that Britain's December disbursement would be suspended pending modifications.[60] Other powers, chiefly France and Belgium, immediately followed Britain's lead.[61] As a lame-duck president, Hoover could not agree to any revisions; and Roosevelt refused to do anything until after his inauguration. Strained discussions over resuming payments then ensued between the departing American government and the debtor powers, and the debt issue became a matter of partisan politics in the United States.[62] Although several debtor powers confirmed that they would suspend their payments to the United States, the National Government decided to make its December disbursement.[63] This decision amounted to a tactical move, however, since London intended to press debt elimination once Roosevelt entered the White House. This turn of events came just as the World Disarmament Conference had to contend with the foreign policy implications of Hitler's rise to power and the League had to address the report of its commission of inquiry into the Manchurian crisis.

By December 1933 these questions were resolved, first, by creation of the new constellation of international power that dominated Great Power politics for the rest of the decade and, second, by the inauguration of a British interventionist diplomacy designed to promote peace and security while the Americans and Canadians receded into isolation. In early January 1933 Japanese forces in Manchuria initiated fresh operations to bring all of northeastern China under Japanese control. Coinciding with League consideration of the report from its commission of enquiry, this offensive laid bare Tokyo's claims that it had originally resorted to armed force for reasons of self-defence. The report argued that although some Japanese grievances were justified and that Japanese rights and interests in Manchuria should be recognized, Japan's use of military power had been excessive.[64] It also recommended that Manchuria remain a province under Chinese sovereignty. When the League accepted the report in February, thereby censuring Japanese action, Tokyo immediately renounced its League membership. It also indicated that it would abide by the results of the World Disarmament Conference only if it met Japan's specific requirements for self-defence.

Led by the British, the European powers continued searching for a suitable arms limitation formula.[65] At first, despite Hitler's rise to power, the Germans seemed willing to cooperate. This appearance constituted a policy of delay. Worried about a pre-emptive attack by Germany's anti-revisionist neighbours, Hitler needed breathing space to consolidate his domestic position before embarking on a forward foreign policy. Hence, German delegates received instructions to welcome any proposals but then to study them and seek clarifications.

MacDonald looked for Roosevelt to support an expanded British plan grounded in the 11 December declaration. Despite private comments before his inauguration about restricting certain classes of weapons, the president made a public statement in May in which he left the initiative for arms limitation with the other powers.[66] He did propose that 'all nations of the world should enter into a solemn and definite pact of non-aggression'; but he failed to elaborate and, as arms limitation discussions since 1926 had demonstrated, pacts needed to be supported by more than words. The World Disarmament Conference stumbled onward, and in October, the Nazi revolution now complete, Hitler took Germany out of both the conference and the League.

While Far Eastern and disarmament questions stymied the powers during 1933, economic diplomacy also proved barren. There were two dimensions: stalemate over war debts and multilateral means to reverse the Depression. In May 1932, before Lausanne, Stimson and MacDonald had struck upon the idea of holding a World Economic Conference after the American elections to examine issues other than war debts and reparations: 'commodity prices, international exchange, trade impediments and kindred subjects.'[67] Preparations began in the autumn of 1932, and, after his election, Roosevelt endorsed the initiative.[68] Thus, with American support, the World Economic Conference was set to open in London in June. War debts, however, rose again to bedevil Anglo-American relations. In January Roosevelt had indicated a willingness to treat British disbursements to date as payments towards reducing the principal of British war loans; only the remainder of the principal had to be repaid. But in subsequent discussions, the Americans contradicted themselves about the sum the British should pay annually. Roosevelt suggested $18 million; his experts, on the other hand, bandied about sums up to $25 million.[69] Prompted by Chamberlain, who had not relented on cancellation, the National Government agreed to a token payment in June pending revision of the 1923 agreement.[70] On the 15th, just three days after the World Economic Conference had opened, the British sent $10 million in silver bullion to the United States.

MacDonald, Chamberlain, and most of their cabinet colleagues reckoned that this conference's success would help to revive trade and provide a foundation for debt revision. Very quickly, however, currency stabilization overwhelmed the discussions, a function of the United States's having gone off the gold standard in April.[71] By 30 June Cordell Hull, Roosevelt's secretary of state and the head of the American delegation, had worked out an agreement with MacDonald and Chamberlain whereby the pound would be pegged at $4.25, a figure suggested by the president. Two days later, Roosevelt had second thoughts; arguing that conference agreements might intrude on American sovereignty in domestic policy, he reneged.[72] The Roosevelt 'torpedo' destroyed the conference and angered the British.[73] The net result was that another round of Anglo-American debt negotiations in October proved fruitless through intransigence on both sides; the British made another token disbursement in December, pending revision.[74] Although Roosevelt publicly announced that this second payment did not mean a default, American legal authorities ruled otherwise. Britain made no payments thereafter, and, since Roosevelt judged domestic economic issues more important, war debts disappeared as an overriding issue in Anglo-American relations. The Americans could not compel payment; the British and other debtors refused to pay.[75] All that transpired was the passage of a bill, the Johnson Act, sponsored by congressional isolationists, which denied defaulting foreign powers access to the American money market.[76]

Thus, as 1933 ended, Germany and Japan had left the League; the World Disarmament Conference had gone into suspended animation (it met briefly in June 1934 before adjourning forever); and war debts and reparations ceased being a matter of first importance. In Britain, Sir Robert Vansittart, the Foreign Office permanent under-secretary, Sir Norman Warren Fisher, his counterpart at the Treasury, and Sir Maurice Hankey, the secretary of both the cabinet and the Committee of Imperial Defence (CID), worried about protecting British global interests.[77] More than a decade of international arms limitation conferences, tied to retrenchment, suggested that the armed forces might be unable to meet new international challenges. Under their prompting, their political masters created the CID Defence Requirements Sub-Committee (DRC) to examine and suggest remedies for meeting defence deficiencies.[78] Its membership comprised Vansittart, Warren Fisher, Hankey, and the three services chiefs (Admiral Sir Ernle Chatfield, General Sir Archibald Montgomery-Massingberd, and Air Marshal Sir Edward Ellington). It began meeting on 14 November 1933 and sent its first report to the cabinet on 28 February 1934.[79]

The DRC proposed more than £70 million in extra spending to allow for balanced air, land, and sea forces to shield the home islands, prepare for a continental commitment, and protect sea routes to the empire and overseas markets.[80] Setting a target date of 1939 to achieve this goal – when the DRC thought Hitler's Germany would be ready for war – the

DRC's technical recommendations involved developing sufficient armed strength to provide the government with the ability to deter possible enemies from imperilling British interests. In this regard, the DRC identified two possible threats: Germany, 'the ultimate potential enemy,' and Japan. Explicitly excluded were defence preparations against France, Italy, and the United States – powers that posed no threat to Britain. Beyond its technical proposals, for instance, a program of battleship construction within the limits of the London naval treaty, the DRC also established a set of strategic principles on which British foreign policy came to rest until after Neville Chamberlain rose to the premiership in May 1937. These principles devolved almost solely from a political debate involving Vansittart and Warren Fisher.

Warren Fisher opined that an Anglo-Japanese accommodation was essential for British security in the Far East – a course that, not surprisingly, would limit RN spending. He asserted that Japan posed the immediate threat to the empire through its actions in China, that it possessed regional naval superiority thanks to the Washington and London naval treaties, and that no other power seemed willing to join with Britain to oppose Japanese ambitions. Indeed, Warren Fisher showed special contempt for the United States, a reaction to Roosevelt's economic diplomacy over the World Economic Conference and war debts: 'the U.S.A. are a serious obstacle to our getting on to terms with Japan; and I believe that we have got to "disentangle" ourselves from the U.S.A. They are no use to us, but make use of us – to our detriment – vis à vis Japan.'[81] Vansittart, on the other hand, although feeling the Americans were unreliable, saw little advantage in needlessly antagonizing Washington. To him, Germany represented the principal worry. 'The order of priorities which put Japan first pre-supposed that Japan would attack us after we had got into difficulties elsewhere,' he told his colleagues. '"Elsewhere" therefore came first, not second; and elsewhere could only mean Europe, and Europe could only mean Germany.'[82] Thus, to Vansittart's mind, Britain needed assistance to balance German and Japanese zeal. Other powers could help. Because France and Italy shared concerns about Hitler, they could probably be counted on in containing Germany.[83] Admittedly, the Far East presented a different question. But Britain could not trust in Japanese goodwill, and attempts to align with Japan, especially if unsuccessful, would achieve nothing but annoying the Americans. Washington later might be prepared – or forced – to involve itself in East Asian affairs beyond statements of principle like 'non-recognition.' As this would aid British interests, it was better to improve British defences in the Far East and avoid approaching Tokyo. Telling in both the DRC deliberations and its report was the absence of any reference to Canada and the contribution that Ottawa might make to imperial defence; in the minds of those making British foreign and defence policy, giving it strength, and paying for it, Canada had receded from active involvement in the political affairs of the world.

Vansittart's vision of a strategic basis for British foreign policy triumphed in the DRC – its report omitted Warren Fisher's anti-American outburst. Admittedly, cabinet evaluation of its conclusions produced changes to the proposed balanced build-up of British forces: alarm over potential air attacks on Britain resulted in increased spending on the Royal Air Force (RAF) and less on the RN and army.[84] None the less, in terms of the strategic principles contained in the report, Vansittart's view of how foreign and defence policy should be pursued won the day. He triumphed, despite Chamberlain's seeking of support for what were now Treasury arguments about a formal Anglo-Japanese condominium in east Asia.[85] Vansittart carefully presented the case for the efficacy of the balance of power in maintaining peace and security, and in the process won support from MacDonald, Baldwin, and Simon.[86]

In terms of the North Atlantic triangle, the course of international politics over the next eighteen months did not disabuse the British of the belief that they could count little on the United States and Canada. As a second London naval conference had to meet sometime in 1935, preliminary British, American, and Japanese conversations were held between October and December 1934. Chamberlain pressed his concept of Anglo-Japanese cooperation until the eve of these discussions;[87] but Japanese demands for naval equality showed the merit of Vansittart's appeal for circumspection in the Far East. Still, even a hint that the British were willing to find a modus vivendi with the Japanese produced paroxysms of disapproval from Roosevelt. In the midst of these talks, he told Norman Davis, a leading American delegate: 'Simon and a few other Tories must be constantly impressed with the simple fact that if Great Britain is even suspected of preferring to play with Japan to playing with us, I shall be compelled, in the interest of American security, to approach public sentiment in Canada, Australia, New Zealand and South Africa in a definite effort to make these Dominions understand clearly that their future security is linked with us in the United States.'[88] Roosevelt's discomfort disappeared when the Japanese announced that they would not renew the London treaty in 1935 unless their demands for equality were met.[89] London cared little about American unease. Words had to be backed by actions, and, except for resistance to Japanese demands for formal equality – which Tokyo had every intention of achieving – Washington offered nothing on which the British could depend to assist them in preserving international stability. Ottawa appeared more realistic. As Bennett had commented a year earlier: 'Canada is not an important member of the League except that we are an active member from the North American Continent. Our military prowess in the next war is regarded as of little concern ... What can one man do who represents only ten and a half millions of people.'[90]

The events of 1935 confirmed that Britain could not rely on 10 million Canadians or 150 million Americans. From London's perspective, the year was dominated by three major issues: Hitler's declaration of rearmament in March, the onset of the Abyssinian crisis in October, and the end of the Washington-London naval system in December. In each case, neither the United States nor Canada saw it in its interests to meet these problems by collective action with Britain and other powers. Indeed, as each North American power embraced political isolation while jealously guarding what its leaders saw as its sovereign rights in foreign policy, each probably contributed to the diplomatic successes of the three totalitarian powers. Thus, when Hitler announced German rearmament, the British, French, and Italians met in hurried conference at Stresa. Seeking to create a counterbalance to Germany, they reaffirmed their opposition to unilateral revision of Versailles. But Washington refused to back Stresa. Even before Hitler's action, in February, when the British and French proposed non-intervention pacts for central Europe and the Danube basin plus a prohibition against aerial bombardment of cities, Hull told Simon: 'I do not see how I could usefully comment in a public statement on what is in the first instance a European political development.'[91] Ottawa's reaction was no better. When the League established the Committee of Thirteen after Stresa 'to render [the] Covenant more effective in organisation of collective security and to define in particular the economic and financial measures which might be applied, should in future a State ... endanger the peace by unilateral repudiation of its international obligations,' Canada agreed to join.[92] But as Bennett told W.A. Riddell, the Canadian advisory officer at Geneva, Canada would 'avoid any position involving acceptance of sanctions policy in advance.'[93]

Canadian-American reluctance to help stymie assaults on the existing international order continued after the Abyssinian crisis erupted. The Italians assumed they had been given a free hand in East Africa via Stresa and earlier discussions with the French.[94] Sir Samuel Hoare, the new British foreign secretary, and Pierre Laval, his French opposite number, wanted to avoid a rupture with Benito Mussolini, the Italian dictator; accordingly, they concocted a secret 'plan' in December to cede two-thirds of Abyssinia to Italy.[95] When their proposal became public, both foreign secretaries were forced to resign; the East African crisis continued till May 1936, when the Italians conquered all of Abyssinia. Hoare and Laval were culpable in many ways for failing to resolve this crisis. For instance, while understandable in *realpolitik* terms – Italian control of Abyssinia did not threaten either power's imperial interests – their 'plan' undermined League collective security. From Hoare's perspective, however, part of the reason for combining with Laval lay in Washington and Ottawa. Although Roosevelt privately shared misgivings about Italian resort to arms, he would not support explicit economic sanctions against Mussolini's regime, chiefly an oil embargo, because of congressional opposition and the traditional American distaste for blockade.[96] Bennett supported Riddell in endorsing League-enforced sanctions; but in the Canadian election of 15 October, twelve days after the beginning of Italian operations, King and the Liberals were re-elected.[97] King immediately reversed Canadian support for sanctions, the decisive vote on the League committee examining their implementation. With the League unable to act and Washington refusing to support sanctions, Hoare fell back on the expedients of 'old diplomacy.' When his successor, Anthony Eden, then tried to galvanize the League into opposing Italy, the result was Anglo-Italian estrangement, the collapse of Stresa, the beginning of Italo-German rapprochement, and the scotching of a cardinal element of DRC strategy – ignoring Italy in British defence planning.

The second London Naval Conference occurred in the midst of the Abyssinian crisis. By this time, following DRC arguments about overlooking the United States in British defence planning, British naval concern centred on the ambitions of Japan and Germany. In the preceding June, just as Baldwin succeeded MacDonald as prime minister, the British had concluded a naval agreement with the Germans: Germany restricted its surface fleet to 35 per cent of that of the RN, while Britain accepted equality in submarines.[98] This agreement produced fissures in the Stresa front – though nothing like those caused by Italy's enthusiasm for enlarging its East African empire, evident after December 1934 – and it gave the RN a two-power standard towards both Germany and Japan. To perpetuate RN superiority over the IJN, the British earlier had circulated proposals as a basis for discussion at the London conference: the three major naval powers would outline their separate needs based on 'a unilateral declaration as to [their] building program over a fixed period of years'; this disclosure would occur in terms of the 'sense of security' necessary to meet their unique defence requirements.[99] British experts supposed that Japan, a regional power, had fewer requirements than either Britain for the United States, each of whom had global interests.

None the less, the London conference centred on Japan's demand for absolute equality with the RN and USN.[100] When the British and Americans refused to concede, Japan left. The conference resulted in an Anglo-American agreement that, reaffirming RN-USN parity, allowed for increases in strength should the international situation change for the worse. Beyond this extension, however, there was no hint of Anglo-American cooperation. Under the pressures of public opinion, Roosevelt was hesitant to push ahead with substantial naval construction. 'U.S. naval policy between 1936 and 1938 was cautious to the point of timidity,' a recent analysis argues. 'The warning that U.S. negotiators had consistently posed to Japan throughout the London proceedings, that it could never hope to win a naval race in a treaty-less period, remained the barest bluff.'[101] In Britain, the DRC met throughout 1935 and, again, Vansittart and Warren Fisher played leading roles. In another report, ready by 21 November, it argued that given changing international circumstances, British policy had to avoid simultaneous conflict with Germany, Italy, and Japan.[102] Tied to this recommendation were proposals to go beyond rectifying defence deficiencies and begin a program of rearmament. Immediately after the Japanese departure, and before Anglo-American conversations ended, this report went to the cabinet Committee on Defence Policy and Requirements. The committee endorsed DRC thinking and concluded that the RN had to be brought up to the approved standard by 1939 so that the fleet could meet coincident Japanese and 'European' threats; the RAF had to be further expanded; and the army should be strengthened for both home defence and the dispatch of an expeditionary force 'to deny the enemy of advanced bases in the Low Countries.'[103] The discussions producing these conclusions mentioned nothing about possible assistance from either the United States or Canada; indeed, the DRC report argued that the Americans 'are more isolationist at heart than ever.'

After early 1936 the diplomatic difficulties confronting Britain in Europe and the Far East mounted.[104] In March 1936, while Abyssinia diverted European attention, Hitler remilitarized the Rhineland. Then, in the summer, a civil war in Spain erupted, which produced covert

Italian and German support for the right-wing rebels. In July 1937 the Japanese struck south of the Great Wall to bring all of China under their control. The following November, Mussolini and Hitler having patched up their differences, there emerged the Italo-German 'Axis' on the continent. This rapprochement smoothed Hitler's way to bludgeon Austria into union with Germany in March 1938, another violation of the Paris Peace Settlement. Six months later Hitler demanded the Sudetenland, the predominantly German-speaking region of western Czechoslovakia. At the Munich conference on 29–30 September 1938, the zenith of 'appeasement,' Chamberlain and the French premier, Edouard Daladier, ceded the Sudetenland to Germany; the quid pro quo was Hitler's promise of no further territorial revisions, a mutual guarantee of the rump of Czechoslovakia, and his signature on an Anglo-German agreement renouncing war between the two powers. Until Munich, Hitler's policies generally had been perceived as justified to modify an overly harsh peace settlement. But when his forces annexed the Czechoslovak rump on 15 March 1939, Chamberlain and his advisers understood that limits had to be put on German ambitions. Two weeks later, the British, with the French, issued a guarantee of the sovereignty of Poland, the next obvious German target. When Hitler's armies invaded Poland on 1 September 1939, the British and French issued an ultimatum to desist. When it was ignored, Britain and France declared war on Germany on 3 September. The Second World War had begun.

British leaders in the late 1930s, especially Chamberlain, have been severely criticized for failing to oppose the totalitarian powers, indeed, for 'appeasing' them in their ambitions; the net result of such supposed near-sightedness was the Polish crisis in September 1939.[105] A result of hindsight, this simplistic assessment ignores the realities of domestic and international politics that constrained British diplomacy. Until September 1939 British foreign policy generally followed the dictates of the November 1935 DRC report to avoid simultaneous conflict with Germany, Italy, and Japan. In the background lay the efforts to rearm, a process designed to strengthen Britain's position and deter Berlin, Rome, and Tokyo from endangering British interests. Although the ends of policy were never disputed, the methods of attaining them became a subject of intense debate within the government. For instance, the date by which British rearmament should be concluded became a matter of contention driven by fiscal strictures and varying perceptions of threat drawn from not always accurate intelligence assessments.[106] Thus, the idea emerged in 1936 that rearmament might be slowed down so as to reach full strength by 1942. Such a view found its basis in new assessments of Germany's industrial capacity and armed forces suggesting that Hitler could not possibly be ready for war before that date. Naturally, stretching out rearmament would create less difficulty for the Treasury.

Beyond these essentially narrow issues affecting the tactics of foreign policy lay the more important consideration of strategy. After the first DRC report, Vansittart's beliefs about the balance of power dominated policy-making.[107] This dominance stemmed partly from the fact that these ideas conformed to the traditions of British diplomacy, which were largely unquestioned by a range of men in positions of authority. It also came from Vansittart's authority within the Foreign Office, a result of his close ties with MacDonald and Baldwin which permitted him to eclipse both Simon and Hoare. But Abyssinia weakened his position, and powerful critics emerged who reckoned that Foreign Office advisers had too much influence and that the politicians should reassert control over policy-making. It is not surprising that Hoare was prominent in this group.[108] More important, other leaders surmised that dependence on the balance of power was unreliable; a different diplomacy was required. In this regard, Neville Chamberlain was crucial.

By the time he had succeeded Baldwin as prime minister in May 1937, Chamberlain had decided that a better means of reducing the threats posed by Germany, Italy, and Japan was through bilateral arrangements to meet these powers' legitimate concerns. As he asked Parliament in early 1938: 'Are we to allow these two pairs of nations to go on glowering at one another ... allowing the feeling ... to become more and more embittered until at last the barriers are broken down and the conflict begins which many think would mark the end of civilization? Or can we bring them to an understanding of one another's aims and objects, and to such discussion as may lead to a final settlement?'[109] In December 1937 Chamberlain, supported by Eden, engineered Vansittart's removal and replaced him with a career diplomat, Alexander Cadogan, who also distrusted the balance of power. This move does not mean that Chamberlain lacked understanding about the need for strong armed forces to support his diplomacy and defend British interests.[110] But it is to say that Chamberlain was willing to compromise with the totalitarian powers while having at his back what he reckoned was a military deterrent. Moreover, finding allies to maintain the balance could not ensure success. Working with France over Abyssinia and the United States in the economic issues of 1932–4, he found that powers sharing British concerns could be as much a hindrance as a help.[111] And suffusing all this was the fact that the British public seemingly had little desire for involvement in another continental war, a reluctance evident in the opposition in both Parliament and the country to the government's rearmament policies after 1936. Herein lay *in toto* the basis of the late 1930s variant of appeasement.

Of course, 'appeasement' failed. Some responsibility resides with Chamberlain: he bypassed the Foreign Office to run foreign policy from Downing Street (which led to Eden's resignation in February 1938); possessing unshakeable confidence in his abilities and ideas, he sometimes dismissed good advice from others; and he did not appreciate the extent of Hitler's ambitions until it was too late. But on the latter point, he held no monopoly; Cadogan recorded when the Germans marched into Prague in March 1939: 'I must say it is turning out – at present – as Van[sittart] predicted and as I never believed it would.'[112] None the less, the real responsibility lay with the German chancellor, since the Second World War, at least in Europe, can be considered Hitler's war.[113] Hitler gambled that he could establish German hegemony on the continent piecemeal by a combination of threatening and using force; he enjoyed success until he threatened Poland. Thus, in September 1939 he misjudged British determination to block his aggrandizement. Although Chamberlain might have entertained the possibility of a negotiated peace in the autumn of 1939, the general public, Parliament, and anti-Nazi senior cabinet ministers like Winston Churchill, the arch-anti-appeaser appointed first lord of the Admiralty as the British ultimatum expired, were ready to fight.

In the late 1930s the Americans and Canadians retreated further into isolation. Although Roosevelt understood the dangers posed by Hitler, he had no desire to involve the United States in another European war. Moreover, even if he had wanted to undertake an active role in preserving European peace and security, congressional isolationists, mirroring the attitudes of American public opinion, presented a powerful impediment. For instance, in October 1937, in response to the Japanese attack on China, the president publicly suggested a worldwide 'quarantine' on aggressors. But when the speech provoked vociferous criticism from American isolationists, he quickly receded into ambiguity.[114] Undeterred, Roosevelt then secretly approached Chamberlain about calling an international conference to limit arms, ensure equal access to raw materials, and establish neutral and belligerent rights should war break out.[115] Failing to provide for enforcement, however, Roosevelt only echoed Hoover's unhelpful 1932 disarmament scheme. 'The plan appeared to me fantastic and likely to excite the derision of Germany and Italy,' Chamberlain noted in his diary. 'They might even use it to postpone conversations with us and if we were associated with it they would see it as another attempt on the part of the democratic bloc to put the dictators in the wrong.'[116]

As Chamberlain saw the United States, so he saw Canada. After the Abyssinian crisis, King's government evaded interventionist diplomacy. Deprecating anything smacking of an imperial foreign policy, and avoiding any contribution to imperial defence, its only specific overseas commitments were its obligations assumed under the League Covenant. But as Abyssinia had shown, Ottawa would not involve itself in League efforts to maintain international peace and security. In fact, after October 1935 King's League policy centred on weakening those provisions of the Covenant designed to enforce peace.[117] At the May 1937 Imperial Conference, King did not hide the direction his diplomacy would take. After genuflecting to 'the pride in common traditions' within the empire, he observed: 'There is outspoken rejection of the theory that whenever and wherever conflict arises in Europe, Canada can be expected to send armed forces overseas to help solve the quarrels of continental countries about which Canadians know little, and which, they feel, know and care less about Canada's difficulties, and particularly so if a powerful country like the United States assumes no similar obligations.'[118] Chamberlain held King to be 'the weakest vessel in the team.' He was told privately by the Canadian premier that 'if [Hitler] should ever aggress in a way to injure us, Canadians would swim the Atlantic rather than be prevented from coming to our aid.'[119] To avoid giving such aid, however, King and O.D. Skelton, his chief diplomatic adviser, unabashedly supported British appeasement policies. Thus, after Munich, while admitting there were 'weaknesses' in the agreement and that each power had looked after its own narrow national interests, Skelton could observe: 'Whatever criticisms may be made of Chamberlain and Daladier's course, surely we must recognize that they, and particularly Chamberlain, worked for peace and achieved it.'[120]

Although Chamberlain's ministry saw little advantage in counting on either the Roosevelt administration or the King government at that moment, the two North American powers might be of use in the future. Despite the Johnson Act, it was thought the United States could economically augment the British defence preparations. Here lay the reason for the British signature on an Anglo-American-Canadian agreement in

November 1938, promoted by Hull since 1935 to increase trade among the three North Atlantic powers.[121] At a lower level, secret naval conversations were held earlier in 1938 in London during which information was shared about fleet sizes, strategy, and technical issues.[122] Then in June 1939, following the Prague crisis, the announcement of the Polish guarantee, and the reintroduction of conscription in Britain, a second set of naval discussions occurred in Washington. The Admiralty learnt that if European war broke out, the USN main fleet would be concentrated at Pearl Harbor to discourage Japanese adventurism while some of its cruisers would patrol the western Atlantic. Moreover, should Britain find itself at war with Germany, Italy, and Japan, Washington would send its fleet to Singapore if London dispatched a suitable 'token' force. Of course, these initiatives would benefit Britain only after hostilities commenced. Roosevelt sensed this concern. Thus, despite American isolationist sentiment and his personal dislike of Chamberlain, he tried to show solidarity with Britain. Accordingly, when King George VI visited the United States in June 1939 – a trip used by London to improve Britain's image there – the president responded with public displays of friendliness.[123]

This desire to augment British diplomatic strength lay in the background of the main lines of British foreign and defence policy in 1938–9. After the Japanese attack on China began in July 1937, Chamberlain's government, through the CID and the Chiefs of Staff Committee, worked to construct a defensive perimeter in East Asia and the western Pacific to protect British colonies, investments, and Australia and New Zealand.[124] In Europe, it pushed ahead with rearmament, especially as it related to the RAF, and after Prague it aligned with France. In the latter case, British leaders sought in essence to reconstruct the pre-1914 anti-German alliance; by the summer of 1939, this policy required an approach to Bolshevik Russia.[125] Yet Anglo-French efforts were half-hearted at best – a result of the ideological distaste that Chamberlain and others had for Joseph Stalin's regime. Neither London nor Paris would meet Moscow's price for an agreement: a free hand in the Baltic states and Poland. Berlin was willing to oblige, which resulted in the Nazi-Soviet non-aggression pact of 23 August 1939. Assured of Russian forbearance in the east, Hitler's Germany readied its assault on Poland; ten days later, Britain and France declared war on Germany.

While the British side of the triangle had at first looked to deter Germany's forward policies and then, after March 1939, prepared for the worst, the Canadian-American sides had not been idle. Isolationist restraints on American foreign policy did not extend to the western hemisphere, where the United States had decided material and strategic interests. Many of Roosevelt's diplomatic efforts after 1933 had been directed towards improving American ties with the Latin-American powers, chiefly through his 'Good Neighbor' policy.[126] But largely for defensive reasons, he did not ignore the northern dominion. In the summer of 1936, he implicitly extended the Monroe Doctrine to Canada.[127] In early 1938, just before the first low-level Anglo-American naval discussions, he arranged for the chiefs of the Canadian army and RCAF to visit Washington – in mufti, at King's insistence – to exchange information with their American opposite numbers.[128] In August 1938, at Kingston, Ontario to receive an honorary degree from a local university, Roosevelt explicitly extended the Monroe Doctrine northward: 'the United States will not stand idly by if domination of Canadian soil is threatened by any other empire.'[129] In addition, given his interest in naval affairs, he ordered USN officers to study how best to ensure the inviolability of the eastern and western coastal waters of Canada, including the colony of Newfoundland. By the time that war in Europe broke out, the United States included Canada in its defence planning.

King tried to steer a course between Britain and the United States; while heading a government desirous of saving public money, he also endeavoured to build up adequate forces for home defence. Thus, he was sincere in telling Chamberlain at the 1937 Imperial Conference that Canadians, or at least English-Canadians, would want to assist Britain should it be attacked. At the same time, abhorring war, he wanted to do everything possible to keep Canada out of another European struggle. Until the summer of 1939, the second line of thought informed Canadian diplomacy. As a recent assessment of his pre-war defence policy argues: 'King's task was to locate the elusive point of balance between doing too little and too much.'[130] Although this strategy produced a cabinet 'Canadian Defence Committee' to coordinate more effectively foreign and defence policy and moderate defence spending, King's government did little of substance in either Anglo-Canadian or Canadian-American relations. Because King and Skelton wanted to protect their vision of Canadian diplomatic sovereignty, they prevented joint planning with either London or Washington – the exchange of information in Washington in early 1938 notwithstanding. All King would do was give verbal support to the British and Americans – for instance, that given to Chamberlain at the time of Munich.[131] But words without action only isolated Canada politically from the other powers in the triangle.

Hitler's policies in the six months after Prague forced Washington and Ottawa to make hard decisions. American isolationism and Roosevelt's belief that the British and French would be able to handle the Germans led, after 3 September 1939, to policies designed to support the Allied war effort, such as the so-called Cash and Carry bill.[132] But the president had no intention of seeing the United States drawn into what he believed was a purely European struggle. All he intended to do was to protect the western hemisphere while helping Britain and its allies and hurting the Germans. As the 1939 naval talks had shown, however, his government was prepared to take an active role should Britain find itself at war with both the Axis powers and Japan. Devoid of altruism, his thinking involved protection of American interests and prevention of a major shift in the world balance of power that would rebound unfavourably on the United States. He thus followed a policy of 'double-edged neutrality,' and it would take the fall of France in June 1940 and the parlousness of British survival to stimulate him to do more. The Canadian case was different, a result of the dominion's leading position in the empire and the large pro-British element in the country. As European tensions increased after March 1939, Canadian opinion outside Quebec was 'educated by Adolph Hitler' about the threat of Nazi Germany.[133] In the year after Munich, a major shift in Canadian attitudes, reflected in King's cabinet, occurred, from support for isolation to support for intervention on Britain's side. As two of King's most sympathetic chroniclers have argued, the Canadian decision to declare war on Germany – seven days after Britain did so in line with Ottawa's sovereignty in foreign policy – was 'a self-evident national duty.'[134] Canada thus followed the other 'white' dominions in supporting Britain's armed struggle against Germany.

At the close of a difficult decade, the North Atlantic triangle was entering an uncertain phase in September 1939. Adding to this uncertainty was the fact that Britain's uneasy relationship with the two North American powers was transforming. As it had been in 1914, the British Empire was at war; again, Canada had agreed to join the 'mother' country; and again, the United States decided to remain neutral but supportive of a British-led anti-German coalition. Unlike the situation in 1914, however, Britain was engaged in a struggle for survival with only one other Great power, France, at its side. The Americans in 1939 were willing to support Britain for the narrowest reasons of national self-interest, in order to wring every benefit possible for their country. That Roosevelt had unilaterally extended the American defensive perimeter in the western hemisphere to include Canada indicated that for the first time the United States was delivering on its potential as a Great Power. For his part, King had not abandoned his desire to entrench Canada's sovereign status by keeping Ottawa distant from the dictates of London. He might have found it necessary and expedient to join in the war against Britain's enemy, but he would not abandon the gains he (and Bennett, though King would not admit it) had made for Canada since 1930. The course of the Second World War would determine the extent of the North Atlantic triangle's transformation.

NOTES

1 P.M. Kennedy, 'The Tradition of Appeasement in British Foreign Policy, 1865–1939,' *British Journal of International Studies*, 2(1976), 195–215.

2 B.J.C. McKercher, '"No Eternal Friends or Enemies": British Defence Policy and the Problem of the United States, 1919–1939,' *Canadian Journal of History*, 28(1993), 257–93; D. Reynolds, *The Creation of the Anglo-American Alliance, 1937–1941: A Study in Competitive Cooperation* (London, 1981); D.C. Watt, *Succeeding John Bull: America in Britain's Place, 1900–1975* (Cambridge, 1984), 60–89.

3 Robert Dallek, *Franklin Roosevelt and American Foreign Policy, 1932–1945* (Oxford, 1979), 3–20.

4 Cf. I.M. Drummond and N. Hillmer, *Negotiating Freer Trade: The United Kingdom, the United States, Canada, and the Trade Agreements of 1938* (Waterloo, Ont., 1989); C.P. Stacey, *Canada and the Age of Conflict*, Vol. II: *1921–1948. The MacKenzie King Era* (Toronto, 1981), 129–35.

5 J.R. Columbo, ed., *Columbo's Canadian Quotations* (Edmonton, 1974), 48.

6 King to Tweedsmuir [governor-general], 2 October 1936, in J. Eayrs, *In Defence of Canada*, Vol. II: *Appeasement and Rearmament* (Toronto, 1965), 39.

7 B.J.C. McKercher, 'From Enmity to Cooperation: the Second Baldwin Government and the Improvement of Anglo-American Relations, November 1928 – June 1929,' *Albion*, 24(1992), 64–87.

8 D. Carlton, *MacDonald Versus Henderson: The Foreign Policy of the Second Labour Government* (New York, 1970), 104–14; C. Hall, *Britain, America, and Arms Control, 1921–37* (London, 1987), 69–75.

9 For instance, Campbell [British Embassy, Washington] telegrams to Henderson [foreign secretary], 19, 20, 23 November 1929, Henderson telegrams to Campbell, 16, 22, 26 November 1929, Henderson dispatch to Campbell, 25 November 1929; all *Documents on British Foreign Policy*, Series II, Vol. I (hereafter in the style *DBFP II*, I), 140–1, 144–7; Atherton [U.S. embassy,

London] telegram (334) to Stimson, 20 November 1929, Herbert Hoover Presidential Papers [Hoover Presidential Library, West Branch, Iowa] (hereafter HHPP) 999.

10 MacDonald diary, 17 January 1930, MacDonald MSS PRO [Public Record Office, Kew] 30/69/1753; Stimson diary, 17 January 1930, with memorandum, Stimson MSS [Sterling Library, Yale University, New Haven, CT] 12.

11 R.G. O'Connor, *Perilous Equilibrium: The United States and the London Naval Conference of 1930* (Lawrence, KS, 1962), 62–108; S.W. Roskill, *Naval Policy Between the Wars*, Vol. II (London, 1977), 37–70.

12 G.C. Kennedy, 'The 1930 London Naval Conference and Anglo-American Maritime Strength, 1927–1930,' in *Arms Limitation and Disarmament, 1899–1939: Restraints on War*, ed. B.J.C. McKercher (Westport, CT, 1992), 149–71.

13 B.J.C. McKercher, 'Between Two Giants: Canada, the Coolidge Naval Conference, and Anglo-American Relations in 1927,' in *Anglo-American Relations in the 1920s: The Struggle for Supremacy*, ed. idem. (London, Edmonton, 1990), 81–124.

14 Stimson 'Memorandum of conversation at the Prime Minister's Office,' 30 January 1930, Stimson MSS 12.

15 Ralston telegram to King, 21 January 1930, *Documents on Canadian External Relations*, Vol. 4 (hereafter in the style *DCER* 4), 721.

16 MacDonald to Ralston, 2 April 1930, Ralston to MacDonald, 5 April 1930, both MacDonald MSS PRO 30/69/1440.

17 B.J.C. McKercher, *Transition: Britain's Loss of Global Preeminence to the United States, 1930–1945* (Cambridge, forthcoming), ch. 2. Cf. D. Marquand, *Ramsay MacDonald* (London, 1977), 628–37; J. Middlemas and J. Barnes, *Baldwin: A Biography* (London, 1969), 625–7.

18 D. Artaud, *La question des dettes interalliées et la reconstruction de l'Europe (1917–1929)*, Vol. II (Paris, 1978), 901–8; B. Kent, *The Spoils of War: The Politics, Economics, and Diplomacy of Reparations, 1918–1932* (Oxford, 1989), 287–303.

19 Larkin [Canadian high commissioner, London] telegram to King, 9 August 1929, *DCER* 4, 756–8.

20 King telegram to Larkin, 19 January 1930, ibid., 765.

21 Hoover moratorium diary, 5–20 June 1931, HHPP 1015. Cf. E.W. Bennett, *Germany and the Financial Crisis, 1931* (Cambridge, MA, 1962); Kent, *Spoils of War*, 338–42.

22 Thomas [dominions secretary] telegram to Bennett, 22 June 1931, Bennett telegram to Thomas, 26 June 1931, both *DCER* 5, 535–8.

23 MacDonald to Stimson, 8 June 1931, Stimson MSS Reel [microfilm edition: Sterling Library, Yale University, New Haven, CT] 81. In this chapter, the

references to the Stimson diary are from the original MSS; those to his private papers are from microfilm copies.

24 Treasury memorandum, 'German Reparations,' undated [but August 1931], T [Treasury Archives, Public Record Office, Kew] 172/1747,

25 M. Vaïsse, 'La Société des Nations et la désarmament', in UN Library, Geneva, and Graduate Institute of International Studies, *The League of Nations in Retrospect: La Société des Nations: Rétrospective* (Berlin, 1983), 245–65; J.W. Wheeler-Bennett, *Disarmament and Security since Locarno, 1925–1931* (London, 1932), 43–9.

26 B.J.C. McKercher, 'Of Horns and Teeth: the Preparatory Commission and the World Disarmament Conference, 1926–1934,' in *Arms Limitation and Disarmament: Restraints on War, 1899–1939*, ed. idem (Westport, CT, 1992), 177–82.

27 Henderson to Tyrrell [British ambassador, Paris], 10 November 1930, Henderson MSS FO 800/282.

28 Cecil [head, British delegation] telegram to Henderson, 24 November 1930, Cadogan [British Delegation] despatch to Henderson, 25 November 1930, *British Documents on Foreign Affairs*, pt. II, ser. J, vol. 3 (hereafter in the form *BDFA* II, J3), 314–18.

29 Stacey, *Age of Conflict*, II, 56–9; R. Veatch, *Canada and the League of Nations* (Toronto, 1975), 81–90, 126–42.

30 Bennett telegram to Ferguson, 23 September 1931, *DCER* 5, 460.

31 J. Hilliker, *Canada's Department of External Affairs*, Vol. I: *The Early Years, 1910–1946* (Montreal, Kingston, 1990), 172–3.

32 *Proposal of the French Delegation* (5 February 1932), LND [League of Nations Published Document: League of Nations Archives, Palais des Nations, Geneva] Conf.D.56. Cf. Bennett, *German Rearmament*, 97–9.

33 Cf. *Naval Commission: Report to the General Commission* (28 May 1932), LND Conf.D.121.; *Land Commission: Report to the General Commission* (7 June 1932), LND Conf.D.122; *Air Commission: Report to the General Commission* (7 June 1932), LND Conf.D.123.

34 *Proposal by the German Delegation concerning Qualitative Disarmament*, LND Conf.D.124.

35 Memorandum, 'Attitude To Be Adopted by the United Kingdom Delegation,' 31 March 1932, CAB 27/509.

36 MacDonald diary, 1 May 1932, MacDonald PRO 30/69/1753; Stimson diary, 16 April – 1 May 1932, Stimson 21.

37 *Declaration by Mr Gibson concerning President Hoover's Proposal* (20 June 1932), LND Conf.D.126. Gibson was the senior American delegate. Cf. Hoover's holograph drafts of the speech, plus Stimson-Gibson telephone conversa-

tion, 20 June 1932 (3:00 pm), both HHPP 1002; Stimson diary, 18–22 June 1932, Stimson 22.

38 *Statement of Views of His Majesty's Government in the United Kingdom regarding President Hoover's Proposal* (7 July 1932), LND Conf.D.133.

39 Dupré telegrams to Bennett, 28 June, 6, 21 July 1932, Bennett telegram to Dupré, 30 June 1932, all *DCER* 5, 476, 477–8.

40 Hoover moratorium diary, 6 May 1931, 'Proposed Statement,' 5 June 1931, both HHPP 1013.

41 Chamberlain to Hilda [his sister], 6 December 1931, 14 January 1932, both NC [Neville Chamberlain MSS, University of Birmingham Library, Birmingham] 18/1/764, 767; Leith-Ross [chief economic adviser, Treasury] to Vansittart [now FO permanent under-secretary], 14 November 1931, Leith-Ross T 188/16; Simon memorandum, 'Reparations and War Debts – A Bird's Eye View,' 29 December 1931, Simon FO 800/285.

42 P.J. Cain and A.G. Hopkins, *British Imperialism: Crisis and Deconstruction, 1914–1990* (London, 1993), 76–93; I.M. Drummond, *British Economic Policy and the Empire, 1919–1939* (London, 1972), 188–220; R. Rhodes James, *The British Revolution: British Politics, 1880–1939* (London, 1977), 519–22.

43 Cmd.4126; 'German addition to Political Clause accepted by British and French Delegations ... July 8,' *DBFP II*, III, 420. Cf. anonymous minute, 'Undertakings entered into at Lausanne (other than those contained in the published documents),' undated, T 172/1788.

44 'Notes of a Meeting ... on April 23, 1932,' 'Record of a Conversation at Villa Besinges,' 23 April 1932, both Simon MSS FO 800/286. Cf. 'Memorandum of a Meeting, April 15, 1932,' Stimson R82.

45 Cf. Passfield [dominions secretary] telegram to King, 11 July, 3 September 1929, both *DCER* 4, 213–14.

46 See 'Extracts from Minutes of Meetings of Prime Ministers and Heads of Delegations,' 13 November 1930, *DCER* 4, 302–6.

47 F. Capie, *Depression and Protectionism: Britain between the Wars* (London, 1983); Drummond, *British Economic Policy*, 96–107; idem., *Imperial Economic Policy, 1917–1939: Studies in Expansion and Protection* (London, 1974), 219–89; Middlemas and Barnes, *Baldwin*, 669–85.

48 Drummond, *British Economic Policy*, 103.

49 See Stacey, *Age of Conflict*, II, app. A, 432–5.

50 Chamberlain to his wife, 16 August 1932, NC 1/26/474.

51 Cf. Casey [Australian diplomat] to Bruce [Australian prime minister], 26 April 1928, in *My Dear P.M.: R.G. Casey's Letters to S.M. Bruce, 1924–1929*, ed. W.J. Hudson and J. North (Canberra, 1980), 337; Dawson [editor, *Times*] to Stevenson [*Times*'s correspondent], 11 June 1928, Stevenson MSS [*Times*

Archives, London]; Willingdon [former governor-general, Canada] to Clark
[British high commissioner, Ottawa], 12 October 1931, Clark MSS [British
Library of Economic and Political Science, London] 1.

52 For instance, Chamberlain to Ida [his sister], 21 August 1932, NC 18/1/795.

53 I.H. Nish, *Japan's Struggle with Internationalism. Japan, China, and the League of
    Nations, 1931–3* (London, 1993), 23–43; C. Thorne, *The Limits of Foreign Policy:
    The West, the League, and the Far Eastern Crisis of 1931–1933* (New York, 1973),
    131–272.

54 Cf. Committee of Imperial Defence memorandum, 'Defence of Singapore,'
    8 December 1930, Deputy Chiefs of Staff Report, 'The Situation in the Far
    East,' 22 February 1932, both CAB 53/22.

55 Stimson note, 7 January 1932, *Papers Relating to the Foreign Relations of the
    United States. Japan, 1931–1941*, vol. I, 76.

56 On Stimson's understanding, see Stimson diary, 9 January 1932, Stimson
    MSS 20; on British views, see Wellesley [FO Far Eastern expert] memoran-
    dum, 3 December 1931, Simon minute, 25 December 1931, both *DBFP II*, IX,
    31–3, plus n9. Simon's policy concerning 'non-recognition' later became a
    cause célèbre, since Stimson claimed it paved the way for the crises of the
    late 1930s; cf. F. Alexander, 'Simon-Stimson Myth: Japanese Aggression in
    Manchuria and Anglo-American Relations, 1931–1934,' *Australian Outlook*,
    9(1955), 5–28; R.A. Hecht, 'Great Britain and the Stimson Note of January 7,
    1932,' *Pacific Historical Review*, 38(1969), 177–91.

57 Simon to MacDonald, 6 October 1932, Vansittart to Simon, 6 October 1932;
    both Simon FO 800/287.

58 'Extract from a speech by Sir J. Simon ... November 10, 1932,' 'Speech by Sir
    J. Simon ... November 17, 1932,' *DBFP II*, IV, 263–5, 287–95.

59 See records of the meetings 2–11 December 1932, and the 'declaration,' in
    ibid., 308–78.

60 Simon telegrams to Lindsay [British ambassador, Washington], 4, 9 Novem-
    ber 1932, *BDFA*, II, C11, 311–13.

61 Cf. the French and Belgian notices, both 15 November 1932, both ibid., 319–
    20, 322.

62 On Anglo-American strain, see Stimson diary, 23 November 1932, Stimson
    MSS 24; Lindsay telegram (468–9) to Simon, 24 November 1932, *BDFA*, II,
    C11, 322–4. On Hoover-Roosevelt problems, see Hoover memorandum,
    22 November 1933 [but 1932], Roosevelt to Hoover, 21 December 1932, both
    HHPP 1013. Cf. E.A. Rosen, 'Intranationalism vs. Internationalism: The
    Interregnum Struggle for the Sanctity of the New Deal,' *Political Science
    Quarterly*, 81(1966), 274–97.

63 See Cmd. 4203, 4210, 4211, 4215, 4216, 4217.

64 Nish, *Japan's Struggle*, 223–30; Thorne, *Limits*, 333–6.
65 McKercher, 'Horns and Teeth,' 188–91; G. Weinberg, *The Foreign Policy of Hitler's Germany*, Vol. I: *Diplomatic Revolution in Europe, 1933–36* (Chicago, 1970), 37–53.
66 Lindsay telegrams (67–8, 70, 73) to Simon, 30, 31 January 1933, *BDFA*, II, C12, 140–3; 'Roosevelt to the Heads of Nations Represented at the London and Geneva Conferences,' 16 May 1933, in *Franklin D. Roosevelt and Foreign Affairs*, Vol. I, ed. E.B. Nixon (Cambridge, MA, 1969), (hereafter in the style *FDRFA*, I), 126–8. Cf. Vansittart to Simon, 23 May 1933, Simon FO 800/291.
67 Simon dispatch (740) to Lindsay, 30 May 1932, ibid. Cf. Stimson diary, 24–26 May 1932, Stimson MSS 22; Hoover draft telegram to Mellon [U.S. ambassador, London], 24 May 1932, with Feis [economic adviser, State Department] minute to Stimson, nd [?24 May 1932], both Stimson R82.
68 Stimson to Roosevelt, 9 December 1932; Feis minute, 23 December 1932, with addendum, 27 December 1932; Feis memorandum, January 1933; Feis memorandum, 24 January 1933; all Feis MSS [Library of Congress, Washington, DC] 123.
69 On Roosevelt's figure, Lindsay telegrams to Simon, 30, 31 January 1933, *BDFA*, II, C12, 140–3; on that of his advisers, Leith-Ross [in Washington] telegram for Treasury, 2 May 1933, ibid., 186–7.
70 Cabinet Committee on the British Debt, Meeting 10, 17 May 1933, CAB 27/548; Cabinet Meeting, 9 June 1933, CAB [Cabinet Archives, Public Record Office, Kew] 23/76; Chamberlain to Ida, 17 June 1933, NC 18/1/831. Cf. Dallek, *Roosevelt*, 40–1, 44, 48.
71 McKercher, *Transition*, ch. 5.
72 See Moley [U.S. delegate] telegram to Washington, 30 June 1933, Roosevelt telegram to Hull, 2 July 1933, both *FRUS 1933*, I, 665–6, 673–4; Roosevelt telegrams to Phillips [under-secretary of state], 30 June, 2 July 1933, Phillips telegram to Roosevelt, 1 July 1933, all *FDRFA*, I, 265–7, 268–9.
73 MacDonald to Bledisloe [a friend], 31 July 1933, MacDonald PRO 30/69/679; Chamberlain to Ida, 15 July 1933, NC 18/1/836.
74 FO memorandum, 'General Outline of the Main Developments of the War Debt Negotiations since October 1933,' *BDFA*, II, C12, 265–7.
75 Actually, one power, Finland, continued payments.
76 P.G. Boyle, 'The Roots of Isolationism: A Case Study,' *Journal of American Studies*, 6(1972), 41–50.
77 See FO 'Memorandum on the Foreign Policy of His Majesty's Government in the United Kingdom,' 19 May 1933, in 'Papers Prepared for the Use of the Chiefs of Staff in their Annual Review of Imperial Defence (1933)' [CID 112-B], 30 June 1933, CAB 4/22.

78 Cabinet conclusion 62(33), 15 November 1933, CAB 23/77.
79 'Defence Requirements Sub-Committee. Report' [DRC 14], 28 February 1934, CAB 16/109. It is interesting to note that the DRC held its first meeting the day before the cabinet formally agreed to its creation.
80 On the work of the DRC, see G. Post, Jr, *Dilemmas of Appeasement: British Deterrence and Defense, 1934–1937* (Ithaca, NY, 1993), 32–8, 43–8.
81 Warren Fisher to Hankey [DRC 16], 12 February 1934, CAB 16/109. Cf. 'Note by Sir Warren Fisher as an addendum to the Defence Requirements Committee Report' [DRC 19], 17 February 1934, ibid.
82 DRC Meeting 3, 4 December 1933, ibid.
83 Cf. A.L. Goldman, 'Sir Robert Vansittart's Search for Italian Cooperation against Hitler, 1933–36,' *Journal of Contemporary History*, 9: 3(1973), 93–130.
84 'Report on Defence Requirements,' 31 July 1934, CAB 16/110.
85 Cf. 'Note by the Chancellor of the Exchequer on the Report of the Defence Requirements Committee' [DC(M)(32) 120], 20 June 1934, CAB 27/511.
86 See Vansittart memorandum, 'The Future of Germany' [CP 104(34)], 7 April 1934, CAB 24/248; Vansittart to Simon, 14 May 1934, CAB 21/388; Simon memorandum [DC(M)(32) 118], 14 June 1934, CAB 27/510. Cf. MacDonald and Baldwin's comments in DC(M)(32) 50th Meeting, 25 Jun 1934, CAB 27/507.
87 Chamberlain memorandum, 'The Naval Conference and Our Relations with Japan,' n.d. [but early August 1934], NC 8/19/1.
88 Roosevelt to Davis, 9 November 1934, Davis MSS [Library of Congress, Washington] 51.
89 S.E. Pelz, *Race to Pearl Harbor: The Failure of the Second London Naval Conference and the Onset of World War II* (Cambridge, MA, 1974), 132–51; Roskill, *Naval Policy*, II, 295–9.
90 From December 1933; quoted in Stacey, *Age of Conflict*, II, 160.
91 Hull to Simon, 7 February 1935, Simon FO 800/290. Cf. Simon to MacDonald, 11 February 1935, ibid.
92 Riddell telegram to Bennett, 17 April 1935, Skelton telegram to Riddell, 20 April 1934, both *DCER* 5, 357, 359–60.
93 Bennett telegram to Riddell, 27 April 1935, ibid., 362.
94 For instance, D.C. Watt, 'The Secret Laval-Mussolini Agreement of 1935 on Ethiopia,' *Middle East Journal*, 15(1961), 69–78.
95 M.L. Roi, '"A Completely Immoral and Cowardly Attitude": The British Foreign Office, American Neutrality, and the Hoare-Laval Plan,' *Canadian Journal of History* 29(1994), 333–51.
96 Roosevelt to Hull, 10 October 1935, *FDRFA*, I, 3, 17–18. Cf. H.B. Braddick, 'A

New Look at American Policy during the Italo-Ethiopian Crisis, 1935–1936,' *Journal of Modern History*, 34(1962), 64–73.

97 Cf. Eayrs, *Defence of Canada*, II, 3–33; Stacey, *Age of Conflict*, II, 180–8; Veatch, *Canada and the League*, 143–69.

98 Cf. E. Haraszti, *Treaty-Breakers or 'Realpolitiker'? The Anglo-German Naval Agreement of 1935* (Boppard am Rhein, 1974).

99 Cf. Craigie [FO naval expert] minute, 19 March 1935, FO [Foreign Office Archives, Public Record Office, London] 371/18732/2878/22; FO-Admiralty memorandum, 'Questions of Naval Limitation, with Relation to the Possible Holding of a Conference for the Limitation of Naval Armament,' 30 March 1935, FO 371/18732/3205/22.

100 Pelz, *Race to Pearl Harbor*, 125–64; Roskill, *Naval Policy*, II, 284–321.

101 M.W. Berg, 'Protecting National Interests by Treaty: The Second London Naval Conference, 1934–1935,' in McKercher, *Arms Limitation*, 221.

102 DRC Third Report, 21 November 1935 [CP26(36)], CAB 24/259.

103 DPR(DR) Report, 12 February 1936, ibid.

104 Representative of this vast literature are E. Haraszti, *The Invaders: Hitler Occupies the Rhineland* (Budapest, 1983); D. Little, *Malevolent Neutrality: The United States, Great Britain, and the Origins of the Spanish Civil War* (Ithaca, 1985); P. Lowe, *Great Britain and the Origins of the Pacific War: A Study of British Policy in East Asia, 1937–1941* (London, 1977); S. Newman, *The British Guarantee to Poland: A Study in the Continuity of British Foreign Policy* (London, 1976); F. Paulhac, *Les Accords de Munich et les Origines de la Guerre de 1939* (Paris, 1988). Above all is the magisterial D. Cameron Watt, *How War Came: The Immediate Origins of the Second World War, 1938–1939* (London, 1989).

105 Cf. 'Cato,' *Guilty Men* (London, 1940); W. Murray, *The Change in the European Balance of Power, 1938–1939: The Path to Ruin* (Princeton, 1984).

106 Cf. Post, *Dilemmas*, 247–330.

107 B.J.C. McKercher, 'The Last Old Diplomat: Sir Robert Vansittart and the Verities of British Foreign Policy, 1903–1930,' *Diplomacy and Statecraft* 6(1995), 1–38.

108 Hoare to Chamberlain, 17 March 1937, NC 7/11/30/74.

109 Quoted in W.R. Rock, *Chamberlain and Roosevelt: British Foreign Policy and the United States, 1937–1940* (Columbus, OH, 1988), 8.

110 Cf. Chamberlain to Hilda, 25 April 1937, NC 18/1/1003.

111 Reynolds, *Anglo-American Alliance*, 9.

112 Cadogan diary, 26 March 1939, in *The Diaries of Sir Alexander Cadogan, 1938–1945*, ed. D. Dilks (London, 1971), 163.

113 Watt, *How War Came*; Weinberg, *Hitler's Germany*, II.

114 Rock, *Chamberlain and Roosevelt*, 33–4.
115 Ibid., 73–7. See Eden to Lindsay, 25 January 1938, Eden MSS FO 954/29/US/38/11.
116 Chamberlain diary, 19 February 1938, NC 2/24A.
117 Eayrs, *Defence of Canada*, II, 34–47; Veatch, *Canada and the League*, 170–80.
118 Quoted in Stacey, *Age of Conflict*, II, 205.
119 Chamberlain to Ida, NC 18/1/1008.
120 Skelton memorandum, 3 October 1938, *DCER*, 6, 1100–03.
121 Drummond and Hillmer, *Freer Trade*, esp. 151–67.
122 On the staff talks, see M. Murfett, *Fool-Proof Relations: The Search for Anglo-American Naval Cooperation during the Chamberlain Years, 1937–1940* (Singapore, 1984), 125–51 passim.
123 D. Reynolds, 'FDR's Foreign Policy and the British Royal Visit to the USA, 1939,' *Historian*, 45(1983), 461–72.
124 B.J.C. McKercher, '"Our Most Dangerous Enemy": Britain Pre-eminent in the 1930s,' *International History Review*, 13(1991), esp. 776–7.
125 S. Aster, *1939: The Making of the Second World War* (London, 1973); Watt, *How War Came*, 162–478 passim.
126 D. Haglund, *Latin America and the Transformation of U.S. Strategic Thought, 1936–1940* (Albuquerque, NM, 1984).
127 S.W. Dziuban, *Military Relations between the United States and Canada, 1939–1945* (Washington, DC, 1959), 3.
128 Eayrs, *Defence of Canada*, II, 180–3.
129 'Speech of the President,' 18 August 1938, *FDRFA*, 11, 70.
130 W.A.B. Douglas, *The Creation of a National Air Force: The Official History of the Royal Canadian Air Force*, II (Toronto, 1986), 131.
131 King telegram to Chamberlain, 29 September 1939, *DCER*, 6, 1099.
132 Dallek, *Roosevelt*, 200–5; Reynolds, *Anglo-American Alliance*, 63–92.
133 Stacey, *Age of Conflict*, II, 264–6.
134 J. Granatstein and R. Bothwell, '"A Self-Evident National Duty": Canadian Foreign Policy, 1935–1939,' *Journal of Imperial and Commonwealth History*, 3(1975), 212–33.

5

Not an Equilateral Triangle: Canada's Strategic Relationship with the United States and Britain, 1939–1945

JOHN ALAN ENGLISH

In early June 1940, in one of the oddest operations of the Second World War, the Hudson's Bay Company supply vessel *Nascopie* transported a Canadian landing party, with three machine-guns, sixty rifles, and 10,000 rounds of ammunition, to Ivigtut in the Danish possession of Greenland.[1] The party consisted of two Royal Canadian Mounted Police constables, four civilians, and one army artillery officer travelling incognito in civilian clothes. Their task was to prevent the Ivigtut cryolite mines from falling to the Germans, who had overrun Denmark in April. Shortly after the *Nascopie*'s arrival, however, the United States Coast Guard cutter *Campbell* sailed into harbour to offload a three-inch gun and several crew members who had been invited by mine administrators to serve as guards. None of the arms aboard the *Nascopie* was consequently distributed in Greenland, which by early April 1941 had virtually become an American protectorate.

In many ways the Ivigtut affair illustrated Canada's broader strategic dilemma during the Second World War. Although Greenland lay athwart North Atlantic convoy routes, to the obvious concern of Anglo-Canadian naval and military planners, it also lay within the boundaries of the western hemisphere as defined by the War Plans Division of the United States General Staff. To complicate matters further, the Ivigtut mines constituted the world's principal source of natural cryolite, essential for producing aluminum, and hence Allied aircraft. Anxious to ensure that neither the Germans nor their puppets gained access to these mines, the British considered the military protection of Ivigtut absolutely vital. Indeed, the aluminium controller for the United Kingdom had urgently warned officials of Alcan, the Aluminum Company of Canada, of the dangers of destructive raids; they, in turn, brought the matter to the attention of the Canadian minister of finance, Colonel J.L. Ralston. It was generally felt, however, that Canadian rather than British occupation would be more palatable to American official and public opinion. Accordingly, the Canadian Chiefs of Staff (COS) met with the minister of national defence on 12 April to discuss how a small-scale occupation of Greenland might be carried out. The plan drawn up called for an expeditionary force, designated Force 'X,' of one infantry company and some artillery.

Meanwhile, the Americans were attempting to secure British acquiescence to a diametrically opposed policy. On 13 April 1940 the American secretary of state, Cordell Hull, suggested to the British ambassador, Lord Lothian, that no intervention take place; it might provide a precedent for Japan to seize Asian possessions administered by other Nazi-occupied European nations, particularly the Dutch East Indies. In a press interview following this meeting, Lothian allowed that neither Britain nor Canada would move into Greenland unless German occupation appeared imminent. More concerned about national autonomy than cryolite, the Canadian cabinet reacted characteristically. Meeting in the absence of Prime Minister William Lyon Mackenzie King, then at Virginia Beach, it observed that Lothian had committed the impropriety of pretending to speak for Canada. Ottawa quickly dispatched a reproachful telegram to London and informed Washington that Lothian had not been authorized to speak on Canada's behalf. On 13 April the Canadian minister in Washington, Loring Christie, called on Hull to dispel any misapprehensions created by the ambassador's statement.

Three days later, at Britain's urging, Ottawa demonstrated its autonomy. Christie informed the State Department: 'in view of the danger of Greenland being made a base for attack, the necessity of protecting the cryolite mining operations essential for aluminum production, and the necessity of assisting the local administration in obtaining supplies and marketing its products, we [the Canadian Government] had been considering the possibility of local action for these purposes, with no thought of a permanent occupation or political control.'[2] The Americans were further assured that Canada would act as 'trustee for a restored and independent Danish government.'[3] This time, American reaction was swift. While some U.S. officials openly commented that the Canadian initiative smacked of an attempt to garner advantage for Alcan,[4] others condemned it as an affront to the status quo guaranteed by the Monroe Doctrine. On 19 April Christie was told unequivocally that the State Department regarded Canada's proposed action as 'highly inadvisable' and that it 'would be glad to learn that Canada felt it unnecessary to take any action.'[5] Ottawa informed London on 23 April that plans to occupy Greenland were being suspended.

Unaware of what had transpired, King raised the issue with Roosevelt at Warm Springs, Georgia, on the same day, this during their first meeting of the war. King allowed that Canada had 'undertaken, in correspondence with Britain, to see that men were supplied who could be of service about the mine in protective ways,' and that the Canadian ship that supplied Greenland annually would shortly be delivering more than it had done previously. Roosevelt replied that the Americans would also be sending a ship, stressing that 'if a real danger arose, [Roosevelt would] have to leave it to the British to deal with submarines, etc., at sea.'[6] He added that he did not think either North American power should make efforts to take possession of Greenland. The only Canadian action encouraged by Roosevelt was for the dominion to follow America's example by appointing a consul to Greenland. King did not demur. In fact, when visiting Washington from 28 to 29 April, he was disturbed to discover that External Affairs had instructed Christie's legation to inform the State Department of Canada's intention to prepare a Greenland defence force. He also learned about Force 'X.' 'Apparently,' he recorded in his diary, 'Ralston being concerned about aluminum and Skelton [under-secretary of state for external affairs and an ardent Canadian nationalist] zealous to have Canada rather than England handle Greenland matters ... had between them gone farther than I think was wise. I thought the position taken by the Americans was wise ... Clearly our people h[ave] been a little over-zealous in preparing for a little war on Canada's own account.'[7] When he returned to Ottawa, he was even more amazed by the advanced state of readiness of plans for the military occupation. Within the War Committee of the cabinet, moreover, he encountered considerable resistance to his decision, taken on 2 May, instructing the Canadian COS to demobilize Force 'X'.

On the same day, Vincent Massey, the Canadian high commissioner in London, received a letter from Anthony Eden, the dominions secretary, requesting that Canada consider the immediate dispatch of an expedition to Greenland to take control of the cryolite mines. The British discounted U.S. objections that such intervention would afford Japan a pretext for intervention in Southeast Asia, since London had already occupied the Danish Faeroe Islands. Eden none the less suggested that the Canadian force be described as a relief expedition carrying supplies for the local population and that the Americans be advised after the fact.

On 9 May several members of the War Committee joined Ralston in urging that Canada proceed with the expedition 'whether viewed with favour by the United States or not.'[8] Convinced that neither the Canadians nor the British appreciated what the Americans 'were doing to keep the Pacific quiet against Japan,' King reckoned that it was 'just matters of this kind which ma[de him] feel the importance of not going abroad if that can be avoided.' Such failure to comprehend the 'larger world situation' thrust Canada 'into the difficult cleft-stick position.' When Ralston and Charles Power, the associate minister of national defence, raised the matter again on 14 May, he 'made it clear that we had previously settled the policy of the Government, which was that our action was to parallel that of the U.S.'[9]

Nevertheless, on 3 June the Canadian chargé d'affaires in Washington was summoned to the State Department, where he was bluntly told that Roosevelt would be 'very angry' if Canada pursued the occupation of Greenland.[10] As the assistant secretary of state, Adolf Berle, explained, the Americans had been shocked to learn that despite previous assurances, Canadian troops had landed in Greenland. He went on to lecture the chargé on the inappropriateness of 'this type of 1890 imperialism,' adding that 'the days of Cecil Rhodes had passed.'[11] In fact, the Americans had been informed in advance about the exact composition of the *Nascopie* landing party, but exaggerated accounts of the activities of the lone army officer in mufti had confused State Department officials. There is strong reason to believe, however, that the State Department suspected that the Canadian government had deliberately inflated the German threat to carve out an economic sphere of interest in Greenland. Berle pressed the War and Navy departments for further American action on the grounds that failure to so would invite Canadian occupation. In September 1940 Hull reaffirmed that Washington would not recognize the right of any third government to interfere in Greenland's affairs. A final Canadian offer to provide for the defence of the cryolite mines in May 1941, a period when the German battleship *Bismarck* was prowling the North Atlantic, was rejected by a still-neutral United States.

The Greenland affair reflects the cold reality of Canada's strategic position and the Anglo-American relationship during the Second World War. In endeavouring to be the linchpin between the two great powers, the dominion tended to find itself squeezed as though in a vice, ineluctably bending towards the stronger jaw. Although King initially embraced the American connection to counter British power and influence – for

him, the major threat to Canadian autonomy – the United States quickly
assumed a grander imperial stance, pushing Canada aside. Of course,
the external policies of King's government helped to hoist Canada with
its own petard. Whereas Prime Minister Sir Robert Borden claimed
national status for Canadians on the grounds of their Great War contribution, King's insistence on exercising autonomy independent of the
Commonwealth closed the one avenue by which Canada might have
gained a strategic voice during the Second World War. Coupled with
King's obsessive fear of overseas conscription, given its potential threat
to national unity and his political power base, this policy ensured that
the country 'backed' haphazardly into the war.[12] Initial reluctance to go
beyond a moderate war effort, largely because of financial considerations and the specious concept of 'limited liability,'[13] condemned the
Royal Canadian Air Force (RCAF) to colonial status and left both it and
the Royal Canadian Navy (RCN) to struggle for their own autonomy.
Early failure to strike a proper diplomatic-military balance within Canada's war machinery similarly limited the government's ability to apply
leverage at the grand strategic level, even though Canada went on to
field a small but powerful overseas army, the fourth-largest air force,
and the world's third-ranking navy.[14] Such aspects, rarely attracting the
serious attention of Canadian scholars,[15] are integral to an understanding of Canada's strategic relationship to Britain and the United States
during the Second World War.

The Greenland affair not only exposed the limits of Canadian autonomy and power, but also revealed the extent to which King personally
intervened in such matters. Indeed, the policies of the Canadian government were to a remarkable degree the idiosyncratic policies of King.[16] A
deeply religious spiritualist who regarded harmony and unity as the
natural state of humanity, he manifested an abiding suspicion of British
imperialists while retaining late Victorian affection for the monarchy
and British Liberal statesmen. A devoted supporter of Sir Wilfrid Laurier, a loyalty that helped his rise to power, he never forgot that his political base was firmly anchored in Quebec. Although not an emotional
nationalist, King constantly sought autonomy for Canada. As late as the
1937 Imperial Conference, he refused to agree to defence pledges in
advance, to the extent that Neville Chamberlain's government interpreted his policy of 'calculated confusion' as meaning Britain could no
longer count on Canada.

The truth was that neither King nor Skelton had the slightest interest
in military affairs. Their penchant was diplomacy and foreign policy, the

major reason why King became external affairs minister as well as premier and why Skelton became the most powerful civil servant in Canadian history. According to Stacey, both men 'would have understood those Chinese intellectuals who, we are told, regard soldiers as an inferior race of beings whose proceedings deserve only the contempt of civilized men.'[17] If King was less a man of the sword – he and Skelton supported British appeasement in the late 1930s[18] – he evidently never doubted that Canada would ultimately assist Britain in a great war. Neither does it appear that he wished to cultivate American relations to the exclusion of the Commonwealth. Like Borden, he envisioned a linchpin role for Canada as interpreter between the United States and Britain. Skelton, on the other hand, preferred to see Canada within an American rather than a British orbit. For him, foreign policy boiled down to economic policy, which left it inseparable from domestic policy.[19] This attitude produced a cleavage with the Canadian military establishment, which more clearly than most saw that Canadian public opinion would ultimately accept, even demand, the overseas commitment of armed forces. Thus, although Newfoundland was strategically important to Canada's security, the attending heads of the Canadian armed forces were expressly forbidden, by Skelton of all people, to discuss the defence of the crown colony with British authorities.[20] This lack of harmony between foreign and military policy forfeited Canada's chances for a strategic voice in the Second World War.

On 24 August 1939 Skelton produced a paper entitled 'Canadian War Policy,' which proposed certain 'forms and objectives' in the event of Canadian participation in hostilities. Assuming there would be immediate consultation with Britain and France, and 'discreet consultation with Washington,' he advocated giving primacy to the defence of Canada. The possibility of aiding Newfoundland and the West Indies also lay, in his view, within 'the measure' of Canadian 'capacity.' Skelton further recommended that 'if any military action is to be taken overseas, it should be, in the first instance, in the air service rather than by military contingents.' The 'announcement of an immediate and intensified programme of building planes and training men for air service and for a Canadian air force operating in France,' he added, 'would be effective from the standpoint both of military value and of consolidation of public opinion.' Skelton envisioned Canada's making its greatest national effort in the economic field. Concentrating on the provision of 'munitions, raw materials and foodstuffs' would underpin the contribution 'most effective to our allies and consistent with Canadian interests.' It also amounted to a blueprint for 'limited liability' war, a discredited policy abandoned by the British six months earlier.[21]

When King read Skelton's paper to the cabinet, apparently without consulting the Canadian COS, it won general approval. On 1 September the cabinet also considered a COS submission entitled 'Canada's National Effort (Armed Forces) in the Early Stages of a Major War.' Noting that Britain intended to dispatch an expeditionary force to France, this submission advocated raising a Canadian army corps of two divisions and ancillary troops for overseas service. On 5 September the Cabinet Defence Committee, chaired by King, informed the COS that pending Parliament's decision, the government was prepared to adopt measures only for the defence of Canada. King reportedly voiced his displeasure with their recommendations, pointing to its dissimilarity with Defence Scheme Number 3, which had been amended in 1937 to provide for a 'Mobile Force' of one cavalry (until 1939) and two infantry divisions, primarily for the direct defence of Canadian territory (although recognizing the contingency that this force could and might be deployed overseas). Meanwhile, certain highly significant measures had already been taken. On 25 August Royal Navy (RN) warships received authorization to use Halifax harbour. After Germany's attack on Poland on 1 September, the entire 'Mobile Force' was mobilized. Two days later, when Britain declared war on Germany, a secret order approved by the cabinet ordered Canadian coastal commanders to take 'all necessary defence measures which would be required in a state of war.' For all practical purposes Canada was at war.[22]

On 3 September King asked Chamberlain by telegraph how the dominion might possibly provide assistance. Three days later, the British requested naval and air support and made a tactful plea for the immediate dispatch of 'a small Canadian [fighting] unit which would take its place along side the United Kingdom troops' and technical units (signals, engineers, ordnance, medical, and transportation) for attachment to British formations. On 15 September, five days after Canada had declared war, the cabinet appointed a subcommittee chaired by Ralston to draft a war program for the nation, which gave priority to the provision of supplies and financial aid. Canada also offered technical units, providing that Britain agreed to absorb all costs associated with them while they were not under Canadian command. Although the last item on the list referred to the organization and training of an expeditionary force, the Canadian COS had already been instructed on 16 September to dispatch the 1st Canadian Infantry Division overseas to fight with the

British Expeditionary Force (BEF). The ferocity of the Nazi assault on Poland made the situation more urgent. It had also raised the spectre of overseas conscription within King's cabinet.[23]

The sorely pressed British government, which initially requested Canada to assist in the individual training of air crew, including 2,000 pilots per year, now proposed a grander scheme based on earlier Air Ministry war planning. On 26 September Chamberlain personally appealed to King to have Canada participate in the British Commonwealth Air Training Plan (BCATP), designed to qualify annually 30,000 British, Canadian, Australian, and New Zealand air crew for service with the Royal Air Force (RAF). To King, whose 1937 rearmament program accorded primacy to the RCAF, which by 1939–40 garnered nearly half of all service appropriations, the proposal seemed a godsend. Convinced of the military merits of air power, King asserted in March 1939 that 'the days of great expeditionary forces of infantry crossing the oceans are not likely to recur.' With Skelton, King believed that an air commitment would involve fewer casualties and hence lessen any requirement for conscription. Though regretting that the British proposal had not been made earlier 'so that [Canada's] war effort would have been framed on these lines instead of having to head so strongly into expeditionary forces at the start,' he cabled his approval in principle on 28 September.[24]

During the first few weeks of the war, Canadians had assumed that the RCAF would field an expeditionary formation akin to that of the army, which reflected Canadian Corps organization in 1914–18. Indeed, British efforts to establish air training bases and flying programs in Canada between 1936 and 1939, along the lines of the 1917 Royal Flying Corps (Canada), had encountered considerable resistance. In 1936 King's government refused a request to establish a training school for airmen on Canadian territory, stating that Canada intended to establish air training schools of its own. A second British initiative proved more fruitful, if not less acrimonious, and enabled RAF personnel to be trained at RCAF facilities while continuing to allow untrained Canadians to be accepted into the RAF each year.[25] Although overtaken by the outbreak of war, this scheme provided the precedent for the BCATP and the often heated negotiations associated with its inception. King's outburst on 31 October 1939 – 'This is not our war' – underlined the basically frugal Canadian approach at that time: to limit involvement to financial, economic, and garrison assistance. He even succeeded in getting the British to acknowledge publicly that Canadian participation in the BCATP 'would provide for more effective assistance toward ultimate victory than any other form of military cooperation which Canada ... [could] give.'[26]

In negotiating the hugely expensive RCAF command and administration of the BCATP, however, King proved too clever by half. Urging the British to form RCAF squadrons overseas at the request of the Canadian government, he argued that the financial burden of the BCATP in Canada absolved him from absorbing their costs. He insisted instead that the British pay for maintaining RCAF squadrons overseas and bear the cost of RCAF aircrew salaries. As might be expected, the resultant shortage of Canadian ground crews in Britain complicated the creation of all-Canadian squadrons. King's action placed RCAF graduates of the BCATP, and the fighting echelon of the RCAF itself, at the disposal of the RAF. Only through a gradual, painful process of 'Canadianization' did the RCAF regain a measure of administrative control over its forces abroad. The establishment of No. 6 (Canadian) Group within Bomber Command on 1 January 1943 proved a major step in this direction. In April Canada belatedly agreed to bear the entire cost of the RCAF overseas, which by late 1944 had grown to forty-six squadrons. Within No. 83 Composite Group, RAF 2nd Tactical Air Force, fifteen out of twenty-nine squadrons were RCAF, though virtually no Canadians served in group headquarters. To the end of the war, the RCAF remained a fragmented auxiliary force, thanks mainly to King's handiwork. By August 1944 there were over 17,000 Canadian aircrew in the RAF compared with 10,000 on strength in RCAF units. As Skelton foresaw at the BCATP inception, a scheme he thought presented an opportunity for sharing in the direction of the war, Canada's failure 'to pay the piper' condemned the RCAF to colonial status for the most of the war.[27]

While the BCATP was being negotiated, King made his first foray into the grand strategic realm by responding positively to Hitler's peace offensive launched on 6 October 1939. Hoping that the German initiative would produce negotiations to end the war, King urged Chamberlain to formulate counter-proposals rather than reject outright Hitler's overtures. After consulting Skelton, King sent his own peace proposal to Chamberlain on 8 October. Conceived along 'the lines of [the Canadian] Industrial Disputes Act' and League of Nations procedures, it advocated 'a form of compulsory consideration not arbitration [by a committee of neutral powers], permitting opportunity for public opinion to be brought to bear.' Although King never expected much to come of this proposal, but personally felt obliged to make it anyway, British officials probably looked upon it with a certain amount of bewilderment. In Stacey's words, they 'undoubtedly regarded his scheme as the height of naïvete, as indeed it was'; for to 'speak of stopping Hitler by the mobilisation of public opinion, in October 1939, was enough to take any practical person's breath away.' When Chamberlain consulted Canada on his proposed reply to Hitler, neither King nor Skelton considered it positive enough respecting war aims and conditions of peace. British refusal to modify this reply, which essentially declared further negotiations futile, prompted King to conclude that such consultation amounted to little more than comment and should be stopped.[28]

Between the conquest of Poland and the German invasions of Denmark and Norway in April 1940, a period of 'Phoney War,' Ottawa displayed little interest in influencing the higher direction of a conflict expected to last three years.[29] Created in 1939 to coordinate the Anglo-French war effort, the Supreme War Council remained a distant forum in which 'France and the United Kingdom ... each ... represented by the Prime Minister and one other Minister, and other Allied Powers, perhaps, by their Ambassadors,' deliberated upon policy. This situation disturbed Lester Pearson, Massey's secretary in London, who warned that failure to assume a larger part in directing the war would render Canada little more than a supplier of soldiers and pilots. He blamed Ottawa's 'peacetime avoidance of consultation on foreign policy and defence' for bringing about this state of affairs. King obviously held other views on how to promote Canadian autonomy; for he continually discouraged Chamberlain's proposals to convene a conference of Commonwealth prime ministers.[30] It was through such consultative bodies, of course, that Borden had converted the battlefield triumphs of the Canadian Corps into the reality of nationhood during the Great War. Within the Imperial War Cabinet, instituted by David Lloyd George in 1917, Borden provided a strategic voice for Canada.[31]

Although orders-in-council passed late in 1939 under the Visiting Forces Act of 1933 and the War Measures Act of 1914 authorized Canadian troops to serve under the commander-in-chief (C-in-C) of the BEF, no evidence exists to indicate that King sought membership on the Supreme War Council, which Canada's status under the League Covenant and the Statute of Westminster may have warranted.[32] Any request for more say in the higher direction of the war might have sparked demands for an increased Canadian war effort, which King, preoccupied by political challenges at home, desperately hoped to avoid. In Quebec, Premier Maurice Duplessis played on conscription fears and called an election for October 1939 over the issue of increased federal wartime powers. His subsequent defeat owed much to the announcement by federal Quebec ministers that they would resign if his party won, thus leaving Quebecers prey to the malice of English-Canadian conscriptionists. King faced a second challenge when the Ontario provincial government passed a resolution in January 1940 condemning his war effort as lackadaisical. In response, King called a snap federal election, which caught his political opponents off guard and resulted in a landslide victory on 26 March 1940.[33] While campaigning in February, however, King had made it clear that he did not wish to be consulted by the British on policy towards Norway, which he considered a 'distinctly European ... [question that] should be kept as between France and Britain themselves.'[34] When the Germans attacked Norway in April, barely two weeks after his election win, he did not even bother to call a meeting of the cabinet War Committee.[35]

The Allies' humiliating defeat in the Norwegian campaign toppled Chamberlain's government. On 10 May, the day Winston Churchill became prime minister, the Germans unleashed their lightning war in the west. Holland surrendered four days later, and Belgium capitulated on 28 May. By 4 June the BEF had been routed from Dunkirk, and on 17 June, seven days after Italy entered the war on Germany's side, the collaborationist Vichy French government of Marshal Henri Pétain sued for peace. These cataclysmic events shook Canada to its core. The cabinet War Committee, which did not meet regularly before May 1940, met eight times before the month was out. On 17 May King declared that the 'Empire was in extremis,' and the cabinet agreed to raise a third division and form a Canadian corps overseas. During the Dunkirk evacuation, the government announced that a fourth division would also be recruited. In June Parliament passed the National Resources Mobilization Act (NRMA), empowering the government to mobilize all material resources and conscript manpower. But financial and home defence concerns no longer predominated, as emphasis shifted to imperial defence and Canada acceded to British requests to provide garrisons for Iceland, Bermuda, and Jamaica.[36] When London asked for destroyers to defend Britain against invasion, Canada immediately dispatched its entire naval force at the time: four detroyers. Even Skelton agreed to leaving Canada bare to shore up Britain, and he opposed having the Americans undertake the protection of Canadian coasts lest they not do as much for beleaguered Britain. Limited liability, except concerning overseas conscription, had been abandoned.[37]

From the fall of France in June 1940 to the invasion of the Soviet Union in June 1941, a dark period when the British Empire stood alone against the Axis powers, Canada was Britain's greatest ally. Yet despite Canada's relative geographical security, King's government refused to take an active part in the higher direction of the war. Fearful of compromising Canadian autonomy, King opposed any equivalent of the former Imperial War Cabinet. When the Australian prime minister, Robert Menzies, proposed such a body to consider strategic matters, King countered that he would require advice from his COS as to who were most needed in Canada. He also expressed reservations about being separated from his cabinet colleagues and being unable to deal with domestic divisions. That Canadian participation could lead to commitments without any real authority, 'responsibility without power,' as he put it, further concerned King. He recommended that individual ministers raise matters as necessary with their British counterparts. On 29 July 1941 the Canadian Cabinet War Committee formally rejected Menzies's proposal. This action all but ensured that the Anglo-French Supreme War Council would be replaced not by a Commonwealth body modelled on the Imperial War Cabinet but, rather, by the British War Cabinet and the British COS, with Churchill as overlord.[38]

Although Churchill declared himself willing to consider the formation of an imperial war cabinet, he did not favour the idea. He was reluctant to share power and rightly feared that permanent Commonwealth membership on such a body would erode his authority and create additional complications, especially in regard to enlisting American support in Europe. This dominance was exactly why Menzies had called for an imperial war cabinet; for he had attended British War Cabinet meetings in early 1941 and thought they left far too much to Churchill's highly personal direction. Churchill, who subsequently used King's arguments against Menzies,[39] assuaged the Australians by proposing an imperial conference for the summer of 1941. When King explained that he could not leave Canada because of the conscription issue, the conference was cancelled. Shortly thereafter Churchill indicated that although dominion prime ministers could always attend the British War Cabinet, ministers other than prime ministers could not. This ruling effectively prevented the creation of a permanently operating imperial war cabinet, since dominion prime ministers could not leave their respective nations for extended periods. Both South Africa and New Zealand joined Canada in opposing such an arrangement.[40]

Unlike King, who had added the External Affairs portfolio to his position as prime minister, Churchill donned the mantle of minister of defence, a post unencumbered by a working department. He thus not only chaired his small War Cabinet, but was also ex officio chairman of the COS Committee which, in his words, 'for the first time ... assumed its due and proper place in daily contact with the Executive Head of Government, and in accord with him had full control over the conduct of the war and the armed forces.'[41] Using military members of the cabinet secretariat as his staff and making their superior, General Sir Hastings Ismay, his personal COS and a member of the COS Committee, Churchill achieved a degree of political-military integration unmatched in America or Canada.[42] Other War Cabinet ministers shouldered substantial parliamentary responsibilities and heavy wartime administrative duties associated with their respective departments. As the war progressed, the British War Cabinet became decreasingly important in directing strategy, which became almost exclusively the purview of Churchill and his COS. Therefore, Churchill became the primary channel through which the dominions received strategic information. When the Australians finally won the right to have their high commissioner attend War Cabinet meetings, they found that he gained little information on the actual conduct of the war. Canada, which did not seek 'the right to be heard ... in the formulation and the direction of policy,' continued to rely on Massey's receiving daily briefings from the dominions secretary, a practice that King had forbidden before the war.[43]

In contrast with Britain's war machinery, that of Canada operated almost bereft of professional military advice. The Emergency Council established on 30 August 1939, which replaced the Canadian Defence Committee originally set up in 1935,[44] considered questions of general policy and coordinated wartime activities. Chaired by King, it comprised Ralston, Ernest Lapointe, the minister of justice, T.A. Crerar, the minister of mines and resources, Norman Rogers, the minister of national defence, and Raoul Dandurand, the Senate government leader. In a further reorganization on 5 December 1939, the Cabinet War Committee superseded the Emergency Council.[45] Initially, the membership of these two bodies was the same, but from May 1940 it grew to include C.D. Howe, minister of munitions and supply, and the newly appointed minister of air, Charles Power, and minister of naval services, Angus Macdonald.[46] Ralston later assumed the defence portfolio on the death of Rogers, and J.L. Ilsley replaced Ralston at Finance. In general, the War Committee comprised the most experienced and influential ministers of the cabinet which, unlike its British equivalent, continued meeting throughout the war. These ministers, including Louis St Laurent, who succeeded Lapointe in November 1941, were highly competent, honest, and dedicated to winning the war; but, collectively, they possessed scant military experience or understanding of war. Howe jealously controlled an essentially civilian department. Ralston, who had commanded a battalion in the Great War with distinction, exhibited little interest in strategic aspects and submerged himself in administrative detail. The result was that the War Committee collectively tended to examine Canadian military affairs in microscopic detail from a domestic perspective.[47]

In practice, though the War Committee's composition tended to remain fixed, ministers attended as required. While Skelton and his successor, Norman Robertson, regularly sat in, King's senior military advisers were not present on a regular basis until the war was nearly three years old. In many ways this fact reflected both the low esteem in which the Canadian COS were held and the eternal tension that existed between them and the influential Department of External Affairs.[48] Before the war, Skelton and his colleagues had always eyed military professionals with suspicion, considering their activities antithetical to the policy of no commitments. The military, conversely, believed that war was approaching and presumed that this imminence justified advance joint planning. Gauging that Canadian-American cooperation would ultimately involve Britain, they were reluctant to jettison a well-established and certain British military connection for a more nebulous American one. Unfortunately, early in the war, the Canadian COS were too often ignored when they should have been consulted. They were rarely invited to attend the War Committee before 17 June 1942, when the latter agreed that 'for a stated period' they should attend the first and third meetings of each month.[49] Thus the COS attended about forty-five of the 167 War Committee sessions until this body dissolved in April 1945. To the end, King, the complete civilian, never appreciated their presence.[50]

Roosevelt, a former assistant secretary of the navy who came to rely heavily on the advice of military advisers, may have been among the first to remind King of their importance. King's first encounter with the president occurred on 7 November 1935, barely three weeks after his Liberal party's election sweep. To fulfil a campaign promise to negotiate a trade agreement with the United States within ninety days of taking office, King had rushed to Washington. On 15 November King and Hull signed a commercial accord in the presence of the president and his cabinet. The next summer, Roosevelt reciprocated by visiting Quebec City to meet King and the governor-general, Lord Tweedsmuir. In March

1937 King again travelled to Washington, where he stayed with Roosevelt. Throughout this period King emphasized to the Americans that he wished to play the role of conciliator in Anglo-American relations, an idea reiterated at the Imperial Conference of 1937. On 17 November 1938 two new trade deals, one Anglo-American and an expanded Canadian-American agreement based upon the 1935 accord, were signed. King stayed at the White House. Both leaders would meet fifteen more times by 1945.[51]

Roosevelt's interest in Canada revolved around more than trade or personal friendship; he raised the issue of defence in each of their meetings from Quebec City to the outbreak of war in Europe. At Quebec, he related a story about certain senators telling him that the United States would have to 'go in and help' if Japan attacked British Columbia.[52] At Chautauqua, New York, on 14 August 1936 he extended the Monroe Doctrine to Canada: 'Our closest neighbours are good neighbours. If there are remoter nations that wish us not good but ill, they know that we are strong; and they know that we can and will defend ourselves and defend our neighbour.'[53] In March 1937 Roosevelt raised the question of an Alaska highway, pointing to the military advantages of such a route in case of trouble with Japan. Evidently shocked by the state of Canada's west-coast defences and Pacific forces when he visited Victoria by destroyer the following September, he registered considerable concern about the British Columbia coastal link to Alaska. After this trip, Roosevelt took the unusual step of personally arranging staff talks between senior Canadian and American military officers about U.S.-Canadian defence.[54] In August 1938, during a visit to Kingston, Ontario, he further declared 'that the people of the United States would not stand idly by if domination of Canadian soil is threatened by any other empire.' In November and June of the following year, Roosevelt again broached the matter of defence with King, indicating his desire to see the port facilities of Halifax made available to the United States Navy (USN).[55]

In August 1939 the navalist Roosevelt embarked upon yet another personal reconnaissance, this time to eastern Canada and the Labrador coast of Newfoundland. As he had on his visit to Victoria, he travelled by warship in the company of naval officers, ostensibly on a holiday. But the origin of the cruise, he later recounted, 'was that he had found to his surprise that none of his naval officers seemed to have been in those waters or to know anything about them, so he wanted to get them interested in studying this area.' His immediate purpose was to have them 'spy out the land' to see what the coastal defence of eastern Canada and Newfoundland involved. Except for telephoning him on 5 September to ascertain whether Canada was officially at war, however, Roosevelt had no further contact with King until the German assaults on Denmark and Norway. King recorded that on 23–24 April 1940 at Warm Springs, Georgia, the president expressed additional concerns about the 'inadequacy' of Canadian coastal defences posing 'a real danger to the United States.' King noted that Roosevelt 'knew exactly from personal observation ... much about the nature of the coasts.'[56]

Dunkirk and the fall of France left Roosevelt and his defence planners pessimistic about Britain's survival against German air and ground assault. Fear of a compromise peace hung in the air. When Churchill pleaded for forty or fifty old destroyers on 15 May to help stave off invasion, Washington anxiously signalled back that he not let the British fleet fall into German hands. Confronting the possibility of a two-front war, the United States faced the ancient dilemma of Great Powers: whether to reinforce failure or husband resources to fight successfully another day. The British had already made this decision when they refused appeals to send additional fighter squadrons to France. The complicating problem for the Americans was that Britain possessed in the RN the one instrument that could inflict harm upon a United States at war with Japan. Canadians, who had never in their wildest dreams envisioned Britannia's trident being used against them, were less concerned. Indeed, Canadian policy in large part presumed the traditional security of the dominion behind the protective shield of the RN. Even the Dunkirk-prompted passage of the NRMA, which conscripted for home defence, leaving volunteers to fight overseas, pointed in this direction. Deep down, Canadians knew that the Americans would come to their assistance. Demonstrating as much, the United States Congress in September 1940 enacted a sweeping draft law that symbolized the total commitment of the nation.[57]

As might be expected of the leader of a Great Power in such circumstances, Roosevelt moved as decisively as he could to shore up American defences.[58] Unable because of the Neutrality Acts to comply with a Canadian request for aircraft for the BCATP, which Britain could not now supply, his administration began sending mounting quantities of war materiel overseas. On 24 May, just after Canada's four destroyers sailed for British waters, the president asked King to despatch an emissary to Washington to discuss the eventuality of a British surrender or compromise peace. In ensuing meetings, Roosevelt urged that King enlist other dominion leaders to pressure Churchill for assurances that the British and French fleets would be dispersed to the empire before being allowed to fall into German hands. 'At this moment, if at no other,' observed Stacey, Canada found itself in a linchpin role 'with a vengeance.' Again, as in the Greenland affair, the 'difficult cleft-stick position' proved highly uncomfortable. Though instinctively revolted at the thought that the United States was 'seeking to save itself at the expense of Britain,' King passed on Roosevelt's concerns to Churchill in couched terms. The latter replied with his defiant 'we shall never surrender' speech in the House of Commons on 4 June, the final day of the Dunkirk evacuation.[59] Equally intent as Roosevelt on preventing the French navy from falling into German hands, on 27 June, he ordered Operation 'Catapult,' which sank most of Vichy's fleet at Oran on 3 July.[60]

On 14 June the Canadian War Committee finally expressed serious concern about the defence of Newfoundland, identifying an immediate need for Canadian-American staff conversations on the defence of the Atlantic coast.[61] Although the State Department proved cool to Canadian overtures, on 3 July 1940 Roosevelt gave permission for American and Canadian military authorities to conduct informal staff talks in secret. Canadian officers stressed during these conversations, as they did to the Canadian War Committee, that North America's first line of defence lay in Britain and that any major attack on Canada's east coast was unlikely before the summer of 1941.[62] The Americans, for their part, made it clear that they were not prepared to jeopardize their own expansion plans by supplying arms to Canada. The British, meanwhile, vainly appealed to King to make some public representations on their behalf for the transfer of American destroyers. When Roosevelt reportedly expressed disappointment that Canada had not cared to comment on the destroyer question, King immediately lent his support to the British request. On 16 August, after announcing that the United States was holding conversations with Britain about acquiring naval and air bases for western hemispheric defence and conducting separate talks with Canada,[63] Roosevelt invited King to meet him on the following evening at Ogdensburg, New York. On an inspection tour, the president had evidently decided upon this initiative independently, without any suggestion from Ottawa.[64]

Although the Ogdensburg meeting produced a press release rather than a treaty or an agreement,[65] it signalled a changing of the guard in Canadian external relations.[66] Roosevelt proposed the immediate establishment of the Permanent Joint Board of Defence (PJBD), composed of military and civilian representatives from both countries, to study and make recommendations for the coordinated defence of the United States and Canada. The initiative was entirely Roosevelt's. His military chiefs, apparently, were concerned more about the Axis threat to Latin America, especially Brazil, than Canada. As for King, in rushing to Ogdensburg he consulted neither his political colleagues nor his COS, who were on record from 1938 as having urged closer military Canadian-American cooperation on Pacific defence. Ironically, the PJBD proved most important in the period of American neutrality, when it submitted several formal recommendations to both governments. After Pearl Harbor, liaison between national headquarters tended to take precedence over the deliberations of this essentially advisory body. Thus, while the PJBD continued to meet frequently during 1942, it made only one of thirty-three wartime recommendations after 1943.[67]

As a result of a decision on 27 August 1940, the PJBD prepared two basic defence plans. The first, 'Joint Canadian-United States Basic Defence Plan – 1940,' dated 10 October 1940 (so-called Basic Plan No. 1), addressed the contingency of Britain's being overrun or the RN's losing control of the North Atlantic. During the spring of 1941 PJBD service members drafted a secondary plan, 'Joint Operational Plan No. 1,' to implement the basic plan. On 15 April a version of this plan, the 'Montreal Revise,' vested the 'strategic direction' of all land and air forces in the chief of staff of the United States Army, subject to prior consultation with the appropriate Canadian heads of service.[68] Meanwhile, the RAF had defeated the Luftwaffe in the Battle of Britain, and the British Army continued to chalk up impressive victories in the Western Desert, Somaliland, and Abyssinia. By September 1940 the United States had also formally agreed to transfer fifty obsolete destroyers to Britain in exchange for ninety-nine-year leases on a series of bases running from Newfoundland to British Guiana.[69] The secret American-British Conversations (ABC) that followed in Washington between January and March 1941 had also produced a plan known as ABC-1, which stipulated that in the event of American belligerency in a two-ocean war, the priority of both Allies would be to defeat the Third Reich.[70]

The ABC development overshadowed Ogdensburg, reflecting the Churchill-Roosevelt special relationship that had been quietly blossoming since 1939 to the derogation of the Roosevelt-King association.[71] Churchill's inspired leadership during Britain's darkest hour greatly influenced the congressional passage of the Lend-Lease Act on 11 March 1941, which, with ABC-1, marked the beginning of the great Anglo-

American wartime coalition termed the 'Grand Alliance.' The exclusion of dominion representatives from Anglo-American military staff conversations, under way in London when King met Roosevelt at Ogdensburg, indicated the degree of deference the Americans were prepared to show lesser powers. Although British representatives carefully referred to themselves as the 'United Kingdom' delegation, the Americans deliberately called them 'British,' considering them representatives of the Commonwealth. In short, ABC-1 reserved unto the American and British high commands the power to formulate and execute strategic policies and plans should the United States enter the war.[72] The Americans evidently were also responsible for a decision not to allow dominion officers to attend ABC sessions as observers. They preferred that the dominions be represented by service attachés through the medium of the British Joint Staff Mission (BJSM) in Washington. When Ottawa remonstrated against this aspect of ABC-1, suggesting a separate Canadian military mission in Washington, the Americans refused to receive it. Ironically, while Canada argued its position largely on the basis of Ogdensburg, the Americans countered that such representation would be 'out of place' given the existence of the PJBD.[73]

It has been suggested that American antagonism towards a Canadian military mission in Washington reflected resentment of Canada's refusal to accept American strategic direction concerning the second basic defence plan prepared by the PJBD. ABC-1 had rendered 'Basic Plan No. 1' obsolete. A new plan, 'Joint Canadian-United States Basic Defence Plan No. 2,' confusingly referred to as ABC-22, was accordingly drawn up for the United States and Canada within the parameters of ABC-1.[74] Put forward in a first draft by American service members of the PJBD on 10 April, ABC-22 gave the United States unqualified strategic control over Canadian forces.[75] Although Canadians were not told, the Americans planned to incorporate Newfoundland, the maritime provinces, the Gaspé peninsula, and British Columbia within their northeast and western defence commands. Canadian strategic control of naval forces was to be limited to the coastal defence of Canada and Newfoundland. Since Ottawa had accepted U.S. strategic direction under the 'Montreal Revise,' the Americans concluded that the same would apply in ABC-22. From Canada's perspective, the two scenarios were quite different. Since ABC-1 postulated concerted American-Commonwealth action to defeat the Axis, Canada balked at granting the Americans strategic control of its forces under ABC-22.[76] After several uncomfortable exchanges, the matter was settled through military channels, though not to the satisfaction of American officers. Should the United States enter the war, ABC-22 provided for coordinatiing Canadian-American military efforts through 'mutual cooperation.'[77]

The heavy neutral hand of the United States continued to be felt throughout 1941. By the Anglo-American agreement on bases signed in London on 27 March 1941, the United States established a security zone in the western Atlantic. On 7 July, fifteen days after Germany attacked the Soviet Union, American marines relieved British garrisons in Iceland, Trinidad, and British Guiana. Concurrently, work began on constructing air bases in Greenland and military installations in Bermuda and the West Indies. Under the main agreement, the Americans additionally acquired six leased areas in Newfoundland, including the naval base at Argentia. When the British initially informed the Canadian government on 13 July 1940 that they were contemplating such a cession, Ralston recommended it to King without consulting the Canadian COS who, for military reasons, retained serious reservations. In fact, two days after the Ogdensburg meeting, Newfoundland agreed to place its forces under Canadian command for defence purposes. By January 1941 American troops had begun to infiltrate the crown colony under the umbrella of Ogdensburg. In April, notwithstanding a protocol that recognized Canada's special responsibility for Newfoundland's defence,[78] Roosevelt ordered additional troops to non-leased areas of the island, without reference to Canada, ostensibly to ward off German raiders. The following October the U.S. chief of naval operations requested the Canadian chief of the air staff to place all RCAF forces assigned to ocean escort duty under the C-in-C of the U.S. Atlantic Fleet.[79] As late as February 1942 General Hugh Drum, commander of the U.S. Eastern Theatre of Operations, recommended that all forces in Newfoundland be placed under the command of an American officer 'without any limitation.' Ultimately, Canadian COS insistence on the principle of mutual cooperation, set forth in ABC-22, ensured Canada's predominant influence within Newfoundland.[80]

On a grander plane, Canadian-American cooperation flagged. Having declined Churchill's invitation to attend the Imperial War Conference held earlier in the summer,[81] King learned from the British high commissioner to Canada on 6 August 1941 that the British premier was en route to rendezvous with Roosevelt off Argentia, Newfoundland. Contrary to what he had intimated to King at Hyde Park the previous April,[82] the president was not travelling to meet Churchill by way of Ottawa. Angered at being ignored by both parties, King characteristically vented his ire and sense of rejection mainly upon the British. He accepted, for example, Roosevelt's rather lame explanation that he had considered leaving by cruiser from Quebec, but thought better of it after realizing that taking one head of a dominion government to a conference with Churchill would be unfair to the others. That the two Great Powers were now prepared to collaborate without Canada none the less prompted King to reconsider Commonwealth relations. He performed an abrupt about-face and arranged a visit to Britain that lasted from 20 August to 7 September. Before leaving Canada, he even suggested that an early meeting of Commonwealth prime ministers should be held.[83] In Britain, King attended several meetings of the War Cabinet and received from Churchill a full account of the Argentia meeting that led to the declaration of the 'Atlantic Charter.' He informed the great man that he 'could see the embarrassment [he] would have been to other parts of the Empire' had he been allowed to attend. After returning to Canada, he announced to the press that the Commonwealth 'had in existence ... in actual practice the most perfect continuous conference of Cabinets that any group of nations could possibly have.'[84]

In September 1941, as had been agreed at Argentia, the Americans assumed strategic control of the western Atlantic; this move released British ships for duty in the eastern Atlantic and the Mediterranean. On 11 September the USN moved beyond protecting American commerce by escorting ships of other flags in Atlantic convoys. As the USN had effectively joined the Commonwealth's North Atlantic convoy escort organization, the RCN's Newfoundland Escort Force passed two days later under the strategic direction of the C-in-C United States Atlantic Fleet in accordance with the provisions of ABC-1. Transfer of the major part of the RCN to American command does not appear to have greatly concerned either King or the War Committee. On U.S. entry into the war, however, most American ships were withdrawn for service in other theatres, leaving only two Coast Guard cutters for ocean escort duty. Canada's contribution meanwhile had grown, as had RCN dissatisfaction with what was perceived as the USN's unjustified operational arrogance. RCN officers began to claim a greater strategic voice in the control of their service. Although the RCN provided 48 per cent of escort forces compared with the RN's 50 per cent and the USN's 2 per cent in the Battle of the Atlantic, the Americans remained reluctant to let the northwestern Atlantic revert to Canadian control. The system of command set up in 1941 thus lasted until March 1943, when the Atlantic Convoy Conference convened in Washington. These discussions produced the Canadian North West Command, headed by Canada's only Allied commander-in-chief of the war, Rear-Admiral L.W. Murray.[85]

Also in 1941 the United States exerted pressure on Canada over Vichy France's continued administration of the islands of St Pierre and Mique-lon. Although the British had openly urged their peaceful *ralliement* to Charles De Gaulle's Free French forces after September 1940, some Americans held other opinions. Cordell Hull resented Britain's support of De Gaulle; and Admiral William Leahy, soon to be Roosevelt's per-sonal COS, had developed pronounced anti-Gaullist views as ambassa-dor to Vichy. Neither Britain nor Canada wished to take action against the islands without American concurrence. The May 1941 discovery of a high-power radio transmitter on the islands increased Anglo-Canadian concern for the security of transatlantic convoy routes. The Canadian COS prepared contingency plans for a possible expedition and recom-mended the early occupation of the islands. The PJBD concurred in November that the radio station constituted a threat to Canadian and American interests. Hull's fear that such action might drive Vichy into the arms of Hitler none the less stopped the War Committee from sanc-tioning Canadian military intervention. For his part, De Gaulle sought to safeguard French sovereignty by ordering Vice-Admiral E.-H. Muselier, recently arrived in Halifax with several Free French ships, to 'rally' the islands without reference to any other authority. Muselier's peaceful conquest of the islands on Christmas Day sparked a diplomatic furore. Convinced that Canada had somehow connived with the Free French, Hull demanded that King evict Muselier. King, equally angry at the Free French, denied collusion and declined to take any action without Anglo-American support. As both powers remained poles apart on the issue, nothing was done.[86]

After Operation Barbarossa and Pearl Harbor ushered in 'a real world war' in 1941,'[87] it was too late for Canada to claim a voice in the higher direction of the war. An initial plan drafted by the State Department indicated as much when it advocated a Supreme War Council made up of representatives from the United States, Great Britain, China, and Rus-sia.[88] When the new British ambassador, Lord Halifax, recommended that the dominions be given status equal to Britain, Hull retorted that too large a group would render the council unwieldy. The 'Arcadia' Conference held in Washington from 22 December 1941 to 14 January 1942 decided the issue; Churchill and Roosevelt created the Combined Chiefs of Staff (CCS) Committee with responsibility to determine the strategic direction of the Allied war effort. Basically, the CCS consisted of the British COS and the American Joint Chiefs of Staff (JCS)[89] set up in imitation. Their most important decisions were taken during a series of major conferences at which Roosevelt and Churchill presided. Permanent CCS headquarters were located in Washington, where the JCS met in regular session with the heads of BJSM service delegations in Washington; these officials represented their respective British chiefs. The head of the BJSM, Field Marshal Sir John Dill, represented both Churchill as minister of defence and the British COS collectively. Given such a structure, which led the BJSM to consider themselves grist between two large millstones,[90] a Canadian military mission appeared extraneous to the Americans.

The Canadian government was neither consulted nor informed about the establishment of the CCS. Such information as was received came through informal contacts with the BJSM. Perhaps because of the firmness with which the JCS rejected Australian and New Zealand pleas for representation,[91] King never lodged a formal protest. Even a suggestion by the Canadian chief of the general staff (CGS), Lieutenant-General K. Stuart, to form a joint Commonwealth staff encountered the accepted External Affairs view that anything short of separate Canadian representation would constitute a reversal of policy. The COS contended, none the less, that a joint staff would provide a 'more practical basis for more effective representation of the Canadian services in joint planning and allocation than would the establishment of a separate Canadian staff group.'[92] Roosevelt and Churchill agreed eventually to allow one Canadian officer to represent the Canadian War Committee before the CCS. The irony was that this officer represented a political and civil authority in front of a largely military authority. In July 1942 the Americans agreed to accept the Canadian Joint Staff (CJS) in Washington, not officially designated a 'mission' or paralleled by any American equivalent in Ottawa. Although the JCS in August 1942 advised their staff planning, intelligence, and public relations agencies to maintain liaison with the CJS, the BJSM remained the main avenue by which Canadians received information on the higher direction of the war. Indeed, even Canada's paltry representation on three out of the ten major subcommittees of the CCS owed a great deal to the Commonwealth connection.[93]

Three other combined boards of which Canada was initially unaware also emerged from the 'Arcadia' Conference. The Munitions Assignments Board (MAB), operating directly under the CCS, coordinated the allocation of weapons and equipment to various theatres of war. It comprised a Washington component and a subordinate London component that reassigned bulk allocations to European allies and the dominions. The other boards included the Combined Shipping Adjustment Board and the Combined Raw Materials Board. Although Canada made determined efforts to gain entry to the MAB based on its standing as the third greatest producer of munitions among the western allies,[94] it failed to gain American approval. A compromise solution to allow limited Canadian membership on the London component also failed, owing to interdepartmental bickering at Ottawa.[95] In the end, Canada accepted American advice to abandon its quest for membership on the MAB in exchange for representation on the less important and ill-starred Combined Production and Resources Board (CPRB) set up in June 1942.[96] Canada also became a member of the Combined Food Board (CFB), established at the same time as the CPRB without Canadian consultation.[97]

Although Canada was the only nation apart from the United States and Britain to achieve combined board membership, it proved an empty honour. Neither the CPRB nor the CFB was particularly important. Despite 'functionalism,' which should have netted Canada a seat on the MAB,[98] the dominion's martial voice counted for little. Neither did Canada receive much information from the important strategic conferences at Casablanca in January 1943, Washington in May, and Cairo and Teheran in November–December. At the conference held in Quebec City from 14–24 August 1943 Canada acted as host. Churchill's earlier proposal for King and his COS to attend all plenary sessions and for the Canadian COS to attend all plenary meetings of the CCS was vetoed outright by Roosevelt on the grounds that a Canadian presence would provide a precedent for admitting China, Brazil, Mexico, and the other dominions. When Roosevelt apparently informed King that rather than risk potential embarrassment, he would prefer not to come to Canada at all, King wilted. Still, King could record 'that Churchill and Roosevelt being at Quebec, and myself acting as host, will be quite sufficient to make clear that all three are in conference together and will not only satisfy but will please the Canadian feeling, and really be helpful to me personally.'[99] The reality, however, was different. At a Cabinet War Committee meeting on 11 August 1943, attended by Churchill, King stated that his government had accepted that the higher direction of the war was exercised by the British prime minister and the president of the United States.[100]

King's government was thus left to project the best image it could to a public clamouring for a larger Canadian role.[101] Partly in response to calls to get Canadian soldiers into action for reasons of honour (American ground forces were fighting in North Africa) and postwar prestige,[102] and partly to reduce the adverse effect of continued inaction upon troop morale, in 1943 the Canadian government arranged to have the 1st Canadian Infantry Division and 1st Canadian Army Tank Brigade replace British formations slated for the assault on Sicily. The original intent was for them to return from the Mediterranean to disseminate battle experience to the First Canadian Army for the invasion of France; but the erroneous perception that casualties would be lighter in Italy prompted Ottawa to pressure British military authorities into accepting an unwanted Canadian corps for service in the Italian theatre.[103] The ramifications of this blatantly political move were that it forced the resignation of General A.G.L. McNaughton, the commander of the First Canadian Army, and, in turn, relegated that formation to a 'follow-up' as opposed to an assault role in the invasion of Europe.[104] Neither would the Canadian corps in Italy fight a corps battle before the Canadian government began agitating in May 1944 for its early repatriation to the First Canadian Army.[105]

Meanwhile, the circumstances of McNaughton's departure, compared with those surrounding the appointments of generals Dwight Eisenhower, Bernard Montgomery, and Henry Maitland Wilson to high command, prompted several External Affairs mandarins to write a memorandum in early 1944 on the question of Canada's relationship to the supreme direction of the war. Whereas Canada had readily received British opinion in the former case, they pointed out, it had not been consulted in the selection of supreme allied commanders charged with the direction of land, air, and sea operations in which Canadian forces would participate. To correct this situation, they recommended the establishment of a joint staff mission (JSM) in London accredited to Eisenhower's headquarters for purposes of top-level liaison. Although the Canadian COS expressed practical military reservations as to how the JSM would actually work, Roosevelt and Churchill were advised that the Canadian government was considering setting up a JSM in London to serve as a channel of communication between the Canadian COS and the supreme commands in Britain and the Mediterranean. In response, Roosevelt forwarded a JCS comment, on which he had annotated his agreement, that the establishment of a London-based JSM was an Anglo-Canadian affair, and that all communications between the Canadian COS and supreme commanders had still to go through the CCS. Churchill, while welcoming the idea of a JSM, agreed that it should not circumvent the CCS in communicating with supreme commands. Not surprisingly, the commander of the First Canadian Army, who had not been consulted, objected to the JSM's effecting liaison with Eisenhower's headquarters on the grounds that as the senior Canadian commander in the field, he had been charged with this responsibility. None the less, while the JSM provided a valuable link with the British COS, it failed to develop as originally envisioned. The less ideal but more practical idea of having Canadian officers assume staff positions at Allied headquarters was never pursued. As Stacey intimated, however, had military advice been heeded at an earlier stage, a more sensible arrangement could probably have been worked out.[106]

Canada's exclusion from higher Allied planning left the King government in a strategic void.[107] Ottawa received no advance warning of Anglo-American landings in North Africa. Neither was the decision to invade Sicily conveyed to King after the Casablanca conference. Most humiliating of all, the Canadian prime minister was actually roused from his sleep in the early hours of 6 June to be told that the invasion of Normandy had commenced. Churchill had chosen not to share the closely guarded secret of the exact date of D-day. The irony of this situation is that, while Churchill was obviously at fault, King's difficulty was of his own making. His persistent refusal to expand traditional Commonwealth channels of communication for fear of compromising Canadian autonomy ensured the primacy of a personal connection to Churchill with its inherent shortcomings. In accepting the exclusion of his government from the 1943 Quebec conference, King may have also given the British prime minister the impression that he could speak for Canada, as Roosevelt evidently wished him to do. Having failed to project a strategic voice through Commonwealth machinery before the United States had entered the war, Canada was unable to change the situation after being effectively silenced at 'Arcadia.'[108] The dominion, in short, did not change horses midstream during the Second World War; rather, it remained unmounted, struggling ever more frantically to stay afloat in high water.

King's attempt to counterbalance America with Britain, moreover, backfired on the home front. In contrast to his treatment of the British before the war, he inadvertently allowed the Americans to bulldoze their way into Canada. Before long, the Americans had made deep inroads through major, and often dubious, undertakings: the Alaska Highway; the northeast air ferry routes to Britain; the northwest air staging route to Alaska and the Soviet Union; associated northern weather stations; and the CANOL oil distribution system designed to provide oil from Norman Wells for U.S. forces in Alaska and western Canada.[109] By 1942 there were 15,000 Americans in Canada, including over 11,000 troops building the Alaska Highway. Early in 1943 impatient with the progress of the northwest staging route, the Americans pressed for a change in Canadian policy restricting the use of their army engineers. Canada yielded and, by mid-year, 33,000 American army personnel were working in northwest Canada. As might be expected, the scale of the American effort posed a substantial threat to Canadian sovereignty as airbases were constructed and contracts let without reference to Ottawa. In March 1943 a worried King took the unusual step of inviting the British high commissioner, just returned from visiting the Canadian northwest, to assess the American presence. Acting on the suggestion that the Canadian government should rightly be concerned, the War Committee appointed a regular military officer in May as special commissioner for defence projects in the north-west responsible for exercising effective national control over all American activities.[110]

Partly to counter growing American influence in its northwest, Canada in the same year agreed to participate in an operation to recapture the Aleutian island of Kiska. Japanese seizure of Kiska and Attu in June 1942 had alarmed citizens on both sides of the U.S.-Canadian border. Under the terms of ABC-22, Canada had dispatched several RCAF squadrons to Alaska to meet this threat.[111] After a Japanese submarine shelled Estevan Point on Vancouver Island on 20 June, the government additionally deployed excessively large numbers of men and equipment on the Pacific coast to appease frightened voters. This decision was taken against the advice of the COS, who correctly cautioned that Japanese operations in the northeast Pacific were defensive rather than offensive.[112] At the height of this crisis, the CGS, who belonged at the seat of government to provide military advice, went west to take personal command of coastal defences. While he may have decided on his own to take this action, such an unprofessional expedient reflected poorly on Canada's war machinery.[113] Significantly, several days after American and Canadian troops had stormed ashore at Kiska on 15 August 1943, the COS recommended the disbandment of Canada's two coastal defence divisions. As for the 13th Canadian Infantry Brigade's expedition to Kiska, King discovered to his chagrin that the original proposal initiating Canadian participation came through his own creation, the PJBD. More significant symbolically, the brigade was organized along U.S. Army lines and Canadian soldiers fitted with American equipment trained in accordance with U.S. command and staff doctrine. The commanding general of the U.S. Western Defense Command, Lieutenant-General John L. De Witt, even refused initially to allow the Canadian CGS to inspect the brigade to pronounce it fit for action.[114]

Although King increasingly expressed alarm that the Americans intended to take Canada 'out of the orbit of the British Commonwealth of Nations into their own orbit,'[115] he continued rejecting British overtures for closer imperial cooperation. At the only prime ministers conference of the war, at London in May 1944, he complained about more numerous British representatives weakening dominion representation. In terms reminiscent of 1937, he opposed establishing any new Commonwealth machinery or reintroducing older forms like the Committee of Imperial Defence with dominion representation. Instead, he continued to extol the virtues of the 'continuing conference of cabinets' made possible by modern means of communication.[116] King's inflexibility no doubt derived from his yearning to preserve Canadian autonomy for domestic reasons; but as this approach over time had developed into an obsession, it prevented him from fully perceiving the extent to which the still mighty British Empire had declined. In these circumstances, the British had necessarily to be more accommodating of Canadian aspirations than those of the more powerful Americans. Regardless, the effect of King's approach to Commonwealth cooperation placed Canada in the unenviable position of a passive receiver of information and direction during the Second World War.

The one period in which Canada could have gained a strategic voice was that following the fall of France to the Japanese attack on Pearl Harbor and Hong Kong in December 1941. The situation warranted such an initiative, and King's government, having just received a decisive mandate from the Canadian people, would have been ideally suited to act. Had King chosen to support Menzies, Churchill could hardly have denied Canada and Australia representation on a Commonwealth council of war. The plain fact was, however, that King remained more interested in domestic affairs and issues of national prestige than in military matters. Canada's war machinery, in failing to harmonize military strength with diplomatic pretensions, differed markedly from British and American war machinery. The War Committee not only operated with a lack of military knowledge and advice, but it tended generally to overmanage military affairs even after subjecting them to the most excruciatingly detailed examination, often from a domestic perspective. Contrary perhaps to King's original hope, the PJBD did not provide

Canada with additional leverage vis-à-vis either the United States or Great Britain. To his personal surprise and dismay, King also discovered too late the overarching nature of the Roosevelt-Churchill relationship. The Grand Alliance did not need a linchpin, and Canada was left to keep up appearances. In striving for autonomy at all costs in military as well as civilian spheres, without appreciating the subtleties of the former, King ensured for Canada only a tactical role during the Second World War.

NOTES

This work could not have been completed without the generous assistance of the SSHRC.

1 Detailed accounts can be found in C.P. Stacey, *Arms, Men and Governments: The War Policies of Canada, 1939–1945* (Ottawa, 1974), 367–70; idem, *Canada and the Age of Conflict: A History of Canadian External Policies*, Vol. II: *1921–1948: The Mackenzie King Era* (Toronto, 1984), 308–9; James Eayrs, *In Defence of Canada: Appeasement and Rearmament* (Toronto, 1967), 167–72; S.W. Dziuban, *Military Relations between the United States and Canada, 1939–1945* (Washington, DC, 1959), 149–55.
2 Eayrs, *Defence*, 168.
3 Stacey, *Arms*, 368.
4 A Canadian official stated later that the Aluminum Company of Canada had originally proposed and practically organized 'the unfortunate *Nascopie* expedition.' Dziuban, *Military Relations*, 151.
5 Stacey, *Arms*, 368; Eayrs, *Defence*, 168.
6 Stacey, *Arms*, 368. Cf. Dziuban, *Military Relations*, 153.
7 Eayrs, *Defence*, 169; Stacey, *Arms*, 368.
8 Eayrs, *Defence*, 170.
9 Ibid.
10 Stacey, *Arms*, 369.
11 Eayrs, *Defence*, 171; Dziuban, *Military Relations*, 152.
12 J.L. Granatstein, *The Ottawa Men: The Civil Service Mandarins, 1935–1957* (Toronto, 1982), 121–2. The Canadian diplomat Hume Wrong, who later promoted the 'functional principle' as the capstone of his government's foreign policy, was almost ashamed of the way Canada backed into the war. Cf. J.L. Granatstein, 'Hume Wrong's Road to the Functional Principle,' in *Coalition Warfare: An Uneasy Accord*, ed. K.E. Neilson and R.A. Prete (Waterloo, Ont., 1983), 53–77.

13 'Limited liability,' most adroitly advanced by British military theorist B.H. Liddell Hart, presumed the superiority of the defence over the offence and proposed committing only minimal British land forces to the direct assistance of European allies at a critical juncture. This concept exerted a powerful appeal for a variety of reasons, among them the still vivid memories of Great War slaughter, mistrust of the French, interservice rivalry, army unpreparedness for continental operations, an accepted military need to buy time, and Treasury concern for financial and economic stability. John A. English, *The Canadian Army and the Normandy Campaign: A Study of Failure in High Command* (New York, 1991), 22–3, 35. Although the limited liability concept undoubtedly impressed King and his External Affairs advisers, it failed to convince the Canadian military. See, for instance, A.H. Bourne, 'Limited Liability War,' *Canadian Defence Quarterly*, 3(1939), 282–90.

14 On a per capita basis, Canada provided three times as much financial assistance to Britain as did the United States.

15 Except Stacey, upon whose extensive research and work this chapter is largely based; and Adrian Preston in his unfootnoted 'Canada and the Higher Direction of the Second World War, 1939–1945,' *Journal of the Royal United Services Institute*, 110 (February 1965), 28–44.

16 Stacey, *Age of Conflict*, II, ix. Cf. J.L. Granatstein, *Canada's War: The Politics of the Mackenzie King Government, 1939–1945* (Toronto, 1975).

17 Stacey, *Age of Conflict*, II, 275.

18 Ibid., 215–16; on appeasement, see P.M. Kennedy, *The Rise and Fall of Great Powers: Economic Change and Military Conflict from 1500 to 2000* (London, 1989), 409–13.

19 Stacey, *Age of Conflict*, II, 8–14, 31, 173–9, 213–18, 235–6; Granatstein, *Ottawa Men*, 28–39, 62–91. On Skelton's tendency towards neutralism, see Eayrs, *Defence*, 54; Granatstein, 'Hume Wrong,' 67–8.

20 Stacey, *Age of Conflict*, II, 3–56, 65–72, 83–9, 202–11; idem, *Arms*, 89.

21 Stacey, *Age of Conflict*, II, 257; idem, *Arms*, 8–9.

22 Idem, *Arms*, 8–10, 12–13.

23 Idem, *Age of Conflict*, II, 16, 39, 272–3, 537–9; idem, *Arms*, 9–14, 144. News of Polish reverses caused Mackenzie King to observe on 7 September: 'Found Council more favourable to an expeditionary force than I had imagined they would be, and growing feeling that it might become inevitable. I was also surprised to find considerable feeling for conscription or saying nothing against conscription'; idem, *Arms*, 13.

24 Idem, *Age of Conflict*, II, 200, 274; idem, *Arms*, 19–29; F.J. Hatch, *Aerodrome of Democracy: Canada and the British Commonwealth Air Training Plan, 1939–1945* (Ottawa, 1983), 1–26; C.P. Stacey, *Official History of the Canadian Army in the*

Second World War, Vol. I: *Six Years of War: The Army in Canada, Britain and the Pacific* (Ottawa, 1966), 13, 36, 58–61, 65; J.W. Pickersgill, *The Mackenzie King Record*, Vol. I: *1939–1944* (Toronto, 1960), 30, 38–59.

25 Stacey, *Arms*, 81–9.

26 Pickersgill, *Mackenzie King Record*, I, 30, 59; Stacey, *Six Years*, 13, 36, 65; idem, *Age of Conflict*, II, 292–6; idem, *Arms*, 20–9, 252.

27 Stacey, *Arms*, 53, 252–307; idem, *Age of Conflict*, II, 354–6; and W.S. Carter, *Anglo-Canadian Wartime Relations, 1939–1945: RAF Bomber Command and No. 6 (Canadian) Group* (New York, 1991), 21–45, 53, 129–77.

28 Stacey, *Age of Conflict*, II, 276–8; Eayrs, *Defence*, 155–62.

29 'Record of a Visit to United Kingdom of Canadian Minister of National Defence 18 April to 9 May 1940,' Norman Rogers MSS [Queen's University Archives (QUA), Kingston, Ontario].

30 Stacey, *Arms*, 140–5.

31 Stacey, *Age of Conflict*, I, 202–16.

32 Ibid., 275; idem, *Arms*, 140, 211–12.

33 J.L. Granatstein, et al., *Twentieth Century Canada* (Toronto, 1986), 272–3.

34 Stacey, *Age of Conflict*, II, 280–1.

35 Idem, *Arms*, 31–2.

36 Minutes of the Cabinet War Committee Meeting, 14 June 1940, Power MSS [QUA].

37 Stacey, *Arms*, 31–7; idem, *Age of Conflict*, II, 298–9.

38 Idem, *Arms*, 146–8. A British proposal (November 1940) to resurrect the Supreme War Council, with dominion high commissioners and representatives from the exiled governments of Poland, Belgium, Holland, Norway, Greece, Czechoslovakia, and the Free French, was rejected outright by King's government. It added its objection to any postwar security commitments.

39 Minutes of the Cabinet War Committee Meeting, 10 September 1941, Power MSS.

40 Stacey, *Arms*, 146–9; idem, *Conflict*, II, 318; Preston, 'Higher Direction,' 104–8.

41 Stacey, *Arms*, 115; S.P. Huntington, *The Soldier and the State: The Theory and Politics of Civil-Military Relations* (New York, 1957), 433.

42 Peter Gretton, *Former Naval Person: Winston Churchill and the Royal Navy* (London, 1968), 285–6; Huntington, *Soldier*, 320, 323, 327–9.

43 Stacey, *Arms*, 117, 146–7, 154–5, 180.

44 Ibid., 69.

45 The War Committee was the most important of ten cabinet committees. The others were War Finance and Supply, Food Production and Marketing, Fuel

and Power, Shipping and Transportation, Price Control and Labour, Internal Security, Legislation, Public Information, and Demobilization.

46 The unified Department of National Defence, created as a cost-cutting measure in 1922, proved unwieldy by the summer of 1940 and had to be subdivided into separate departments to enhance efficiency.

47 Stacey, *Arms*, 112–22, 139; idem, 'Canadian Leaders of the Second World War,' *Canadian Historical Review*, 1(1985), 69.

48 The Canadian COS Committee, established in January 1939, superseded the Joint Staff Committee set up in 1927. It comprised the chief of the general staff, the chief of the air staff, and the chief of the naval staff, the most senior among them acting as chairman. There were minor changes during the war. Stacey, *Arms*, 69, 117–18, 126–9.

49 Private Secretary of the Minister of National Defence for Air to Chief of the Air Staff, 18 June 1942, Power MSS.

50 Stacey, *Arms*, 71, 99–100, 115, 128–9.

51 J.L. Granatstein and Norman Hillmer, *For Better or for Worse: Canada and the United States to the 1990s* (Toronto, 1991), 105–18.

52 Ibid., 141–2.

53 Dziuban, *Military Relations*, 3.

54 The first visit occurred in secrecy in January 1938, with the Canadian CGS, Major General E.C. Ashton, and the chief of the naval staff, Commodore P.W. Nelles, travelling separately to Washington in civilian clothes. Eayrs, *Defence of Canada*, 180–3.

55 Granatstein and Hillmer, *For Worse*, 103–4, 123–6.

56 Ibid., 125–6, 135–6.

57 Stacey, *Age of Conflict*, II, 308–11; Granatstein and Hillmer, *For Worse*, 136–7. In May 1939 Britain also had conscripted for the first time in peacetime. Canada's NRMA, in fact, created a fractured army that clearly exposed the superficial unity of Canada.

58 A Gallup Poll conducted in May 1941 indicated that 79 per cent of Americans opposed entering the war voluntarily. Roosevelt had also felt obliged to pander to isolationist sentiments in the 1940 election campaign. From 1941 Roosevelt tended to take executive actions that presented Congress with a series of faits accomplis. C. Thorne, *Allies of a Kind: The United States, Britain, and the War against Japan, 1941–1945* (Oxford, 1978), 93.

59 Stacey, *Arms*, 328–32. Churchill's reference to 'our Empire beyond the seas, armed and guarded by the British Fleet ... carry[ing] on the struggle, until, in God's good time, the New world, with all its power and might, steps forth to the rescue and the liberation of the Old' delighted Roosevelt. Yet Churchill commented to King the next day: 'if America continued neutral

and we were overpowered, I cannot tell what policy might be adopted by pro-German administration such as would undoubtedly be set up.' When King relayed this portion of Churchill's message to Roosevelt, the American pronounced it 'alarming and distressing,' but he expressed the hope that Churchill had meant what he said in the Commons. Ibid., 331.

60 See A.J. Marder, *From the Dardanelles to Oran* (London, 1974), 179–88.
61 Minutes of War Cabinet Committee Meeting, 14 June 1940, Power MSS. On the outbreak of war in Europe, Canada requested and obtained the Newfoundland government's approval for the RCAF to overfly the colony and use its airport facilities. The Canadian Joint Staff Committee had raised the issue of the defence of Newfoundland in 1938, but nothing concrete had developed. When the COS again broached the matter in April 1939, the minister's office informed them that he was 'not prepared at the moment, to deal with the question.' Stacey, *Arms*, 92–3, 135, 332.
62 Minutes of the Cabinet War Committee Meeting, 26 July 1940, Power MSS.
63 Anglo–American service liaison had been established as early as December 1937. Dziuban, *Military Relations*, 20; Thorne, *Allies*, 39. In August 1940 Roosevelt dispatched military representatives to Britain to discuss plans for cooperation in the event America entered the war. E.B. Potter and C.W. Nimitz, *Sea Power: A Naval History* (Englewood Cliffs, NJ, 1960), 549.
64 Stacey, *Arms*, 332–8; idem, *Conflict*, II, 231, 311.
65 Canada published it in its Treaty Series, incorporating it in an order-in-council; Roosevelt saw it as an executive arrangement not subject to Senate ratification.
66 C.P. Stacey, 'The Turning Point: Canadian-American Relations during the Roosevelt-King Era,' *Canada: An Historical Magazine*, 1(1973), 1–9.
67 Stacey, *Arms*, 75, 342–8.
68 Ibid., 349.
69 Potter and Nimitz, *Sea Power*, 548.
70 The full title of ABC-1 was 'United States-British Staff Conversations, Report.' Dziuban, *Military Relations*, 103; Thorne, *Allies of a Kind*, 77–8; Arthur Bryant, *The Turn of the Tide 1939–43: A Study Based on the Diaries and Autobiographical Notes of Field Marshal the Viscount Alanbrooke, K.G., O.M.* (London, 1957), 250.
71 J.P. Lash, *Roosevelt and Churchill 1939–1941: The Partnership that Saved the West* (New York, 1976), 21–4, 34, 51, 62; Thorne, *Allies of a Kind*, 77–8, 96, 111–13, 119; E.A. Cohen, 'Churchill and Coalition Strategy in World War II,' in *Grand Strategies in War and Peace*, ed. P.M. Kennedy (New Haven, CT, 1991), 43–67. Cf. R.E. Sherwood, *The White House Papers of Harry Hopkins* (London, 1948), Vol. I, 127–8, 142.

72 The 'C' in ABC did not stand for Canada. It probably stood for 'conversations,' 'conference,' or even 'Commonwealth.' Dziuban, *Military Relations*, 103.

73 Minutes of the Cabinet War Committee Meeting, 2 and 29 October 1941, Power MSS; Stacey, *Arms*, 159–60, 354–47. At the time of the 'Montreal Revise,' American military members of the PJBD had accepted the exchange of army and air force missions. Worried that this action might set a precedent for similar missions by other 'British Dominions and ... American Republics,' the State Department suggested, instead, the establishment of permanent offices in Washington for the Canadian military members of the PJBD. Ibid., 355.

74 Dziuban, *Military Relations*, 106.

75 Under this arrangement, the RCN would not have been able to move a warship from the west to the east coast without American authorization. Nor would the army have been able to move a field unit from Winnipeg to Quebec. Stacey, *Arms*, 354.

76 Minutes of the Cabinet War Committee Meeting, 27 May 1941, Power MSS.

77 The War Cabinet approved ABC-22 on 15 October 1941. Ibid., 15 October 1941; Stacey, *Arms*, 349–54.

78 The Canadian COS made strong representations concerning Canada's vital interest in Newfoundland. Their counsel was ineffectual, since the Americans remained adamant in demanding broad military operational power, including legal jurisdiction over British subjects; however, the Americans agreed to respect Canadian interests. Stacey, *Arms*, 358–60.

79 King related that the governor of Newfoundland had urged Canada to assert its interests in Newfoundland vis-à-vis the United States. Minutes of the Cabinet War Committee Meeting, 29 October 1941, Power MSS.

80 Stacey, *Arms*, 129, 135, 344–5, 348, 357–67; Minutes of the Cabinet War Committee Meeting, 9 October 1941, Power MSS.

81 Minutes of the Cabinet War Committee Meeting, 24 June 1941, Power MSS.

82 Here Roosevelt and King issued the 'Hyde Park Declaration': the United States and Canada would coordinate their defence production efforts on the basis of each one's providing the other with the materiel that it was best able to produce. See Granatstein and Hillmer, *For Worse*, 145–8; Robert Bothwell, '"Who's Paying for Anything These days?" War Production in Canada, 1939–1945,' in *Canada's Defence: Perspectives on Policy in the Twentieth Century*, ed. B.D. Hunt and R.G. Haycock (Toronto, 1993), 125–6.

83 Minutes of the Cabinet War Committee Meeting, 13 August, 10 September 1941, Power MSS.

84 Stacey, *Arms*, 149–51; Minutes of the Cabinet War Committee Meeting, 10 September 1941, Power MSS.

85 W.G.D. Lund, 'The Royal Canadian Navy's Quest for Autonomy in the North West Atlantic: 1941–43,' in *The RCN in Retrospect, 1910–1968*, ed. J.A. Boutilier (Vancouver, 1982), 138–57; Stacey, *Arms*, 312–14; idem, *Age of Conflict*, II, 354–5.

86 Stacey, *Arms*, 370–3; idem, *Age of Conflict*, II, 302–6; Granatstein, *Ottawa Men*, 96–106; Granatstein and Hillmer, *For Worse*, 149–50; Sherwood, *Hopkins*, I, 456–66; Thorne, *Allies of a Kind*, 108–9.

87 A.J.P. Taylor, *The Origins of the Second World War* (London, 1963), 336.

88 Sherwood, *Hopkins*, I, 467.

89 Huntington, *Soldier*, 317–29, 337.

90 The British Joint Staff Mission comprised the British Admiralty delegation, the RAF delegation, and the British army staff. From July 1942 Leahy acted as chairman of the JCS and provided naval balance. Alex Danchev, *Very Special Relationship: Field Marshal Sir John Dill and the Anglo-American Alliance 1941–44* (London, 1986), 10, 12–16, 19–25, 58; Stacey, *Arms*, 161–2.

91 Churchill reputedly developed a 'morbid fear' that the CCS would gang up on him. Danchev, *Dill*, 22.

92 Minutes of the Cabinet War Committee Meeting, 14 January 1942, Power MSS.

93 Ibid., 11 March, 4 June 1942; Stacey, *Arms*, 162–7, 354–7. Canada was the only dominion represented on the Combined Shipbuilding Subcommittee. It was also represented on the Combined Communications Board and the Combined Meteorological Subcommittee. The Combined Shipbuilding Subcommittee, however, comprised six American and six British and Canadian members; the Combined Communications Board was similarly composed of six American representatives and six from the United Kingdom, Canada, Australia, and New Zealand.

94 Canada produced five times as many munitions as Australia, India, South Africa, and New Zealand combined, but it accounted for only 5 per cent of the small arms and other infantry weapons produced by the United States, Britain, and Canada. In comparison, the British produced 34 per cent and the Americans 62 per cent. Canada did produce 20 per cent of motor vehicles.

95 Minutes of the Cabinet War Committee Meeting, 11 March, 11 June, 1, 15, 7 July, 19 August, 2 September 1944, Power MSS.

96 King reported that Roosevelt had agreed to Canada's having full representation on the MAB; Harry Hopkins thought otherwise: that Canada should forgo the MAB for the CPRB. Ibid., 29 April 1942. Roosevelt suggested that

American representatives on the CPRB would speak for North America, including Canada; Minutes of the Cabinet War Committee Meeting, 11 June 1942, Power MSS.

97 Stacey, *Arms*, 162, 167–78; Danchev, *Dill*, 82–3.

98 'Functionalism' postulated that a country's voice should be commensurate with its contribution to the war effort and its influence greatest in those areas where it is most directly concerned. Cf. Granatstein, *Ottawa Men*, 93, 126–33; idem, 'Hume Wrong's Road.'

99 Stacey, *Arms*, 182.

100 Minutes of the Cabinet War Committee Meeting, 11 August 1943, Power MSS; Stacey, *Arms*, 178–84; idem, *Age of Conflict*, II, 326–34, 337–8.

101 On 17 December 1941 the Manitoba legislature passed a resolution demanding conscription for overseas service. Stacey, *Arms*, 46, 400. King reacted by calling a national plebiscite in which he asked to be released from his earlier promise not to introduce such conscription. Though he won his release handily, Quebec's disenchantment was such that he then adopted the policy of 'not necessarily conscription, but conscription if necessary.' King stood his ground or dragged his feet on this issue, depending on one's point of view, until the autumn of 1944, when critical troop shortages in fighting formations could no longer be met by the volunteer system. Faced with the prospect of either ordering conscripts overseas or seeing his government break up, he chose the former.

102 External Affairs officials argued in January 1943 that Canada's influence in the postwar world would suffer if the nation made no demonstrable contribution to victory. Stacey, *Arms*, 42, 229.

103 Fear that casualties would create a requirement for overseas conscription caused King to write: 'The more our men participate in the campaign in Italy, the fewer there are likely to be who will be involved in the crossing of the Channel, which, as Churchill says, will be a very tough business.' Ibid., 237.

104 Minutes of the Cabinet War Committee Meeting, 19 August 1942, Power MSS.

105 G.W.L. Nicholson, *The Canadians in Italy* (Ottawa, 1956), 656–60; English, *Normandy Campaign*, 143–53, 181–2.

106 Stacey, *Arms*, 185–96.

107 Minutes of the Cabinet War Committee Meeting, 25 March 1943, Power MSS.

108 Stacey, *Arms*, 153–4, 180–1, 557–9; idem, *Six Years*, 494–505; idem, *Age of Conflict*, I, 334.

109 Both the RCAF and the RAF had serious reservations about the practicabil-

ity of northeast air ferry routes to Europe: Minutes of the Cabinet War Committee Meeting, 3 June 1942, Power MSS. So did the CCS: Stacey, *Arms*, 377.

110 Granatstein and Hillmer, *For Worse*, 153–6.

111 The Japanese thrust towards the Aleutians was a diversionary effort in support of the Midway operation fought on 4 June. USN intelligence had broken Japanese codes and provided early warning of these naval deployments. Stacey, *Arms*, 48.

112 Minutes of the Cabinet War Committee Meeting, 24 June 1942, Power MSS. Mackenzie King personally 'emphasized the danger of under-estimating the strength of Japanese operations on the Pacific Coast.' Ibid., 4 June 1942. This action contrasted sharply with Churchill's brave and sensible decision to risk uncovering Britain and dispatch the bulk of the British army to fight in the Middle East.

113 See ibid., 20 February, 3, 4 June 1942. Cf. J.L. Granatstein, *The Generals: The Canadian Army's Commanders in the Second World War* (Toronto, 1993), 225–6.

114 Stacey, *Arms*, 47–8, 116, 133–4, 388–91, 411; idem, *Six Years*, 173–5, 183–6; Galen Perras, 'Canada as Military Partner: Alliance Politics and the Campaign To Recapture the Aleutian Island of Kiska,' *Journal of Military History*, 3(1992), 423–54. The landing at Kiska was unopposed.

115 Stacey, *Arms*, 387.

116 Ibid., 155–6; idem, *Age of Conflict*, II, 363–7.

6

From World War to Cold War: Cooperation and Competition in the North Atlantic Triangle, 1945–1949

LAWRENCE ARONSEN

At the end of the Second World War, Canada, Great Britain, and the United States were in basic agreement on the matter of the new political order. These powers understood that their wartime 'special relationship' did not extend to the world at large, and that if independent nation-states continued as the main actors in the international arena, some kind of formal organization would be necessary in the years ahead to resolve inevitable tensions and hostilities.[1] It was also apparent that steps taken at the end of the war to promote postwar security would likely determine the course of history for several years to come. Middle powers like Canada were excluded from the earliest discussions about the creation of the United Nations (UN), a new international organization designed to replace the League of Nations. By 1944 the British and the Americans, supported by the Canadians, agreed on a General Assembly whose membership was open to all countries, a Security Council that extended permanent positions to the Great Powers and allowed for electing non-permanent representatives from the General Assembly, a Secretariat, and an International Court of Justice. Beyond these general principles, each country held differing views about what authority the UN should have on issues related to the vital interests of the Great Powers and the priorities of social and economic functions as means to promote international stability. National security, the ideology of liberal internationalism, and the personalities of President Franklin Roosevelt and of the prime ministers, William Lyon Mackenzie King of Canada and Winston Churchill of Great Britain, were the key determinants of their respective policies towards international organization.

Considerable support for the UN existed in the United States, generated by a resurgence of the Wilsonian ideology of liberal internationalism within the State Department, the media, and private-interest groups.[2] The movement reached its peak by 1945 and the cornerstone of its appeal for the American public lay in the vision of a revitalised League of Nations. American indifference to the League during the inter-war period had been a major cause of that organization's ineffectiveness in dealing with aggression. Liberal internationalists were therefore moti-vated by a reading of what has been described as the 'lessons of the past' and a vague sense of guilt that the United States had not lived up to its responsibilities. These latter-day Wilsonians recognized that in the pro-cess of creating a viable international organization the United States would have to surrender some of its sovereignty.[3] But in the end, argued the internationalists, the United States would gain greater national secu-rity while establishing itself as the world's foremost advocate of the rule of law and morality in the conduct of affairs among nations.[4]

Individual leaders played a part in the formation of the UN, and nobody was more important than Roosevelt. The president's basic premise about postwar collective security was that the world should avoid regional and formal alliances and spheres of influence and rely primarily on an all-inclusive international organization. Roosevelt was neither an advocate of one-world government nor an uncritical sup-porter of the Wilsonian idea of internationalism. He originally envi-sioned a world dominated by only two superpowers – the United States and Great Britain. This view was later expanded to include the Soviet Union and China, which formed the core of his concept of the 'four policemen.' While acknowledging the membership of all nations, the president believed that the only workable system of collective security would be one dominated by the Great Powers, each with the right to exercise the veto over the demands of lesser powers.[5]

A less charitable interpretation suggests that the United States as a capitalist society was motivated by the need to make the world safe for trade and investment and therefore 'sought to advance its national inter-ests in the guise of performing erstwhile international obligations.'[6] It is argued that America's pursuit of internationalism served only the inter-ests of corporations at home and was designed to integrate other coun-tries into a hierarchical three-tiered dependency mould.[7] American isolationists, however, offered several criticisms at the time about how involvement in international organizations like the UN would compro-mise American interests rather than advance them. This view also over-looks the concessions the United States made to Britain and Canada in the formulation of the Charter at the San Francisco Conference.

Great Britain was less influenced by domestic considerations than was the United States in the creation of UN policy. There is a striking absence of any great debate in the British experience between isolationists and internationalists, or of pressure from public opinion and the media to act decisively to implement a new system of collective security. The views of the Labour party opposition were inconsequential to Conservative policy on this issue. Liberal internationalism or the Wilsonian version of it was never part of the political culture or debates about Britain's proper role in the world. Policy was generally determined by Britain's security requirements in the European context, its desire to hold on to as much of the empire as was politically possible, and a deep sense that Britain was entering an uncertain period and that in all likelihood its position in relation to other powers was in decline. This approach to foreign policy transcended changing Conservative and Labour governments from 1945 to 1951.[8]

It was Churchill who defined and implemented British policy from Dumbarton Oaks to the final negotiation of the Charter in San Francisco. In so doing he played a role similar to that of Roosevelt, who was guiding American policy towards the UN. Churchill's scepticism of international organization, however, combined with a lack of concern for understanding the technical details of the plans for the new world organization meant that much of the day-to-day negotiations leading up to the San Francisco Conference were left in the hands of secondary figures from the Foreign Office.[9]

The prime minister's strongly stated opinions about the postwar collective security system overlapped with those of the United States. It was less out of conviction than out of necessity, however, that Churchill agreed with Roosevelt about the organization of the General Assembly, Great Power domination of the Security Council, and the use of the veto. Ultimately it was a clear calculation of British interests that led Churchill to follow the American diplomatic initiatives. The prime minister believed that supporting the United States in its efforts to promote international organization was a means of ensuring American participation in European affairs after the war.[10] Britain would not have the capability to maintain the balance of power in Europe if the United States returned to isolationism after the war. The British believed, moreover, that by 'going along' with the Americans they would have a greater chance of securing financial assistance to facilitate the postwar economic recovery, to maintain its own status as a near Great Power in Europe, and perhaps hold on to at least part of the empire.[11]

There were some significant but not well-publicized differences between the two nations leading up to the final signing of the Charter in October 1945. The British were less sanguine than the Americans about the inclusion of China as a permanent member of the Security Council or the future effectiveness of the UN in resolving disputes with the Soviet Union. In an effort to promote Great Power unity, the United States acknowledged some of the concerns of its London ally, especially on the issue of Commonwealth representation in the Security Council beyond the single vote held by Britain. The United States conceded changes by making provisions for up to six non-permanent members, one of which at any given time would likely be a Commonwealth member. Furthermore, the United States deferred to British requests for flexibility in the Charter to allow for regional alliances as reflected in the drafting of Article 51 at the San Francisco Conference.[12]

The British, however much they preferred to cultivate the theme of the 'special relationship' that existed between their country and the United States, quickly recognized its limitations by the time of the San Francisco Conference. Two major issues produced sharp disagreements. First, the Churchill government was alarmed by the American proposal to include within the Charter a substantive 'human rights' clause. This addition was summarily rejected by the British on the grounds that it opened up opportunities for compromising national sovereignty and that it would prove difficult to take collective action to enforce. More importantly, if a 'human rights' clause could be enforced by sanctions or diplomatic pressure, it would seriously undermine the control of colonial subjects in Africa and Asia. The British were particularly concerned about Roosevelt's Yalta proposal to use the UN to implement a trusteeship to administer former enemy territories; in Churchill's mind these territories potentially included the remaining colonies within the empire. Upon being informed of the American report on trusteeships, Churchill refused to allow 'thrusting interfering fingers,' into the running of the empire.[13] Roosevelt, who did indeed consider the idea of using the offices of the UN to promote decolonization, candidly admitted: 'we will have more trouble with Great Britain after the war than we are having with Germany now.' In the end, however, the trusteeship proposal was narrowly defined to apply to territories formerly under the control of the Axis bloc.[14]

Canada did not play a central role in the early planning of the postwar collective security system. Although the other North Atlantic triangle allies kept their junior partner informed, Canada was not invited to the

Dumbarton Oaks conference and had only a modest impact on the drafting of the final charter at the San Francisco conference.[15] Given Canada's status as a middle power, its greatest influence was in the drafting of articles related to the interests of that particular group of countries. The dominion's most notable successes were in the drafting of Article 23 (the inclusion of six non-permanent members of the Security Council) and Article 44 (the requirement that countries who were not sitting on the Security Council be allowed to participate in council discussions if their troops were involved in peacekeeping duties).

Within the North Atlantic triangle the Canadian government generally leaned towards the American position and on several occasions expressed reservations about the British approach to postwar collective security. Canadian officials were particularly concerned with Churchill's emphasis on regional alliances and his idea that all the Commonwealth countries be represented only by Great Britain. Some External Affairs officials viewed Britain as a declining, reactionary power unwilling to give up the empire and implement social reforms at home. If Britain continued on its destructive course, it was conceivable that Canada some day would emerge as the leader of the Commonwealth nations.[16] But whatever negative views the Canadians had, they did not publicly offer their criticism of the British position at the San Francisco Conference, as did the New Zealanders and Australians. Instead, the Canadians always put the interest of creating a viable UN organization, which to succeed required the cooperation of the Great Powers, ahead of any excessively idealistic visions of a new world order based on law and morality.

Despite American indifference to Canadian requests for inclusion in the Dumbarton Oaks conference and a place on the planning boards of key organizations such as the UN Relief and Rehabilitation Committee, Canada worked much more closely with the United States than with Britain. These closer ties on matters related to creating the UN reflected similar interests, ideology, and personal views of key government officials. Mackenzie King remained sceptical of the American presence in the Canadian north during the Second World War, but rising stars in External Affairs like Lester Pearson and Louis St Laurent were less cautious about the Americans. After working with the Washington officials on the Food and Agriculture Organization and the International Civil Aviation Organization, the Canadians concluded that the American commitment to the principle of international organization, however flawed, was greater than that of any other power.[17]

Canada's shift to liberal internationalism correlated with its status as a rising middle power with an expanding export-oriented economy. From Ottawa's perspective, international organization would establish rules and regulations that in the end would favour countries of Canada's size, especially in their relations with Great Powers. A UN created largely under the direction of State Department officials, even with several shortcomings, would at least ensure that America did not return to isolationism, as it had after the First World War. On economic matters involving the UN, John Holmes writes that 'self-interest and internationalist convictions led both Americans and Canadians to support measures to open the clogged channels of trade and finance.'[18] It was towards this end that Canada and the United States became the leading proponents of the UN Economic and Social Council (UNESOC). Canada agreed with the United States that economic problems were a major obstacle to maintaining peace and that the Security Council should look after only matters of the most pressing significance. One of the first tasks of UNESOC was to sponsor preliminary trade talks between wartime allies and draft a proposal for a new international trade organization.[19]

The North Atlantic allies believed that the UN would be best able to resolve immediate political crises, and for long-term stability to prevail, the highest priority should be given to reconstructing and stabilizing the world capitalist economy. Among the three countries there was a basic consensus about the new economic realities of the postwar world: that the war had strengthened America's economic position to the point that no other combination of countries was its equal; that the United States would have to take the lead in reconstructing the postwar world economy, and a return to economic nationalism of the interwar period would be folly; and that the best way to improve the world economy was to allow each country to specialize in what it produced best and create an open door for trade and investment. The new trading and financial system would require adjustments to reflect the specific interests of each country.

Each country's contribution to the new world economic order was determined by a particular combination of ideology, interests, and personalities. Within the State and Commerce departments the ideology of the 'open door' – the liberalization of international trade and investment – came to dominate the foreign economic policy of the Roosevelt and Truman administrations. Outside the executive branch these views were widely supported in the American media, academic circles, and those larger corporations with international interests. Yet despite the firm resolve of American presidents to pursue the agenda of economic internationalism, the division of powers outlined in the American Constitution allowed for a Congress less committed to the new international economic order to have considerable input into the formulation and implementation of foreign economic policy.[20]

The idea that an 'open door' for trade and investment would lead to 'peace and prosperity' was elaborated on by Harry S. Truman. 'A durable peace,' noted the American president, 'cannot be built on an economic foundation of exclusive blocs, discriminatory policies, prohibitive barriers, autarchy, and economic warfare.'[21] The president's views were a restatement of classical liberal theory about the ideal conditions under which nation-states could pursue their economic interests. Each country would freely compete with others bound by commonly accepted rules and regulations. The role of the United States was to be a catalyst to bring about the proper conditions through the creation of organizations like the Bretton Woods system and the General Agreement on Trade and Tariffs. In the end, all countries would have more productive economies, they would be economically interdependent, and peace and prosperity would prevail.[22]

Historians have debated what purposes this new 'open door' economic ideology served. Left-revisionists, for example, have argued that the survival of the American capitalist economy was dependent on foreign economic expansion. This expansion was essentially a zero-sum game in that it benefited the United States at the expense of less developed countries. After the Second World War the United States, unlike any other country, was able to dominate export markets, dictate the terms of investment, and extract raw materials at favourable prices. Less economically developed countries or those countries that had suffered wartime damages to their industries had to buy manufactured goods at high American prices given the absence of foreign competition.[23]

Neo-realist historians, on the other hand, have suggested that the new economic policy served the economic interests of all the members of the capitalist bloc as well as specific American geopolitical/strategic objectives. From this perspective, the Truman administration defined as the immediate postwar national security objective the economic reconstruction of western Europe and East Asia, hoping thereby to avoid a return to the instability of the 1930s which had set the stage for the Second World War. It was only under such conditions of international 'peace and prosperity' that the United States would be able to keep its military expenditures to a minimum and rely on the UN Security Council in the event of an international emergency. With the onset of the Cold War by 1947, the objective of American foreign trade and investment policy shifted to the containment of the expansionist Communist bloc. Neo-realist historians acknowledge that on some occasions national security policy overlapped with specific corporate interests, but they find that ultimately the continued survival of the liberal capitalist nations transcended all other concerns during the early Cold War crises.[24]

In contrast to the situation in the United States, postwar British governments were much more divided about the prospects of economic internationalism. Within the Conservative party, 'old-line Tories' believed that American multilateralism would cause severe economic dislocations within the empire. They favoured a postwar economic order built on extending imperial preferences on a bilateral basis with sterling as the main currency. Representing the interests of the British Federation of Industries and the London Chamber of Commerce, these critics also expressed scepticism about the ability of war-damaged British industry to compete favourably with American manufacturing and technology.[25]

The left wing of the Labour party, led by Emmanuel Shinwell and Aneurin Bevan, was equally critical. They warned that an 'American imposed capitalist world order' would restrict British trade practices like the letting of large-volume import contracts by government agencies. More important, under the new economic order Britain would be forced to accept convertibility of the pound. If the pound weakened in relation to the dollar, as it did in 1946 and 1947, the British would be forced to restrict imports or cut back domestic spending on welfare state programs.[26] Despite criticism from within their parties, the governments of Churchill and Clement Attlee, his socialist successor, espoused the principles of economic internationalism, but not to the same degree as the Truman administration or for quite the same reasons. Liberal internationalist ideology was less important to London economic planners than a calculation of the political and strategic advantages that cooperation with the United States would bring. The British, whether Tory or Labour, were always 'economic realists' to the extent that they recognized the decline of the British economy because of the war and the preeminent position occupied by the United States. A remarkable degree of agreement existed between the reform wing Tories and the trade unionist wing of the Labour party on the need for Britain to accept a new international order with international controls on trade barriers, payments, and currency valuations. This consensus on foreign economic policy in part reflected the influence of Lord Keynes, who warned the incoming Labour government of an impending 'financial Dunkirk' if aid from the United States was not immediately forthcoming.[27]

In addition, future long-term pressures encouraged cooperation. It was unrealistic to expect, for example, that the postwar welfare state could be financed simply by implementing a more progressive income tax and that the success of the social democratic experiment would rest primarily on continued expansion of foreign trade. The Bevan socialists, much to their credit, saw the retreat into empire protectionism as impeding trade and reducing economic growth. Also, the Labour government in 1945, like its Conservative predecessor, recognized the need to compromise British foreign economic policy in order to secure American assistance in the growing confrontation with the Soviet Union.[28]

The Labour party recognized the inevitability of the new multilateral trading system but did everything possible to push for British interests. Ideally, from the democratic socialist perspective, multilateralism would work properly only in an international environment of centrally planned economies. Given an imperfect world of socialist and traditional capitalist nations, however, the Labour party settled for much less. Specifically, the British preference in the difficult reconversion period after the war was that the United States should commit itself to maintaining the currency reserves of its foreign trading partners. It would also be helpful if the United States pushed for horizontal tariff reductions that would be implemented simultaneously by all participating countries.[29] Much to the dismay of the Attlee government, little progress was made on these matters in 1945 and 1946.

From 1945 to 1949 several economic issues preoccupied Canadian foreign policy officials, including monetary and exchange policy, international investment, commerce, commodities exchange, control of cartels, and international labour standards. Like the Americans, the Canadians had a strong ideological conviction about the connection between 'peace and prosperity' and the creation of a viable international trading system. The Canadian approach to foreign economic policy was nicely summarized by the reconstruction minister, C.D. Howe, in the 1945 White Paper on Employment and Income: 'International security and freedom from threat of war are the first objects of collaboration and are essential prerequisites of international prosperity.' It was towards this end that the government 'pressed and is continuing to press actively for a wide collaboration in the reciprocal reduction and removal of trade barriers.'[30]

The first step was to create an international economic organization comparable to the UN and comprising the same members in which all would agree to the reduction of tariffs and other discriminatory measures standing in the way of maximized trade. But unable strictly to follow the multilateralist principles required of this new commercial system, Canada found itself resorting to bilateral agreements that did not meet the optimistic expectations it had had in 1945. Historic ties with the British Empire and unforeseen balance of payments difficulties dictated that throughout much of the postwar period Canada should follow a course of pragmatism and compromise in its pursuit of national economic interests.

As a member of the dollar bloc, Canada had to balance its traditional ties with Great Britain and the sterling bloc with the constantly shifting commercial policies of the United States. The importance of economic ties with Great Britain was reflected in the fact that over 50 per cent of Canada's prewar trade was tied to the sterling bloc. For much of the first half of the twentieth century, Canadian prosperity depended on maintaining an export surplus with Great Britain; this favourable set of circumstances allowed Ottawa to convert its surplus pounds sterling into dollars to finance the trade deficit with the United States.[31] To help in the restoration of postwar commercial equilibrium within the North Atlantic triangle, Ottawa officials extended a $1.25 billion loan to Britain, cancelled a debt in excess of $400 million incurred under the British Commonwealth Air Training Plan, and negotiated a wheat export agreement below market value. To maintain diplomatic harmony within the North Atlantic triangle, Canadian officials on occasion attempted to moderate trade disputes between Great Britain and the United States.

The source of Canada's strongly held convictions about the need for expanded postwar trade lay in certain 'lessons from the past' about the consequences of the Great Depression. Ottawa officials, as did their American counterparts, grounded ideological convictions in a practical consideration of economic self-interest that reflected the impact of the Second World War on the national economy. 'In order to maintain full employment in this country,' C.D. Howe reminded his fellow citizens, 'Canada had to contribute fully to every international (economic) arrangement.'[32]

The extensive diversification and expansion of the economy that occurred from 1939 to 1945 was described by a Bank of Nova Scotia study as 'Canada's second industrial revolution.'[33] Growth in industrial output imposed new pressures on the Canadian government to expand markets abroad. Over 5,000 new manufacturing plants were built across

Canada, and the total value of industrial production more than doubled from $3.4 billion to $8.25 billion. Given this unprecedented expansion, 'the Canadian economy is more dependent on international trade than any other nation,' observed Brooke Claxton, an adviser to the prime minister. 'Foreign trade accounted for 25% of our income before the war and today it must account for 35% ... The world cannot have too much trade.'[34] American exports, by contrast, had varied from 4 per cent to 12 per cent as a percentage of GNP throughout the twentieth century.[35]

A 'special relationship' on postwar economic issues developed between Canada and the United States which in several respects separated the two countries from their common British ally. Washington officials were willing to extend special concessions to Canada for several reasons. Improved trade relations with Canada meant new opportunities for the hundreds of American corporations that had located north of the border since the 1920s. In the air-atomic age Canada was singled out by American national security planners for its strategic geographic location and its willingness to coordinate defence policies through the Permanent Joint Board of Defence (PJBD) and the Military Cooperation Committee (MCC). Also appreciated were Ottawa's efforts to provide strategic resources and industrial defence production to America's rearmament program after 1947. Canada emerged from the war as the United States's strongest supporter of the new multilateral order. On this point one State Department official observed that 'there appears to be a clear community of interests between Canada and the United States in the broad field of international economic relations.' He therefore recommended to the secretary of state that 'in formulating postwar economic policies, close and continuous consultation with our best trading customer appears essential.'[36]

In May 1945 the two countries exchanged diplomatic notes that outlined the general principles for coordinating their respective demobilizations and economic reconversions.[37] To conserve key materials, such as high-grade steel and industrial equipment required in the conversion to peacetime production, the United States imposed export controls. Canada received an AA-4 priority rating similar to that given to the largest American industries, however, which allowed it to continue importing scarce materials on the same basis as it had done during the war. Provisions were also made to help the dominion with the disposal of surplus wartime stores arising from orders placed by the War Production Board before the war ended. Owing to its weaker economic position and the dangerous effects of the insatiable demand and more dynamic price structure of its neighbour to the south, Canada was allowed to maintain controls on the export of key commodities. The State Department privately concluded that the provisions of the two diplomatic notes 'constitute an extremely valuable concession to Canadian industry ... and it is unfortunate that we are not prepared at this moment with specific requests for concessions from Canada.'[38]

America was not always as cooperative in its approach to Great Britain's economic conversion. Throughout the last year of the war the United States disallowed British use of lend-lease materials for use in manufacturing; this restriction could have been a means of strengthening gold and dollar reserves and made for an easier transition to a peacetime economy. The British were not consulted before the abrupt cancellation of the lend-lease program in August 1945. Financial aid to compensate for the loss of lend-lease was also unsatisfactory to the British. Although the United States agreed to extend a $3.75 billion loan in 1946, it was much less than the $3 billion grant and $5 billion loan that London officials were expecting. Except for some very tentative plans discussed in 1944, the United States and Britain for the most part did not coordinate their foreign trade policies to accommodate the shift from defence to civilian production reduction that occurred in 1945–6.[39]

Several other economic issues contributed to the decline of the 'special relationship' between Great Britain and the United States. Throughout 1946 and 1947 the Attlee government firmly rejected American efforts to coordinate the British recovery program with the commercial and financial policies of the western European allies. Moreover, Washington officials increasingly came to resent the Labour government's encouragement of the German labour union movement and imposition of statist economic policies in its German occupation zone.[40] The 1947 International Trade Organization / GATT negotiations brought further tension when the British made it clear that they were unwilling to lower the number of imperial preferences, particularly on items that traded in large volume. Multilateral negotiations were severely strained at times, and it was only with some difficulty that compromises were reached on the practice of state trading, the adoption of subsidies, and the use of safeguards to remedy balance-of-payments problems. In the end, concessions and compromises almost cancelled virtually any benefits the new trading order would bring to the western allies. In contrast, British interests, particularly in maintaining the sterling bloc, were well served to the extent that historian Richard Gardner concluded that the new GATT system provided 'little practical benefit' to American trade.[41]

Canadian officials were agreeable to the outcome of the negotiations in Geneva, but they quickly became disillusioned with further trade talks in Havana, Torquay, and Annecy from 1947 to 1949. During the course of these negotiations Ottawa officials expressed impatience with the 'foot-dragging' of the British representatives. Dana Wilgress, the chief Canadian negotiator, commented that 'the United Kingdom has secured the unenviable reputation of being the most backward of all participants in the granting of tariff concessions.' The Americans, on the other hand, sought only 'modest concessions,' enough to mollify public demand for the recognition of at least some American interests.[42]

Such complaints were added to a list of Canadian trade disputes with Great Britain. Despite the generous terms of a 1946 $1.25 billion loan, the British did not respect the seriousness of the Canadian dollar shortages in the spring of 1947 and were reluctant to reschedule drawing on the loan. Later that year a British food mission travelled to Ottawa and according to one secret memo, was prepared to use strong-arm tactics, such as breaking long-term trade contracts to reduce Canadian agricultural and timber imports.[43] Ottawa officials were particularly disappointed when the Labour government negotiated trade agreements for Polish bacon, Scandinavian timber, and Russian canned salmon; all were items traditionally imported from the Canadian west.

Canada's shift to a 'special economic relationship' with the United States was dictated by circumstance and necessity rather than any preconceived continentalist convictions about weakening traditional cultural and economic ties with Britain.[44] By 1947 Canada was faced with several unexpected developments which led to a serious balance of payments crisis. The loan of 1946 paid in currency tied to the American dollar contributed to a rapid decline in Canada's gold and dollar reserves. The problem was complicated the next year, when the British withdrew from convertibility, thereby eliminating an important source of hard currency. At the same time Canadian imports from the United States rapidly increased, in part because the British were unable to offer a wide range of products that were acceptable to the Canadian consumer. These developments set the stage for a fundamental restructuring of the North Atlantic economic triangle. The solution to the balance-of-payments crisis was to seek closer bilateral economic arrangements with the United States: the 1947–8 Customs Union negotiations, an increase in Canadian resource exports to the United States, and the implementation of a policy to encourage more American capital investment.[45]

Within two years of the Second World War, the Grand Alliance had virtually disintegrated, only to be replaced by a bipolar struggle between the western capitalist countries and the Communist bloc states led by the Soviet Union. Expectations for continued international cooperation through the UN proved to be unrealistic, as did the American dream of a peaceful, interdependent world tied together by trade and investment. The threat posed by the expansion of Soviet power into the Middle East and eastern Europe marked the beginning of a new chapter of economic and military cooperation between the North Atlantic allies. Great Britain was the first of the North Atlantic allies to recognize the danger of the Soviet-sponsored coups in eastern Europe, the effect of Moscow's control of the Communist movements in France and Italy, Russian pressure on Turkey to extend concessions on the Dardanelles, and the continued presence of the Red Army in northern Iran. The way in which Britain and its two closest allies, Canada and the United States, responded to the Soviet threat and the steps the three allies took collectively to ensure their security were determined by several factors: leadership, ideology, economic interests, and concerns related to strategic geographic location.

Several reasons have been offered by historians to explain how Great Britain came to be the first of the North Atlantic allies to raise questions about Soviet occupation policies in eastern Europe and diplomatically to confront Joseph Stalin, the Soviet leader, about respecting earlier wartime agreements. Internationally, the strategic location of the British Empire in relation to long-standing Russian ambitions in the Mediterranean/Middle East and the surprisingly quick communization of eastern Europe made some kind of confrontation virtually inevitable. Warren Kimbell has emphasized the role of domestic political considerations. Although Churchill had reached a spheres-of-influence deal with Stalin in 1944, the prime minister quickly reversed course in March 1945 and engaged in anti-Soviet posturing to strengthen his position in the upcoming elections.[46] Other historians have suggested that Churchill and his foreign secretary, Anthony Eden, were genuinely alarmed by the arrest of non-Communist political activists in Poland, the Soviet-engineered coup in Romania, and the obstruction of British Control Mission in Bulgaria, all of which occurred within a few days of the Yalta accords.[47]

Poland was the test case of Stalin's intentions, since it was ostensibly in defence of that country's sovereignty that the British declared war on Germany in 1939. The Polish issue highlighted for Churchill the basic dilemma of postwar British foreign policy. 'Great Britain and the British

Commonwealth,' observed the prime minister, 'are very much weaker militarily than Soviet Russia, and have no means, short of another general war, of enforcing their point of view.' As was the case during the Second World War, 'we cannot ignore the position of the United States. We cannot go further in helping Poland than the United States is willing or can be persuaded to go.'[48]

Among the North Atlantic allies it was the British government that first condemned the undemocratic tactics of the Polish Communist party; for its efforts it was subjected to a barrage of propaganda from Pravda and the Soviet Foreign Office. Some Soviet specialists have speculated that Stalin had singled out Britain because it was the weaker of the two wartime allies and would be easily isolated given the American preoccupation with domestic issues. It has also been suggested that the appeal of the middle-of-the-road social reforms of a Labour government in power was more dangerous to the Soviet-sponsored march to the collectivist utopia than the example of the reactionary policies of the American capitalists. But whatever reasons motivated Stalin, the British had to deal with still another obstacle in relations with their former ally.[49]

Despite the transition from the Churchill government to the Attlee government, there was little difference in the British respective assessment of Soviet intentions and capabilities and the need to 'hold the line' – later described by the Americans as containment – against further Communist expansion. Both governments had a similar overall strategic concept about the conduct of foreign policy, the relative decline of British power in relation to the other major powers, and the necessity of working as closely as possible with the United States to contain Soviet power.

Before assuming office in July 1945, many members of the Labour party subscribed to the view that the UN would provide the best means to resolve disputes among the Great Powers. Also, left-wing stalwarts like Aneurin Bevan and Emmanuel Shinwell believed that the Kremlin harboured less animosity towards the Labour party than it did towards the Churchill Conservatives.[50] But the moderate wing of the Labour party quickly realized that the responsibilities of office dictated that balance-of-power considerations outweighed social democratic ideological convictions about the ideal relationship with the Kremlin.

Attlee entrusted major foreign policy decisions to his foreign secretary, Ernest Bevin, a strong British nationalist and representative of the moderate wing of the Labour party. Bevin proved to be a quick foreign policy study, and almost immediately he recognized the imperialist nature of Soviet foreign policy and that its concern with security was obsessive. He was particularly concerned about Soviet designs in areas where the British had strategic interests, such as the Mediterranean and the Middle East.[51] At the same time Bevin emphasized that the threat was political and that the Russians' experience of war was so horrific that they would avoid a conflict in the immediate future at all costs. In part his scepticism about the Soviets stemmed from his dealings with Communists in the trade union movement in the 1930s. Contributing to his realpolitik education in matters involving the Soviet Union were the seasoned advisers in the Foreign Office and Chiefs of Staff. Reports about the treatment of social democratic parties in eastern Europe, the revival of Communist military activity in Greece, and Soviet efforts to promote the subversion of British interests throughout the Middle East greatly alarmed the new foreign secretary.[52]

Bevin agreed completely with Churchill that Britain could not indefinitely 'hold the line' against the Soviets on its own and that the Foreign Office should impress upon the Americans the importance of a coordinated effort and the need to 'educate' the Americans about the nature of Soviet behaviour in Europe.[53] Towards this end, the British shared intelligence with the Americans on Communist movements in Europe and worked closely with high-level American military authorities. A low-level propaganda operation was conducted by the American Information Department of the Foreign Office, which attempted to influence opinion on a wide range of foreign policy issues at the popular and elite levels.[54]

Bevin and his Foreign Office diplomats took every opportunity to educate the Truman administration about the Communist threat and the need for joint action, but sometimes to little effect. In preparation for the September 1945 London Foreign Ministers Conference, Secretary of State James Byrnes was advised by the Foreign Office that the Soviet foreign minister, Vyacheslav Molotov, would be particularly intransigent on issues related to the application to eastern European countries of the Declaration on Liberated Europe's principle for 'free and unfettered elections.' The secretary ignored these warnings, and he was not receptive to the British recommendation to issue a joint statement condemning Soviet unwillingness to hold open elections in Bulgaria and Romania. Sometimes, however, the objectives of the Foreign Office were pursued by others in a non-official capacity, the best example being Churchill's famous 'Iron Curtain' address at Fulton, Missouri, in February 1946. While the British Foreign Office was pleased that Churchill's ominous warnings about Communist imperialism resonated deeply throughout the United States, it was disappointed that public opinion and the media were not yet ready to respond to the former prime minister's call for a military alliance of 'English-speaking peoples.'[55]

The turning point in the British effort to coordinate its containment policy with that of the United States came with the issue of the continued presence of Soviet troops in the northern Iranian province of Azerbaijan. When the Iranian government protested the occupation before the Security Council in January 1946, it was Bevin who first stood up to the Russians. The British confrontation was designed to marshal world opinion against the Soviet Union and to impress upon American opinion, the media, and Congress that of all western democracies only the British had the courage and integrity to stand up for the universal principle of national self-determination. If the Americans could be mobilized on the Iranian issue, the British would be in a better position to protect their oil and strategic interests in the Middle East. Bevin's spirited oratory in January and February 1946 was favourably reported in the American media and well received by some in the Republican party. Shortly thereafter, Byrnes sent a blunt note to the Kremlin demanding the immediate withdrawal of Soviet troops. Thus for the first time the United States joined Britain in a public demonstration of resolve to pressure the Soviet Union to live up to its wartime agreements.[56]

The next international crisis that drew the United States closer to supporting British interests in the Mediterranean was the Greek civil war between the Communist National Liberation Front and the Royalist Tsaldaris government. The United States traditionally had shown little interest in Greece, preferring that the British assume responsibility for affairs in the region. After the war, Bevin undertook a series of measures to keep the American State Department informed. In December 1945 the British embassy in Washington explained the difficult economic situation facing the government in Athens and asked if the Truman administration could offer technical advisers and economic aid. Byrnes cautioned against any economic aid at that time, arguing that the Greek government should clean up its own economic house first.[57]

Throughout the fall of 1946 the Truman administration was advised by London of the growing political unrest between the Tsaldaris government in Athens and the Communist insurgents backed by Yugoslavia and Albania. While the Labour government continued to support the monarchist-oriented regime in Athens, unexpected circumstances dictated a fundamental shift in London's strategic policy. The devastating winter of 1946–7 and alarming reports from the chancellor of the Exchequer about Britain's uncontrolled budget deficit forced a major reassessment of America's foreign commitments. In February 1947 the Foreign Office sent two notes to the State Department explaining that economic assistance to the Greek government would be terminated after March. Assistant Secretary of State Dean Acheson later recalled that these communications raised issues requiring 'the most major decision with which we have been faced since the war.'[58] Events moved rapidly in Washington. On 12 March Truman announced before a joint session of Congress a new economic and military aid bill 'to support free people who are resisting attempted subjugation by armed minorities or outside pressures.' Thus the origins of the Truman doctrine lay partly in the decline of British power and the Labour government's efforts to redress the imbalance of power in the old world with the economic and military power of the new world.[59]

From 1945 to the spring of 1947 the United States did very little to educate its English-speaking wartime allies about the causes of Soviet expansionism, the threat it posed to the global balance of power, and the need for a collective response. There were few, if any, domestic pressures to force a reassessment of relations with the Soviet Union. The politics and policies of reconverting the wartime economy almost totally preoccupied the Truman administration in the first year after the war and prevailed over the warnings of the State and War departments. Truman's abrasive personality, as revealed in his famous encounter with Molotov in April 1945, caused a temporary setback in postwar cooperation with the Soviets, but it did not stand in the way of improved relations later that year.[60]

Public opinion and Congress, notably the eastern European minorities in Michigan and New York, were quite vocal on the issue of Poland but carried little political weight. Even the expansionist nature of the capitalist system, which presumably would lead to a conflict with Communism, was not reflected in the Truman administration's sincerely held beliefs that the Soviets would participate in the Bretton Woods and GATT negotiations. Until the Iranian crisis in the spring of 1946, Truman believed that the Soviet Union was a problem, but only one of several international problems, and that it was not a direct threat to American national security.[61]

America's isolated strategic-geographic location, its status as the world's leading superpower and its assessment of Soviet intentions and capabilities led to some fundamental disagreements between Washington and London officials about best way to deal with the Soviet Union in the period immediately following the war. American State Department officials, for example, were less inclined than the British to view the communization of eastern Europe as fundamentally altering the global balance of power. If Stalin had designs on Poland, that was tragic for the Poles, but the Soviet dictator had his own legitimate security interests and the American administration did not think this issue was worth a major breakdown in relations between the two countries.[62]

Several factors stood in the way of the United States's forging of a cohesive diplomatic strategy with the British to deal with the Soviets. Roosevelt's efforts to curry Stalin's support at Yalta by baiting Churchill had appealed to those who believed that the British were simply intransigent imperialists. After the war influential elements in Congress, public opinion, and the media continued to raise questions about British imperialist practices in South Asia and the Middle East. While Truman did not share these Anglophobic sentiments, Byrnes on occasion provoked the Labour government. The British were largely ignored at the Potsdam Conference and later, in the autumn, Byrnes did not inform Bevin in advance of the agenda at the December 1945 Moscow Foreign Ministers Conference.[63]

The United States began to reassess its relations with Britain during the Mediterranean and Middle East crises of 1946. At the beginning of the Iranian crisis the Truman administration continued to avoid British overtures for a coordinated diplomatic response to force the removal of Soviet troops from the northern province of Azerbaijan. Washington officials viewed the situation as still another of the traditional Anglo-Russian rivalries in the Near East. By March 1946, however, several events had transpired – Stalin's speech denouncing capitalist countries as warmongering and the reports submitted by the Iranian government of growing Soviet troop movements – to occasion a reassessment in Washington of its 'hands off' approach. The United States finally joined forces with Great Britain and through various diplomatic channels began strongly to reprimand the Soviets.[64]

British weakness throughout the Mediterranean area and American willingness to 'redress the balance of the old world' led to the next step in the coordinated Anglo-American effort to contain Communist expansion: the promulgation of the Truman Doctrine in March of 1947. Designed specifically to provide $400 million in military aid to Greece and Turkey, the wording of the doctrine left open the possibility that the United States would come to the assistance of other countries facing internal subversion or external aggression.[65] If the rhetoric of the Truman Doctrine implied the beginning of a new global strategy to contain Communist expansion through the use of military aid, the highest priority was given to maintaining the stability of western Europe by economic means. A unilateral endeavour, however, was never the intention. The United States was prepared to make a substantial financial commitment to the recovery of Europe, but Truman's new secretary of state, George Marshall, emphasized in his address at Harvard University in June 1947 that European participants must also take the initiative in overcoming traditional economic barriers and coordinate their economic recovery. At that particular juncture all three north Atlantic allies were in agreement about the political and psychological nature of the Communist threat, the importance of using economic instruments of policy to contain it, and the necessity for the United States to provide financial assistance to what came to be known as the European Economic Recovery Program (ERP). This new direction in policy was to have immediate consequences for relations with Great Britain and led to unanticipated new developments in economic relations with Canada.

The threat of a Communist takeover was greatest in France and Italy, and the economic crisis facing Germany was much worse than it was elsewhere in Europe, but it was Bevin who first took up Marshall's offer to organize a European response. Britain itself did not need Marshall Plan money to contain Communism at home. Instead, financial assistance was important for Britain to preserve its Great Power status, which in turn was necessary for maintaining the balance of power in Europe. Recognizing that American national security interests were now dependent on what the British had to offer – strategic air bases, a diplomatic corps with highly trained Soviet specialists, and the global presence of the empire – Bevin realized that his government was in a much better position to resist multilateralism and further integration into the continental European economy. To be sure, the United States requested access to strategic resources of the Commonwealth and empire countries and further commitments to reduce foreign debts, balance budgets, and impose restrictions on domestic wage demands; but in the end, compromise and consensus prevailed. Only on a few issues was the United States able to gain any concessions from Great Britain, one instance being the Labour government's shelving of its plans to nationalize the Ruhr coal mines in Germany.[66]

Overall, the British fared quite well from the Marshall Plan. Bevin drafted the first response to Marshall's request asking for $29 billion.

Truman, sympathetic but practical minded when facing Congress, asked for a $17 billion appropriation. From 1948 to 1951 Congress approved funding for $13.3 billion, of which Britain, the largest of the European beneficiaries, received $3.2 billion. This aid allowed Britain to import high-demand commodities from dollar-bloc countries, unjam bottlenecks, maintain financial stability, and control inflation. Economists have not been able to determine precisely the relationship to the European recovery; suffice it to say that among the ERP countries industrial and agricultural production increased by one-third during those years.[67]

Canada was not faced with the same problems as the European countries were of restoring a war-ravaged economy and of the threat posed to internal political stability by the Communist-dominated Labour Progressive party and militant trade unions. Consequently, Canadian requests to be included in economic planning during the initial stages of the ERP in September 1947 came as somewhat of a surprise to those in Washington.[68] Ottawa officials were primarily concerned about the expansion of Communism abroad and believed that the most effective policy was reliance on economic instruments of policy. As St Laurent explained, Communism appealed primarily to the 'unfortunate and oppressed.' The best way to deal with this political threat, therefore, was to 'remove the social evils which provide the breeding ground for Communist support.'[69]

As noted in the previous section, domestic economic factors weighed heavily in the determination of Canadian foreign policy during the early Cold War period, especially because of the growing balance-of-payments problems in the summer and fall of 1947. Canadian officials believed that if the Truman administration made provisions for European countries to use their Marshall Plan monies, paid in U.S. dollars, to purchase Canadian wheat and other foodstuffs, this would be a major step towards restoring the imbalance in Canada's hard-currency account. From the second quarter of 1948 to the second quarter of 1950, US$1.155 billion flowed into Canada as payment under the 'Off-Shore Purchases' clause of the Marshall Plan, and the impact on Canada's dollar account was not inconsequential. By March 1949 reserves of gold and U.S. dollars had reached $1,065 million and the Canadian government was able to lift import restrictions on a wide range of American products. Overall, the effect of the ERP in 1948 had been to maintain Canadian overseas trade for a number of basic commodities at a level not far below that of 1947.[70]

The off-shore provisions clause of the Marshall Plan provides the best example of the 'special relationship' that existed between Canada and the United States, standing in contrast to Canadian relations with Great Britain. There was little action or even communication between Great Britain and Canada from 1945 to 1947 on the issue of determining the causes of Soviet expansion and the best methods to deal with it. Mackenzie King informed the British about the Gouzenko spying incident, and the British in turn briefed King and provided intelligence reports about the state of Soviet espionage in Europe. For a brief period, the Labour government approached Canada about the possibility of a new agreement on the research and development of atomic energy. Overall, however, little was done to enlist further Canadian involvement in the containment of the Soviet Union. It was enough for the British to get agricultural imports and financial assistance from Canada and other matters – the formulation and implementation of the containment strategy and the task of 'educating' the Americans were best left to skilled diplomats in the Foreign Office.[71]

By 1947 the Liberal government in Ottawa recognized that a fundamental shift in the North Atlantic economic triangle had developed. Not only had the United States emerged as the dominant economic power, but in the years ahead the Americans would be much more receptive to Canadian economic concerns than Great Britain would be. This attitude was particularly notable when the State Department defended Canadian interests in the midst of the Truman administration's efforts to persuade Congress about the advantages of international trade liberalization during the 1947 GATT negotiations. Although the Canadians imposed their own bilateral trade restrictions, in apparent violation of the spirit of the GATT, the State Department supported a special $300 million export-import bank loan and even made provisions to the 1938 trade agreement to allow Ottawa to impose new import restrictions. Despite these protectionist measures taken by Canada, 'both from the economic and the defense point of view,' argued one State Department report, 'we should continue to urge Congress to give us the flexibility under the European Recovery Program which will permit purchases in Canada of materials in short supply.'[72]

Congress was the major obstacle to closer continental economic ties. In 1947 State Department officials believed that the best way to convince Congress was to remind members that 'whatever benefits and advantages Canada gained from the United States relationship were given in our own self interest.'[73] Towards this end, these officials explained that Canada was the United States's largest trading partner, and by helping the northern dominion America's largest foreign market was being protected. Furthermore, in time of crisis, Canada's strategic raw materials and industrial defence production would be assets to the Americans' war-making capability. Finally, by helping Canada, the United States was demonstrating to the rest of the world 'the ability of democratic freedomloving nations to live, work, and progress together towards lasting peace and prosperity.'[74]

Growing fears about the imminent outbreak of another major war in Europe prompted Canadian, American, and British officials early in 1948 to consider the need for a regional defence organization. Collective security concerns supplanted preconceived ideological convictions about multilateralism, the interests of the British Empire, or the restrictive pressures from domestic interest groups. Historians have exhaustively documented the American enthusiasm for adopting military instruments of policy to deal with Communist expansion; it was the Canadian and British governments, however, that first proposed the creation of a North Atlantic defence pact. The United States, for its part, was primarily concerned about the security of the western hemisphere and, in contrast to its irresolution regarding the North Atlantic defence pact, always took the initiative to promote closer military ties with Canada.[75]

The Labour government and British Chiefs of Staff did not envisage a direct Soviet military attack on western Europe before 1950, but war could none the less break out by accident or miscalculation, in which case the Red Army would quickly overrun the French and German forces. The Attlee government argued that under these uncertain conditions the ERP could not proceed effectively without the guarantee of a significant military presence to ensure the national security and psychological well-being of western Europe. The British Chiefs of Staff and the Foreign Office consistently attempted to inform the Truman administration on these points and on the need to continue the deployment of American troops in Germany.[76] British officers had sentimental attachments to the idea of imperial fraternity, but military relations with Canada were not of any great consequence to British planning until the 1948 NATO negotiations.

In the immediate postwar period British officials were not entirely successful in their efforts to continue the close wartime relationship with the American military. The Truman administration was anxious to demobilize as quickly as possible, not to provoke the Russians into thinking that they were secretly engaged in military planning with the

British. In September 1945 Truman gave orders to dissolve the wartime Combined Boards, and the by the end of 1945 the Combined Chiefs of Staff was reduced to a skeleton operation. Most damaging to the British was American reluctance to continue sharing information about the development and testing of atomic weapons, prompting the Labour government to set out on its own program in 1947. Given the absence of an American commitment to the defence of western Europe, the British Chiefs of Staff proposed that an arsenal of at least 200 atomic bombs would be the best means of deterring a Soviet first-strike attack.[77]

Despite indifference on the part of the Truman administration, British military authorities persisted in seeking closer ties with their American counterparts. The Chiefs of Staff strongly supported continuing the operation of the British Joint Staff Mission in Washington after the war. As an effort to cement further military ties between the two countries, the Labour government welcomed the 1946 agreement between General Carl Spaatz of the United States Army Air Force and Air Marshal Tedder, chief of the RAF's Air Staff, to prepare four East Anglian bomber bases for American use in the event of an emergency.[78] The British made several proposals in July 1946 for informal secret military meetings which culminated in General Montgomery's secret discussions with American officials in September. For the first time since the war tentative agreements were reached on strategic planning and standardization of military equipment. The next year the British Joint Planning Staff was successful in convincing the Americans that the two countries should coordinate their defence plans for the Middle East. A further British initiative resulted in the 1947 UKUSA agreement which established a global division of labour on matters related to the gathering of communications intelligence.[79]

By 1947 Great Britain and the United States were becoming tied militarily and diplomatically by a secret but informal alliance. The next step was to unify the western allies into a comprehensive regional security pact in which the three North Atlantic allies would play a leading role. Following on Canadian disillusionment with the Soviet use of the veto and other delaying tactics in the UN, External Affairs official Escott Reid outlined in July 1947 a proposal for a new regional security organization. He made it clear that the alliance was to include more than just the 'English-speaking peoples,' as Churchill had suggested in his 1946 'Iron Curtain' address. Reflecting Canadian enthusiasm for linking national security with domestic economic considerations, the North Atlantic military alliance would also promote economic and cultural ties.[80]

Washington officials paid little attention to these Canadian proposals, but they took seriously Bevin's warnings in December 1947 that economic aid would not be enough to stop further Communist expansion in Europe. To restore a sense of security to a demoralized Europe, the British foreign secretary argued for a defence pact between the major western European nations. But in the end the formation of the Brussels Pact in March 1948 was meant to be simply a stop-gap measure until direct American involvement was secured, a point that Bevin continued to make in his secret communications with Washington. The foreign secretary later acknowledged that only a narrow circle of officials knew of these British initiatives to promote a larger North Atlantic alliance, and he preferred to leave the impression that it was the Americans who were the driving force behind it.[81]

Important as these British initiatives were, it was the impact of other international developments – the Czech coup in February, Soviet pressures on Norway in early March, and growing Communist unrest in France and Italy – that led the United States to participate in preliminary NATO discussions with Canada and Great Britain in the spring of 1948. By June, however, American interest in a new collective security organization was beginning to wane. In fact, at least one observer believed that if it had not been for effective diplomatic efforts on the part of the Canadians and the British, full American participation in the NATO alliance never would have come about.[82]

The Canadian, American, and British proposals for a draft of the NATO charter were completed in July 1948 and submitted to the other western allies for their consideration. With the final ratification of the treaty in April 1949, Britain had achieved its central aim of moving the NATO negotiations ahead as quickly as possible and formalizing American commitment to the security of Europe. Canada was pleased that NATO provided an ideal framework for middle powers to exert their interests and was particularly satisfied with Article 2 of the Charter which promoted closer economic and cultural ties between countries. The Truman administration, albeit with some initial reluctance on the part of Congress, welcomed NATO because it increased the chances for success of the Marshall Plan. An additional benefit to the United States was that European countries would be obliged to increase their own defence budgets to meet NATO obligations, and direct American military aid would be kept to a minimum. As late as April 1950 the United States had allocated only $42 million to its NATO allies under the Military Assistance Plan.[83]

The formation of NATO marked a significant turning point in relations among Canada, Great Britain, and the United States. The Canadian and British governments quickly realized that roles had been reversed in the North Atlantic triangle. Before 1949 it was the Canadians and British who educated the Americans about their Cold War duties and responsibilities. As the United States became more assertive militarily and increasingly gave direction as to the way its allies should participate in the great struggle with the Soviet Union, Canada and Britain more than before acted with a degree of caution and moderation. This 'diplomacy of constraint' was aimed at trying to limit the excesses of the American containment doctrine – its application, the use of certain instruments of policy, and the inflated Cold War rhetoric.[84]

National security considerations – specifically strategic nuclear weapons policy, North American air defence, and industrial defence mobilization planning – were primary factors in determining the course of Washington's relations with Canada and Britain after 1948. Although the United States shared little nuclear weapons information with Britain after the passage of the 1946 MacMahon Act, the Department of Defense continued to work with Britain and Canada on secret chemical and biological weapons research at the test centre in Suffield, Alberta.[85] In 1949 the United States updated its strategic war plans to reflect its new NATO commitments. Defence plans Offtackle and Dropshot emphasized the importance of defending Great Britain and the need to use British airbases to launch atomic attacks against the Soviet Union. By 1949 there were 180 American B-29 bombers stationed at seven British airfields. Under the guidelines of Offtackle and Dropshot, in the first thirty days of the next world war American bombers operating out of British bases in East Anglia and the Middle East were scheduled to deliver 453 atomic bombs on Soviet targets.[86]

More than Great Britain or other NATO allies, Canada assumed a 'special relationship' in postwar American defence planning. In the event of a Soviet attack on the western hemisphere, the National Security Council conducted its planning on the premise that the northern dominion was an extension of the United States to be protected at all costs. Given Canada's strategic-geographic location in the 'air-atomic-age,' less attention was paid to naval and land-based military operations than to drawing up plans for the defence of Canadian air space. The United States generally took the initiative in coordinating continental strategic planning, while Canada took the first steps to promote the continental integration of its own resource and industrial defence production.

In contrast to the Truman administration's indifference to maintaining the Combined Chiefs of Staff ties to Britain, Washington officials approached Ottawa in June 1945 with a proposal to continue the operation of the PJBD into the postwar period. To update the western-hemisphere wartime defence plans (ABC-22), the United States persuaded Canada to form a 'Military Cooperation Committee' to work on a new Basic Security Plan.[87] The following year the two countries participated in Operation Muskox, a joint military training exercise in the Arctic. It was not until 1951, however, that Canada agreed to allow basing rights in Newfoundland for American bombers and made the commitment to undertake a joint North American air defence program.

Several factors explain why Canada moved more slowly than the British towards establishing military commitments with the Americans. Mackenzie King was by temperament deliberate and cautious, and generally he acted accordingly; he was also uneasy about the long-term impact of the United States on Canadian sovereignty. The Canadian prime minister was, moreover, genuinely concerned about unnecessarily provoking the Soviet Union, and he approached all major Cold War crises with the hope that diplomatic and economic solutions would prevail. Canadian officials were well aware that in the event of a major Soviet-American confrontation Canada could become the Belgium of the next world war. The Canadians were less concerned than the British about maintaining the balance of power in Europe, but they were concerned with keeping Soviet bombers out of Canadian skies. Another restraining factor was related to national defence: as a middle power, Canada did not want to be caught in an unequal bilateral military alliance with the United States, preferring to work within a larger regional defence framework. NATO would provide a countervailing force against the excesses of American power. As the external affairs minister, Lester Pearson, observed: 'for Canada there was always security in numbers.'[88]

From 1945 to 1950 Canada defined its 'special relationship' with the United States primarily in economic terms. When the Truman administration reversed the decline in military spending in 1947, Ottawa officials quickly realized that there would be new opportunities to improve its balance-of-payments position and promote industrial diversification. The first step was taken in April 1947 when Mackenzie King suggested to Truman that the 'dollar gap' problem could be alleviated by increasing exports to the United States of aluminum, lead, zinc, and copper.[89] The next year Canadian Industrial Defence Board officials approached

Washington with a request to form a new bilateral organization designed to coordinate Canadian resource and industrial production with the requirements of the American rearmament program. This move led to the signing of still another bilateral agreement in April 1949, bringing into operation the Joint Industrial Mobilization Planning Committee (JIMPC). Several subcommittees were created which began work on drawing up plans that coordinated continental industrial mobilization with the war plans drawn up by the American Joint Chiefs of Staff. Although operation of the JIMPC remained limited in scope throughout the first year, the framework was laid for further continental integration to meet the defence mobilization demands of the Korean War.[90]

The perception of a shared threat, mutual security needs, and the prospects for certain economic advantages determined the course of interaction between the North Atlantic allies from 1945 to 1949, but in time of Cold War crisis the ties that bound the three allies remained uneven. The strongest economic links in the North Atlantic triangle were those forged between Canada and the United States, while the United States and Britain were closer on military matters. It is interesting to note that the weakest link in both areas was between the two Commonwealth partners. Economically, Britain did little to facilitate closer trade relations, the Labour government preferring to conclude more favourable deals with other European countries, much to the dismay of the Canadian negotiators. Even though Canada compromised its own gold and dollar reserves to help in the postwar recovery of Britain, this assistance was simply taken for granted.

Britain's approach to Canada on military matters followed a larger pattern of weakened relations with Commonwealth countries both within and outside the NATO alliance. In 1946 London made appeals to coordinate defence planning with member countries, but as historian Jack Granatstein has pointed out, this was no more than 'a transparent dodge' to get Canada and the other dominions to assume a disproportionate share of defence costs to shore up a crumbling empire.[91] In former years Britain had been able call on support of the empire, but owing to a particular set of challenges the early postwar period posed for national security, little was done to forge a renewed sense of Commonwealth solidarity with countries like Canada. Canada had given Britain substantial assistance during the war, but in an age of uncertainty dominated by strategic weapons technology, it had little to offer, possessing neither the atomic deterrent nor the vast economic resources of the United States. In the light of the unsurpassed military and economic power of the United States, it was to that country that Britain first turned to meet its own security needs, defined primarily as maintaining the balance of power in Europe and the Middle East.

The extensive publication of new monographs on Anglo-American and Canadian-American relations over the past decade has had a substantial impact on the development of Cold War historiography. British efforts to educate the Truman administration and allow it to set up military bases provide additional evidence to substantiate Geir Lundestad's 'empire by invitation' thesis.[92] The opening of British documents also seems to discredit the left-revisionist contention that the Truman administration took the initiative in interpreting Soviet foreign policy as provocative and opportunistic, if not outright expansionistic. On the basis of evidence now available, it seems that European estimates of Soviet intentions and capabilities, at least in the early Cold War period, were closer to the mark than were those of the Americans.[93]

Another point related to the larger historiographical debates concerns the perceived use of coercive diplomacy by the United States and the negative effect of American economic expansion on other countries. American integration of Canada's resource and industrial defence production, undertaken largely on the initiative of the Ottawa government, was particularly beneficial to the host country. In the key economic categories of housing starts, inflation, and dollar strength, from 1945 to 1950 Canada surpassed the United States. Studies carried out by the Department of Trade and Commerce and the Dominion Bureau of Statistics indicate that American-controlled high-technology industries, such as automobiles, electronics, and oil refining, recorded the highest rates of productivity in North America as measured by output per man-hour. By the end of 1950 Canadian unemployment, at just over 2 per cent, compared favourably with the slightly higher rate in the United States.[94]

The two North American countries, together with Britain, reached a level of cooperation that peaked with the tripartite NATO negotiations, the efforts to coordinate chemical and biological warfare research and development in western Canada, and the 1948 agreement to standardize screw threads. 'The standardization of screw threads may sound trivial,' observed Canada's General A.G.L. McNaughton, 'but it was one of the greatest things we ever did.'[95] Although the three countries also worked closely together within larger multilateral organizations, such as the UN, GATT, and NATO, they never quite fulfilled Churchill's vision of an English-speaking alliance. Even during the crisis years of 1948–9 the three allies tended to seek out bilateral ties rather than larger multilateral agreements related to economic mobilization and strategic doctrine.

After 1946 the United States assumed an increasingly dominant position in the North Atlantic triangle, but its strength did not mean that Britain and Canada invariably deferred to higher authority. The Truman administration's excessive use of Cold War rhetoric in 1947 prompted Canadian officials in 1947 to 'tell the United States to stop rocking the boat or driving holes in its bottom.'[96] On economic matters the British remained the main obstacle to the implementation of a multilateral trading system. At times the Labour government engaged in bilateral trade practices that offended the Americans, most notably the decision to export Rolls-Royce jet engines to the Soviet Union in 1947. As for relations in the Far East, the British Foreign Office in 1949 established diplomatic ties with the Mao Tse-tung Communists, thereby undermining the American policy of non-recognition. By 1949 the North Atlantic triangle had become somewhat less intimate and more troubled than it had been during the Second World War. Yet despite a slight erosion in relations and the fact that the three allies did not always pursue identical interests, their commonality of purpose in the end far surpassed that of their Communist adversaries.

NOTES

1 For a discussion of what constitutes a 'special relationship' and what its underlying causes are, see David Reynolds, 'A "Special Relationship"? America, Britain and the International Order since the Second World War,' *International Affairs*, 62(1985–6), 2–17. For a discussion of the application of the 'special relationship' concept to Canadian-American relations, see Lawrence Aronsen, 'The "Indispensable Ally": American National Security and Economic Relations with Canada, 1945–1963,' unpublished manuscript, 14–52.

2 On the rise of internationalism, see Robert Divine, *Second Chance: The Triumph of Internationalism in America during World War II* (New York, 1967).

3 Ernest May, *Lessons of the Past: The Use and Misuse of History in American Foreign Policy* (New York, 1973), 9–17.

4 This point is discussed in Arthur Ekirch, *Ideas, Ideals, and American Diplomacy: A History of Their Growth and Interaction* (New York, 1966). For a criticism of American foreign policy as being too moralistic and legalistic, see George Kennan, *American Diplomacy, 1900–1950* (Chicago, 1951).

5 Robert Dallek, *Franklin D. Roosevelt and American Foreign Policy, 1932–1945*

(New York, Oxford, 1979), 419–21, 434–40, 510–11, 519–23; Thomas Camp-bell, *Masquerade Peace: America's UN Policy, 1944–1945* (Tallahassee, FL, 1973), 1–25.

6 Quoted in Gabriel Kolko, *The Politics of War: The World and United States For-eign Policy, 1943–1945* (New York, 1968), 46.

7 For example, David Horowitz, *Empire and Revolution* (New York, 1969), 232–58; Thomas McCormick, *America's Half-Century: United States Foreign Policy in the Cold War* (Baltimore, 1989), 43–99.

8 Ritchie Ovendale, ed., *The Foreign Policy of the British Labour Government, 1945–1951* (Leicester, 1984), 1–20; Joseph Frankel, *British Foreign Policy, 1945–1973* (New York, 1975), 175–200.

9 David Dilks, ed., *The Diaries of Sir Alexander Cadogan, 1938–1945* (New York, 1971), 653, 670, 688, 705.

10 On this point see, Robert Hathaway, *Ambiguous Partnership: Britain and Amer-ica, 1944–1947* (New York, 1981), 40–1.

11 Geoffrey Goodwin, *Britain and the United Nations* (New York, 1957), 45–8; E.J. Hughes 'Winston Churchill and the Formation of the United Nations Organization,' *Journal of Contemporary History*, 9(1974), 177–94.

12 Goodwin, *United Nations*, 14–48.

13 U.S. Department of State, *Foreign Relations of the United States* (hereafter *FRUS*), *1945: Malta and Yalta* (Washington, DC, 1955), 793.

14 Dallek, *Roosevelt*, 429.

15 Canadian historians tend to overemphasize the role their diplomats played at the San Francisco Conference. For example John Holmes, *The Shaping of Peace: Canada and Search for World Order, 1943–1957*, Vol. I (Toronto, 1979), 229–95; Clyde Eagleton, 'Canada in the Making of the United Nations,' *University of Toronto Law Journal*, 7(1948), 329–51.

16 For example, Escott Reid, *On Duty: A Canadian at the Making of the United Nations, 1945–1946* (Toronto, 1983), 33, 46, 67–76; J.L. Granatstein, 'Canada and Peacekeeping: Image and Reality,' in *Canadian Foreign Policy: Historical Readings*, ed. idem (Toronto, 1986), 232–3.

17 John English, *Shadow of Heaven: The Life of Lester Pearson*, Vol. I: *1897–1948* (Toronto, 1992), 273–81; J.L. Granatstein, *A Man of Influence: Norman A. Rob-ertson and Canadian Statecraft, 1929–68* (Toronto, 1981), 144–56.

18 Holmes, *Shaping of Peace*, 270.

19 F.H. Soward and Edgar McInnis, *Canada and the United Nations* (New York, 1957), 29.

20 On this point see Robert Pastor, *Congress and the Politics of U.S. Foreign Eco-nomic Policy, 1929–1976* (Berkeley, 1980); F.O. Wilcox, *Congress, the Executive and Foreign Policy* (New York, 1971).

21 Truman, quoted in U.S. Department of State, *Bulletin*, 26(August 1945), 279–80.

22 This point is elaborated on in U.S. Department of State, *Proposals for Expansion of World Trade and Employment, November 1945* (Washington, DC, 1945); Clair Wilcox, *A Charter for World Trade* (New York, 1949).

23 See Fred Block, *The Origins of International Economic Disorder: A Study of United States International Monetary Policy from World War II to the Present* (Berkeley, 1977); Thomas Paterson, 'The Quest for Peace and Prosperity: International Trade, Communism, and the Marshall Plan,' in *Politics and Policies of the Truman Administration*, ed. Barton Bernstein (Chicago, 1970), 78–112; William A. Williams, 'The Large Corporations and American Foreign Policy,' in *Corporations and the Cold War*, ed. David Horowitz (New York, 1964), 41–60. For a critique of the 'open door' thesis, see Alfred Eckes, 'Open Door Expansionism Reconsidered: The World War II Experience,' *Journal of American History*, 59(1973), 909–24.

24 The major neo-realist studies of American foreign economic policy include Robert Pollard, *Economic Security and the Origins of the Cold War, 1945–1950* (New York, 1985); Thomas Zeiler, *American Trade and Power in the 1960s* (New York, 1992).

25 Richard Gardner, 'Sterling-Dollar Diplomacy in Current Perspective,' in *The 'Special Relationship': Anglo-American Relations since 1945*, ed. W.R. Louis and Hedley Bull (Oxford, 1986), 187–8.

26 Richard Clarke, *Anglo-American Economic Collaboration in War and Peace, 1942–1949* (Oxford, 1982), 66–88, 149–66.

27 R. Bullen and M.E. Pelly, eds, *Documents on British Policy Overseas, 1946* (London 1987), 36.

28 Hugh Dalton, *High Tide and After: Memoirs, 1945–1960* (London, 1962), 74–87; R.F. Harrod, *The Life of John Maynard Keynes* (New York, 1951), 496 ff.

29 The Labour party's postwar foreign economic policies are discussed in Allan Bullock, *Ernest Bevin: Foreign Secretary, 1945–1951* (London, 1983), 121–6, 202–5, 393–467.

30 C.D. Howe, 'Employment and Income with Special Reference to the Initial Period of Reconstruction,' in *Canadian Foreign Policy, 1945–1954*, ed. R.A. Mackay (Toronto, 1971), 52–3.

31 John Bartlett Brebner, *North Atlantic Triangle: The Interplay of Canada, the United States, and Great Britain* (New York, 1945; Toronto, 1966), 230–49; R.D. Cuff and J.L. Granatstein, *American Dollars: Canadian Prosperity* (Toronto, 1978), passim; Robert Bothwell and John English, 'Canadian Trade Policy in the Age of American Dominance and British Decline, 1943–1947,' *Canadian Review of American Studies*. 8(1977), 54ff.

32 Howe, 'Address,' 19 November 1946, file 45, vol. 157, C.D. Howe Papers, National Archives of Canada (hereafter NAC).

33 'Canada's Industrial Expansion,' *Monthly Review of the Bank of Nova Scotia* (June 1948), 1–4. See also Homer Fox, 'Canada's Economy in 1945,' *Foreign Commerce Weekly* (22 January 1945), 6–9.

34 Claxton, 'Address,' 27 August 1943, vol. 18, MG 26 Nl, NAC.

35 U.S. Department of Commerce, *Historical Statistics of the United States: Colonial Times to 1957* (Washington, DC, 1961), 542–66.

36 Atherton to Secretary of State, 11 September 1947, file 842.5151/9–1147, RG 84, National Archives of the United States (hereafter NARS).

37 Canada, *Treaty Series, 1948*, No. I: *Exchange of Notes*, 7 and 15 May 1945 (Ottawa, 1948), 3–6.

38 Parsons to Atherton, 3 May 1945, file 842.20 Defense/5–345, RG 59, NARS.

39 Hathaway, *Ambiguous Partnership*, 182–201, 230–48.

40 Carolyn Eisenberg, 'Working Class Politics and the Cold War: American Intervention in the German Labor Movement, 1945–49,' *Diplomatic History*, 7(1983), 283–306.

41 Gardner, 'Sterling–Dollar Diplomacy,' 360.

42 Wilgress to Secretary of State for External Affairs, 23 September 1947, in *Documents on Canadian External Relations*, ed. Norman Hillmer and Donald Page, Vol. 13: *1947* (Ottawa, 1992), 1176–7.

43 B.W. Muirhead, *The Development of Postwar Canadian Trade Policy* (Montreal, 1992), 23.

44 For critical analysis of the Canadian government's shift to economic continentalism, see Donald Creighton, *The Forked Road: Canada, 1939–1957* (Toronto, 1977), 140–70.

45 Lawrence Aronsen, 'An Open Door to the North: The Liberal Government and the Expansion of American Foreign Investment, 1945–1953,' *American Review of Canadian Studies*, 22(1992), 167–98.

46 Warren Kimbell, ed., *Churchill and Roosevelt: The Complete Correspondence*, Vol. 3 (Princeton, 1984), 546–51; idem, 'Naked Reverse Right: Roosevelt, Churchill, and Eastern Europe from Tolstoy to Yalta – and a Little Beyond,' *Diplomatic History*, 9(1985), 17-20.

47 See, for example, Desmond Donnelly, *Struggle for the World* (New York, 1965), 155–8; Victor Rothwell, *Britain and the Cold War* (London, 1982), 178–9.

48 Martin Gilbert, *Winston S. Churchill*, Vol. VII: *Road to Victory, 1941–1945* (London, 1986), 1230–1.

49 Soviet policy towards Great Britain is discussed in Rothwell, *Cold War*, 241–60; Fraser Harbutt, *The Iron Curtain* (New York, 1986), 95–110.

50 Raymond Smith and John Zametica, 'The Cold Warrior: Clement Attlee

Reconsidered, 1945–7,' *International Affairs*, 61(1985), 237–52; Raymond Smith, 'A Climate of Opinion: British Officials and the Development of British Soviet Policy, 1945-7,' *International Affairs*, 64(1988), 631–47.

51 Frank Roberts, 'Ernest Bevin as Foreign Secretary,' in *The Foreign Policy of the British Labour Government, 1945–1951*, ed. R. Ovendale (Leicester, 1984), 29–38; Bullock, *Bevin*, 105–7, 117, 159, 191–2.

52 Peter Boyle, 'The British Foreign Office View of Soviet-American Relations,' *Diplomatic History*, 3(1979), 307-20; Ray Merrick, 'The Russia Committee of the British Foreign Office and the Cold War, 1946–7,' *Journal of Contemporary History*, 20(1985), 453–65.

53 The 'holding the line' concept was developed by Frank Roberts, British chargé d'affaires in Moscow, 1945–7.

54 Philip Taylor, 'The Projection of Britain Abroad, 1945–1951,' in *British Foreign Policy, 1945–1956*, ed. Michael Dockrill and John Young (New York, 1989), 9–27; Robert Hathaway, *Great Britain and the United States: Special Relations since World War II* (Boston, 1990), 22–3.

55 Harbutt, *Iron Curtain*, 185-91.

56 Terry Anderson, *The United States, Great Britain, and the Cold War* (London, 1981), 98–103.

57 Ibid., 148–9.

58 Acheson to Marshall, 24 February 1947, *FRUS, 1947*, vol. V, 45.

59 Historians have offered widely different assessments of the effectiveness of British diplomacy. At least one historian plays down the clever diplomatic maneuovring of the British and argues that the British served 'as kind of a front for the United States in order that American policies not appear provocative.' See Bruce Kuniholm, *The Origins of the Cold War in the Near East* (Princeton, 1980), 383. Other historians have provided evidence suggesting the Greek crisis was in good measure due to British ineptness in not supporting the more moderate reformist elements in Athens. See Melvyn Leffler, *A Preponderance of Power: National Security, the Truman Administration, and the Cold War* (Stanford, 1992), 73–4.

60 John Lewis Gaddis, *The United States and the Origins of the Cold War, 1941–1947* (New York, 1972), 205–6.

61 Robert Donovan, *Conflict and Crisis: The Presidency of Harry S. Truman, 1945–1948* (New York, 1977), 55, 128, 161–2; Leffler, *Preponderance of Power*, 31–8, 46–52.

62 Arthur Bliss Lane, *I Saw Poland Betrayed* (Indianapolis, 1948); Hugh De Santis, *The Diplomacy of Silence: The American Foreign Service, the Soviet Union, and the Cold War, 1933–1947* (Chicago, 1983), 186–97.

63 Bullock, *Bevin*, 199–200.

64 Historians have given several reasons for the American reversal on the

Iranian crisis by March 1946. Cf. Stephen McFarland, 'A Peripheral View of the Origins of the Cold War: The Crises in Iran, 1941–47,' *Diplomatic History*, 4(1980), 333–51; Gary Hess, 'The Iranian Crisis of 1945–46 and the Cold War,' *Political Science Quarterly*, 89(1974), 117–46; Justus Doenecke, 'Iran's Role in Cold War Revisionism,' *Iranian Studies*, 5(1972), 96–111.

65 One view is that the Truman Doctrine was more rhetoric than a major shift in cold war policy. Cf. John Lewis Gaddis, 'Was the Truman Doctrine a Real Turning Point?' *Foreign Affairs*, 52(1974), 386–402.

66 W.C. Cromwell, 'The Marshall Non-plan: Congress and the Soviet Union,' *Western Political Quarterly*, 32(1979), 422–43; Peter Wiler, 'British Labour and the Cold War: The Foreign Policy of the Labour Governments, 1945–1951,' *Journal of British Studies*, 26(1987), 54–82.

67 Harry Price, *The Marshall Plan and Its Meaning* (Ithaca, 1955), 104–7; Charles Kindleberger, 'The Marshall Plan and the Cold War,' *International Journal*, 24(1968), 369–82; Scott Newton, 'Post-War Reconstruction: How Successful Was the Marshall Plan?' *History Today*, 33(1983), 11–15.

68 Stone to Pearson, 12 June 1947, Wrong to Pearson 20 June 1947, in Hillmer and Page, *Canadian External Relations*, Vol. 13, 415–20.

69 Quoted in Lawrence Aronsen and Martin Kitchen, *The Origins of the Cold War in Comparative Perspective: American, British and Canadian Relations with the Soviet Union, 1941–48* (London, 1988), 184.

70 J.D. Gibson, *Canada's Economy in a Changing World* (Toronto, 1948), 291.

71 Denis Smith, *The Diplomacy of Fear: Canada and the Cold War, 1941–1948* (Toronto, 1988), 101–12.

72 'Canadian Dollar Problem,' 29 November 1947, file FW 611.4231/11–5947, RG 59, NARS.

73 Foster to Wailes, 31 December 1947, file 850, RG 84, NARS.

74 Mosser to Truman, 4 March 1949, OF, box 238, file OF 48-B, 1948–50, Harry S. Truman Library.

75 D.C. Watt, 'Britain, the United States and the Opening of the Cold War,' in Ovendale, *Foreign Policy*, 56–59; Joseph Jockel, *No Boundaries Upstairs: Canada, the United States and the Origins of North American Air Defence, 1945–1958* (Vancouver, 1987), 6–29.

76 Richard Best, Jr, *"Co-operation with Like-Minded Peoples": British Influences on American Security Policy, 1945–1949* (New York, 1986), 30–1.

77 Margaret Gowing, *Independence and Deterrence: Britain and Atomic Energy, 1945–1952*, Vol. I (London, 1974), 92–111, 215; N.J. Wheeler, 'British Nuclear Weapons and Anglo-American Relations, 1945–54,' *International Affairs*, 62(1985–6), 71–2.

78 Harry Borowski, *Hollow Threat: Strategic Air Power and Containment before Korea* (Westport, CT.,1982), 102; John Greenwood, "The Emergence of the

Postwar Strategic Air Force, 1945–1953," in *Air Power and Warfare: The Proceedings of the Eighth Military History Symposium*, ed. Alfred Hurley and Robert Ehrhart (Washington, DC, 1979), 217–18.

79 James Bamford, *The Puzzle Palace: A Report on America's Most Secret Agency* (New York, 1983), ch. 8.

80 Escott Reid, 'The Creation of the North Atlantic Alliance, 1948–1949,' in Granatstein, *Historical Readings*, 158–82.

81 Best, *British Influences*, 7–8.

82 on this point, see Martin Folly, 'Breaking the Vicious Circle: Britain, the United States, and the Genesis of the North Atlantic Treaty,' *Diplomatic History*, 12(1988), 7–8. The Canadian viewpoint is discussed in Lester Pearson, *Mike: The Memoirs of the Right Honourable Lester B. Pearson*, Vol. II: *1948–57* (Toronto, 1973), 44–7.

83 Lawrence Kaplan, *A Community of Interests: NATO and the Military Assistance Program, 1948–1951* (Washington, DC, 1980), 41–9.

84 The term is taken from Denis Stairs, *The Diplomacy of Constraint: Canada, the Korean War, and the United States* (Toronto, 1974).

85 'Defence Research Report,' 13 April 1953, O.M. Solandt Papers, vol. 2425 RG 24, Department of National Defence Records, NAC.

86 Steven Ross, *American War Plans, 1945–1950* (New York, 1988), 128–9.

87 Joseph Jockel, 'The Canada-United States Military Cooperation Committee and Continental Air Defence, 1946,' *Canadian Historical Review*, 64(1983), 352–77.

88 Pearson, *Memoirs*, II, 32–3.

89 Mackenzie King to Truman, 23 April 1947, file 711.42/4–2347, RG 84, NARS.

90 Minutes of the Second Meeting of the JIMPC, 8 August 1950, entry 31 JIMC file, RG 304, NARS.

91 J.L. Granatstein, *How Britain's Weakness Forced Canada into the Arms of the United States* (Toronto, 1989), 60.

92 Geir Lundestad, *The American Empire* (London, 1990).

93 D.C. Watt, 'Britain and the Historiography of the Yalta Conference and the Cold War,' *Diplomatic History*, 13(1989), 67–98; 'Stalin Blamed for Cold War,' *New York Times*, 3 March 1989; Jeffrey Hart, 'While America Slept,' *National Review*, 15 September 1989, 32–6.

94 *Dominion Bureau of Statistics Report*, 21 December 1953, file 200-12-2, vol. II, RG 49, NAC; 'The Establishment of New Manufacturing Firms in Canada,' 6 December 1950, Industrial Reports file 18, RG 49, NAC.

95 John Swettenham, *McNaughton*, Vol. III (Toronto, 1969), 188.

96 Escott Reid memorandum, 30 August 1947, in Hillmer and Page, *Canadian External Relations*, Vol. 13, 381.

7

From the Korean War to Suez: Anglo-American-Canadian Relations, 1950–1956

MARTIN KITCHEN

In the early hours of 25 June 1950 North Korean troops launched an attack across the 38th parallel and captured Seoul two days later. In Washington President Harry Truman and Secretary of State Dean Acheson acted promptly in calling a meeting of the United Nations (UN) Security Council. As the Soviet Union had boycotted the Security Council since January, in protest against UN refusal to admit Communist China, an American-sponsored resolution condemning this breach of the peace and calling for a cease-fire and withdrawal was passed by a vote of 9–0, with Yugoslavia abstaining. Two days later a further American resolution was adopted that recommended that 'the Members of the United Nations furnish such assistance to the Republic of Korea as may be necessary to repel the armed attack and to restore international peace and security in the area.' This time the vote was 7–1, with Yugoslavia opposed and India and Egypt not present. The Indian government announced a few days later that it supported the resolution. The Egyptian ambassador said that his government would have asked him to abstain.

The British government supported these actions. The prime minister, Clement Attlee, and the minister of state at the Foreign Office, Kenneth Younger, visited the foreign secretary, Ernest Bevin, who was in hospital, on the evening of the 25th. They all agreed that Britain should do everything possible to help the United States win full support for a UN action in Korea. Like the Americans, they were convinced that the North Koreans were acting on instructions from Moscow. Since the Soviets were absent from the Security Council, it seemed an excellent opportunity to use the UN to resist Communist aggression.[1]

Truman ordered air and sea cover for South Korea, sent the Seventh

Fleet to patrol the waters between Formosa and the Chinese mainland, and ordered increased military support for the Philippines and Indo-China. These actions were taken several hours before the UN resolution was passed on 27 June. In his public statement the president referred to armed aggression and war directed by 'centrally directed Communist Imperialism.' Many members of the British cabinet felt that his choice of words was most unfortunate and suspected that it was a deliberate attempt to involve Formosa. Bevin hoped that the Americans were planning to become more active in their support of the British in Malaya and the French in Indo-China and welcomed these clear signs that they had ceased to complain about British and French imperialism. The foreign secretary agreed, however, that the UN resolution should apply strictly to Korea.[2]

Although there was widespread support for the UN resolutions throughout the non-Communist world, serious misgivings about the operation soon developed. Since most of the troops in the UN contingent were American, it was essentially an American operation sanctioned by the world body. Since the American commander-in-chief, General Douglas MacArthur, paid scant attention to the directives of his own government, there were serious concerns about the aims of American policy in Asia. Would the powerful China lobby and hard-line Republicans succeed in converting the Korean war into a general anti-Communist crusade and encourage Chiang Kai-shek to launch an attack on mainland China? America was in the grips of anti-Communist hysteria. The Soviets had detonated their first atomic bomb in September 1949. In October Mao Tse-tung had won the civil war. In February 1950 Senator Joseph McCarthy had begun his hearings. The hunt was on for the traitors, spies, fellow travellers, and appeasers who had 'sold out the country' to the Communists. Even George Marshall and Dean Acheson, Truman's secretaries of state, had to listen to blistering attacks in the Senate by right-wing Republicans on their craven and unpatriotic failures to resist Communism.

The new containment policy was adumbrated in NSC-68, a document produced in early 1950 that defined Communism as totalitarian and expansionist, posing as big a danger as Nazi Germany. Massive rearmament was needed to meet this threat. The armed forces of the United States had to match those of the Soviet Union in every respect to allow a 'flexible response' to Communist incursions. Furthermore Communism was not simply to be contained; it had to be pushed back and the Cold War won by the Free World.

The British were very concerned that American involvement in South Korea might drastically weaken the defences of western Europe. In West Germany, which was still disarmed, there was widespread panic since the German Democratic Republic with its 60,000 paramilitary People's Police and twenty-seven 'fraternal' Soviet divisions faced twelve inferior NATO divisions with inadequate air cover. A worried Konrad Adenauer, the West German chancellor, asked the U.S. high commission to provide better defence for the Federal Republic. The logic of the situation was that since the Americans were fully engaged in Korea, Germany would have to be allowed to rearm. This argument did not escape the French, who were appalled at the prospect and strengthened the hand of those who argued that France should be neutral in the east-west conflict. The British had shown no particular interest in Korea until 1950, and the Americans had never seen fit to brief the British government on their policies in the peninsula. Churchill was later to announce proudly that he had 'never heard of the bloody place till I was seventy-four.'[3] The British were far more concerned about Hong Kong, Malaya and Indo China. Moreover they had recognized Communist China as early as January 1950, much to the ire of the Americans. Bevin insisted that Mao was first and foremost a nationalist rather than a Communist and that he might very well prove to be another Tito.

The Canadians, although less concerned about the defence of western Europe and with no immediate interests in Asia, were broadly in agreement with the British and shared many of the same concerns about American policy. At first they doubted whether the Americans would become militarily involved, since Acheson had given a speech to the National Press Club in January in which he defined the American defence perimeter as a line from the Aleutians to Japan, Okinawa, and the Philippines; thus it did not include Korea. In Tokyo in February the minister of external affairs, Lester Pearson, met General MacArthur, who also excluded Korea from the area into which the Americans would not allow the Communists to expand.[4] Like the British, the Canadians were first and foremost concerned to keep American actions in Korea under the aegis of the UN and to restrain the United States from getting embroiled in a large-scale, unilateral campaign against Asian Communism. They also were adamant that given Canada's limited armed forces, they should not be asked to make an extensive contribution to the UN force.

The St Laurent government was further strengthened in its resolve to become involved, however minimally, by reports from the Canadian

Joint Staff in London, which stated that the British government was solidly behind the UN resolution.[5] On 28 June Lester Pearson told the House of Commons that the United States was forced to act on behalf of the UN because the troops foreseen in the Charter did not exist. Although satisfying all but a lone and disgruntled Québécois, M. Pouliot, who spoke out against Canadian involvement in Korea, it was a somewhat disingenuous statement. The Americans had decided to intervene in Korea almost twenty-four hours before the UN resolution, and Truman had told the press that the United States would intervene eleven hours before the resolution was passed. UN intervention was, from the outset, little more than a convenient cover for an American action. It is not the case that the UN decided to support South Korea and then asked its members to take action in support of a state that had been wilfully attacked. The United States had decided, with undue and ill-considered haste, to intervene and then asked for the support of the UN.

The Canadians did not see the situation in this light. Although they had a number of reservations about American policy and objected to being treated as a very junior partner, they decided to support the American initiative because, as the Conservative opposition leader, George Drew, said in the House of Commons, what was at stake was not so much the future of Korea but the future of the UN. Both government and opposition were strongly committed to the ideals of the UN and furthermore were determined to use the UN to restrain the Americans. Thus the Canadian ambassador in Washington, Hume Wrong, made every effort to reduce the number of times the United States was mentioned in the Security Council's third resolution on Korea of 7 July and also objected to the clause in the preamble that 'recommended that Members of the United Nations furnish such assistance to the Republic of Korea as may be necessary to repel the armed attack and to restore international peace and security in the area.'[6] Ottawa was concerned that 'the area' might well be very generously defined by the Americans.

Bevin shared these concerns and instructed the British ambassador in Washington, Oliver Franks, to tell Acheson that although the British government supported the Americans in Korea, it had serious misgivings about their policy towards Formosa. Acheson sent a biting reply via the American ambassador, Lewis Douglas, in which he said 'I want to leave him (Bevin) in no doubt of seriousness with which I view implications of his message and their possible effect on our whole future relationship.'[7] The reservations of both the British and the Canadian governments about U.S. policy in Korea were considerably lessened by the failure of attempts by the Indian and British governments to get the Soviets to mediate. The Soviets meanwhile returned to the Security Council, even though China still had no seat in the UN and their ambassador, Jakob Malik, was as obstructive and tiresome as ever. The British were surprised to hear from the Americans that the fighting in Korea was likely to last for several months, having hoped that the hostilities would be ended before British troops could reach the area. They then committed the 29th Brigade along with naval forces.

The Canadians were even less forthcoming. They agreed to send three destroyers and five North Star transport planes. The military complained bitterly that this action seriously weakened Canada's defensive capacity if it turned out that Korea was merely a Soviet diversion. When Pearson told a State Department official that the three destroyers were no mere token, the latter replied testily 'Okay, let's call it three tokens!'[8] Tokens or not, the modest forces sent by eight other countries fought with distinction and at least showed the world that the UN operation in Korea was not a purely American affair, as the Soviets repeatedly insisted. Truman also needed to show the American people that the United States was not alone in Korea, and given that the American forces were taking a severe beating, he needed all the help he could get. The British were also keen to do everything possible to preserve the much vaunted, and largely mythical, 'special relationship' with the Americans; they feared that if they did not support the Americans in Korea, the western alliance would be in ruins. Attlee made the point very forcefully in his broadcast of 23 July 1950 in which he said: 'If the aggressors get away with it, aggressors all over the world will be encouraged ... The fire that has started in distant Korea may burn down your own house.'[9]

MacArthur's visit to Formosa at the end of July made it seem possible that the fire might well spread. Fortified by his assurances, Chiang announced: 'We are convinced that our struggle against Communist aggressors will end in final victory.'[10] A few weeks later MacArthur send a message to the Veterans of Foreign Wars (VFW) convention in which he announced: 'Nothing could be more fallacious than the threadbare argument by those who advocate appeasement and defeatism in the Pacific that if we defend Formosa we alienate continental Asia.' Such an argument, he said, making a dig at Acheson, could be advanced only by someone who did not understand 'oriental psychology.'[11] Truman quickly ordered MacArthur to withdraw this provocative message, but the damage had been done. It had been widely published and even read into the *Congressional Record*. It strengthened the convictions of those who, perfectly correctly, believed that China would soon be involved in the war.

In the first stages of the war, from June to September 1950, the North Koreans pushed the South Korean (ROK) and UN forces to the Pusan perimeter in the southeast corner of the peninsula. On 15 September MacArthur launched his daring landing at Inchon, on the west coast just below the 38th parallel, which was well behind the enemy lines. The landings were an outstanding success, and the North Korean forces (NKPA) began to disintegrate. NSC-81, which the president had approved a few days before the Inchon landings, outlined operations north of the 38th parallel that would completely smash the NKPA, but it warned that the border should be crossed only if 'there has been no entry into North Korea by major Soviet or Chinese forces, no announcement of intended entry, nor a threat to counter our operations militarily in North Korea.' UN troops were not to cross the Soviet or Chinese borders, and only ROK troops should be employed in the frontier areas.[12]

On 27 September MacArthur was given permission to cross the 38th parallel. Both Truman and Acheson felt that a solution to the Korean problem was close at hand and should not be spoilt by concern over what Acheson called 'a surveyor's line.' On 12 September the Americans had announced that they supported German rearmament, a unified NATO command, and an increased troop strength in Europe. Were the UN forces under American command to stop at the frontier of North Korea, there would be widespread complaints about a 'Europe first' policy and almost certainly a most unpleasant and politically damaging rift between the administration and MacArthur. Acheson wanted to take full advantage of the situation while the Soviets and the Chinese were still caught by surprise, and he believed that a forceful campaign in the north was the best way to deter them from intervening. Once again the administration wanted the UN to approve an American decision, and it found the British more than willing to sponsor a resolution permitting MacArthur to advance north of the 38th parallel. Although Pandit Jawahavlal Nehru, the Indian prime minister, warned Bevin that the Indian ambassador in Peking had been told that if the UN forces crossed the border of North Korea, the People's Army would intervene, the foreign secretary agreed to sponsor the motion that 'all appropriate steps be taken to ensure conditions of stability throughout Korea' and that elections should be held supervised by the UN to establish a 'unified, independent and democratic government.'[13]

The British Chiefs of Staff were seriously worried about extending the war beyond the 38th parallel; they felt that from a military point of view there was no reason why there should not be a pause so that the Chinese might clarify their position. Their reservations were conveyed to Attlee and the minister of defence, Emmanuel Shinwell, during the Labour party conference at Margate. After considerable heart searching the prime minister accepted Bevin's arguments that the American alliance had to be preserved and strengthened at a time when the United States was increasing its commitment to Europe. The British could not afford to look like appeasers, and in any case Bevin was convinced that the Chinese were bluffing. His major concern was that MacArthur would order the bombing of Manchuria and northern China if the People's Republic intervened as the general had assured an astounded British diplomat in Tokyo that he would.[14]

The Canadian position was presented forcefully in an address by Lester Pearson to the General Assembly on 27 September 1950. He insisted that the UN's aim in Korea was to unify the country and ensure free elections. The Communist aggressors in Korea had to be decisively defeated, if necessary by UN forces crossing the 38th parallel. A united Korea had to be free from foreign influence and was not to be a threat to its neighbours. The free governments of Asia were to give every assistance to Korea to set up a suitable system of government.[15] These five principles of Canadian policy were remarkably belligerent and contradictory. The aim of the UN was now no longer to restore the status quo ante bellum but to unify Korea and roll back Communism. How the Soviet Union could possibly witness the American-sponsored destruction of an ally on their borders without considering this 'a menace to Korea's neighbours' is hard to imagine. To add to the confusion, the Canadian government and its UN delegation felt that once the North Koreans had been driven back across the border, the UN forces would have fulfilled their mission. Pearson told the U.S. delegates in New York that his government had instructed him to call for a halt at the 38th parallel. Hume Wrong also had meetings with Acheson and Dean Rusk, the assistant secretary of state of far eastern affairs, and Philip Jessup, the American representative to the UN General Assembly, to explain the Canadian position. That it clearly contradicted the position taken by Lester Pearson in his address to the General Assembly seems to have been forgotten.[16]

Realizing that the Americans were determined to go ahead, Pearson tried to persuade them to reach a compromise. First he suggested that the North Koreans should be given a few days grace to decide whether to accept a cease-fire, failing which the UN forces would invade their country. Then he suggested a halt at the northern neck of Korea, between the 39th and 40th parallels. The Americans first indicated that they would agree to this course of action; then in the General Assembly they called for an immediate invasion of North Korea. Pearson was furious that his peace initiative had failed and felt that he had been cheated and deceived by the Americans. He explained this regrettable behaviour by assuming that the American government was completely subservient to the whims of General MacArthur. This being the case, he felt that the Canadians should in future have as little to do with Korea as possible. Prompted by Hume Wrong, Acheson made a rather lame apology to Pearson about what he described as 'an unfortunate mixup,' but this acknowledgment did nothing to change American policy in Korea.

The resolution, which passed in the General Assembly by forty-seven votes to five with eight abstentions, was extraordinarily vaguely worded. It was not at all clear how the unification of Korea was to be achieved, or what steps could be deemed 'appropriate.' MacArthur had no hesitation in announcing two days later that he intended to 'take such military action as may be necessary to enforce the decrees of the United Nations.'

MacArthur was still convinced that the Chinese were merely bluffing and that in any case his aircraft could destroy all the bridges across the Yalu River and thus prevent them from reaching North Korea. On 9 October, the day that MacArthur crossed the 38th parallel, Bevin told the cabinet that he did not think that the Chinese would intervene and that K.M. Pannikar, the Indian ambassador to China, had not produced any 'hard evidence' that their threat could be taken seriously. Bevin felt that it was politically unacceptable to call for a halt at a time when it seemed that the war was almost won and when a victory in Korea would provide a much-needed boost to the government's popularity.[17] Truman met MacArthur on Wake Island on 15 October armed with a report from the CIA which argued that the Chinese were unlikely to intervene. Before Truman left Washington, the British ambassador, Oliver Franks, had begged him to ensure that no action would be taken outside Korea in the event of a Chinese intervention without the express permission of the president. He also requested that the British be consulted if such action was contemplated. Clearly the British government was worried about MacArthur and his unpredictable and swashbuckling behaviour. Truman, however, was in no mood for caution. He wanted to show his solidarity with the victorious MacArthur on the eve of the November congressional elections and was encouraged by the general's assurances that the war would be over by the end of that month.

MacArthur's predictions seemed to be amply justified. The North Korean capital, Pyongyang, fell on 20 October, and casting all caution aside, MacArthur ordered UN troops to advance to the Yalu. There were still no signs of Chinese intervention, so it was no longer considered necessary to send only South Korean troops to the extreme north. The general euphoria over this rapid advance was marred only by reports of atrocities committed by the ROK armies. Bevin was concerned that public opinion might turn against the UN forces if President Syngman Rhee's South Korean troops were not brought to heel. He called for free elections in both Koreas, to be supervised by the UN, in order to get rid of Rhee. The Americans, determined that Rhee's government must be seen as the legitimate government of South Korea, elected freely under UN supervision, ignored Bevin's strictures.[18] On 5 November 1950 MacArthur announced that Chinese troops had appeared on the battlefields of North Korea and that Chinese-manned MIG-15s were in the skies of the northwest. His immediate reaction was to bomb the Yalu bridges and to order 'hot pursuits' of Chinese aircraft across the border into China. Truman ordered that only the Korean end of the bridges could be attacked, to avoid bombing Chinese territory, but the reaction among America's UN allies was so negative that 'hot pursuits' were banned.

The Canadian government was very concerned that MacArthur's impetuosity and lack of concern for the UN could very well lead to war between the United States and China. Pearson blamed the general for the Chinese intervention in the war on the grounds that the Americans were likely to attack China's hydroelectric stations on the Yalu and that Chinese troops had been sent to protect them.[19] In a position paper prepared in the Department of External Affairs in November for Canada's major diplomatic posts, Pearson insisted that the aim of Soviet policy was to get the western democracies bogged down in a war in Korea and thus seriously weaken the defences of western Europe. But a war with China would be even more disastrous, since world opinion would blame the United States because of its intransigence over Formosa and its refusal to admit China to the UN, in addition to countless provocative statements from MacArthur and the Republican right.[20]

In Britain the reaction was, as usual, much stronger. The Chiefs of Staff were convinced that if MacArthur advanced to the Yalu, war with China would be inevitable. They suggested that UN forces should halt at the 40th parallel beyond which there should be a demilitarized zone (DMZ). Bevin supported this idea and suggested that the DMZ could be patrolled by the UN in collaboration with the Chinese. But it was already too late. American troops had advanced well beyond the 40th parallel, and they did not want to appear to back down in the face of Chinese threats. Furthermore, the Republican right had made substantial gains in the congressional elections, and their inevitable objections to such a scheme could not be ignored. Acheson asked Bevin not to put forward his suggestions at this stage, and the foreign secretary agreed. He knew what pressures the Truman administration was under, and having recently won the battle over hot pursuits, he did not want to press the Americans further.[21]

MacArthur launched what he confidently hoped would be his final offensive on 24 November 1950. Two days later the Chinese counterattacked to devastating effect. MacArthur issued a series of alarming statements from his headquarters in Tokyo calling for the bombing of Manchuria, the use of Kuomintang troops, a blockade of the Chinese mainland, and possibly the use of atomic bombs. This belligerence triggered a fierce political debate in the United States. Was MacArthur justified in claiming that the catastrophe in Korea was due to the fact that he had been hamstrung by timid politicians? What should be America's future policy towards China? Elsewhere there was widespread fear of a third world war and a uneasy feeling that the Soviet Union would exploit the situation to strengthen its hand in Europe. On 30 November Truman told a press conference that he was prepared to use 'every weapon that we have' and that there had been 'active consideration' of the use of the atomic bomb.

Attlee called an emergency cabinet meeting to discuss the situation following a stormy Commons debate in which seventy-six Labour MPs announced that they would not support the government if it approved of an attack on Manchuria or the use of the A-bomb. For the opposition, Churchill warned of the dangers to Europe if the Korean situation got out of hand. The news that Attlee had decided to go to Washington was met with worldwide relief. The prime minister travelled without Bevin, who was too sick to withstand the lengthy flight, and arrived in Washington on 4 December. Attlee found that Truman and Acheson were in full agreement that NATO had to be strengthened and that an American supreme commander had to be appointed as soon as possible. They would not listen, however, to the suggestion that China could be separated from the Soviet Union and should be admitted to the UN; nor would they consider linking a cease-fire along the 38th parallel to these political concessions to China. To do so, they felt, would be tantamount to rewarding aggression and would be political suicide, given the hawkish political climate in the United States after the mid-term congressional elections.

It used to be believed that Attlee's visit to Washington stopped the Americans from using the atomic bomb, but this belief has since been shown to be fallacious. Misunderstandings caused by Truman's press conference had already been cleared up, and the British were assured that the Americans were not seriously considering using the bomb. The final communiqué said that the Americans would keep the British informed about whether they intended to use the bomb, a far cry from the assurance by the president that Britain would be consulted. Small wonder that Acheson described Attlee's response as 'a long withdrawing, melancholy sigh.'[22] Writing privately to Bevin, Attlee insisted that the communiqué was for domestic consumption and was harsher in tone than the discussions warranted and that 'the UK was lifted out of the European queue and we were treated as partners, unequal no doubt in power but still equal in counsel.' This was an unusually optimistic gloss on the proceedings for the laconic prime minister.

The Canadians were equally anxious about the use of the bomb and agreed with the British that the war should be ended as soon as possible. On 2 December the Canadian government sent a memorandum to friendly governments which argued: 'Every opportunity for discussion of the issues with Communist China should be explored. Once the military situation has been stabilised a cease-fire might be obtainable.' It was also suggested that China should be given a seat in the UN along with Formosa.[23] The Canadian position was closer to that of the Americans than to that of the British in its insistence on a stabilization of the front before negotiations began.

In December 1950 the UN established a three-man cease-fire group for Korea. It laid out the 'Five Principles' for a cease-fire in January, which stated that a cease-fire in Korea should be the prelude to a debate on Far-Eastern issues, including Peking's claim to a seat in the UN and the future of Formosa. These topics would be discussed by a committee of Chinese, Soviet, American, and British officials under the auspices of the UN. Foreign troops would be withdrawn from Korea 'in appropriate stages.' The Koreans would decide their own future according to the principles of the UN.[24] The British, who had urged the group to establish such a set of principles, favoured the proposal. Pearson was also optimistic and hoped that the Chinese would find the terms acceptable. He was encouraged by the news that the Americans had agreed to the principles, but he did not realize that they had done so in the hope that they would be rejected by the Chinese.[25] When the Chinese announced that they would not discuss a cease-fire without consideration of broader political issues, the Americans called for a condemnation of Chinese aggression by the UN.

The British government was appalled by this rhetoric. It feared that the Americans, who were again in full retreat following MacArthur's strategic blunder of leaving his X Corps unsupported on the eastern flank, might well abandon Korea and attack China. Public opinion in Britain was increasingly critical of the Americans. The Republican right that had done so well in the recent elections was extremist anti-Communist, and Attlee felt that its hysterical fear of Communism would lead to war. News of ROK atrocities and Truman's threats to use the bomb were further causes for concern, and many were uneasy that the international crisis over Korea would lead to a revival of German power to meet the Soviet threat in Europe. A number of leading figures in the Labour party argued in favour of voting against the United States in the UN. Bevin, who argued that a break with the United States would leave Britain in a disastrously exposed position relative to the Soviet Union, was in failing health and did not have long to live. In his last memorandum on the subject, written on 12 January, he argued: 'We have to imagine what it would be like to live in a world with a hostile Communist bloc, an uncooperative America, a Commonwealth pulled in two directions and a disillusioned Europe, deprived of American support.'[26] On 25 January 1951 Younger obtained a majority in cabinet to vote against the United States in the Security Council. The following day cabinet reversed its decision, partly as a result of the efforts of the chancellor of the Exchequer, Hugh Gaitskell, who considered the anti-Americanism of some of his colleagues 'pathological.' Britain thus did not side with the Communist bloc at the UN on 1 February and dutifully supported the American resolution.

Relations between the Canadians and the Americans were also extremely strained over the UN vote. Like Britain, Canada had tried to get the Chinese to clarify their position and had invited India to act as intermediary. The Americans complained that the Canadians were negotiating behind their backs and that they had not been properly consulted. Pearson replied that the Canadian government was not obliged to inform the United States whenever it consulted a fellow member of the Commonwealth, and that since the Americans had already made up their minds about China, it was hardly necessary to consult them.[27] The Canadians voted for the resolution with almost as many reservations as the British and used the same rather lame argument that as allies of the United States they could exercise a restraining influence on their often erratic partner. Shortly after the UN vote the military situation in Korea stabilized. General Matthew Ridgway's Eighth Army drove the Communists back almost to the 38th parallel. The British were anxious that UN, troops should not cross the parallel before a serious attempt had been made to reach a compromise with the Chinese. The Canadians were similarly worried that the Americans were spoiling for a fight with China and might not be able or willing to restrain MacArthur. Their worst fears were confirmed on 24 March when he announced that if the Chinese did not begin negotiations with the UN, he would destroy China's ports and cities.

The British ambassador to the UN, Gladwyn Jebb, told the Foreign Office that if MacArthur imagined he could get the UN's support for such a policy, 'he must only be conscious of public opinion in the Philippines, some of the banana states and the lunatic fringe of the Republican Party.' Dean Rusk informed the British ambassador in Washington, Oliver Franks, that there was little that could be done to restrain the general, since Congress would not tolerate an attempt to disown him and American help to Europe could become endangered.[28] In Canada, Pearson made a number of public speeches expressing his concerns over the political climate in America and MacArthur's irresponsible behaviour.[29] At the beginning of April the Americans proposed the bombing of Manchurian air bases if such action was deemed essential for the safety of UN troops, and MacArthur threatened a massive demonstration of naval power off the Chinese coast. There was considerable relief in Britain when it was learned that Truman had sacked MacArthur on 11 April for criticizing the administration's policies in Korea in a letter to the Republican minority leader in Congress, Joseph Martin. Herbert Morrison, Bevin's successor, wisely counselled his colleagues not to show their delight at this announcement too openly for fear of making MacArthur into a martyr in the eyes of the still-powerful Republican right.[30] The Gallup Poll showed that 69 per cent of Americans supported MacArthur, and across the nation effigies of Truman were burnt. On MacArthur's return to San Francisco 100,000 people welcomed him. He then travelled to Washington to address a joint session of Congress, but the storm was soon over and, as he said in this speech, like an old soldier he just faded away.[31]

There was a general feeling of relief in the Canadian Parliament that MacArthur had been given the sack, but some concern was expressed about the possible consequences. Writing to Hume Wrong a few days later, Pearson said: 'The events of the next two or three weeks will show whether moderate, wise and healthy influences will prevail over hysteria, prejudice and immaturity. I think the President is going to win on this issue, but if he doesn't, and if the forces which are backing MacArthur prevail, there will be stronger expressions used up here about American policy than have been even contemplated previously.'[32] As noted above, the British were equally delighted that MacArthur had been sacked, but were warned by Morrison that there should be no public expressions of glee for they would only provide rightwing Republicans with further ammunition for attacking the Truman administration for being soft on Asian Communism and led astray by socialist Britain and selfish Europeans.[33] Many of MacArthur's supporters were convinced that Britain had played an important part in their hero's dismissal.

The uproar in the United States over the dismissal of MacArthur died down somewhat when one of his central contentions at the congressional hearing was proved fallacious. The general had insisted that a military stalemate in Korea would lead to a protracted war of attrition in which U.S. casualties would be unacceptably high. General Ridgway withstood two massive Chinese offensives by the skilful and concentrated use of air power and artillery. At the end of May he announced that the Chinese were so exhausted that they could no longer launch a serious offensive south of the 38th parallel.[34] On 18 May Dean Rusk made a speech claiming that the Taiwan government represented the Chinese people and that Peking was a 'slavic Manchukuo on a gigantic scale.' British officials were appalled at this speech, which implied that Washington would never treat with the existing Chinese government, and Herbert Morrison feared that this attitude might mean that the United States was contemplating action against China.

Anglo-American relations were now badly strained. Britain had been obliged to rearm and had introduced prescription charges in April 1951 to meet part of the costs, a move that had led to the resignation of Nye Bevan. Many felt that Britain had been forced by the Americans to accept German rearmament, a widely unpopular move. Rusk's speech was seen as further evidence of American anti-Communist hysteria, which could well drag the west into a catastrophic war. On the other hand, Britain was in no position to impose its will on the United States, and even the idea that British support for the Americans in Asia might lead to American support for the British in Iran proved to be a vain hope. The uncompromising attitude of the Chinese government also did much to strengthen the American case. The British government was unable to convince the Americans that Peking should be invited to the Japanese peace conference and was obliged to accept the American position that neither Chinese government should attend. It was further humiliating evidence of the decline of British influence in Asia.

British fears that the conflict might soon get out of hand fortunately were exaggerated. On 2 May the Soviet ambassador to the UN, Jakob Malik, gave a lift to two U.S. officials as he drove into Manhattan. In the course of conversation over Korea, Malik hinted that the Soviet Union was interested in a negotiated settlement. George Kennan, who was on leave of absence from the State Department, was asked to pursue the conversations in the car, and the Americans came to the conclusion that an armistice might be negotiated. To avoid the embarrassing issue of de facto recognition of the Peking government, it was agreed that the armistice talks should be conducted by the commander in the field, not by diplomats at the UN. The talks began at Kaesong on 10 July. North Koreans was represented by Nam Il, chief of staff to the NKPA, and the UN by Admiral C. Turner Joy. The South Koreans were present at the talks, but America's other allies were absent and ill informed as to what was going on.

The talks proceeded slowly, 'with all the speed of a stiff concrete mix,' as Admiral Joy complained.[35] The main point of dispute was the Communist insistence that Korea should be divided along the 38th parallel. Although the Americans had earlier agreed to this return to the status quo ante bellum, it would mean a withdrawal of UN troops from the Kansas-Wyoming Line, which would leave Seoul open to attack from the north. America's allies, particularly Britain, were anxious that the war should be ended as soon as possible and feared that the Americans might become so frustrated that they would extend the war. In September Morrison visited the United States and irritated his hosts with lectures on the dangers of pushing the Chinese further into the Soviet camp. There was considerable relief in Washington when Labour was ousted and Churchill returned to No. 10 Downing Street in November. The prime minister and his foreign secretary, Anthony Eden, supported American policy towards Korea and insisted that it would be criminal to drop an old ally like Chiang. On the other hand, the Conservative government did not contemplate withdrawing recognition from Peking and was as anxious as its predecessor not to extend the war. A war with China would endanger Hong Kong, weaken the west's defences in Europe, and run the risk of a major war with the Soviet Union. Britain's economic problems made the conclusion of an early peace of primary importance. For all the difference in tone, Conservative policy towards Asia thus remained virtually the same as that of Labour.[36]

In order to break the deadlock in the armistice talks the United States proposed concessions on the inspection issue and 'greater sanctions,' meaning retaliation against the Chinese should they breach the armistice. The Americans wanted to bomb selected targets in China and blockade the coast. The British were highly alarmed at this suggestion and managed to tone down the wording of the warning to the Chinese to read that if the armistice was broken by the Chinese 'in all probability, it would not be possible to confine hostilities within the frontiers of Korea.'[37] One of the major problems at the armistice talks was the question of the POWs. Under Article 118 of the Geneva Convention of 1949 all POWs were to be repatriated at the termination of hostilities. But the Convention did not apply to civil wars, and the problem was further exacerbated by the existence of two Koreas and two Chinas. Many North Korean and Chinese POWs sought asylum in the ROK and Taiwan, and the Americans had no desire to send them back to their Communist homelands, since doing so would give the DPRK and China a degree of legitimacy that Washington stoutly denied. The Communists agreed that lists should be drawn up of those POWs who wished to be repatriated, and they issued a statement granting amnesty to all who returned. This scheme was acceptable to the United States, but in the POW camps, particularly in the huge compound on Koje island, South Korean guards and anti-Communist militants beat and terrorized the prisoners into refusing repatriation. Whereas the Americans assumed that 116,000 of the 132,000 prisoners on Koje would wish to return home, of the 106,000 interviewed only 31,000 were prepared to be repatriated. Clearly the Communists could not accept this humiliating result, but the Americans would not accept that force had been used and saw these results as further proof that the DPRK and China were illegitimate regimes without popular support. One again the armistice talks ground to a halt, this time on the eve of the American presidential campaign in the autumn of 1952.

The Foreign Office was sharply critical of American policy over the POWs and felt that it was endangering the return of British and other UN prisoners. As C.G. Kimball, the head of the Consular Department, said: 'callous as it may seem, I would rather have a few North Korean POWs liquidated by the Communists than delay the liberation of our people.' An official at the Korea desk was even more direct: 'I also feel that the humanitarian argument, that we could not have it on our conscience to force prisoners to return to death or slavery, has been given too much importance.' Eden, typically, wavered on this issue, commenting that he 'did not like the idea of sending back these poor devils to death or worse.' Churchill was adamant that the American position should be supported, and the advocates of forcible repatriation were silenced.[38]

The POW issue became a matter of popular concern when the Communist POWs on Koje rioted and captured the American commander of the camp. The riot was quashed, with considerable loss of life, by combat troops among whom were British and Canadian units. Questions were asked in the Houses of Commons in London and Ottawa. Largely to silence the opposition, the government sent the minister of defence, Lord Alexander, and the minister of state at the Foreign Office, Selwyn Lloyd, to Korea, supposedly on a fact-finding mission. The ministers travelled home via Ottawa, where they gave the Americans a good report, claiming that they had seen no evidence of intimidation or ill treatment, except by Communist POWs. Selwyn Lloyd repeated these anodyne statements in the House of Commons on 1 July. A story in the *Toronto Star* detailed the physical threats used against POWs by the anti-Communists and was repeated in the British Communist *Daily Worker* in an article that attracted considerable attention. The Canadians protested vigorously that their troops had been used to put down the revolt without Ottawa's being consulted. The Canadian officer who had authorized the use of these troops was recalled and forced to take early retirement. Moscow Radio made much of this incident, and Washington felt obliged to make a partial confession of its misdemeanours.[39]

In May the Indians passed on a message from Chou En-Lai asking the British to use their influence to break the deadlock over the POWs. Anxious to bring the war to a close, but wary of antagonizing the Americans, Eden skilfully pursued this idea. With the active participation of the Indians, particularly the ambassador in Peking, K.M. Panikkar, a wily if slippery diplomatist, a proposal was put forward that POWs under the UNC should be screened by a four-power neutral commission. While these negotiations were going on, the UN launched a massive air strike on 23 June 1952 against the hydroelectric plants on the Yalu, highly sensitive targets, since they supplied electricity to both

China and the Soviet Union. The Labour party was in an uproar because the government clearly had known nothing of the preparations for this attack, even though two senior ministers were in Korea during the planning stages. The government was embarrassed, since it could not deny that it had not been consulted. To repair the damage the Americans agreed to appoint a British deputy to General Mark Clark, who had succeeded Ridgway in May 1952, and Dean Acheson apologized profusely to a meeting of MPs in Westminster Hall. The raids effectively ended the talks with Peking over the POWs, and the Chinese roundly condemned the notion of voluntary repatriation, a move that convinced Prime Minister Nehru that there was little to choose between the Chinese and the Americans on the POW question. He resolved to have nothing more to do with the issue.[40]

America's allies were very concerned about the effects of the presidential election on U.S. policy in Korea. The Republican front-runner, Senator Robert Taft, advocated a landing on the Chinese mainland by nationalist forces sponsored by the United States. Adlai Stevenson, the Democratic candidate, supported Truman's policy in Korea and rejected both appeasement and escalation. General Eisenhower, who won the Republican nomination, endorsed John Foster Dulles's policy of rolling back, rather than containing, Communism, and promised to work for the liberation of Soviet satellites. His vice-presidential candidate, Richard Nixon, denounced Stevenson as a graduate of Dean Acheson's 'Cowardly College of Communist Containment.'[41] In September at Cincinnati, in a major speech on Korea, Eisenhower called upon the ROK to play a greater part in the war, which should become a war of Asians against Asians with the United States on the side of freedom. Truman was furious at this attack on his policy and vigorously defended his position on Korea in a series of blistering speeches. At the end of October Eisenhower promised that he would make Korea his first priority, and the widespread belief that he could bring the war to an honourable conclusion was a major reason for his resounding victory.

Encouraged by all the tough talk about 'liberation' during the campaign, Mark Clark demanded an end to all restraints on waging the Korean war and announced that the time had come to 'go for victory.' On 29 September he called for the use of atomic bombs, the bombing of Manchuria, the use of two Kuomintang divisions, an increase in the ROK army, and reinforcements for the UN contingent.[42] Truman agreed that the ROK army should be expanded but rejected all Clark's other suggestions on the grounds that they would be unacceptable to the allies. Eden was absolutely opposed to the idea of putting any more pressure on China, and Lester Pearson, who was now president of the UN General Assembly, saw it as his main task to find a solution to the Korean conflict and to stop any attempt to widen the war.[43]

Angered by the opposition of its allies, the United States sponsored a '21-power resolution' which called upon the North Koreans and the Chinese to 'agree to an armistice which recognizes the rights of all prisoners of war ... to be repatriated and avoids the use of force in their repatriation.' The Indian government would not support the resolution on the grounds that it would be unacceptable to the Communists, and repeated their proposal for a four-power commission of Sweden, Switzerland, Poland, and Czechoslovakia, possibly chaired by an Indian, to supervise the POWs. The British and Canadian governments supported this plan, and Lester Pearson worked tirelessly with Krishna Menon, whom he described as 'a very clever man with a great capacity for constructive action and an almost equal capacity for mischief,' to reconcile the Indian and American positions. It was an effort that earned Pearson the contempt of Dean Acheson, who was strongly opposed to the Indian plan.[44] Both Pearson and Eden were appalled at American intransigence over the POW issue, and Pearson came to the conclusion that the American military was deliberately trying to sabotage the armistice talks.[45] Acheson peevishly told his allies that since the Americans were bearing the brunt of the war, the judgment of American generals should be given decisive weight.

Acheson found himself increasingly isolated. President-elect Eisenhower refused to lend him any encouragement. Pearson and Eden were winning wide support for the Indian resolution. He vented his spleen by describing Pearson as 'an empty glass of water' and Selwyn Lloyd as 'a little Welsh lawyer.' Eden later remarked: 'But for the knowledge that Mr Acheson had just come from a somewhat prolonged cocktail party in his own suite, I should have felt bound to take him up seriously.' He felt that Acheson was falling apart under the pressure of events.[46] Since the Democrats had lost the election, Acheson was in no position to stand up to this united front, and the realization of his powerlessness increased his frustration. Soviet opposition to the Indian proposal made Acheson more sympathetic to it, though he still harboured a deep loathing for the Indians, and after some tinkering with the text the resolution was passed on 3 December with only the Soviet bloc opposed. On 15 December the resolution was rejected by Peking, possibly because of Soviet pressure but also because the Chinese preferred to wait for the induction of the new American administration, which might well reject a compromise solution.

Meanwhile, in September the Americans had successfully tested their first hydrogen bomb. Churchill was worried that, given the talk of liberation and rollback and with Mark Clark straining at the leash, they might be tempted to use it against the Soviet Union, in which case Britain, which was strategically little more than an aircraft carrier for the U.S. Air Force, would be in the front line. The prime minister was therefore determined to call a summit conference to ease the tension and to confirm Britain's status as a Great Power and one of the Big Three. When Eisenhower assumed the presidency, both the Pentagon and the Joint Chiefs of Staff were pressing for the use of atomic weapons in Korea and Manchuria. The president, who favoured an early offensive in Korea, felt that such weapons would have to be used, and he and Dulles issued numerous statements hinting that their use was being considered. Atomic weapons were moved to Okinawa in readiness. The first major act in his administration was to withdraw the Seventh Fleet from the Taiwan straits. Eden sent a sharply worded note of protest to Washington and criticized the American action in the House of Commons. Dulles was sent to London to repair the damage, and he assured the British that the Americans were not thinking of unleashing Chiang.

There is no clear evidence as to why the Communists decided to negotiate. They were faced with the possibility of massive retaliation from the Americans. The British and like-minded allies were trying to reopen the talks on the POWs. The Korean War was a severe drain of Soviet resources. Stalin was beginning a fresh round of domestic purges and wanted to be free of foreign entanglements. On 5 March 1953 Stalin died and at his funeral his successor, Georgi Malenkov, spoke of the possibility of peaceful coexistence. When Chou En-Lai returned from the funeral, the Chinese and North Koreans agreed to the exchange of sick and wounded POWs, as had been proposed by Eden. Civilian detainees were released shortly after. The British government urged the Americans to seize this opportunity and return to Panmunjom to resume the armistice talks. Eisenhower did not take up Churchill's suggestion for a summit, but he did agree to the resumption of the armistice talks. Much to the dismay of the British the talks soon bogged down over the POW issue, the Americans taking a particularly intransigent line. Churchill sent a protest note to Washington and reiterated his call for a summit.[47] Syngman Rhee was also doing his best to sabotage the armistice talks, denouncing them as an attempt to partition his country. Churchill was furious with Rhee and growled: 'If I were in charge, I would withdraw UN troops to the coast and leave Syngman Rhee to the Chinese ... Korea does not matter now.'[48] The Canadians were equally distressed about the American rejection of the UN resolution, which they had done so much to sponsor and the Communists now accepted.[49] In his final attempt to ruin the armistice talks, which were progressing well with both sides showing a willingness to compromise, Rhee ordered the release of 25,000 'non-repatriables,' Communist POWs who did not wish to return home. Lester Pearson protested vigorously in his roles as minister of external affairs and president of the General Assembly. Rhee was bought off by promises of massive American aid, and the armistice was finally signed on 27 July 1953.

Eisenhower claimed that ending the Korean War was his greatest achievement.[50] Perhaps only a man of his enormous stature had the authority to end the war without causing serious political divisions at home. It was a war for which there was no moral justification, which had been fought for ideological reasons with serious misunderstandings on both sides and ended in a stalemate. Truman had dragged the UN into the conflict, although there was no need for him to do so under the terms of the Potsdam agreement, and in doing so he placed a serious strain on his allies and discredited the UN as little more than a blunt instrument of American imperialism. By gaining the much-vaunted 'moral support' of the UN, Truman did not have to win congressional approval for his war and thus greatly strengthened the executive branch.

Far from weakening Communism, the war established China as a first-rate military power; it was less dependent on the Soviet Union than it had been and went ahead with its atomic bomb program. It was a pointless war which solved nothing, and Eisenhower showed his greatness and his skill in ending it quickly, as he had promised he would in his campaign. He was to do the same in 1956 in ending Britain's Suez adventure. The lessons of the two wars are similar. Britain and Canada exercised the diplomacy of constraint with their closest ally, but their influence was minimal. Churchill had called for 'a place on the bridge within reach of the wheel,' but he got no further than a place at the captain's table.[51] The Americans acted in their own interests with no regard for the interests of their allies, and the fact that they came to much the same conclusions about Korea had precious little to do with promptings from London or Ottawa, which were seen as little more than tiresome carping. Korea clearly showed that the United States was a hegemonic power and that the much-vaunted 'special relationship' was the fond illusion of a second-rate power. This lesson was brought home painfully during the Suez crisis.

During the election campaign of 1951 Churchill had launched a scathing attack on the Labour party's policy of 'scuttle.' Mossadeq had recently nationalized the Abadan oil refinery, Britain's largest overseas asset. Nahas Pasha, the Egyptian premier, had renounced the Anglo-Egyptian condominium over the Sudan and denied Britain's right to station troops in Egypt under the treaty of 1936. Attlee had refused to move, arguing that Britain would not have the support of the United States and thus would have to face the opposition of the UN alone. Furthermore, Attlee doubted whether military action would secure the overthrow of Mossadeq and argued that such an action would simply unite Egypt behind him. These were arguments that Anthony Eden would have done well to have heeded in 1956.

From the U.S. perspective, the Russian arms deal with Egypt in the autumn of 1955 did not seem to John Foster Dulles a serious threat, and the State Department sugested, basing its argument on American experience of foreign aid, that it might soon prove to be a liability to the Soviets.[52] For the Israelis, however, the prospect of an Egypt armed with 300 medium and heavy tanks, 200 MIG 15s, fifty Ilyushin bombers, and sundry other military hardware did not inspire confidence.[53] The Israeli chief of staff, Moshe Dayan, believed it would take the Egyptians a mere six months to master these new weapons; other experts argued that it would take much longer, but Israeli policy was dictated by Dayan's worst-case scenario. Planning began at the end of October 1955 for a pre-emptive strike against Egypt, plans that were quickly picked up by British intelligence.[54] David Ben Gurion, the Israeli premier, then had a change of heart. He argued that wars do not end wars, that Israeli aggression would be met by an arms embargo, and, in a curious flight of fancy, that the British might be tempted to side with the Arabs in order to obtain another military base.[55] The operation was called off, and the Israel Defence Force was allowed to raid Syria to keep up morale.

Meanwhile Colonel Gamal Abdul Nasser pushed ahead with his scheme to build the High Aswan Dam. The World Bank agreed that the scheme was economically sound but felt that the German contractors, Hochtief, had underestimated the cost. The World Bank was prepared to advance a loan of $200 million, but Egypt was left with the task of finding another $200 million. Less than one month after the arms deal, the Russians announced that they would put up the money. This move caused Eden to panic; he begged the American ambassador, Winthrop Aldrich, to persuade his government that the western powers would have to finance the deal, or the Soviets would be safely entrenched on the other side of the Northern Tier of the Baghdad Pact.[56] The Americans were not unsympathetic, but they insisted that the project had to be on a sound economic footing and that there should be competitive tendering.

At a meeting with Lester Pearson on 27 March Dulles complained that the British were very 'jittery' in the Middle East, handling negotiations with Jordan over entry into the Baghdad Pact very ineptly and alienating the Saudis over the Buraimi affair. Pearson agreed, suggesting that Eden's problems might be genetic when he remarked with characteristic understatement that his father had been 'quite eccentric.'[57] Eden was indeed becoming obsessed with the idea of Nasser as an Arab Mussolini who was the close ally of the Soviet Union, and he even suggested that he should be murdered.[58] Yet although the Americans disagreed with the alarmist assessments of British intelligence as to Nasser's long-term aims, the CIA cooperated with MI6 in drawing up plans for toppling the Syrian government in collusion with the Iraqis, whom the British also hoped to use to overthrow King Saud of Saudi Arabia. It was agreed that the coup against the Syrian government should take place on 29 October 1956.

In June 1956 Nasser became president of Egypt. Dmitri Shepilov, the new Soviet foreign minister, attended the ceremonies, in the course of which he told Nasser that the Soviet Union was prepared to finance the Aswan Dam with no strings attached. Ahmed Hussein, the Egyptian ambassador in Washington, warned Nasser that if he took up this offer he would be handing Egypt over to a foreign power. He suggested that the Anglo-American offer should be taken up, and Nasser suddenly agreed that the ambassador should return to Washington and tell the Americans that he accepted the terms laid out in their memoranda. Nasser predicted that the terms would be rejected, and he stated that rather than accept the Russian offer he would nationalize the canal in order to finance this mega-project. The president was proved correct, much to Ahmed Hussein's horror and amazement. Bluntly telling him that American public opinion would not accept expenditure on this scale and that the offer was withdrawn, Dulles insisted that the project was far too costly for an economy like Egypt's to sustain and that Egyptians should concentrate on less grandiose projects.[59] Dulles was delighted with this interview, feeling that he had shifted an intolerable burden onto the backs of the Soviet Union and their unfortunate satellites. The British, government was in substantial agreement and withdrew their grants. Without the support of the Americans and the British, the World Bank announced that a loan would not be forthcoming.

Nasser reacted in a way that neither the Americans nor the British had foreseen. On 26 July 1956, while he addressed the crowds in Cairo, Egyptian troops took over the offices of the Suez Canal Co. and the company was nationalized. This news drove Eden 'bananas,' as Sir Dermot Boyle remarked. As chief of Air Staff he had attended a late-night meeting at 10 Downing Street where Eden had pressed for military action against Egypt. There were, however, a number of problems. The army would not be able to send an invasion force for some two months and the RAF needed four weeks to get ready. Only the Mediterranean fleet was ready to sail within a matter of hours. At a cabinet meeting the following day it was pointed out that Nasser had acted perfectly legally in that he had simply offered to buy out the shareholders, offering the share prices as of 25 July.[60] A further problem was that Britain had only three weeks' worth of oil supplies and thus needed to keep the canal open for some time to build up reserves. Nevertheless the cabinet agreed unanimously that military force should be used if necessary against Egypt, even if such a course of action was not supported by either the United States or France.

The Americans felt that Eden was altogether too alarmist. Nasser had as yet done nothing illegal. Only if he made good his threat to imprison pilots and engineers who threatened to leave their posts or if the management of the canal proved to be utterly incompetent was military action justified. The chief of naval operations, Admiral Arleigh Burke, advised the White House that piloting through the canal was very easy, and if the pilots left, it would not be difficult to find replacements. France, with the exception of the Communists and Mendes-France, was united against Nasser. He was hated either for his stand against Israel or because he was thought to be the mastermind behind the Algerian FLN. The socialist government was determined to show that it was tough; the defence staff was anxious to have a crack at Nasser; and Admiral Henri Nomy, chief of the Naval Staff was sent to England, violating the sacred peace of the weekend, to tell the British that the French were determined to take military action against Egypt.

Meanwhile messages from the ambassadors in Washington were far from encouraging. Both Maurice Couve de Murville, who was almost alone in seeing the connection between the Aswan Dam and the canal, and Sir Roger Makins warned that the Americans were likely to want to mediate and said they thought that military action was unjustified at present. President Eisenhower's envoy to London warned Selwyn Lloyd, the foreign secretary, not to take precipitate military action, since it would not be acceptable to world opinion.[61] This warning cut little ice with the government's Suez Committee, and Harold Macmillan told Murphy that the government was not perturbed by the prospect of Russian intervention: 'if we should be destroyed by Russian bombs now, that would be better than to be reduced to impotence by the disintegration of our entire position abroad.' Reaching a histrionic peak, the chancellor of the Exchequer proclaimed that regardless of cost the government was determined to use force in spite of any 'conferences, arrangements, public postures and maneuvers.'[62] Alarmed by this sabre rattling, Eisenhower decided to send Dulles to London to try to persuade the British not to use force and to accept the idea of an international conference on the use of the canal. The Americans were also worried by the attitude of the French government. The premier, Guy Mollet, told the American ambassador, Douglas Dillon, that the Soviet Union was behind the whole affair, that it was as serious as the Berlin Blockade or the Korean War, and that the Americans should recognize this fact and not let France down. The Canadian government made it plain that it did not agree with the British government's grim assessment of the situation, and the high commissioner, General Sir Archibald Nye, reported to the British government that the prime minister, Louis St Laurent, had been sorely tempted to deliver a homily to Eden on the dangers of precipitate action.[63]

In London, Dulles launched into a long tirade against Nasser and insisted that an international waterway like the Suez Canal had to be under international control, but he stressed that force should be used only as a last resort. He brought with him a letter from Eisenhower to Eden which read, in part: 'We recognize the transcendent worth of the canal to the free world and the possibility that eventually the use of force might become necessary in order to protect international rights.' The British interpreted this statement to mean that the president did not rule out the use of force and that they could deal with Dulles, who, they thought, made foreign policy, not the President.[64] As a result of Dulles's visit, the British agreed to an international conference on the use of the canal and were prepared to take the risk that the Soviet Union might attend. They felt that Dulles had come close to their point of view, and Dulles went back to Washington believing that he had calmed them down. Neither side had made its position clear, and there was much wishful thinking both in London and in Washington. The

French felt that Dulles had been successful in his London mission and complained that the British, once again, were backing down and playing the appeasers.

Despite a lack of preparation and problems with the French, planning went ahead for a landing in Egypt, code-named 'Musketeer.' Although the London conference was due to begin on 16 August – and it was scheduled to last for a week – D-Day was set for 15 September. The   aim of the operation was to topple Nasser, after which it was assumed that the allies would have full control over the canal. The Americans' response to these preparations was ambiguous. Admiral A.A. Burke, the chief naval planner, wanted to lend the British the landing craft they badly needed. The French were assured of getting spares for their aircraft. The British were allowed to borrow some radio equipment from NATO. All this seemed to add up to tacit American approval of Musketeer. On the other hand, many senior American officers felt that the Anglo-French operation was doomed to failure.[65] On the eve of the Maritime Conference in London the American position was one of support for the Anglo-French stand, including the possible use of force, provided that the British and French were 'reasonable.'[66] This statement was so vague as to mean almost anything, and the British and French had no clear idea of what the Americans understood to be 'reasonable.' Participants in the Maritime Conference accepted the American proposals that control of the canal should be internationalized, that Egypt should receive a fair financial return, and that any threat of interference with the operation of the canal would be considered a breach of the peace under the terms of the UN charter. A delegation, made up of representatives from Australia, Ethiopia, Iran, Sweden, and the United States, was appointed to present the case to the Egyptian government.

The major remaining problem was how to handle the UN. After much discussion it was agreed that if Nasser turned down the proposals, a meeting of the Security Council should be called. Under the cover of this meeting Britain and France would prepare for war.[67] Dulles felt that the British and French were now in an impossible bind. On the one hand, if they let Nasser 'get away with it,' they would be finished as first-class powers. If, on the other, they seized the canal, they would end up in a hopeless situation. They would alienate all Middle Eastern countries and be obliged to maintain an occupying force that would weaken their own countries. Only the Soviets would benefit. Dulles realized that the problem of the Suez Canal and the removal of President Nasser were two separate issues which had been confused by the British. The five-nation delegation, chaired by the Australian prime minister, Robert Menzies, arrived in Cairo on 2 September and stayed for a week. Their proposals were rejected, and in his reply Nasser suggested preliminary talks about a future conference which would find a solution to the problem on terms acceptable to Egypt. Meanwhile, the Americans were becoming increasingly opposed to the use of force. Dulles wanted the canal to be run by a users' association first known as the Cooperative Association of Suez Canal Users (CASU) and then as the Suez Canal Users' Association (SCUA).

On 2 September Eisenhower wrote to Eden, making it plain that the Americans rejected the idea of using force.[68] Eisenhower made the valid point in a subsequent letter to Eden that the British government was making too much of Nasser. The president wrote: 'Nasser thrives on drama. If we let some of the drama go out of the situation and concentrate on deflating him through slower but sure processes such as I described, I believe the desired results can more probably be obtained.'[69] The constant comparisons between Nasser and Mussolini and in the case of the French, with Hitler, seemed to American officials to be increasingly absurd. To them Nasser was more show than substance, a slightly absurd figure led astray at the Bandung conference in April 1955 by the likes of Nehru, Tito, and Sukharno. Since the Menzies mission had failed and the United States was now strongly against the use of force and did not want to refer the matter to the Security Council, the Americans suggested going ahead with CASU, a scheme that would deprive the Egyptians of more than 80 per cent of the canal revenues.

The British cabinet was now split on what to do next. Macmillan, as the leading hawk, argued that CASU would not work and that force would therefore be necessary. Sir Walter Monckton, as minister of defence, argued that the use of force without the full support of the Americans would be disastrous. Selwyn Lloyd came to the conclusion that Britain first would have to approach the Security Council, but Eden rejected this solution, in part because Dulles was against it, and decided to back SCUA in the hope that the Americans would eventually cooperate.[70] In Washington, the Egyptian ambassador proclaimed that the Users' Association was an 'open and flagrant aggression on Egypt's sovereignty and its implementation means war.' Dulles countered by saying that the Americans did not intend to 'shoot our way through' the canal.[71] The Canadian ambassador, Norman Robertson, was outspoken in his condemnation of the intention to use the 1888 Convention of Constantinople to support the use of force and insisted that the matter should be brought before the UN.[72]

With the Americans consistently watering down the conditions laid down by SCUA, the British decided to go to the Security Council and began to think of finding another and more plausible casus belli. Meanwhile, the French invited Israel to send a delegation to Paris to discuss military action against Egypt. The Israelis, headed by Golda Meir, began these discussions in Paris on 30 September, they found the French vague and poorly briefed, and therefore they turned down the suggestion that they should begin operations against Egypt so that the French and possibly the British could join in later.[73] During the Security Council debate relations between the United States and Britain worsened considerably, as did relations between Britain and France. The Americans wanted a negotiated settlement, but neither the British nor the French seemed to know quite what they wanted. Matters were further complicated by Jordan's request in the night of 10/11 October for British support against Israel, which was readily granted by officials in Amman and Jerusalem. But in Britain the Chiefs of Staff made the obvious point that Britain could not get involved in a war with Israel if they intended to go ahead with Musketeer.[74]

On 14 October a French mission met Eden at Chequers and suggested that the Israelis might be persuaded to attack Egypt. Eden was most impressed by the idea, and the French were amazed to learn that it had not occurred to him before.[75] The Foreign Office, however, was appalled by the French suggestion. The United States would be bound to oppose it, as would the UN. The Commonwealth would be divided over a policy that served French interests in North Africa, not British interests in the Middle East. Eden rejected these objections as typical examples of Foreign Office dithering and travelled to Paris with Selwyn Lloyd to discuss the proposals further with Mollet and Pineau. The French, British, and Israelis conferred at Sèvres from 22 to 24 October. The Israelis agreed to attack Egypt on 29 October and hoped to reach the Canal Zone the following day. The French and British would then call upon the belligerents to withdraw their forces ten miles to the east and west of the Suez Canal. Egypt was to accept an Anglo-French occupation force to secure the canal, even if it agreed to the terms of the ultimatum.

The Israelis began mobilization as soon as the protocol of the Sèvres conference was signed, and the Americans were soon aware that a major operation was afoot. Initially they assumed that the Israelis were planning to seize the West Bank. Intelligence reports of an Anglo-French build-up in Cyprus and unusual cable traffic between Paris and Tel Aviv, coupled with the fact that the British ambassador in Washington had been withdrawn and his replacement was being sent by the slowest possible sea route, made the Americans deeply suspicious, but Eisenhower was still convinced that the British were not so foolish as to be dragged into an attack on Egypt.[76] When the Israelis duly attacked Egypt on 29 October, Dulles suggested to the British and French representatives that the three powers should go the Security Council that day to condemn Israeli aggression. The British and French stalled. In New York Secretary-General Dag Hammarskjold also suggested a meeting of the Security Council, but Sir Pierson Dixon and Bernard Cornut-Gentille argued that they had no instructions and that it was the middle of the night in London and Paris.[77] Eisenhower believed that the French were deeply involved in the Israeli aggression, but he was uncertain about the British. His aim now was to stop the British from becoming involved. Eden wrote to Eisenhower assuring him that he agreed to go to the Security Council, but added: 'Experience however shows that its procedure is unlikely to be either rapid or effective.' The prime minister called for 'decisive action' to stop hostilities.[78] Eisenhower and Dulles correctly assumed that Eden meant that the British and French were ready to take military action to secure the canal.

The British and French duly sent their ultimatums to Israel and Egypt in which the Egyptians were called upon to accept the 'temporary occupation by Anglo-French forces of key positions at Port Said, Ismailia and Suez.' The two countries were given twelve hours to accept these terms, failing which British and French forces would intervene.[79] The American ambassador in London, Winthrop Aldrich, read the text of the ultimatums to Eisenhower over the telephone, adding that the ultimatum to Egypt was 'about as crude and brutal as anything he had ever seen.' Eisenhower thought it was 'pretty rough' and Dulles said it was 'utterly unacceptable.' Eisenhower promptly informed Eden and Mollet that he found their actions reprehensible and informed the press that he completely disassociated himself from their actions.[80] In the Security Council Henry Cabot Lodge demanded that the Israelis should withdraw completely from Egypt and that no country should lend them any assistance whatsoever until they had complied. No nation, he added pointedly, should be permitted to use force in the area. Furthermore, he roundly condemned the Anglo-French ultimatums as inconsistent with the Charter of the UN.[81] Dulles told the British chargé d'affaires that it was a 'brutal affair' and added: 'the British Government has kept us deliberately in the dark about its plans.' Britain and France had to change their policy if they wished to regain the trust of the United States.[82] Dulles then reported to the National Security Council that the Anglo-French demarche marked 'the death knell for Great Britain and France.'

The majority of Commonwealth countries were strongly opposed to the Suez adventure. New Zealand could be counted upon to support Britain under almost any circumstances. In Australia Sir Roy Welensky was enthusiastic, as was Robert Menzies, but many Australian ministers did not share his point of view. In Ottawa Lester Pearson wrote to Norman Robertson in London expressing 'our feeling of bewilderment and dismay at the decision which they have taken ... while the Security Council was meeting in New York; decisions which came as a complete surprise to us and which had not been hinted at in any previous discussions.' St Laurent wrote to Eden condemning the effect British actions had had on the UN, pointing out that they had alienated a large part of the Commonwealth and ruined Anglo-American relations. St Laurent refused to make any comments to the press about Suez, but later in November he told the House of Commons that he was delighted that 'the era when the supermen of Europe could govern the whole world ... is coming pretty close to an end.'[83]

The UN General Assembly met in an emergency special session on the night of 1–2 November at which Dulles condemned Israel, Britain, and France for acting against the Charter. The secretary of state proposed a resolution calling for an immediate cease-fire and withdrawal of all foreign troops from Egypt. The UN was to remain in emergency session to ensure that these conditions were met. The resolution was adopted by sixty-four votes to five (with New Zealand and Australia supporting the three miscreants). Canada and five other nations abstained.[84] Lester Pearson's motive for abstaining was that he considered the wording of the resolution far too vague. He suggested that the UN should seize the opportunity to find a political solution to the questions of Palestine and the Suez Canal and also that a UN force should be sent to the area pending such settlements. These ideas were enthusiastically supported by Dulles, who asked Pearson to draw up a concrete proposal to this effect.[85] As the 1956 American presidential campaign entered its final stages, the Eisenhower administration came under increasing attack from Adlai Stevenson and the Democrats for pursuing an irresolute policy in the Middle East which had alienated the British and the French. Eisenhower wrote to his old friend General Alfred M. Gruenther, who had just retired as NATO supreme commander: 'I believe that Eden and his associates have become convinced that this is the last straw and Britain simply had to react in the manner of the Victorian period. If one has to have a fight, then that is that. But I don't see the point in getting into a fight to which there can be no satisfactory end; and in which the whole world believes you are playing the part of the bully, and you do not even have firm backing of your entire people.'[86] The president here accurately expressed the feelings of most Americans. As Robert Murphy told Alphand: 'The United States wants the success for your enterprise provided that it can succeed with the shortest delay.'[87] Herein lay the core of the Americans' dilemma. On the one hand, they did not approve of the Suez adventure and denounced it as immoral, old-style, western colonialism. On the other hand, they wanted it to succeed, although they had no clear idea of what they meant by success. For the moment, Eisenhower firmly rejected Eden's idea that the UN should take over from Britain and France. He still hoped to stop them from landing in Egypt.[88]

Lester Pearson presented his plan to Hammarskjold over lunch on 2 November, but the response was not enthusiastic. The secretary-general felt that Israel, as an 'aggressive and acquisitive' state, would not accept any further UN observers and in any case was unlikely to survive as a nation. Pearson returned to Ottawa and continued fleshing out his plan. He suggested that the British and French troops on the spot should be joined by contingents from Canada and the United States, which would then be replaced by a proper UN force controlled by a five-nation committee.[89] The Americans could not accept this plan, since they did not want the British and French to land. They also felt that the committee of five would take too long to put in place. Prompted by Cabot Lodge, Pearson therefore put forward a revised plan on the evening of 3 November empowering the UN secretary-general to organize a force to bring about the cessation of hostilities. The resolution to send an expeditionary force was carried with the predictable abstentions but with no contrary votes. The outstanding problem was whether the action could be taken before the British and French had landed.

The British government was now in a sorry jam. The UN was threatening sanctions if it went ahead with the landings. Both Egypt and Israel having agreed to a cease-fire, it was difficult to see why a landing was necessary. The argument that Israel had not agreed to withdraw and that Egyptians therefore had to be killed in order to oblige the Israelis to retreat was not very convincing. The Canadian plan was now seen as a possible cover for the landings as the first stage of a UN solution.[90] The cabinet, uncertain about whether the Israelis had ceased to fight and arguing that they had not withdrawn and had refused to accept the UN force, decided to invade Egypt. From inside 10 Downing Street ministers could hear the vast crowds assembled in Trafalgar Square and pouring down Whitehall chanting 'law, not war' and 'Eden must go' while they made this fateful decision.

Landings in Suez duly went ahead on 5 November, but the pressure from the United States and the UN was such that a cease-fire had to be ordered almost immediately. Harold Macmillan, whom Harold Wilson described as the 'first in and first out,' had warned that pressure on sterling was such that the invasion had to be halted. Eden now imagined that he could use the Anglo-French position in Suez as a 'gage' to make a deal with Hammarskjold and Eisenhower, but neither was interested. Both wanted to clear the Anglo-French forces from Suez immediately and to put UNEF on the ground as soon as possible, an expeditionary force made up of troops from minor nations under Canadian command so as to keep the Soviets out. Eden's assumption that, as soon as the Suez affair was over, relations with the United States would immediately go back to normal was wide of the mark. Indeed, the Americans' continued disapproval made the prime minister particularly angry and hurt. In Washington and the UN they now cut off British diplomats from all but routine business. It was a painful experience for the new ambassador, Sir Harold Caccia, and for Sir Pierson Dixon at the UN.[91] Eisenhower blew hot and cold, and Dulles, whom Selwyn Lloyd visited in hospital after his operation for cancer, asked a dumbfounded foreign secretary why the British had not got on with the job and got rid of Nasser.[92] Dulles believed that the British had succeeded in alienating most the world without achieving anything positive in return and had failed to get rid of a man whom he had described as 'a Hitlerite personality.'[93] In the tough world of international politics a crime that paid was at least partially excusable. The British had proved to be exceedingly incompetent crooks.

Eden, sick, desperately tired, and stuffed full of stimulants, left for a holiday in Jamaica on 23 November. To many, his departure seemed as if the captain was leaving the sinking ship, and the Americans began to think of his successor. R.A. Butler seemed to be the probable choice, but it was generally felt that Harold Macmillan had an outside chance. Eisenhower, who favoured Macmillan, told the U.S. ambassador to talk to both men together, to avoid the charge of favouritism. He insisted, however, that first the British had to withdraw from Suez; then oil supplies to Britain from the Arab states would have to be secured; then, and only then, would the Americans be prepared to talk about financial help for Britain.[94] The Americans kept their word. Once the British announced that they would withdraw from Suez, oil supplies began to flow from the Gulf of Mexico and the Americans gave their full support to a loan of $561.47 million from the International Monetary Fund, with a further $738.53 million in reserve. The American Export-Import Bank loaned a further $500 million, and Britain was allowed to postpone interest payments on American loans.[95] Britain's financial situation was temporarily saved, but it was some time before relations between the two countries were back to normal. The Americans had done what they could to save the Conservative government; for, as secretary to the Treasury, George Humphrey, had pointed out to the president: 'If they throw them out then we have those socialists to lick.'[96] Macmillan was fully aware of his dependence on the United States and was determined to revive the tattered 'special relationship.' His remarkable rationalization of the post-Suez situation was the imaginative fantasy of a classical scholar. 'We are,' he mused, 'the Greeks of the Hellenistic age: the power has passed from us to Rome's equivalent, the United States of America, and we can at most aspire to civilise and occasionally to influence them.' The illusion of the 'special relationship' lived on in spite of the Suez debacle. The Canadians harboured the less exalted illusion that they would continue to exercise a sobering and restraining influence on their allies. This conviction was strengthened when Lester Pearson was awarded the Nobel Prize for Peace for his role in bringing the Suez crisis to an end.

NOTES

1 Alan Bullock, *Ernest Bevin. Foreign Secretary, 1945–51* (London, 1983), 791.
2 Ibid.
3 Lord Moran, *Winston Churchill the Struggle for Survival, 1940–1965* (London, 1968), 423.
4 Denis Stairs, *The Diplomacy of Constraint: Canada, the Korean War, and the United States* (Toronto, 1974), 39; Lester Pearson, *Mike: The Memoirs of the Right Honourable Lester B. Pearson*, Vol. II: *1948–1957* (Toronto, 1973), 145.
5 Stairs, *Constraint*, 46.
6 Ibid., 69.
7 U.S. Department of State, *Papers Relating to the Foreign Relations of the United States, 1955–1957*, (hereafter *FRUS*), Vol. VII, 352; Bullock, *Bevin*, 794.
8 Stairs, *Constraint*, 74.
9 Kenneth Harris, *Attlee* (London, 1982), 455.

10 Royal Institute of International Affairs (hereafter RIIA), *Survey of International Affairs, 1949–50*, (London, 1953) 657–8.

11 John W. Spanier, *The Truman-MacArthur Controversy and the Korean War* (New York, 1965), 73–8.

12 Callum MacDonald, *Korea: The War before Vietnam* (London, 1986), 48–9.

13 Bullock, *Bevin*, 813

14 MacDonald, *Korea*, 33.

15 Stairs, *Constraint*, 120.

16 *FRUS*, vol. VII, 1065; Pearson, *Memoirs*, II, 158–9.

17 MacDonald, *Korea*, 55.

18 Ibid., 34; *FRUS*, vol. VII, 1004.

19 Pearson, *Memoirs*, II, 163.

20 Ibid.

21 *FRUS*, vol. VII, 1228; Bullock, *Bevin*, 820; MacDonald, *Korea*, 37.

22 Bullock, *Bevin*, 823; Dean Acheson, *Present at the Creation* (London, 1969), 480–5. For Attlee's visit to Washington, see *FRUS*, vol. VII, 1361–77, 1392–408.

23 Pearson, *Memoirs*, II, 166.

24 Stairs, *Constraint*, 162–3.

25 Pearson, *Memoirs*, II, 167.

26 Bullock, *Bevin*, 826.

27 Stairs, *Constraint*, 168.

28 MacDonald, *Korea*, 48.

29 Pearson, *Memoirs*, II, 180.

30 MacDonald, *Korea*, 48.

31 Roy Jenkins, *Truman* (London 1986), 187.

32 Pearson, *Memoirs*, II, 182.

33 MacDonald, *Korea*, 48.

34 Ibid., 102.

35 Turner Joy, *How Communists Negotiate* (New York, 1955), 18–20.

36 MacDonald, *Korea*, 131.

37 M.L. Dockrill, 'The Foreign Office, Anglo-American Relations and the Korean Truce Negotiations July 1951–July 1953,' in *The Korean War in History*, ed. James Cotton and Ian Neary (Manchester, 1989), 104.

38 Dockrill, 'Truce Negotiations,' 106.

39 Stairs, *Constraint*, 249–55.

40 Sarvepalli Gopal, *Jawaharlal Nehru*, Vol. I (Cambridge, MA, 1979), 140.

41 Stephen Ambrose, *Eisenhower: Soldier and President* (New York, 1990).

42 *FRUS*, vol. XV, pt.1, 548; MacDonald, *Korea*, 168.

43 Pearson, *Memoirs*, II, 184.

44 Ibid.
45 MacDonald, *Korea*, 171.
46 Ibid.
47 Ibid., 89.
48 Moran, *Churchill*, 423.
49 Stairs, *Constraint*, 277.
50 Stephen Ambrose, *Eisenhower: The President* (New York, 1984), 107.
51 MacDonald, *Korea*, 95.
52 *FRUS*, vol. XIV, 543–9.
53 Moshe Dayan, *Story of My Life* (London, 1976), 147.
54 Keith Kyle, *Suez* (London, 1991), 80.
55 W.R. Louis and Roger Owen, eds, *Suez 1956: The Crisis and Its Consequences* (Oxford, 1984), 147.
56 *FRUS*, vol. XIV, 632–6.
57 Kyle, *Suez*, 101.
58 Anthony Nutting, *No End of a Lesson: The Story of Suez* (London,, 1972), 34–5.
59 *FRUS*, vol. XV, no. 478, 19 July 1956, 867–73; Mohamed Heikal, *Cutting the Lion's Tail* (London, 1986), 119–22.
60 Kyle, *Suez*, 137–8.
61 Ibid., 147.
62 *FRUS*, vol. XVI, no. 33, 31 July 1956, 60–2.
63 Kyle, *Suez*, 156.
64 No. 31, July 1956, *FRUS*, vol. XVI, 69–71. Lord Selwyn-Lloyd, *Suez 1956* (London, 1978), 98; Robert Rhodes James, *Anthony Eden* (London, 1986), 471–3.
65 No. 68, 7 August 1956, no. 72, 9 August 1956, *FRUS*, vol. XVI, 153–6, 165–76.
66 No. 78, 10 August 1956, ibid., 185–7.
67 Kyle, *Suez*, 208.
68 No. 163, 2 September 1956, *FRUS*, vol. XVI, 355–8.
69 No. 192, 8 September 1956, ibid., 435–8.
70 Selwyn-Lloyd, *Suez*, 140.
71 No. 216, 13 September 1956, *FRUS*, vol. XVI, 491–2.
72 Kyle, *Suez*, 252.
73 Matti Golan, *Shimon Peres* (London, 1982), 51; Dayan, *Story*, 158–65.
74 Kyle, *Suez*, 295.
75 Maurice Challe, *Notre Revolte* (Paris, 1968), 27–8; Paul Ely, *Suez … Le 13 Mai* (Paris, 1969), 137–8.
76 No. 395, 28 October 1956, *FRUS*, vol. XVI, 802–4.
77 No. 413, ibid., 840–2.
78 Anthony Eden, *Full Circle* (London, 1960), 525; no. 421, *FRUS*, vol. XVI, 856–7.
79 Kyle, *Suez*, 358.

80 No. 420, no. 430, *FRUS*, vol. XVI, 855–6, 866.

81 UN Security Council, *Proceedings, 749th Session and 750th Session*.

82 No. 437, 30 October 1956, *FRUS*, vol. XVI, 875–6.

83 James Eayrs, *The Commonwealth and Suez* (Oxford, 1964), 417.

84 UN General Assembly, *Official Records. 1st and 2nd Emergency Special Sessions, 1956. 561st and 562nd Plenary Meetings* (1–2 November 1956).

85 Rosalyn Higgins, *UN Peacekeeping. 1946–67 Documents and Commentary. The Middle East* (Oxford, 1969), 228–9.

86 Kyle, *Suez*, 427.

87 No. 127, 6 November 1956, Ministère des Affaires Etrangères [France], *Documents Diplomatiques Françaises, 1956*, vol. III, 213–14.

88 No. 477, 3 November 1956, *FRUS*, vol. XVI, 947–9.

89 Pearson, *Memoirs*, II, 247–51; Michael Fry, 'Canada, the North Atlantic Triangle and the UN,' in Louis and Owen, *Suez 1956*, 306–16. Cf. no. 481, no. 485, both 3 November 1956, *FRUS*, vol. XVI, 960–4.

90 Kyle, *Suez*, 440.

91 No. 575, 14 November 1956, *FRUS*, vol. XVI, 1123–5.

92 Lloyd, *Suez*, 219.

93 Ambrose, *President*, 334.

94 No. 597, 20 November 1956, *FRUS*, vol. XVI, 1169–70.

95 Diane Kunz, 'The Importance of Having Money,' in Louis and Owen, *Suez 1956*, 232.

96 Christopher Hitchens, *Blood, Class, and Nostalgia: Anglo-American Ironies* (New York, 1990), 106, 280.

Afterword

B.J.C. McKERCHER and LAWRENCE ARONSEN

Since publication in 1945 of J.B. Brebner's classic work, the study of North Atlantic triangle relations has been left to Canadian academics who have funnelled their writing into the separate categories of Anglo-Canadian and Canadian-American relations.[1] Books and articles in each of these areas have made reference to those of the other, but none has treated the subject of the North Atlantic triangle as a separate analytical category.[2] The contributors to this collection have integrated several of the above studies in addition to providing new research by focusing on how Ottawa officials conceived and implemented policies designed to resolve and strengthen relations among the three English-speaking countries from 1903 to 1956. Attention has also been paid to the evolution of the North Atlantic triangle in the larger context of the decline of British power and the rise of American strategic and economic power.

Diplomatic relations within the North Atlantic triangle have been concerned with accommodating the interests of the three countries related primarily to military and economic issues. Larger cultural questions have been of significance only in the context of Canada's relationship with the United States and Great Britain but of little consequence for Anglo-American relations. Only one American president, Theodore Roosevelt, occasionally spoke of an 'English-speaking accord,' which outlined the common task of ruling 'colonial peoples' with the ultimate aim of civilizing them.[3] Winston Churchill's periodic calls for solidarity among 'the English-speaking peoples' to confront twentieth-century totalitarian aggression were considered by historians to represent a more acceptable cause, however. Canadians, on the other hand, took cultural relations much more seriously. From the founding of the Imperial Federation League in 1884 to the end of the First World War, English

Canadian nationalists argued that the survival of the country was dependent upon maintaining close intellectual, religious, and political ties to Great Britain as a counter to the spillover of American capital investment and mass culture.[4] This concern over the Americanization of Canadian culture reappeared later in the 1951 Royal Commission *Report on National Development in the Arts, Letters and Sciences*, as well as in the scholarly research of nationalist academics in the 1960s and 1970s; by this time, however, the advantage of maintaining the British cultural connection was no longer cited as the antidote to Americanization.[5]

The changing relations between Canada, Great Britain, and the United States can be explained within three levels of analysis outlined by a political scientist, Kenneth Waltz, in his classic work, *Man, the State and War*.[6] Waltz's first category deals with the role that individuals play in the conduct of international affairs. In the context of North Atlantic triangle relations, an individual's characteristics such as temperament, judgment, and empathy have occasionally been decisive factors. Until the First World War, little was done by particular leaders to define common interests of the three countries and to implement mutually favourable policies. As Roger Sarty has noted, after the controversial settlement of the Alaskan boundary dispute Canadian leaders, regardless of political party, remained suspicious of American intentions. Across the border, President William Howard Taft viewed North Atlantic triangle relations primarily in terms of advancing American economic interests. The American president, in effect, wanted to lure Canada into a reciprocal trade agreement as a way of economically weakening the sterling bloc.[7]

President Woodrow Wilson preferred to view the world in terms of liberal internationalism; in such a situation it would be unnecessary to have 'a special relationship' with any particular country or group of allies. His views on Communism, anti-colonialism, and the 'open door' for trade and investment defined the major issues on which the coherence of the North Atlantic triangle was to depend for the following three decades. Wilson's biographer indicates that he did not get along particularly well with David Lloyd George or Robert Borden.[8] Nor did the crisis of the 1930s depression yield any significant cooperation on matters related to trade liberalization among President Herbert Hoover and Prime Ministers J. Ramsay MacDonald and Richard Bennett; and there was increasing acrimony between Britain and the Canadian leaders, especially at the 1932 Ottawa economic summit conference.

Early in the Second World War, personal relations among President

Franklin Roosevelt and Prime Ministers Winston Churchill and William Lyon Mackenzie King promised to set precedents that would overcome parochial economic and strategic interests. Although these leaders met collectively on only two occasions, at the first and second Quebec conferences, ties were maintained through personal correspondence and diplomatic envoys. Memoirs and published correspondence indicate that each of the three leaders had a genuine respect and admiration for the others.[9] C.P. Stacey does impose certain limits, however, noting that Churchill 'was polite to King' only in so far as the Canadian leader 'could be useful to him.'[10] Throughout the course of the war there were instances in which personal trust, generosity of spirit, and a sincere understanding of the problems of others had a significant impact on relations between countries. Most noteworthy are the generous terms President Roosevelt extended to Prime Ministers King and Churchill in the Hyde Park and lend-lease agreements.

Personal ties between leaders as a factor that contributed to improving relations did not continue much beyond the Second World War. Secretary of State Dean Acheson admired and respected Ernest Bevin and Lester Pearson. Harry Truman in private spoke highly of the political skills of Attlee and Mackenzie King. There is little evidence, however, that personal relationships ameliorated or lessened the Anglo-American differences over the GATT, decolonization, and civil aviation. On these issues, Canada's position was more or less similar to that of the United States, and some historians have emphasized this consonance as a key factor in the strengthening of the continentalist axis in the North Atlantic triangle after the Second World War.[11]

Waltz's second category is composed of domestic factors: party politics, public opinion, economic interest groups, and the media; these elements have been part of Canadian relations within the North Atlantic triangle, but they have been considerably less important for the United States and Great Britain. Canadian public opinion that was openly hostile to the United States was particularly evident after the unfavourable settlement of two issues: the Alaskan boundary dispute in 1903 and the debate over reciprocity in 1911. Greg Johnson, David Lenarcic, and Brian McKercher give considerable weight to the restrictive effects of public opinion on Mackenzie King and R.B. Bennett's policies towards Great Britain during the Chanak crisis in 1921 and the 1931 Manchurian crisis. McKercher also notes the effects of American isolationist opinion and the neutrality legislation passed by Congress as barriers to President Roosevelt's efforts to reach new military agreements with Canada and Great Britain. After 1939 the domestic constraints of policy quickly gave way to the rapidly changing international situation.

The basic premise of Waltz's third category assumes that, given the condition of anarchy, the absence of morality or an effective code of law in the international arena, individual states have tended to focus primarily on their own security, especially on economic and military policies. The twentieth century, characterized by war, limited war, and Cold War, developing against the backdrop of revolutionary changes in weapons technology, is a particularly useful period to study in the context of Waltz's third category. Preoccupation with national security set the stage for three significant departures in the military and economic relations of the North Atlantic triangle: 1917–18, 1940–1, and 1947–8.

Roger Sarty has observed that the most significant development in the North Atlantic triangle prior to the First World War was the diminishing British power in Canada and the consequent decline in Washington's use of coercive diplomacy to settle boundary disputes. American officials at the time assumed that Canada and Britain could actually contribute to continental security through the defence of the northern frontier and the North Atlantic sea lanes. As Greg Kennedy shows, it was only under conditions of wartime crisis, from 1917 to 1918, that North Atlantic leaders moved to redefine and formalize fundamentally military relations. While the United States and Britain looked after grand strategy in the campaigns in western Europe, the three North Atlantic allies participated in some significant new regional defence operations. A division of labour was set up to coordinate air and sea patrols off the Atlantic coast, and agreement was reached on the sharing of intelligence data and the training of aircraft crews. This cooperation was never formalized into long-term treaty commitments, and after 1918 it disappeared as quickly as it had started.

The absence of pressing international issues from 1919 to the end of the 1930s resulted in few developments of lasting significance in North Atlantic triangle military relations. Brian McKercher reminds us of the notable British efforts to encourage greater diplomatic and military cooperation among the three countries, especially from 1936 onward. Some historians have charged that the appeasement policies of the Chamberlain government are at least in part due to the insubstantial support and general indifference of its North Atlantic allies.[12] At that time, much to the dismay of London officials, the rapidly changing balance of power in Europe had little immediate effect on isolationist sentiments within Canada and the United States. The Roosevelt administration could announce its commitment to the defence of Canada as early as 1936, but only as part of a larger strategy to maintain the security of the western hemisphere. The northward extension of the Monroe Doctrine set the stage for an unprecedented peacetime development: the negotiation of the 1940 Ogdensburg Agreement with Canada.

On the basis of the successful Ogdensburg negotiations and what seemed to be the development of close personal ties between Prime Minister Mackenzie King and President Roosevelt, Canadian External Affairs officials were greatly optimistic about the prospects for trilateral cooperation on the major military and strategic issues in the immediate future and beyond. John English has documented how Mackenzie King's preoccupation with domestic politics and general lack of understanding of how Canada could have played a strategic role during Britain's 'finest hour' in 1940–1 set the stage for a decidedly modest role for the remainder of the war. Furthermore, the Americans, especially elements in the State and Navy departments, were quite unwilling to invite the Canadians to sit in on the 1941 Argentia conference negotiations, or to participate on the Combined Chiefs of Staff, or themselves to seek advice on the defence of Newfoundland. While grand strategy was largely the preserve of Stalin, Churchill, and Roosevelt, the Canadians were included in the highest levels of top-secret weapons research, most notably the Manhattan project. Other significant aspects of military relations among the three countries included the coordination of naval strategy in the Pacific and Atlantic oceans, the establishment of joint air-training programs, and the creation of an advanced chemical-weapons research and testing base at Suffield, Alberta.

Canadian efforts to formalize military relations within the North Atlantic triangle became particularly noteworthy with the onset of the Cold War in 1947. During that year diplomatic officials spoke of the need to form a regional security pact outside the United Nations. Shortly after the Czech crisis in February of the following year, negotiations began that would culminate in the signing of the North Atlantic Treaty Organization agreement in April 1949. In contrast to their position in the Second World War, the Canadian leaders participated in the initial top-secret tripartite negotiations and played a key role in later negotiations as well.

North Atlantic economic relations were generally dependent upon normal peacetime factors of supply and demand that affected the flow of trade and investment. From 1917 to 1948, however, war and Cold War fundamentally altered economic relations in that national security considerations often prevailed over the demands of private market forces, interest groups, or regions. The United States emerged as the pre-eminent economic power of the three, and henceforth Canadian and British leaders generally reacted to Washington's initiatives rather than help to set the agenda.

In 1917 the North Atlantic allies looked to Washington to provide leadership and coordinate war production, as a source of supply for scarce capital, and to help to resolve pressing balance-of-payments problems. During the First World War, economic relations for the first time came to be viewed in strategic terms. In keeping with this approach, the Wilson administration extended special emergency loans to Canada and Great Britain, despite the restrictions imposed on foreign lending, and encouraged technology transfer to Canada through the expansion of American branch plants. Canadian and British officials also set up wartime commissions in Washington primarily for the purpose of getting exemptions from American allocation controls imposed on the export of strategic materials. Yet the special relationship in economic relations did not extend into the postwar period, and the three countries made little effort to coordinate the reconversion of their wartime economies. American leadership on matters related to international trade and economic recovery disappeared with the passage of the Emergency Tariff Act in 1921 and the Fordney-McCumber tariff in the following year.[13]

It was only after the outbreak of the Second World War that the United States once again assumed the role of providing economic leadership within the North Atlantic triangle. Problems relating to trade imbalances and currency convertibility were resolved in 1941 through the lend-lease program and special bilateral defence production efforts, such as the Hyde Park agreement. The latter set the stage for the creation of a series of joint industrial defence planning and production agreements that tied the two continental economies far closer together than they had been during the First World War. So successful were these efforts at continental cooperation that by 1943 Canadian and American production totalled more than one and one-half times that of the Axis bloc.[14] The Mackenzie King government fully expected to cooperate in all aspects of wartime economic planning and was taken aback when the British and Americans later excluded Canada from the Combined Production Board and the Combined Food Board.

Historical differences between the discriminatory trading practices of the sterling bloc, led by Great Britain, and American efforts to liberalize international trade, dating from the passage of the 1934 Reciprocal

Trade Act, were put aside until the latter part of the Second World War. It was not until the 1944 Bretton Woods negotiations, followed by the 1947 GATT agreements, that the gap between the two countries began to reappear. Canada emerged as the country most interested in restoring stability and compromise within the North Atlantic triangle. The dramatic realignment of economic power within the North Atlantic triangle in 1945 is the focal point of Lawrence Aronsen's chapter. All three countries recognized that the Second world War fundamentally had changed the economic landscape leading to the emergence of the United States as the dominant economic power, the precipitous decline of Britain, and the emergence of Canada as a major commercial and industrial power. In contrast to the aftermath of the First World War, the United States defined its postwar national security in terms of maintaining international peace and prosperity. Towards this end, the highest priority was given to providing financial assistance to Britain in 1945 and 1946 in order to facilitate conversion to a peacetime economy and sustained economic growth. In return, the British were to agree to international controls on trade barriers, balance of payments levels, and currency valuations. Canada was also motivated to extend financial assistance, but for different reasons arising out of a lingering sense of guilt for the suffering that the mother country had endured and from a clear calculation of economic interest.

By 1947 the onset of the Cold War reassured British and Canadian officials that the United States would not retreat into the economic nationalism that had characterized the interwar period. In short, larger international crises again had immediate consequences for economic relations within the North Atlantic triangle. The economic recovery of Britain and the rest of Europe was viewed almost entirely in terms of stopping the further advance of Communism in two ways: first, by providing stability so that Communist parties from within each country could not be successful through the democratic process; and secondly, by strengthening the economies of western Europe and thereby assuring an adequate industrial defence capacity in time of mobilization, should it be necessary. As the largest recipient of Marshall Plan assistance, Great Britain under the Labour party gained enormously yet without any political commitments attached by the more capitalist-minded Americans. Canada was favoured through the 'off-shore purchases' clause and by several new bilateral agreements to coordinate defence production planning and the export of strategic resources. By 1950 there was considerable stability in the North Atlantic economic triangle: all three countries enjoyed a measure of economic prosperity, stable currencies, and improved balances in trade relations.

The common perception of a Communist threat was not of unlimited effectiveness as a unifier of the North Atlantic triangle. Personal ties between leaders and the ideals of the wartime 'special relationship' held by the public and the media had little effect on determining the proper strategy to fight the limited war in Korea. From the American perspective the decision to respond to the North Korean attack was influenced by overall strategic interests in the Far East, particularly the protection of Japan and the containment of Communist Chinese power. The anti-Communist climate at home provides a context for President Harry Truman's decision to cross the 38th parallel and his hints that atomic weapons could be used in the event of massive Chinese intervention in December 1950.

The British had fewer important strategic interests in the Far East, and the isolated position of the Hong Kong colony was always a reminder of the perils of antagonizing the Communist behemoth to the north. In addition, British and Canadian diplomatic officials shared grave reservations about President Truman's remarks regarding the use of atomic weapons, which on occasion were echoed by commanders in the field as well as the new Eisenhower administration. Both Britain and Canada were well aware that in the 'air-atomic age' they would be in the unenviable position of being the 'Belgium of World War Three.' In the end, both countries sided against their erstwhile ally through the practice of the 'diplomacy of constraint,' which, according to Martin Kitchen, had little effect on the Americans' conduct of the war.

The continuation of the Cold War after Korea, differences over the ends and means of the containment strategy, and the rise of Third World nationalism provided the backdrop to the response of the three English-speaking allies to the 1956 Suez crisis. The confrontation between traditional British imperialism and Arab nationalism eventually led to the most serious disruption in the history of the North Atlantic triangle; this time the United States and Canada aligned themselves against the British. In the aftermath of the 1954 Bandung Conference, the United States increasingly came to define the 'Cold War' as a competition with the Soviet Union for spheres of influence in the the Third World and the support of the non-aligned bloc. It also became less tolerant of any vestiges of traditional European imperialism. In response to President Nasser's seizing of the Suez Canal, the Eden government naïvely assumed it could act with American backing, or at least tacit support, to regain its lost territory. When Britain and France agreed to support the Israeli invasion of Egypt which called for, among other things, the seizure of the Suez Canal, President Eisenhower unhesitatingly described this as an act of 'allied treachery.' In contrast to their implementation of the Marshall Plan to restore the British economy for the purposes of national security, the United States resorted in 1956 to the use of an oil import embargo and the witholding of loans from the Export-Import and World banks.

Canada's response to the Suez crisis was equally harsh, but different measures were employed to deal with the matter. In addition to issuing sharply worded diplomatic notes, the St Laurent government sought a resolution of the crisis within the United Nations rather than within the Commonwealth. Among the media, public opinion, and the ruling Liberal party, many believed that the Suez crisis marked the end of a final chapter in the Canadian 'special relationship' with the mother country and redefined the North Atlantic triangle. Canada's new role as an independent 'peacekeeper' was particularly welcomed by the Americans. 'I think you have done a wonderful thing,' President Dwight Eisenhower wrote in a congratulatory note to Prime Minister St Laurent.[15] By working through the United Nations Security Council and its peacekeeping forces, Canada made it abundantly clear that it would no longer assume Mackenzie King's version of the linchpin role 'to build an alliance of three great democratic groups in the interest of world peace.'[16] After Harold MacMillan replaced Anthony Eden in London, Anglo-American relations improved, but the memories of Suez lingered. When President Lyndon Johnson called for allied support during the early stages of the Vietnam War and the contribution of only token military forces, the recently   elected British Labour government under Harold Wilson firmly rejected this proposal and informed the American leader that a mediated solution, using the offices of the United Nations, was the best solution. After once prodding the Americans about the danger of Soviet expansion in 1947, the British now assumed the 'linchpin' role as Cold War mediator.

Throughout the twentieth century the North Atlantic triangle has evolved through the stages of informal entente and formal alliance to a steady partnership within larger multilateral organizations such as the GATT, NATO, and the United Nations. International relations theory has devoted much of its attention to the causes of conflict, but the diplomacy of the three countries offers much empirical evidence to show why countries remain relatively close allies. The North Atlantic triangle has the distinction of being the twentieth century's longest-standing, mutually cooperative relationship. The triangular partnership was largely defined by Canada as an extension of the 'special relationship' that existed between the United States and Great Britain, always tempered by Ottawa's own calculation of ideology, interests, and sense of historical tradition. In some respects it embodied the ideals of the 1945 United Nations Charter on a more limited scale and still stands as a model for contemporary economic and political conflict resolution.

NOTES

1 The only notable exception is R.N. Kottman, *Reciprocity and the North Atlantic Triangle, 1932–1938* (Ithaca, 1968).

2 See, for example, the recent studies by B.W. Muirhead, *The Development of Postwar Canadian Trade Policy: The Failure of the Anglo-European Option* (Montreal, 1992); J.L. Granatstein and N. Hillmer, *For Better or for Worse: Canada and the United States to the 1990s* (Toronto, 1991).

3 Quoted in H.K. Beale, *Theodore Roosevelt and the Rise of America to World Power* (New York, 1965), 148–9.

4 C. Berger, *Sense of Power: Studies in the Ideas of Canadian Imperialism, 1869–1914* (Toronto, 1970).

5 R. Colins, *Culture, Communication and National Identity: The Case of Canadian Television* (Toronto, 1990); J.H. Thompson, 'Canada's Quest for Cultural Sovereignty; Promotion, Protection and Popular Culture,' in *Seeing Ourselves: Media Power and Policy in Canada*, ed. H. Holmes and D. Taras (Toronto, 1992).

6 K. Waltz, *Man, the State, and War: A Theoretical Analysis* (New York, 1959).

7 This point is developed in G.T. Stewart, '"A Special Contiguous Country Economic Regime": An Overview of America's Canadian Policy,' *Diplomatic History* 6(Fall 1982), 339–58; R.E. Hannigan, 'Reciprocity 1911: Continentalism and America Weltpolitik,' *Diplomatic History* 4(Fall 1980), 1–18.

8 A.S. Link, *Wilson the Diplomatist* (New York, 1963), 110–24.

9 J.W. Pickersgill, ed., *The Mackenzie King Record*, Vol. 1: *1939–44* (Toronto, 1960); G.W. Egerton, ed., *Political Memoir: Essays on the Politics of Memory* (London, 1994); W.F. Kimball, ed., *Churchill and Roosevelt: The Complete Correspondence*, 3 vols (Princeton, 1984).

10 C.P. Stacey, *Canada and the Age of Conflict: A History of Canadian External Policies*, Vol. II: *1921–1948* (Toronto, 1981), 325.

11 See, for example, L. Aronsen, 'The Indispensable Ally: American National Security and Relations with Canada, 1945–1963,' unpublished manuscript.

12 C. Barnett, *The Collapse of British Power* (London, 1972), 218–27; R. Ovendale, *'Appeasement' and the English Speaking World* (Cardiff, 1975), 319–30.
13 H.L. Keenleyside and G.S. Brown, *Canada and the United States* (New York, 1952), 284–5.
14 'Canada's Industrial War Effort: A Year-End Review,' 22 January 1944, vol. l, RG 28a, [National Archives of Canada].
15 President Eisenhower, quoted in Granatstein and Hillmer, *For Better or for Worse*, 188.
16 Quoted in J.H. Thompson and S. Randall, *Canada and the United States: Ambivalent Allies* (Montreal, 1994), 146.

Select Bibliography

Acheson, Dean. *Present at the Creation*. London, 1969.

Adler, Selig. *The Isolationist Impulse: Its Twentieth-Century Reaction*. New York, 1957.

– *The Uncertain Giant, 1921–1941: American Foreign Policy between the Wars*. New York, 1965.

Albion, R.G., and J.B. Pope. *Sea Lanes in Wartime: The American Experience, 1775–1945*. 2nd ed. New York, 1968.

Alexander, F. 'Simon-Stimson Myth: Japanese Aggression in Manchuria and Anglo-American Relations, 1931–1934.' *Australian Outlook*, 9(1955).

Allard, D.C. 'Admiral William S. Sims and United States Naval Policy in World War I.' *American Neptune*, 35(1975).

Ambrose, Stephen. *Rise to Globalism: American Foreign Policy, 1938–1970*. Harmondsworth, 1971.

– *Eisenhower: The President*. New York, 1984.

– *Eisenhower: Soldier and President*. New York, 1990.

Anderson, Terry. *The United States, Great Britain, and the Cold War*. London, 1981.

Aronsen, Lawrence. 'An Open Door to the North: The Liberal Government and the Expansion of American Foreign Investment, 1945–1953.' *American Review of Canadian Studies*, 22(1992).

– 'The "Indispensable Ally": American National Security and Econimic Relations with Canada, 1945–1963.' Unpublished manuscript.

Aronsen, Lawrence, and Martin Kitchen. *The Origins of the Cold War in Comparative Perspective: American, British and Canadian Relations with the Soviet Union, 1941–48*. London, 1988.

Artaud, D. *La Question des Dettes Interalliées et la Reconstruction de l'Europe (1917–1929)*, Vol. II. Paris, 1978.

Aster, S. *1939: The Making of the Second World War*. London, 1973.

Bamford, James. *The Puzzle Palace: A Report on America's Most Secret Agency*. New
York, 1983.

Barnett, C. *The Collapse of British Power*. London, 1972.

– *The Audit of War: The Illusion and Reality of Britain as a Great Nation*. London,
1986.

Bartlett, C.J. *The Long Retreat: A Short HIstory of British Defence Policy, 1945–1970*.
London, 1972.

Beale, H.K. *Theodore Roosevelt and the Rise of America to World Power*. New York,
1965.

Beaver, D.R. *Newton D. Baker and the American War Effort, 1917–1919*. Lincoln,
NE, 1966.

Beckett, I.F.W., and J. Gooch, eds. *Politicians and British Defence Policy, 1945–1970*.
Manchester, 1981.

Bell, A.C. *A History of the Blockade of Germany: and of the Countries Associated with
Her in the Great War, Austria-Hungary, Bulgaria and Turkey*. London, 1937.

Beloff, Max. 'The Special Relationship: An Anglo-American Myth.' In *A
Century of Conflict, 1850–1950: Essays for A.J.P. Taylor*, ed. M. Gilbert. London,
1966.

– *Britain's Liberal Empire, 1897–1921*. London, 1969.

Bennett, E.W. *Germany and the Financial Crisis, 1931*. Cambridge, MA, 1962.

Berg, M.W. 'Protecting National Interests by Treaty: The Second London Naval
Conference, 1934–1935.' In *Arms Limitation and Disarmament: Restraints on War,
1899–1939*, ed. B.J.C. McKercher. Westport, CT, 1992.

Berger, C. *Sense of Power: Studies in the Ideas of Canadian Imperialism, 1869–1914*.
Toronto, 1970.

Best, Jr, Richard. 'Co-operation with Like-Minded Peoples': British Influences on
American Security Policy, 1945–1949*. New York, 1986.

Bliss, M. *A Canadian Millionaire: The Life and Business Times of Sir Joseph Flavelle,
Bart., 1858–1939*. Toronto, 1978.

Block, Fred. *The Origins of International Economic Disorder: A Study of United States
International Monetary Policy from World War II to the Present*. Berkeley, 1977.

Borden, Henry, ed. *Robert Laird Borden: His Memoirs*. Toronto, 1969.

Borowski, Harry. *Hollow Threat: Strategic Air Power and Containment before Korea*.
Westport, CT, 1982.

Bothwell, Robert. *Loring Christie: The Failure of Bureaucratic Imperialism*. New
York, 1988.

– '"Who's Paying for Anything These Days?" War Production in Canada, 1939–
1945.' In *Canada's Defence: Perspectives on Policy in the Twentieth Century*, ed.
B.D. Hunt and R.G. Haycock. Toronto, 1993.

Bothwell, Robert, and John English. 'Canadian Trade Policy in the Age of American Dominance and British Decline, 1943–1947.' *Canadian Review of American Studies*, 8(1977).

Bothwell, R., I.M. Drummond and J. English. *Canada, 1900–1945*. Toronto, 1987.

– *Canada since 1945: Power, Politics, and Provincialism*. Toronto, 1989.

Bourne, A.H. 'Limited Liability War.' *Canadian Defence Quarterly*, 3(1939).

Bourne, Kenneth. *Britain and the Balance of Power in North America, 1815–1908*. London, 1967.

Boyle, P.G. 'The Roots of Isolationism: A Case Study.' *Journal of American Studies*, 6(1972).

– 'The British Foreign Office View of Soviet-American Relations.' *Diplomatic History*, 3(1979).

Braddick, H.B. 'A New Look at American Policy during the Italo-Ethiopian Crisis, 1935–1936.' *Journal of Modern History*, 34(1962).

Brebner, J.B. *North Atlantic Triangle: The Interplay of Canada, the United States and Great Britain*. New York, 1945; Toronto, 1966.

Brown, R.C. *Canada's National Policy, 1883–1900: A Study in Canadian-American Relations*. Princeton, 1964.

– *Robert Laird Borden: A Biography*. 2 vols. Toronto, 1975, 1980.

Brown, R.C., and R. Bothwell. 'The Canadian Resolution.' In *Policy by Other Means: Essays in Honour of C.P.Stacey*, ed. M. Cross and R. Bothwell. Toronto, 1972.

Bryant, Arthur. *The Turn of the Tide, 1939–43: A Study Based on the Diaries and Autobiographical Notes of Field Marshal the Viscount Alanbrooke, K.G., O.M.* London, 1957.

Buchan, A. 'Mothers and Daughters (or Greeks and Romans).' *Foreign Affairs*, 54(1976).

Bullock, Allan. *Ernest Bevin: Foreign Secretary, 1945–1951*. London, 1983.

Burk, K.M. *Britain, America and the Sinews of War, 1914–1918*. London, 1985.

Butler, J.R.M. *Lord Lothian*. London, 1960.

Butterfield, H. *The Whig Interpretation of History*. London, 1931.

Cain, P.J., and A.G. Hopkins. *British Imperialism: Crisis and Deconstruction, 1914–1990*. London, 1993.

Campbell, A.E. *Great Britain and the United States, 1895–1903*. London, 1960.

Campbell, Jr., C.S. *Anglo-American Understanding, 1898–1903*. Baltimore, 1957.

Campbell, Thomas. *Masquerade Peace: America's UN Policy, 1944–1945*. Tallahassee, FL, 1973.

Capie, F. *Depression and Protectionism: Britain between the Wars*. London, 1983.

Carlton, D. *MacDonald versus Henderson: The Foreign Policy of the Second Labour Government*. New York, 1970.

Carnegie, David. *The History of Munitions Supply in Canada, 1914–1918*. Toronto, 1925.

Carter, W.S. *Anglo-Canadian Wartime Relations, 1939–1945: RAF Bomber Command and No. 6 (Canadian) Group*. New York, 1991.

'Cato.' *Guilty Men*. London, 1940.

Churchill, Winston. *The History of the English-Speaking Peoples*. 4 vols. Toronto, 1956–8.

Clarke, Richard. *Anglo-American Economic Collaboration in War and Peace, 1942–1949*. Oxford, 1982.

Coffman, E. 'American Military and Strategic Policy in World War One.' In *War Aims and Strategic Policy in the Great War, 1914–1918*, ed. B.D. Hunt and A. Preston. London, 1977.

Cohen, E.A. 'Churchill and Coalition Strategy in World War II.' In *Grand Strategies in War and Peace*, ed. P.M. Kennedy. New Haven, CT, 1991.

Cohen, Warren I. *The American Revisionists: The Lessons of Intervention in World War I*. Chicago, 1967.

– *Empire without Tears: America's Foreign Relations, 1921–1933*. New York, 1987.

– *America in the Age of Soviet Power, 1945–1991*. Cambridge, 1993.

Coletta, Paolo E. 'The American Naval Leaders' Preparations for War.' In *The Great War, 1914–18*, ed. R.J.Q. Adams. London, 1990.

Colins, R. *Culture, Communication and National Identity: The Case of Canadian Television*. Toronto, 1990.

Constantine, Stephen. 'Anglo-Canadian Relations, the Empire Marketing Board, and Canadian National Autonomy between the Wars.' *Journal of Imperial and Commonwealth History*, 21(1993).

Cook, G.L. 'Sir Robert Borden, Lloyd George and British Military Policy, 1917–1918.' *Historical Journal*, 14(1971).

Cook, Ramsay, ed. *The Dafoe-Sifton Correspondence, 1919–1927*. Altona, Man., 1966.

Costigliola, Frank. 'Anglo-American Financial Rivalry in the 1920s.' *Journal of Economic History*, 37(1977).

– *Awkward Dominion: America's Political, Economic and Cultural Relations with Europe, 1919–1933*. Ithaca, NY, 1985.

Creighton, Donald. 'Decline and Fall of the Empire of the St Lawrence.' *Canadian Historical Association Papers* (1969).

– *Canada's First Century*. Toronto, 1970.

– *The Forked Road: Canada, 1939–1957*. Toronto, 1977.

– *Canada's First Century*. Toronto, 1970.

Cuff, R.D. *The War Industries Board*. Baltimore, 1973.

Cuff, R.D., and J.L. Granatstein. *Canadian-American Relations in Wartime*. Toronto, 1975.

– *American Dollars: Canadian Prosperity*. Toronto, 1978.

Dallek, Robert. *Franklin Roosevelt and American Foreign Policy, 1932–1945*. Oxford, 1979.

Dalton, Hugh. *High Tide and After: Memoirs, 1945–1960*. London, 1962.

Danchev, Alec. *Very Special Relationship: Field Marshal Sir John Dill and the Anglo-American Alliance, 1941–44*. London, 1986.

Dawson, R. MacGregor. *William Lyon Mackenzie King: A Political Biography, 1874–1923*. Toronto, 1958.

Dayer, Roberta. 'The British War Debts to the United States and the Anglo-Japanese Alliance, 1920–1923.' *Pacific Historical Review*, 45(1976).

– *Finance and Empire: Sir Charles Addis, 1861–1945*. New York, 1988.

– 'Anglo-American Monetary Policy and Rivalry in Europe and the Far East, 1919–1931.' In *Anglo-American Relations in the 1920s: the Struggle for Supremacy*, ed. B.J.C. McKercher. London, 1991.

De Conde, Alexander. *A History of American Foreign Policy*, Vol. II: *Global Powers (1900 to the Present)*. 3rd ed. New York, 1978.

De Santis, Hugh. *The Diplomacy of Silence: The American Foreign Service, the Soviet Union, and the Cold War, 1933–1947*. Chicago, 1983.

Dewey, P.E. 'Military Recruiting and the British Labour Force during the First World War.' *Historical Journal*, 27(1984).

Dilks, D., ed. *The Diaries of Sir Alexander Cadogan, 1938–1945*. London, 1971.

Divine, Robert. *Second Chance: The Triumph of Internationalism in America during World War II*. New York, 1967.

Dockrill, M.L. 'The Foreign Office, Anglo-American Relations and the Korean Truce Negotiations, July 1951 – July 1953.' In *The Korean War in History*, ed. James Cotton and Ian Neary. Manchester, 1989.

Doenecke, Justus. 'Iran's Role in Cold War Revisionism.' *Iranian Studies*, 5(1972).

Donnelly, Desmond. *Struggle for the World*. New York, 1965.

Donovan, Robert. *Conflict and Crisis: The Presidency of Harry S. Truman, 1945–1948*. New York, 1977.

Douglas, W.A.B. *The Creation of a National Air Force: The Official History of the Royal Canadian Air Force*. Vol. II. Toronto, 1986.

Dreisziger, N.F., ed. *Mobilization for Total War: The Canadian, American and British Experience, 1914–1918*. Waterloo, Ont., 1981.

Drummond, I.M. *British Economic Policy and the Empire, 1919–1939*. London, 1972.

– *Imperial Economic Policy, 1917–1939: Studies in Expansion and Protection*. London, 1974.

Drummond, I.M., and Norman Hillmer. *Negotiating Freer Trade: The United King-*

dom, the United States, Canada, and the Trade Agreements of 1938. Waterloo, ON, 1989.

Dziuban, S.W. *Military Relations between the United States and Canada, 1939–1945*. Washington, DC, 1959.

Eagleton, Clyde. 'Canada in the Making of the United Nations.' *University of Toronto Law Journal*, 7(1948).

Eayrs, James. *In Defence of Canada*. Vols I, II. Toronto, 1964, 1965.

– *The Commonwealth and Suez*. Oxford, 1964.

Eckes, Alfred. 'Open Door Expansionism Reconsidered: The World War II Experience.' *Journal of American History*, 59(1973).

Eden, Anthony. *Full Circle*. London, 1960.

Egerton, G.W., ed. *Political Memoir: Essays on the Politics of Memory*. London, 1994.

Eisenberg, Carolyn. 'Working Class Politics and the Cold War: American Intervention in the German Labor Movement, 1945–49.' *Diplomatic History*, 7(1983).

Ekirch, Arthur. *Ideas, Ideals, and American Diplomacy: A History of Their Growth and Interaction*. New York, 1966.

English, John. *Shadow of Heaven: The Life of Lester Pearson*, Vol. I: *1897–1948*. Toronto, 1992.

English, John A. *The Canadian Army and the Normandy Campaign: A Study of Failure in High Command*. New York, 1991.

Ewart, J.S. 'Canada, the Empire, and the United States.' *Foreign Affairs*, 6(1927).

– *The Independence Papers*. Vol. I (n.p., n.d.).

Fayle, C.E. *A History of the Great War: Seaborne Trade*. London, 1927.

Feis, Herbert. *The Diplomacy of the Dollar: The First Era, 1919–1932*. Baltimore, 1969.

Ferris, John. 'The Symbol and Substance of Seapower: Great Britain, the United States, and the One-Power Standard, 1919–1921.' In *Anglo-American Relations in the 1920s: The Struggle for Supremacy*, ed. B.J.C. McKercher. London, 1991.

– '"The Greatest Power on Earth": Great Britain in the 1920s.' *International History Review*, 13(1991).

– 'Worthy of Some Better Enemy? The British Estimate of the Imperial Japanese Army, 1919–41, and the Fall of Singapore.' *Canadian Journal of History*, 28(1993).

Folly, Martin. 'Breaking the Vicious Circle: Britain, the United States, and the Genesis of the North Atlantic Treaty.' *Diplomatic History*, 12(1988).

Fowler, W.B. *British-American Relations, 1917–1918: The Role of Sir William Wiseman*. Princeton, 1969.

Frankel, Joseph. *British Foreign Policy, 1945–1973*. New York, 1975.

French, David. *British Economic and Strategic Planning, 1905–1915*. London, 1982.

– *British Strategy and War Aims, 1914–1916*. London, 1986.

– '"Perfidious Albion" Faces the Powers.' *Canadian Journal of History*, 28(1993).
Friedberg, A.L. *The Weary Titan: Britain and the Experience of Relative Decline,
    1895–1905*. Princeton, 1988.
Friedman, Norman. *U.S. Destroyers*. Annapolis, MD, 1982.
Fry, M.G. *Illusions of Security North Atlantic Diplomacy, 1918–1922*. Toronto, 1972.
– 'The North Atlantic Triangle and the Abrogation of the Anglo-Japanese Alli-
    ance.' *Journal of Modern History*, 39(1976).
Fussell, Paul. *The Great War and Modern Memory*. Oxford, 1975.
Gaddis, John Lewis. *The United States and the Origins of the Cold War, 1941–1947*.
    New York, 1972.
– 'Was the Truman Doctrine a Real Turning Point?' *Foreign Affairs*, 52(1974).
– 'International Relations Theory and the End of the Cold War.' *International
    Security*, 17(1992–93).
Gardner, Richard. 'Sterling-Dollar Diplomacy in Current Perspective.' In *The
    'Special Relationship': Anglo-American Relations since 1945*, ed. W.R. Louis and
    Hedley Bull. Oxford, 1986.
Gardner, L.C. *Economic Aspects of New Deal Diplomacy*. Madison, WI, 1964.
Gibson, J.D. *Canada's Economy in a Changing World*. Toronto, 1948.
Gilbert, Martin. *The Roots of Appeasement*. London, 1966.
– *Winston S. Churchill*. Vol. VII: *Road to Victory, 1941–1945*. London, 1986.
Gimblett, R.H. '"Tin-Pots" or Dreadnoughts? The Evolution of the Naval Policy
    of the Laurier Administration, 1896–1911.' Unpublished MA thesis, 1981.
Glazebrook, G.P. *A History of Canadian External Relations*. Vol. I. Toronto, 1966.
Glueck, A.C. 'Pilgrimages to Ottawa: Canadian-American Diplomacy, 1903–13.'
    Canadian Historical Association Papers (1968).
– 'The Invisible Revision of the Rush-Bagot Agreement, 1898–1914.' *Canadian
    Historical Review*, 60(1979).
Goldman, A.L. 'Sir Robert Vansittart's Search for Italian Cooperation against
    Hitler, 1933–36.' *Journal of Contemporary History*, 9:3(1973).
Goldrick, James; and John B. Hattendorf, eds. *Mahan is not Enough*. Newport, RI,
    1993.
Goldstein, Erik. *Winning the Peace*. Oxford, 1991.
Gooch, John. 'The Maurice Debate, 1918.' *Journal of Contemporary History*,
    3:4(1968).
– *The Plans of War: The General Staff and British Military Strategy c. 1900–1916*.
    London, 1974.
– *The Prospect of War: Studies in British Defence Policy, 1847–1942*. London, 1981.
Goodwin, Geoffrey. *Britain and the United Nations*. New York, 1957.
Gordon, D.C. *The Dominion Partnership in Imperial Defense, 1870–1914*. Baltimore,
    1965.

Gough, B.M. 'The End of Pax Britannica and the Origins of the Royal Canadian Navy: Shifting Strategic Demands of an Empire at Sea.' In *The RCN in Transition, 1910–1985*, ed. W.A.B. Douglas. Vancouver, 1988.

Gowen, R.J. 'British Legerdemain at the 1911 Imperial Conference: The Dominions, Defense Planning, and the Renewal of the Anglo-Japanese Alliance.' *Journal of Modern History*, 52(1980).

Gowing, Margaret. *Independence and Deterrence: Britain and Atomic Energy, 1945–1952*, Vol. I. London, 1974.

Graham, W.R. *Arthur Meighen: A Biography*. Toronto, 1960–65.

Granatstein, J.L. *Canada's War: The Politics of the Mackenzie King Government, 1939–1945*. Toronto, 1975.

– *A Man of Influence: Norman A. Robertson and Canadian Statecraft, 1929–68.* Toronto, 1981.

– *The Ottawa Men: The Civil Service Mandarins, 1935–1957*. Toronto, 1982.

– 'Hume Wrong's Road to the Functional Principle.' *Coalition Warfare: An Uneasy Accord*, ed. K.E. Neilson and R.A. Prete. Waterloo, Ont., 1983.

– 'Canada and Peacekeeping: Image and Reality.' In *Canadian Foreign Policy: Historical Readings*, ed. idem. Toronto, 1986.

– *How Britain's Weakness Forced Canada into the Arms of the United States*. Toronto, 1989.

– *The Generals: The Canadian Army's Commanders in the Second World War*. Toronto, 1993.

Granatstein J.L., and R. Bothwell. '"A Self-Evident National Duty": Canadian Foreign Policy, 1935–1939.' *Journal of Imperial and Commonwealth History*, 3(1975).

Granatstein, J.L., et al. *Twentieth Century Canada*. Toronto, 1986.

Granatstein, J.L, and N. Hillmer. *For Better or for Worse: Canada and the United States to the 1990s*. Toronto, 1991.

Greenwood, John. 'The Emergence of the Postwar Strategic Air Force, 1945–1953.' In *Air Power and Warfare: The Proceedings of the Eighth Military History Symposium*, ed. Alfred Hurley and Robert Ehrhart. Washington, DC, 1979.

Grenville, J.A.S. 'Great Britain and the Isthmian Canal, 1898–1901.' *American Historical Review*, 51(1955).

Gretton, Peter. *Former Naval Person: Winston Churchill and the Royal Navy*. London, 1968.

Grieves, K. *The Politics of Manpower, 1914–1918*. Manchester, 1988.

Guinsburg, T.N. *The Pursuit of Isolationism in the United States Senate from Versailles to Pearl Harbor*. New York, 1982.

Haggie, P. *Britannia at Bay: The Defence of the British Empire against Japan, 1931–1941*. Oxford, 1981.

Haglund, D. *Latin America and the Transformation of U.S. Strategic Thought, 1936–1940*. Albuquerque, NM, 1984.

Hall, C. *Britain, America, and Arms Control, 1921–37*. London, 1987.

Halpern, P.G. *The Naval War in the Mediterranean, 1914–1918*. Annapolis, 1987.

Hannigan, R.E. 'Reciprocity 1911: Continentalism and America Weltpolitik.' *Diplomatic History* 4(Fall 1980).

Haraszti, E. *Treaty-Breakers or 'Realpolitiker'? The Anglo-German Naval Agreement of 1935*. Boppard am Rhein, 1974.

– *The Invaders: Hitler Occupies the Rhineland*. Budapest, 1983.

Harbutt, Fraser. *The Iron Curtain*. New York, 1986.

Hardach, Gerd. *The First World War, 1914–1918*. London, 1977.

Harris, Kenneth. *Attlee*. London 1982.

Harris, S.J. *Canadian Brass: The Making of a Professional Army, 1860–1939*. Toronto, 1988.

Harrod, R.F. *The Life of John Maynard Keynes*. New York, 1951.

Hatch, F.J. *Aerodrome of Democracy: Canada and the British Commonwealth Air Training Plan, 1939–1945*. Ottawa, 1983.

Hathaway, Robert. *Ambiguous Partnership: Britain and America, 1944–1947*. New York, 1981.

– *Great Britain and the United States: Special Relations since World War II*. Boston, 1990.

Haycock, R.G. *Sam Hughes: The Public Career of a Controversial Canadian, 1885–1916*. Waterloo, Ont., 1986.

Hecht, R.A. 'Great Britain and the Stimson Note of January 7, 1932.' *Pacific Historical Review*, 38(1969).

Heikal, Mohamed. *Cutting the Lion's Tail*. London 1986.

Hess, Gary. 'The Iranian Crisis of 1945–46 and the Cold War.' *Political Science Quarterly*, 89(1974).

Higgins, Rosalyn. *UN Peacekeeping, 1946–67: Documents and Commentary on The Middle East*. Oxford, 1969.

Hilliker, John. *Canada's Department of External Affairs*. Vol. I: *The Early Years, 1909–1946*. Montreal, Kingston, 1990.

Hillmer, Norman. 'A British High Commissioner for Canada, 1927–28.' *Journal of Imperial and Commonwealth History*, 3(1973).

– 'The Anglo-Canadian Neurosis: The Case of O.D. Skelton.' In *Britain and Canada: Survey of a Changing Relationship*, ed. P. Lyon. London, 1976.

Hitchens, Christopher. *Blood, Class, and Nostalgia: Anglo-American Ironies*. New York, 1990.

Hitsman, J.M. *Safeguarding Canada, 1763–1871*. Toronto, 1968.

Hogan, M.J. *Informal Entente: the Private Structure of Cooperation in Anglo-American Economic Diplomacy, 1918–1928.* Columbia, MO, 1978.

Holmes, H., and D. Taras, eds. *Seeing Ourselves: Media Power and Policy in Canada.* Toronto, 1992.

Holmes, John. *The Shaping of Peace: Canada and Search for World Order, 1943–1957.* Vol. I. Toronto, 1979.

Horowitz, David. *Empire and Revolution.* New York, 1969.

Howard, Michael. *The Continental Commitment: The Dilemma of British Defence Policy in the Era of the Two World Wars.* Harmondsworth, 1974.

Howe, C.D. 'Employment and Income with Special Reference to the Initial Period of Reconstruction.' In *Canadian Foreign Policy, 1945–1954,* ed. R.A. Mackay. Toronto, 1971.

Hudson W.J., and J. North, eds. *My Dear P.M.: R.G. Casey's Letters to S.M. Bruce, 1924–1929.* Canberra, 1980.

Hughes, E.J. 'Winston Churchill and the Formation of the United Nations Organization.' *Journal of Contemporary History,* 9(1974).

Huntington, S.P. *The Soldier and the State: The Theory and Politics of Civil-Military Relations.* New York, 1957.

Hurd, A. *The Merchant Navy.* London, 1929.

Iriye, Akira. *The Globalizing of America, 1913–1945.* Cambridge, 1993.

Jenkins, Roy. *Truman.* London 1986.

Jockel, Joseph. 'The Canada-United States Military Cooperation Committee and Continental Air Defence, 1946.' *Canadian Historical Review,* 64(1983).

– *No Boundaries Upstairs: Canada, the United States and the Origins of North American Air Defence, 1945–1958.* Vancouver, 1987.

Johnson, Paul. *A History of the Modern World.* London, 1983.

Joy, Turner. *How Communists Negotiate.* New York 1955.

Kaplan, Lawrence. *A Community of Interests: NATO and the Military Assistance Program, 1948–1951.* Washington, DC, 1980.

Keenleyside, H.L., and G.S. Brown. *Canada and the United States.* New York, 1952.

Kendle, J.E. *The Round Table Movement and Imperial Union.* Toronto, 1975.

Kennan, George. *American Diplomacy, 1900–1950.* Chicago, 1951.

Kennedy, Greg C. 'The 1930 London Naval Conference and Anglo-American Maritime Strength, 1927–1930.' In *Arms Limitation and Disarmament: Restraints on War, 1899–1939,* ed. B.J.C. McKercher. Westport, CT, 1992.

Kennedy, P.M. *The Rise and Fall of British Naval Mastery.* New York, 1976.

– 'The Tradition of Appeasement in British Foreign Policy, 1865–1939.' *British Journal of International Studies,* 2(1976).

– *The Rise and Fall of the Great Powers: Economic Change and Military Conflict from 1500 to 2000.* London, 1988.

Kent, B. *The Spoils of War: The Politics, Economics, and Diplomacy of Reparations, 1918–1932*. Oxford, 1989.

Keylor, W.R. *The Twentieth-Century World*. Oxford, 1984.

Kimball, W.F., ed. *Churchill and Roosevelt: The Complete Correspondence*. 3 vols. Princeton, 1984.

– 'Naked Reverse Right: Roosevelt, Churchill, and Eastern Europe from Tolstoy to Yalta – and a Little Beyond.' *Diplomatic History*, 9(1985).

Kindleberger, Charles. 'The Marshall Plan and the Cold War.' *International Journal*, 24(1968).

– *The World in Depression, 1929–1939*. Los Angeles, 1973.

Klein, Ira. 'Whitehall, Washington, and the Anglo-Japanese Alliance, 1919–1921.' *Pacific Historical Review*, 41(1972).

Kolko, Gabriel. *The Politics of War: The World and United States Foreign Policy, 1943–1945*. New York, 1968.

– *Main Currents in Modern American History*. New York, 1984.

Kolko, Gabriel, and Joyce Kolko. *The Limits of Power: The World and United States Foreign Policy, 1945–1954*. New York, 1972.

Kuniholm, Bruce. *The Origins of the Cold War in the Near East*. Princeton, 1980.

Kyle, Keith. *Suez*. London 1991.

LaFeber, Walter. *The Search for American Opportunity, 1865–1913*. Cambridge, MA, 1993.

Lane, Arthur Bliss. *I Saw Poland Betrayed*. Indianapolis, 1948.

Lash, J.P. *Roosevelt and Churchill, 1939–1941: The Partnership that Saved the West*. New York, 1976.

Leffler, M. 'Political Isolationism, Economic Expansionism, or Diplomatic Realism: American Policy toward Western Europe, 1921–1933.' *Perspectives in American History*, 8(1974).

– *A Preponderance of Power: National Security, the Truman Administration, and the Cold War*. Stanford, 1992.

Lentin, A. *Lloyd George, Woodrow Wilson and the Guilt of Germany: An Essay in the Pre-History of Appeasement*. Baton Rouge, LA, 1985.

Levin, N. Gordon. *Woodrow Wilson and World Politics: America's Response to War and Revolution*. New York, 1968.

Link, A.S. *Wilson the Diplomatist*. New York, 1963.

– *Wilson: Campaigns for Progressivism and Peace, 1916–1917*. Princeton, 1965.

– *Woodrow Wilson: Revolution, War and Peace*. Arlington Heights, IL, 1979.

Little, D. *Malevolent Neutrality: The United States, Great Britain, and the Origins of the Spanish Civil War*. Ithaca, 1985.

Louis, W.R., and Roger Owen, eds. *Suez 1956: The Crisis and Its Consequences*. Oxford 1984.

Lowe, P. *Great Britain and the Origins of the Pacific War: A Study of British Policy in East Asia, 1937–1941.* London, 1977.

Lower, A.R.M. *Colony to Nation.* Toronto, 1957.

Lund, W.G.D. 'The Royal Canadian Navy's Quest for Autonomy in the North West Atlantic: 1941–43.' In *The RCN in Retrospect, 1910–1968,* ed. J.A. Boutilier. Vancouver, 1982.

Lundestad, Geir. *The American Empire.* London, 1990.

MacDonald, Callum. *Korea: the War before Vietnam.* London 1986.

Mackinnon, C.S. 'The Imperial Fortresses in Canada: Halifax and Esquimalt, 1871–1906.' PhD thesis, University of Toronto, 1965.

Maddox, Robert J. *William E. Borah and American Foreign Policy.* Baton Rouge, LA, 1969.

Mansergh, N. *Survey Of British Commonwealth Affairs: Problems of External Policy, 1931–1939.* London, 1952.

Marder, A.J. *The Anatomy of British Sea Power: A History of British Naval Policy in the Pre-Dreadnought Era, 1880–1905.* New York, 1940; new ed., London, 1964.

– *Portrait of an Admiral: The Life and Papers of Sir Herbert Richmond.* Cambridge, MA, 1952.

– *From Dreadnought to Scapa Flow.* London, 1961.

– *From the Dardanelles to Oran.* London, 1974.

Marquand, D. *Ramsay MacDonald.* London, 1977.

Martel, Gordon. 'The Meaning of Power: Rethinking the Decline and Fall of Great Britain.' *International History Review,* 13(1991).

May, Ernest. *Lessons of the Past: The Use and Misuse of History in American Foreign Policy.* New York, 1973.

McCallum, R.B. *Public Opinion and the Last Peace.* London, 1944.

McCormick, Thomas. *America's Half-Century: United States Foreign Policy in the Cold War.* Baltimore, 1989.

McFarland, Stephen. 'A Peripheral View of the Origins of the Cold War: The Crises in Iran, 1941–47.' *Diplomatic History,* 4(1980).

McKercher, B.J.C. 'Wealth, Power, and the New International Order: Britain and the American Challenge in the 1920s.' *Diplomatic History,* 12(1988).

– 'Between Two Giants: Canada, the Coolidge Conference, and Anglo-American Relations in 1927.' In *Anglo-American Relations in the 1920s: The Struggle for Supremacy,* ed. idem. Edmonton, London, 1990.

– '"Our Most Dangerous Enemy": Great Britain Pre-eminent in the 1930s.' *International History Review,* 13(1991).

– 'From Enmity to Cooperation: the Second Baldwin Government and the Improvement of Anglo-American Relations, November 1928 – June 1929.' *Albion,* 24(1992).

- '"A Greater and a Higher Ideal": Esme Howard, Imperial Unity, and Canadian Autonomy in Foreign Policy, 1924–27.' In *Power, Personalities and Policies: Essays in Honour of Donald Cameron Watt*, ed. M.G. Fry. London, 1992.
- 'Of Horns and Teeth: the Preparatory Commission and the World Disarmament Conference, 1926–1934.' In *Arms Limitation and Disarmament: Restraints on War, 1899–1939*, ed. idem. Westport, CT, 1992.
- '"No Eternal Friends or Enemies": British Defence Policy and the Problem of the United States, 1919–1939.' *Canadian Journal of History*, 28(1993).

Merrick, Ray. 'The Russia Committee of the British Foreign Office and the Cold War, 1946–7.' *Journal of Contemporary History*, 20(1985).

Middlemas, J., and J. Barnes. *Baldwin: A Biography*. London, 1969.

Miller, A.J. 'The Functional Principle in Canada's External Relations.' *International Journal*, 35(1980).

Miller, Carman. *The Canadian Career of the Fourth Earl of Minto: The Education of A Viceroy*. Waterloo, 1980.

- *Painting the Map Red: Canada and the South African War, 1899–1902*. Montreal, Kingston, 1993.

Miller, K.E. *Socialism and Foreign Policy: Theory and Practice in Britain to 1931*. The Hague, 1967.

Miller, R. 'Britain and the Rhineland Crisis, 7 March 1936: Retreat from Responsibility or Accepting the Inevitable?' *Australian Journal of Politics and History*, 33(1987).

Moran, Lord. *Winston Churchill the Struggle for Survival, 1940–1965*. London, 1968.

Morton, Desmond. *Ministers and Generals: Politics and the Canadian Militia, 1868–1904*. Toronto, 1970.

- *The Canadian General: Sir William Otter*. Toronto, 1974.
- *Canada and War*. Toronto, 1981.
- 'The Canadian Military Experience in the First World War, 1914–1918.' In *The Great War, 1914–18*, ed. R.J.Q. Adams. London, 1990.

Morton, Desmond, and J.L. Granatstein. *Marching to Armageddon: Canadians and the Great War, 1914–1919*. Toronto, 1989.

Muirhead, B.W. *The Development of Postwar Canadian Trade Policy: The Failure of the Anglo-European Option*. Montreal, 1992.

Murfett, M. *Fool-Proof Relations: The Search for Anglo-American Naval Cooperation during the Chamberlain Years, 1937–1940*. Singapore, 1984.

Murray, W. *The Change in the European Balance of Power, 1938–1939: The Path to Ruin*. Princeton, 1984.

Neary, Peter. 'Grey, Bryce, and the Settlement of Canadian-American Differences, 1905–1911.' *Canadian Historical Review*, 49(1968).

Neatby, H.B. *William Lyon Mackenzie King, 1924–1932: The Lonely Heights.* Toronto, 1970.

Neilson, Keith. 'Russian Foreign Purchasing in the Great War: A Test Case.' *Slavonic and East European Review,* 60(1982).

– *Strategy and Supply.* London, 1985.

– '"Greatly Exaggerated": The Myth of the Decline of Great Britain before 1914.' *International History Review,* 13(1991).

– '"Pursued by a Bear": British Estimates of Soviet Military Strength and Anglo-Soviet Relations, 1922–1939.' *Canadian Journal of History,* 28(1993).

Newman, S. *The British Guarantee to Poland: A Study in the Continuity of British Foreign Policy.* London, 1976.

Newton, Scott. 'Post-War Reconstruction: How Successful Was the Marshall Plan?' *History Today,* 33(1983).

Nicholson, G.W.L. *The Canadians in Italy.* Ottawa, 1956.

– *Canadian Expeditionary Force: The Canadian Army in the First World War, 1914–1919.* Ottawa, 1960.

Nish, Ian. *Alliance in Decline: A Study in Anglo-Japanese Relations, 1908–1923.* London, 1972.

– *Japan's Struggle With Internationalism: Japan, China, and the League of Nations, 1931–3.* London, 1993.

Norrie, Kenneth, and Douglas Owram. *A History of the Canadian Economy.* Toronto, 1991.

Nutting, Anthony. *No End of a Lesson: The Story of Suez* London, 1972.

O'Connor, Raymond G. *Perilous Equilibrium: The United States and the London Naval Conference of 1930.* Lawrence, KS, 1962.

Offer, A. *The First World War: An Agrarian Interpretation.* Oxford, 1989.

Osgood, R.E. *Ideals and Self-Interest in America's Foreign Relations.* Chicago, 1953.

Ovendale, R. *'Appeasement' and the English Speaking World.* Cardiff, 1975.

– ed. *The Foreign Policy of the British Labour Government, 1945–1951.* Leicester, 1984.

Parrini, C.P. *Heir to Empire: The United States Economic Diplomacy, 1916–1923.* Pittsburgh, 1969.

Parsons, E.B. 'Why the British Reduced the Flow of American Troops to Europe in August–October, 1918.' *Canadian Journal of History,* 12(1977).

Pastor, Robert. *Congress and the Politics of U.S. Foreign Economic Policy, 1929–1976.* Berkeley, 1980.

Paterson, Thomas. 'The Quest for Peace and Prosperity: International Trade, Communism, and the Marshall Plan.' In *Politics and Policies of the Truman Administration,* ed. Barton Bernstein. Chicago, 1970.

Paulhac, F. *Les Accords de Munich et les Origines de la Guerre de 1939.* Paris, 1988.

Pearson, Lester. *Mike: The Memoirs of the Right Honourable Lester B. Pearson*. Vol. II: *1948–57*. Toronto, 1973.

Pelz, S.E. *Race to Pearl Harbor: The Failure of the Second London Naval Conference and the Onset of World War II*. Cambridge, MA, 1974.

Penlington, N. *Canada and Imperialism, 1896–1899*. Toronto, 1965.

Perkins, Bradford. *The Great Rapprochement: England and the United States, 1895–1914*. New York, 1968.

Perras, Galen. 'Canada as Military Partner: Alliance Politics and the Campaign to Recapture the Aleutian Island of Kiska.' *Journal of Military History*, 3(1992).

Pickersgill, J.W., ed., *The Mackenzie King Record*. Vol. I: *1939–1944*. Toronto, 1960.

Pinder, John. 'Prophet Not without Honour: Lothian and the Federal Idea.' In *The Larger Idea: Lord Lothian and the Problem of National Sovereignty*, ed. John Turner. Exeter, 1988.

Pollard, Robert. *Economic Security and the Origins of the Cold War, 1945–1950*. New York, 1985.

Post, Jr, G. *Dilemmas of Appeasement: British Deterrence and Defense, 1934–1937*. Ithaca, NY, 1993.

Potter, E.B., and C.W. Nimitz. *Sea Power: A Naval History*. Englewood Cliffs, NJ, 1960.

Prang, Margaret. *N.W. Rowell: Ontario Nationalist*. Toronto, 1975.

Preston, Adrian. 'Canada and the Higher Direction of the Second World War, 1939–1945.' *Journal of the Royal United Services Institute*, 110(February 1965).

Preston, R.A. *Canada and 'Imperial Defense': A Study of the Origins of the British Commonwealth's Defense Organization, 1867–1919*. Toronto, 1967.

– *The Defence of the Undefended Border: Planning for War in North America, 1867–1939*. Montreal, London, 1977.

Price, Harry. *The Marshall Plan and Its Meaning*. Ithaca, 1955.

Reid, Escott. *On Duty: A Canadian at the Making of the United Nations, 1945–1946*. Toronto, 1983.

Reynolds, David. *The Creation of the Anglo-American Alliance, 1937–1941: A Study in Competitive Cooperation*. London, 1981.

– 'FDR's Foreign Policy and the British Royal Visit to the USA, 1939.' *Historian*, 45(1983).

– 'A "Special Relationship"?: America, Britain and International Order since the Second World War.' *International Affairs*, 62(1985–6).

– *Britannia Overruled: British Policy and World Power in the 20th Century*. London, 1991.

Rhodes James, R. *The British Revolution: British Politics, 1880–1939*. London, 1977.

– *Anthony Eden*. London 1986.

Rider, P.E. 'The Imperial Munitions Board and its Relationship to Government, Business and Labour, 1914–1920.' PhD thesis, University of Toronto, 1974.

Robbins, Keith. *Appeasement*. Oxford, 1988.

Rock, W.R. *British Appeasement in the 1930s*. London, 1977.

– *Chamberlain and Roosevelt: British Foreign Policy and the United States, 1937–1940*. Columbus, OH, 1988.

Roi, M.L. '"A Completely Immoral and Cowardly Attitude": The British Foreign Office, American Neutrality, and the Hoare-Laval Plan.'*Canadian Journal of History*, 29 (1944).

Rosen, E.A. 'Intranationalism vs. Internationalism: The Interregnum Struggle for the Sanctity of the New Deal.' *Political Science Quarterly*, 81(1966).

Roskill, S.W. *The Strategy of Sea Power*. London, 1962.

– *Naval Policy between the Wars*. 2 vols. London, 1968, 1977.

Ross, Steven. *American War Plans, 1945–1950*. New York, 1988.

Rothwell, Victor. *Britain and the Cold War*. London, 1982.

Ryan, H.B. 'A New Look at Churchill's "Iron Curtain" Speech.' *Historical Journal*, 22(1979).

Sarty, Roger. 'The Naval Side of Canadian Sovereignty, 1909–1923.' *The Niobe Papers*. Vol. 4: *Oceans Policy in the 1990s: An Atlantic Perspective*. St. John's, Nfld, 1992.

– 'Silent Sentry: A Military and Political History of Canadian Coast Defence, 1867–1945. PhD thesis, University of Toronto, 1982.

– '"There Will be Trouble in the North Pacific": The Defence of British Columbia in the Early Twentieth Century.' *BC Studies*, 61(1984).

– 'Entirely in the Hand of the Friendly Neighbour': The Canadian Armed Forces and the Defence of the Pacific Coast, 1909–1939.' Unpublished paper, 1990.

– 'The Origins of the Royal Canadian Navy: The Australian Connection.' In *Reflections on the Royal Australian Navy*, ed. T.R. Frame, J.V.P. Goldrick, and P.D. Jones. Kenthurst, NSW, 1990.

– 'Canadian Maritime Defence, 1892–1914.' *Canadian Historical Review*, 71(1990).

Sarty, Roger, and Michael Hadley. *Tin-Pots and Pirate Ships: Canadian Naval Forces and German Sea Raiders, 1880–1918*. Montreal, Kingston, 1991.

Scheinberg, Stephen. 'Invitation to Empire: Tariffs and American Economic Expansion in Canada.' In *Enterprise and National Development: Essays in Canadian Business and Economic History*, ed. Glenn Porter and Robert D. Cuff. Toronto, 1973.

Schurman, D.M. *The Education of a Navy: The Development of British Naval Thought, 1867–1914*. Chicago, 1965.

Schwabe, Klaus. *Woodrow Wilson, Revolutionary Germany, and Peace-Making, 1918–1919*. Chapel Hill, NC, 1985.

Selwyn-Lloyd, Lord. *Suez 1956*. London, 1978.

Sherwood, R.E. *The White House Papers of Harry Hopkins*, Vol. I. London, 1948.

Shrader, C.R. '"Maconochie's Stew": Logistical Support of American Forces with the BEF, 1917–18.' In *The Great War, 1914–18*, ed. R.J.Q. Adams. London, 1990.

Skelton, O.D. 'Current Events: Canada and the Making of War and Peace.' *Queen's Quarterly*, 28(July 1920).

Smith, Denis. *The Diplomacy of Fear: Canada and the Cold War, 1941–1948*. Toronto, 1988.

Smith, Gaddis. 'Canada and the Siberian Intervention, 1918–1919.' *American Historical Review*, 64(1959).

Smith, Raymond. 'A Climate of Opinion: British Officials and the Development of British Soviet Policy, 1945–7.' *International Affairs*, 64(1988).

Smith, Raymond, and John Zametica. 'The Cold Warrior: Clement Attlee Reconsidered, 1945–7.' *International Affairs*, 61(1985).

Smythe, D. *Pershing: General of the Armies*. Bloomington, IN, 1986.

Soward, F.H., and Edgar McInnis. *Canada and the United Nations*. New York, 1957.

Spanier, John W. *The Truman-MacArthur Controversy and the Korean War*. New York 1965.

Spiers, E.M. *Haldane: An Army Reformer*. Edinburgh, 1980.

Stacey, C.P. *Canada and the British Army, 1846–1871: A Study in the Practice of Responsible Government*. Rev. ed. Toronto, 1963.

– *Official History of the Canadian Army in the Second World War*. Vol. I: *Six Years of War: The Army in Canada, Britain and the Pacific*. Ottawa, 1966.

– 'The Turning Point: Canadian-American Relations during the Roosevelt-King Era.' *Canada: An Historical Magazine*, 1(1973).

– *Arms, Men and Governments: The War Policies of Canada, 1939–1945*. Ottawa, 1974.

– *Canada and the Age of Conflict: A History of Canadian External Policies*. 2 vols. Toronto, 1977, 1981.

– 'Canadian Leaders of the Second World War.' *Canadian Historical Review*, 1(1985).

Stairs, Denis. *The Diplomacy of Constraint: Canada, the Korean War, and the United States*. Toronto, 1974.

Stewart, A.R. 'Sir John A. Macdonald and the Imperial Defence Commission of 1879.' *Canadian Historical Review*, 35(1954).

Stewart, G.T. '"A Special Contiguous Country Economic Regime": An Overview of America's Canadian Policy.' *Diplomatic History* 6(Fall 1982).

Stone, Ralph. *The Irreconcilables: The Fight against the League of Nations.* Lexington, KY, 1970.

Sumida, J.T. *In Defence of Naval Supremacy.* London, 1989.

– 'Forging the Trident: British Naval Industrial Logistics, 1914–1918.' In *Feeding Mars: Logistics in Western Warfare from the Middle Ages to the Present,* ed. J.A. Lynn. Boulder, CO, 1993.

– 'British Naval Operational Logistics, 1914–1918.' *Journal of Military History,* 57(1993).

Swettenham, J.A. *To Seize the Victory: The Canadian Corps in World War I.* Toronto, 1965.

Tallman, R.D. 'Warships and Mackerels: The North Atlantic Fisheries in Canadian-American Relations, 1867–1877.' PhD thesis, University of Maine, 1971.

Taylor, A.J.P. *The Origins of the Second World War.* London, 1963.

– *English History, 1914–1945.* Oxford, 1965.

Taylor, Philip. 'The Projection of Britain Abroad, 1945–1951.' In *British Foreign Policy, 1945–1956,* ed. Michael Dockrill and John Young. New York, 1989.

Terraine, J. *Douglas Haig, the Educated Soldier.* London, 1963.

Thompson, J.H. *The Harvests of War: The Prairie West, 1914–1918.* Toronto, 1978.

Thompson, J.H., and S. Randall. *Canada and the United States: Ambivalent Allies.* Montreal, 1994.

Thompson, J.H., and Allen Seager. *Canada, 1922–1939: Decades of Discord.* Toronto, 1985.

Thorne, Christopher. *The Limits of Foreign Policy: The West, the League and the Far Eastern Crisis of 1931–1933.* New York, 1973.

– *Allies of a Kind: The United States, Britain, and the War against Japan, 1941–1945.* London, 1978.

Thornton, A.P. *The Imperial Idea and Its Enemies: A Study in British Power.* London, 1959.

Trask, D.F. *Captains and Cabinets.* Columbia, 1972.

Travers, Tim. 'The Evolution of British Strategy and Tactics on the Western Front in 1918: GHQ, Manpower and Technology.' *Journal of Military History,* 54(1990).

– *How the War Was Won: Command and Technology in the British Army on the Western Front, 1917–1918.* London, 1992.

Tucker, G.N. *The Naval Service of Canada.* Vol. 1. Ottawa, 1952.

Turner, John. *British Politics and the Great War: Coalition and Conflict, 1915–1918.* New Haven, CT, 1992.

UN Library, Geneva, and Graduate Institute of International Studies *The League of Nations in Retrospect: La Société des Nations: Rétrospective.* Berlin, 1983.

Van Alstyne, R.W. 'Private American Loans to the Allies, 1914–1916.' *Pacific Historical Review*, 2(1933).

Veatch, Richard. *Canada and the League of Nations*. Toronto, 1975.

Vinson, J.C. *The Parchment Peace: The United States and the Washington Conference, 1921–1922*. Athens, GA, 1955.

Waltz, K. *Man, the State, and War: A Theoretical Analysis*. New York, 1959.

Watt, D.C. 'The Secret Laval-Mussolini Agreement of 1935 on Ethiopia.' *Middle East Journal*, 15(1961).

– *Succeeding John Bull: America in Britain's Place, 1900–1975*. Cambridge, 1984.

– 'Britain and the Historiography of the Yalta Conference and the Cold War.' *Diplomatic History*, 13(1989).

– *How War Came: The Immediate Origins of the Second World War, 1938–1939*. London, 1989.

Webber, G.C. *The Ideology of the British Right, 1918–1939*. London, 1986.

Weinberg, G. *The Foreign Policy of Hitler's Germany*. Vol. I: *Diplomatic Revolution in Europe, 1933–36*. Chicago, 1970.

Wells, Jr, S.F. 'British Strategic Withdrawal from the Western Hemisphere, 1904–1906.' *Canadian Historical Review*, 49(1968).

Wheeler, N.J. 'British Nuclear Weapons and Anglo-American Relations, 1945–54.' *International Affairs*, 62(1985–6).

Wheeler-Bennett, J.W. *Disarmament and Security since Locarno, 1925–1931*. London, 1932.

Widenor, W.C. *Henry Cabot Lodge and the Search for an American Foreign Policy*. Berkeley, 1980.

Wigley, P.G. *Canada and the Transition to Commonwealth: British-Canadian Relations, 1917–1926*. Cambridge, 1977.

Wilcox, Clair. *A Charter for World Trade*. New York, 1949.

Wilcox, F.O. *Congress, the Executive and Foreign Policy*. New York, 1971.

Wiler, Peter. 'British Labour and the Cold War: The Foreign Policy of the Labour Governments, 1945–1951.' *Journal of British Studies*, 26(1987).

Williams, Rhodri. *Defending the Empire: The Conservative Party and British Defence Policy, 1899–1915*. New Haven, CT, 1991.

Williams, William Appleman. 'The Legend of Isolationism in the 1920s.' *Science and Society*, 18(1954).

– *The Tragedy of American Diplomacy*. New York, 1959.

– 'The Large Corporations and American Foreign Policy.' In *Corporations and the Cold War*, ed. David Horowitz. New York, 1964.

Williams, W.J. *The Wilson Administration and the Shipbuilding Crisis of 1917: Steel Ships and Wooden Steamers*. Lewiston, NY, 1992.

Williams, W.J. 'American Destroyer Programs during World War I.' Unpublished paper presented at the Naval History Symposium, Annapolis, MD, 21–23 October 1993.

Wilson, Joan Hoff. *American Business and Foreign Policy, 1920–1933*. Lexington, KY, 1971.

Woodward, David R. 'Did Lloyd George Starve the British Army of Men prior to the German Offensive of 21 March, 1918?' *Historical Journal*, 27(1984).

– *Trial By Friendship: Anglo-American Relations, 1917–1918*. Kentucky, 1993.

Wright, C.W. 'American Economic Preparations for War, 1914–1917 and 1939–1941.' *Canadian Journal of Economics and Political Science*, 8(1942).

Zeiler, Thomas. *American Trade and Power in the 1960s*. New York, 1992.

Contributors

LAWRENCE ARONSEN, Associate Professor of History at the University of Alberta, is the co-author (with Martin Kitchen) of *The Origins of the Cold War in Comparative Perspective*. He is now engaged in a major study of the development of United States air power in the post-1945 period, looking specifically at the evolution of the B-52 bomber.

JOHN A. ENGLISH is the author of the acclaimed *On Infantry* and co-author of *On Infantry: Revised Edition*. He is the main Canadian contributor to *The D-Day Encyclopedia*, and his book *The Canadian Army in the Normandy Campaign* has just been published in Canadian paperback as *Failure in High Command*. He is currently series adviser to the 'Praeger Series in War Studies' and an adjunct professor of history and war studies at Queen's University and the Royal Military College.

GREGORY JOHNSON, currently teaching history at the University of Alberta, is a graduate of the University of British Columbia and York University. He has written on various aspects of Canadian foreign policy and is currently completing a book on the impact of the struggle for the Pacific on Canada's relations with Britain and the United States during the Mackenzie King era.

GREG KENNEDY, a sessional lecturer at the Royal Military College of Canada, is finishing his PhD in history (University of Alberta). His dissertation concerns Anglo-American maritime relations in the Pacific Ocean during the 1930s. He has already published a number of scholarly articles on American, British, and Canadian naval and diplomatic topics, and he is completing the late Barry D. Hunt's unfinished book on the Royal Navy during the First World War.

MARTIN KITCHEN, Professor of History at Simon Fraser University, has written extensively on nineteenth- and twentieth-century international history. Among his more than a dozen books are *A World in Flames: A Short History of the Second World War in Europe and Asia, Europe between the Wars: A Political History,* and *Nazi Germany at War.*

DAVID LENARCIC, a graduate of the University of Toronto and York University, was recently a post-doctoral fellow at the Laurier Centre for Military, Strategic, and Disarmament Studies. He is currently a part-time faculty member of the History Department at Wilfrid Laurier University and is completing a book on the making of Canadian peacekeeping policy during the 1950s and 1960s.

B.J.C. McKERCHER, Associate Professor of History at the Royal Military College of Canada, has written widely on Anglo-American and Anglo-Canadian relations in the twentieth century. The general editor of the 'Praeger Series on Diplomacy and Strategic Thought,' he is completing *Transition: Britain's Loss of Global Preeminence to the United States, 1930–1945,* which is scheduled to appear in 1996.

ROGER SARTY is Senior Historian at the Directorate of History, National Defence Headquarters, Ottawa. He was part of the team that produced *The Creation of a National Air Force,* volume 2 of *The Official History of the Royal Canadian Air Force,* and is now the team leader of the Royal Canadian Navy official history project. Publishing widely on Canadian defence and foreign policy history, he co-authored (with Michael Hadley) *Tin-Pots and Pirate Ships: Canadian Naval Forces and German Sea Raiders, 1880–1918.*

Index

Given the nature of this book, there are no separate entries for 'Canada,' 'Great Britain,' the 'North Atlantic Triangle,' and the 'United States of America.'

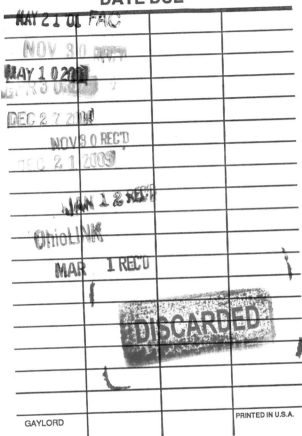

CONTRIBUTORS

Lawrence Aronsen	Martin Kitchen
John Alan English	David A. Lenarcic
Gregory A. Johnson	B.J.C. McKercher
Greg C. Kennedy	Roger Sarty

'Britain, the United States, and Canada have always had a "special relationship" based on history, culture, and language. ...To understand the North Atlantic triangle in the changing world between 1902 and 1956, we must examine how the complex relationship of Britain, the United States, and Canada evolved during this crucial time, how that relationship matured, and how the triangle influenced global politics beyond its confines at a difficult time in international history.'

From the Introduction

UNIVERSITY OF TORONTO

ISBN 0-8020-6957-6

9 780802 069573